AF863213

Politically Motivated Justice

Artem Galushko

Politically Motivated Justice

Authoritarian Legacies and Their Role in Shaping Constitutional Practices in the Former Soviet Union

ASSER PRESS

Springer

Artem Galushko
Kyiv, Ukraine

ISBN 978-94-6265-458-7 ISBN 978-94-6265-459-4 (eBook)
https://doi.org/10.1007/978-94-6265-459-4

Published by T.M.C. ASSER PRESS, The Hague, The Netherlands www.asserpress.nl
Produced and distributed for T.M.C. ASSER PRESS by Springer-Verlag Berlin Heidelberg

© T.M.C. ASSER PRESS and the author 2021
No part of this work may be reproduced, stored in a retrieval system, or transmitted in any form or by any means, electronic, mechanical, photocopying, microfilming, recording or otherwise, without written permission from the Publisher, with the exception of any material supplied specifically for the purpose of being entered and executed on a computer system, for exclusive use by the purchaser of the work.
The use of general descriptive names, registered names, trademarks, service marks, etc. in this publication does not imply, even in the absence of a specific statement, that such names are exempt from the relevant protective laws and regulations and therefore free for general use.

This T.M.C. ASSER PRESS imprint is published by the registered company Springer-Verlag GmbH, DE part of Springer Nature.
The registered company address is: Heidelberger Platz 3, 14197 Berlin, Germany

Preface

This book addresses authoritarian legacies of politically motivated justice and its unwritten practices that have re-emerged in the recent trials related to both political (abuse of public office, assembly, etc.) and ordinary criminal charges (corruption, organized crime and others) against prominent opposition leaders in many former Soviet republics. Taking into account that in any country all trials are more or less related to politics, my research differentiates between trials on political issues (political trials that are not necessarily arbitrary) and politicized partisan trials (arbitrary trials against political opponents). The monograph, thus, adopts a broad definition of a political trial, which includes all trials that are related to politicians and political matters such as elections, regime change, activities of parties and other political organizations. The book focuses on a separate group of partisan trials that are politicized (i.e., politically motivated) and which are used by governments to restrain political opposition and dissent.

The topic of politicized criminal justice in the former Soviet Union is of increasing academic and research significance. International reports on massive arbitrary arrests[1] of protestors and opposition leaders in Belarus,[2] persecutions of political opponents in Russia that could become even more repressive in the context of the

[1]As of December 2020, more than 30,000 persons have been detained in Belarus for participating in peaceful rallies since the beginning of the presidential elections campaign in May. Belarus-Analysen Nr. 53 vom 21.12.2020, S. 17–20. https://www.laender-analysen.de/belarus-analysen/53/bericht-des-menschenrechtszentrums-wiasna-human-rights-situation-in-belarus-november-2020/. Accessed 29 December 2020.

[2]Step Vaessen (2020) Belarus mass arrests fail to stop protests. Aljazeera. https://www.aljazeera.com/news/2020/09/belarus-mass-arrests-fail-stop-protests-200915140123728.html. Accessed 22 December 2020.

recent poisoning attempt of the Russian opposition activist Alexei Navalny,[3] an 11-year jail sentence for the former President of Kyrgyzstan Almazbek Atambaev,[4] as well as ongoing criminal proceedings against the former President of Ukraine Petro Poroshenko[5] have raised questions about the possible selective justice and politically motivated nature of these proceedings. A number of human rights organizations and think tanks such as Amnesty International,[6] Human Rights Watch[7] and Freedom House[8] have conducted research and reported on the issue of political prisoners and arbitrary justice in the former communist bloc. Allegations about politically motivated justice in the former USSR have also attracted significant attention in the course of the Trump-Ukraine impeachment inquiry in the USA.[9] As a recent development, the arrests and detention of government critics in times of the COVID-19 global pandemic have also become a major issue in many countries and regions nowadays, given that detention facilities with poor sanitation can become contagion zones that could expose political opponents, who are arbitrarily deprived of their liberty, to a higher risk of viral transmission.[10] Arbitrary detentions of protestors in Belarus and Russia were still ongoing at the time of the book preparation and publication.

---

[3]Deutsche Welle (2020) Angela Merkel says Novichok Poisoning of Russia's Navalny was Attempted Murder. https://www.dw.com/en/navalny-novichok-germany-russia/a-54794283. Accessed 22 December 2020. *See also* BBC News (2020) Russia Far East Protest over Governor's Arrest, sec. Europe. https://www.bbc.com/news/world-europe-53373132. Accessed 22 December 2020.

[4]Catherine Putz (2020) 11-Year Sentence for Former Kyrgyz President Atambayev's Role in Early Release of Aziz Batukayev. https://thediplomat.com/2020/06/11-year-sentence-for-former-kyrgyz-president-atambayevs-role-in-early-release-of-aziz-batukayev/. Accessed 22 December 2020.

[5]Peter Dickinson (2020) Atlantic Council. What Could the Prosecution of Petro Poroshenko Mean for Ukrainian Democracy? https://www.atlanticcouncil.org/blogs/ukrainealert/what-could-the-prosecution-of-petro-poroshenko-mean-for-ukrainian-democracy/. Accessed 22 December 2020.

[6]Amnesty International (2019) Ukrainian Filmmaker Oleg Sentsov and others Freed in Ukraine/Russia Prisoner Swap. https://www.amnesty.org/en/latest/news/2019/09/russiaukraine-filmmaker-oleg-sentsov-and-others-freed-in-prisoner-swap/. Accessed 22 December 2020.

[7]Human Rights Watch (2020) Russia: Dozens of Journalists Detained for Peaceful Protests. https://www.hrw.org/news/2020/07/10/russia-dozens-journalists-detained-peaceful-protests. Accessed 22 December 2020. *See also* Human Rights Watch (2020) Tajikistan: Intensified Pressure on Dissidents' Families. https://www.hrw.org/news/2020/07/09/tajikistan-intensified-pressure-dissidents-families. Accessed 22 December 2020.

[8]Zselyke Csaky (2020) Freedom House Report. Nations in Transit 2020. Section 'Justice in the Service of Politics. https://freedomhouse.org/report/nations-transit/2020/dropping-democratic-facade#Justice. Accessed 22 December 2020.

[9]See the Trump-Ukraine Impeachment Inquiry Report of the US House of Representatives Permanent Select Committee on Intelligence, Pursuant to H. Res. 660, December 2019. https://intelligence.house.gov/uploadedfiles/20191203_-_full_report___hpsci_impeachment_inquiry.pdf. Accessed 22 December 2020.

[10]The UN News (2020) Political Prisoners should be among First Released in Pandemic Response, Says UN Rights Chief. https://news.un.org/en/story/2020/04/1061002. Accessed 22 December 2020. *See also* Front Line Defenders (2020) COVID-19—Attacks on HRDs in a Time of Pandemic. https://www.frontlinedefenders.org/en/campaign/covid-19-attacks-hrds-time-pandemic. Accessed 22 December 2020.

The book begins with the origins of communist politicized justice from the early Soviet 'agitation trials' and the subsequent Moscow show trials replicated in the communist satellite countries until the late Soviet trials against dissidents. Based on this analysis, I identify main types of politicized trials and their core unwritten practices during Communism. The book demonstrates the pervasive and subversive character of such practices, which even three decades after the fall of Communism can lead to the split of a legal system into two parallel orders of formal and informal rules in the post-Soviet states that disrespect the rule of law. Therefore, the core message of the book is that the communist practices of politicized justice have survived the collapse of the USSR and can still be exposed in the recent trials against opposition in the transitional former Soviet republics. The legal assessment of authoritarian traditions of politicized justice is very timely. In various former Soviet republics, ruling elites weaponized politicized justice against their critics who are facing violations of their constitutional rights in proceedings that look similar to Stalinist show trials against 'people's enemies.'

With regard to the limitations of my research, it deals only with proceedings initiated by national authorities against political parties, acting or former politicians. Although it is reported that journalists, business actors and human rights activists from NGOs also often become the target of politically motivated justice in the former Soviet Union, limitation of the present research scope only to politicians and political parties allows examining in more detail the so-called hidden political agenda usually alleged by prosecuted opposition politicians. Cases selected in the post-Soviet states are related to prominent politicians, because it helps test the hypothesis that trials against politicians in authoritarian and transitional-hybrid regimes of the former Soviet Union stem from a parallel system of justice and its unwritten practices used by post-Soviet elites to remove formidable political opponents.

The book is aimed at legal practitioners such as transnational human rights activists, prosecutors and judges, as well as historians, rule-of-law experts, postgraduates and university professors that teach courses on post-Soviet politics and comparative legal institutions. Potential readers can gain from the book information, which is useful in assessing the interdisciplinary phenomenon of politically motivated criminal justice in transitional and authoritarian post-Soviet republics. Namely, the book will provide a comprehensive account of the historical origins of Soviet arbitrary criminal justice, its informal unwritten practices that survived the fall of Communism and which have manifested themselves in the recent trials against political opposition in the post-Soviet states. Most importantly, the book offers a list of criteria that can equip those interested in the subject with the knowledge how to assess future allegations about politically motivated justice at various stages of criminal proceedings.

Kyiv, Ukraine Artem Galushko

Acknowledgements This book is based on a doctoral dissertation I defended at the Central European University (CEU). I would like to thank my mentors, colleagues, classmates and professors who took an interest in my research, as well as dedicated their personal time and valuable insights to make my work better. During my research stays in Germany, Sweden, Hungary and Myanmar, I have met people whose kind support and attention mean a lot to me. While the very existence of communist crimes and legacies is often denied or trivialized, until now, this book is an endeavor to commemorate victims of totalitarian regimes and to denounce all attempts at the reconstruction and glorification of such regimes nowadays.

Introduction

Despite introducing new democratic constitutions and constitutional courts shortly after the fall of Communism, many former Soviet republics still display authoritarian practices of arbitrary persecution against political opposition. The *puzzle* to address in this context is the absence of similar practices of politicized justice in established democracies that have also experienced a communist or another totalitarian regime in the past. This book focuses on the communist legacy of unwritten conventionalities that cause systemic legal deficiencies incompatible with the rule of law in Europe. The main premise of my research is that the transitional post-Soviet states have failed to introduce legal reforms necessary to dismantle unwritten communist practices of politically motivated justice whose supra-constitutional standing now makes it impossible to guarantee successful democratic transformations in these countries.

The goal of my research is to provide a theoretical framework for comparing trials against politicians in such established democracies as Germany and Austria with those in transitional states such as Ukraine and Belarus. The key component of my comparative research is to identify unwritten extra-legal practices that are incompatible with the 'common European heritage of the Rule of Law'[11] and may cause democratic backsliding in the former Soviet republics. The ultimate goal of this analysis is to reveal the roles performed by 'political trials' in the so-called countries in transition and established democracies. In order to achieve this goal, I develop my own concept of '*Twofold Constitutionalism*,' which explains the communist legacy of politicized show trials. With this novel theoretical framework at hand, my research develops criteria to evaluate 'politically motivated trials' and give recommendations on measures that should be taken to prevent the phenomenon of politicized justice in transitional post-Soviet countries.

The *novelty of this research* manifests itself in the analysis of political justice from a comparative legal perspective. Existing previous research was limited to individual cases and missed identifying common characteristics of political trials in the former communist bloc. The European Court of Human Rights has already reviewed

[11] See the European Convention on Human Rights (ECHR), opened for signature 4 November 1950 (entered into force 3 September 1953) (the Preamble). http://www.hri.org/docs/ECHR50.html. Accessed 22 August 2020.

applications concerning politicized justice in the former USSR.[12] Because the issue remains on the democratization agenda of the post-communist states, my research will offer criteria to be used by the policy community to evaluate future allegations about political persecutions. In order to address the issue of politically motivated justice, I seek to answer the following *research question*: What is the role of political trials in the context of transitioning from state repression to the rule of law? A series of case studies help test my *hypothesis* that, as opposed to established democracies where trials against politicians usually lead to constitutional dialogue and reconciliation, trials against politicians in transitional former communist countries reveal a parallel system of justice whose largely unwritten rules, conventionalities, judicial and prosecutorial practices are inherited from the communist times and now hinder a successful post-communist transition.

In my research, I use several *key definitions* while exploring the phenomenon of politicized justice in the former Soviet Union. In particular, I use Ron Christenson's definition of politically motivated justice, whose goal is 'not only legal but also political in a direct sense…[, because] the law was being used merely as an alibi.'[13] In this context, my research differentiates between a 'political trial' and a 'politically motivated/politicized/arbitrary trial'. On the one hand, 'political trial' is a trial, which is related to issues of politics and not necessarily arbitrary by its nature ('something is called political if it is thought to relate in a particularly intensive way to the interests of the community.').[14] An example of such trial proceedings related to politics would be criminal trials (trials within the rule of law) of heads of states and government for acts of states, trials against former dictators and perpetrators of state-induced crimes. On the other hand, 'politically motivated/politicized (arbitrary) trial' would be 'a regime's attempt to incriminate its foe's public behavior with a view to evicting him from the political scene'.[15] Politicized trials are 'used…to denote prosecutions brought against political opponents in general for the purpose of eliminating them.'[16] In its turn, the Soviet show trial, which has been studied in this book, 'is a propaganda arm of political terror…[, whose] aim is to personalize an abstract political enemy, to place it in the dock in flesh and blood and, with the aid of a perverted system of justice, to transform abstract political-ideological differences into easily intelligible common crimes. It both incites the masses against the evil embodied by the defendants and

---

[12]In particular, ECtHR (the European Court of Human Rights), *Ilgar Mammadov v Azerbaijan,* 22 May 2014, Case No. 15172/13; ECtHR, *Tymoshenko v Ukraine*, 30 April 2013, Case No. 49872/11; ECtHR, *Lutsenko v Ukraine*, 3 July 2012, Case No. 6492/11; ECtHR, *Khodorkovskiy v Russia,* 31 May 2011, Case No. 5829/04 and ECtHR, *Gusinskiy v Russia,* 19 May 2004, Case No.70276/01.

[13]*See* Christenson R. (1999) Political Trials: Gordian Knots in the Law, revised, expanded, subsequent edn. Routledge, New Brunswick, NJ, p. xiii.

[14]Kirchheimer O. (1968) Political Justice: The Use of Legal Procedure for Political Ends, new edn. Princeton University Press, p. 25.

[15]Ibid., p. 46.

[16]Laughland J. (2008) A History of Political Trials: From Charles I to Saddam Hussein, new edn. Peter Lang Oxford, Oxford, p. 17.

frightens them away from supporting any potential opposition.'[17] Soviet type show trials covered in this research can be characterized by construed facts, wide publicity, invented facts, theatricality and judgments prepared in advance.

Among various categories of politically motivated trials, my research focuses only on a separate group of *politicized partisan trials* that are used by governments against political opposition. Furthermore, the book provides analysis of the Soviet legacy of *show trials* that were the most vivid example of politicized partisan trials during the Soviet times. This, in turn, is closely related to the *limitations of my research.* This book, in particular, focuses only on criminal cases initiated by national authorities of the selected Western European countries and former Soviet republics against political parties, acting or former politicians in *2010–2015* when political opposition both in Belarus and Ukraine claimed it became a victim of politically motivated justice. Although it is reported that human rights activists from national NGOs also often become target of politically motivated justice in the former Soviet Union,[18] limitation of the present research scope only to politicians and political parties allows examining in more detail the so-called 'hidden [political] agenda'[19] often alleged by prosecuted opposition politicians. Thus, this research covers 'political cases' that took place in *2010–2015* in the selected jurisdictions. Cases selected in the former Soviet Union are related to popular politicians, because it helps test the hypothesis that trials against politicians in the former Soviet Union are qualitatively different from those conducted in Western Europe due to a parallel system of justice and its unwritten practices that are used by post-Soviet ruling elites to remove formidable, popular political opponents.

Chapter 1 of the book provides an overview of the current state of research in the field, the explanation of my research methodology as well as relevant terminology, key features and the classification of political trials in general. The aim of the first chapter is to provide a theoretical framework for comparing trials against politicians in Western Europe with those in the former USSR. Several steps are taken to outline the framework of my research. *First*, the chapter refers to scholars who have already analyzed the phenomenon of political justice in various countries. *Second*, based on the already existing theories offered by these authors I give my own definition of a political trial to describe differences that exist between political trials in Western Europe and in the former Soviet Union. *Third*, this chapter offers the research methodology I intend to use in order to analyze recent political cases in the selected former Soviet republics and countries of Western Europe. The goal of this

---

[17] Hodos G. (1987) Show Trials: Stalinist Purges in Eastern Europe, 1948–1954, 1st edn. Praeger, New York, p. xiii.

[18] See Human Rights House Network (2014) Strengthening of repression against non-governmental and political activists in Azerbaijan. https://humanrightshouse.org/articles/strengthening-of-repression-against-non-governmental-and-political-activists-in-azerbaijan/. Accessed 22 December 2020.

[19] See the ECtHR, the final judgment in the case '*Khodorkovskiy v. Russia*', 31 May 2011, Case No. 5829/04, p. 64, para 255. http://hudoc.echr.coe.int/sites/eng/pages/search.aspx#{%22appno%22:[%225829/04%22],%22itemid%22:[%22001-104983%22]}. Accessed 22 December 2020.

analysis is to reveal roles performed by political trials in the so-called countries in transition and established Western democracies.

Chapter 2 presents detailed analysis of communist show trials, their categorization and the Soviet legacy of '*Twofold Constitutionalism.*' This chapter offers a critical assessment of the Soviet system of criminal justice and its trials. My analysis of these trials is made in chronological order—from most representative early Soviet 'show trials' against 'people's enemies' to a regional 'model show trial' in communist Hungary and persecution of political dissidents in the late Soviet period of 'Brezhnev's Stagnation' and 'Perestroika.' One of the aims of this chapter is to demonstrate that the Soviet system of political justice became an unwritten constitution of the USSR. To achieve this aim, the chapter provides two outcomes. *First*, it makes a categorization of the above-mentioned political trials with a special emphasis on victims of politically motivated justice and goals pursued by these trials. *Second*, the chapter analyzes major legal features that were peculiar to political justice during the communist regime. Categorization of political trials under Communism and their features helps me scrutinize my hypothesis that, unlike in Western European states, trials against politicians in selected former Soviet republics can reveal a split into a nominal written Constitution and its informal unwritten counterpart.

Chapter 3 proceeds with the description of facts, procedural history and reasoning behind judgments in selected cases as well as their legal analysis in the framework of the relevant case law by the European Court of Human Rights. The chapter provides an analysis of two cases from each of the four jurisdictions within my research (Ukraine, Belarus, Germany and Austria). Cases from Belarus are analyzed by using the legal approach of the European Court of Human Rights as if the country joined the European Convention on Human Rights. This concluding part of the book demonstrates the difference between the roles performed by political trials in transitional former Soviet republics and in Western European democracies as well as offers legal criteria to evaluate future allegations about politically motivated justice.

My research argues that the phenomenon of politically motivated justice is interconnected with the ongoing crisis of constitutionalism in transitional post-Soviet states. The crisis is demonstrated by several *relevant constitutional law theories*. For instance, Alexei Trochev developed a theory of *'Non-Linear Development'* to explain the ups and downs of the post-Soviet constitutionalism.[20] Trochev analyzes several inconsistencies in the development of the Constitutional Court of the Russian Federation. In particular, the Court loses and regains its authority in circles. While judges of the Court are empowered within the formal Russian judicial hierarchy, there is also a simultaneous weakening of democratic institutions in Russia. Finally, officials from the executive and judicial branches simply refuse to enforce some decisions of the Court and continue applying norms that have been already recognized as unconstitutional. Trochev explains that the above-mentioned inconsistencies are the result of constantly changing political priorities that influence the system of justice,

---

[20]Trochev A (2011) Judging Russia: The Role of the Constitutional Court in Russian Politics 1990–2006, reissue edn. Cambridge University Press, Cambridge.

the low legal awareness of the general population and enormous socio-political transformations that took place after the collapse of the Soviet Union.

Andrey Medushevsky offered another theory of '*Nominal Constitutionalism*,' which is also relevant for my research on the Soviet legacy of declaratory laws. Medushevsky rightly observes that constitutional rights and freedoms mostly remained unenforceable in practice during the Soviet times. Soviet constitutions, thus, played only a nominal role when the Communist Party used them to hide numerous human rights violations and present a fake image of the Soviet Union as a country where rights and freedoms were respected. Medushevsky concludes that the nominal status of the Soviet constitutions was exposed by the Soviet dissident movement, whose demonstrative implementation (Russian: v yavochnom poriadke) of declaratory constitutional norms was prosecute*d* as a crime or a social deviation.[21] This politicized justice against all dissenting voices continued until the very collapse of the Soviet Union in 1991.

Another relevant theory of '*Failing Constitutionalism*' and '*Constitutionalization of Politics*' was offered by Armen Mazmanyan, who studied the Soviet legacy of legal nihilism, political legalism and embedded formalism. Mazmanyan warns us that the process of the post-Soviet democratization might be compromised 'through undemocratic and unconstitutional channels.'[22] The Soviet legacy manifests itself in various constitutional deficiencies such as the defective design of constitutional courts, irresponsible political leadership and formalistic approach to law viewed by the post-Soviet ruling elites merely as an instrument to secure their political interests. Taking into account that these deficiencies became part of the local legal culture in many former Soviet republics, Mazmanyan effectively argues that it is possible to get rid of the Soviet legal culture by focusing more on constitutional concepts and principles rather than on formal rules and procedures. The post-Soviet judiciary could play a decisive role in this regard if it goes beyond the text of written constitutions and promotes constitutional principles instead.

My research offers a separate theory, which can explain the phenomena of 'nominal constitutionalism,' 'sham constitutions,' 'failing constitutionalism,' 'non-linear development' of constitutional courts and 'constitutions without constitutionalism' in criminal justice of transitional post-Soviet states. Although there is much more to constitutionalism than criminal law, I believe that a specific focus on politicized criminal justice can help reveal the absence of the rule of law in relation to such key values of any constitutional democracy as freedom of political speech and opinion, independent and professional judiciary, principle of legality or no punishment without law, right to counsel, presumption of innocence and the equality of all before the law. My theory of '*Twofold Constitutionalism*' emphasizes the duality of

---

[21] Andrei Medushevsky (2011) Stalinizm kak model. Obozreniye izdatelskogo proekta ROSSPEN. Istoriya stalinizma, *Vestnik Evropy*, no. 30. https://magazines.gorky.media/vestnik/2011/30/stalinizm-kak-model-obozrenie-izdatelskogo-proekta-rosspen-istoriya-stalinizma.html. Accessed 24 December 2020.

[22] Mazmanyan A (2012) Failing constitutionalism: From political legalism to defective empowerment. Global Constitutionalism, 1(2), pp. 313–333. https://doi.org/10.1017/S2045381711000128, p. 313.

the Soviet legal system rooted in the traditional division of Russian law into formal law usually borrowed from abroad and informal mostly unwritten common law. I will use the previous research on the Soviet system of criminal justice to show that the Soviet constitutions were twofold. The first written and official part of the Soviet constitutions played only a nominal role by legitimizing the communist regime in the Soviet Union and abroad. The second informal and mostly unwritten part included customary law and other conventionalities of political justice that were superior to all written laws.

This introduction sets out the main elements of my theoretical framework, which is further developed in the chapters. The concept of '*Twofold Constitutionalism*' developed in this book addresses the puzzle of dualistic constitutions in transitional post-Soviet states. The split of a legal system into two parallel legal orders of formal and informal norms raises the question about the role played by formal written constitutions and informal practices in such countries. Is it possible to expose 'imitated democracies' by studying 'political trials'? By answering this question in Chaps. 1–3 of this book, it seeks to analyze constitutional mechanics in the times of post-communist transition from a dictatorship to the rule of law.

Given the above-mentioned considerations, this introductory section presents two *preliminary outcomes* of my research. The first outcome is the concept of '*Twofold Constitutionalism*,' which offers a novel argument that the communist extra-legal practices, described in detail in Chaps. 1–3, attained in the Soviet Union a constitutional rank, because they could prevail over the formal (nominal) written constitutions. This created two co-existing legal orders of informal and formal norms when the former could replace the latter any moment depending on political expediency, the interpretation by various state agencies and systemic changes that 'justified' political interventions in the legal system. The supremacy of the informal legal order was revealed in politicized trials against actual or potential opponents of the communist regime that were persecuted regardless of their actual guilt or innocence.

The second preliminary outcome of this book is that the informal order of politically motivated justice was so entrenched that it survived the fall of Communism and manifested itself in politicized trials against opposition in transitional former Soviet republics. It has several significant repercussions. *First*, if the extra-legal practices of politicized justice have a constitutional rank in the transitional post-Soviet states, it means that the supreme written law of these countries can be easily rendered null and void for political considerations. This affects not only victims of politicized justice, but also ordinary citizens whose constitutional rights and freedoms can be routinely disregarded, as they remain only on paper. *Second*, although many authoritarian post-Soviet governments declared that they observed the rule of law by adopting new democratic constitutions and establishing constitutional courts, the theory of '*Twofold Constitutionalism*' exposes the false nature of these 'new democracies' and questions the legitimacy of political regimes in these countries. In this context, 'political trials' appear to be an ultimate test to check whether a country has the genuine rather than the declaratory rule of law. Chapter 1 seeks to explain how written (formal) norms interact with unwritten (informal) practices and under which conditions the latter can prevail over the former. Most significantly, that chapter also presents my own theoretical framework to assess the complex phenomenon of politically motivated justice and identify differences between political trials in transitional post-Soviet states and established Western democracies.

Kyiv, Ukraine Artem Galushko

Contents

About the Author

Artem Galushko is a postdoctoral researcher at the Max Planck Institute for the Study of Religious and Ethnic Diversity in Germany. His current research project is related to legacies of politically motivated justice in post-Soviet Eurasia and the impact of international legal frameworks on the former communist states. His research interests lie in comparative constitutional law, focusing on the relationship between criminal justice and authoritarian legacies, public international law, minority rights protection and international criminal law. He has received a doctoral degree in juridical science (S.J.D.) from the Central European University (CEU) in Budapest, Hungary, and LL.M. at the University of Saarland (UdS) in Saarbruecken, Germany. In 2017, the Yehuda Elkana Centre for Higher Education has selected Artem for the Global Teaching Fellowship, during which he was teaching International Law for students of LL.M. and LL.B. programs during one semester at the Law Department of the Yangon University in Myanmar. Prior to undertaking the S.J.D. program at CEU, Artem has worked for a number of international organizations in Ukraine, including the United Nations Children's Fund (UNICEF), Winrock International, the Soros Foundation and the National Democratic Institute for International Affairs (NDI).

Abbreviations

ÁVH	Communist State Protection Authority of Hungary (Hungarian: *Államvédelmi Hatóság*)
BVerfGE	Constitutional Court of the German Federal Republic (German: *Bundesverfassungsgericht*)
CDU	Christian Democratic Union (German: *Christlich Demokratische Union Deutschlands*)
CHEKA (Bolshevik Security Service)	All-Russian Extraordinary Commission (Russian: *Vserossiyskaya Chrezvychaynaya Komissiya*)
CoE	Council of Europe
Cominform	Communist Information Bureau of the Communist and Workers' Parties
CPI	Corruption Perceptions Index
CPT	European Committee for the Prevention of Torture and Inhuman or Degrading Treatment or Punishment
ECHR	European Convention on Human Rights
ECtHR	European Court of Human Rights
ENEMO	European Network of Election Monitoring Organizations
EU	European Union
FPÖ	Freedom Party of Austria (German: *Freiheitliche Partei Österreichs*)
FRG	Federal Republic of Germany (German: *Bundesrepublik Deutschland, BRD*)
GDR/DDR	German Democratic Republic, (German: *Deutsche Demokratische Republik*)
GG	Basic Law for the Federal Republic of Germany (German: *Grundgesetz*)

GULAG	Principle Administration of Camps (Russian: *Glavnoye Upravleniye Lagerey*)
KPD	Communist Party of Germany (German: *Kommunistische Partei Deutschlands*)
NEP	New Economic Policy
NKVD	People's Commissariat for Internal Affairs, the successor of OGPU (Russian: *Narodnyy Komissariat Vnutrennikh Del*)
NPD	National Democratic Party (German: *Nationaldemokratische Partei Deutschlands*)
NYT	New York Times
OG	Supreme Court of Austria (German: *Oberster Gerichtshof*)
OGPU	Joint State Political Directorate under the Council of People's Commissars of the USSR (Russian: *Obyedinyonnoye gosudarstvennoye politicheskoye upravleniye pri Sovnarkome SSSR*)
OSCE	Organization for Security and Cooperation in Europe
ÖVP	People's Party of Austria (German: *Österreichische Volkspartei*)
Politburo	Political Bureau (Russian: *Политбюро*)
SFRY	Socialist Federal Republic of Yugoslavia
SRD	Socialist Reich Party of Germany (German: *Sozialistische Reichspartei Deutschlands*)
Venice Commission	European Commission for Democracy through Law
WJP	World Justice Project

Chapter 1
Phenomenon of Politically Motivated Justice and Its Relevance for the Rule of Law in the Former USSR

Contents

Abstract This chapter provides an overview of the phenomenon of politically motivated justice and a general classification of political trials. The aim of the chapter is to develop a conceptual framework for identifying constitutional practices and roles played by trials against politicians and political parties in established democracies and in transitional states of the former USSR. Several steps are taken to outline the framework of my research. *First*, the chapter gives a succinct summary of the existing research on politically motivated justice and my contribution to the debate. *Second*, based on the already existing theories I give my own definition of a political trial in the context of the post-communist transition to the rule of law. *Third*, it offers a novel research concept I use in the next chapters in order to analyze recent political cases in the selected former Soviet republics and countries of Western Europe. The main goal of this analysis is to demonstrate the subversive character of politicized criminal justice which can override constitutional provisions and undermine democratic transformations in transitional former Soviet republics.

Keywords Rule of law · Politically motivated criminal justice · Constitutional law · Belarus · Ukraine · Post-communist transition

© T.M.C. ASSER PRESS and the author 2021

A. Galushko, *Politically Motivated Justice*,
https://doi.org/10.1007/978-94-6265-459-4_1

1.1 Introduction

This chapter provides a theoretical framework for comparing 'political trials' (i.e. trials related to politics) in Western Europe with those in the former USSR. Several steps are taken to outline the framework of my research. *First*, the chapter refers to scholars who have already analyzed the phenomenon of political justice in various countries. *Second*, based on the already existing theories offered by these authors I give my own definition of a 'political trial' to describe differences that exist between political trials in Western Europe and in the former Soviet Union. *Third*, this chapter offers the research methodology I intend to use in order to analyze recent political cases in the selected former Soviet republics and countries of Western Europe. The goal of this analysis is to reveal roles performed by political trials in transitional countries and established democracies.

I understand that the concept of the post-Soviet transition remains controversial almost three decades after the collapse of the Soviet Union, as the uniform title of a 'state in transition' probably fails to catch a great diversity of transitional paths chosen by the fifteen sovereign states that emerged from the Union of Soviet Socialist Republics after its disintegration in 1991. Nevertheless, the task of this book is not to disqualify or justify the transition concept in the context of post-communist transformations in the former Soviet republics. My conceptualization of post-Soviet political regimes presented in this book as 'transitional-hybrid' or 'authoritarian' relies on the classification of the Freedom House, whose latest report "*Nations in Transit 2020*"[1] on democratic reforms in the 29 formerly communist countries has identified that among former Soviet republics only Latvia, Lithuania and Estonia have become consolidated democracies. The fact that the three Baltic states have achieved their long-standing strategic goals by joining both the European Union and NATO in 2004 can explain the relative success of these countries in terms of their 'constitutional Westernization' since 1991. According to the Freedom House rating, Ukraine, Moldova and Georgia have transitional or hybrid regimes, Armenia is a semi-consolidated authoritarian regime, while the rest of the post-Soviet states including Russia have consolidated authoritarian regimes. This also explains the selection of Belarus (a consolidated authoritarian regime) and Ukraine (a transitional or hybrid regime), whose comparison could reveal the divergent impact of the communist legacies in different republics of the former Soviet Union.

The main puzzle to be addressed here is the phenomenon of '*sham or failed constitutions*' and '*constitutions without constitutionalism*' in many former Soviet republics, which despite their democratic constitutions and constitutional courts still display authoritarian practices of arbitrary justice. In order to resolve this puzzle, this book explains how formal (written) and informal (unwritten) norms interact with each other and under which conditions the latter set of norms can prevail over the other. The key conclusion of this chapter on the Soviet legacy of politically motivated justice is that informal practices prevail over formal norms when law enforcement officials are unable or unwilling to resist political interventions. Ultimately, I will elaborate

[1] Freedom House 2020.

on my own concept of "*Twofold Constitutionalism*" to explain the Soviet legacy of politicized show trials. With the theoretical framework at hand I will speculate about measures that should be taken to prevent the phenomenon of politically motivated justice in the former Soviet Union.

1.2 Definitions and Classifications of Politically Motivated Trials

Prior to making any comparison between the Soviet tradition of show trials and political trials in Western Europe, this section introduces my own definition of a political trial, which I will further use in this book. Taking into account that in any country all trials are more or less related to politics, it is important to differentiate between trials on political issues (political trials) and politicized partisan trials. In terms of politicized partisan justice, a definition given by *Eric Posner* focuses on prosecution of political opponents, where "[i]n the typical political[ly motivated] trial, a person is tried for engaging in political opposition or violating a law against political dissent, or for violating a broad and generally applicable law that is not usually enforced, enforced strictly, or enforced with a strict punishment, except against political opponents of the state or the government."[2] At the same time, Posner distinguishes a broader notion of political criminal trials during emergencies when "defendants...are not merely political opponents but are in fact also public threats...to the entire constitutional system or to the well-being of many people."[3] Although *Otto Kirchheimer* describes "[t]he classic political trial...[as] a regime's attempt to incriminate its foe's public behavior with a view to evicting him from the political scene",[4] he also acknowledges the possibility of a broader concept, under which "something is called political if it is thought to relate in a particularly intensive way to the interests of the community."[5] Other researchers make the same distinction between political and arbitrary (politicized) trials.

Ron Christenson, whose research focuses on the Western tradition of political justice, differentiates between two types of political trials. The first group of trials conducted within the rule of law is "'political' either because the subject matter was a crime or conspiracy against the state or because the investigation was politically motivated."[6] The second group of partisan trials is politicized, "because...[their] aim was not only legal but also political in a direct sense...[and] the law was being used merely as an alibi."[7] *John Laughland* points out that his concept of political trials is "not used, as it commonly is, to denote prosecutions brought against political

[2] Posner 2005, p. 76.
[3] Ibid., p. 106.
[4] Kirchheimer 1961, p. 46.
[5] Ibid., p. 25.
[6] Barna and Pető 2015, p. 25.
[7] Ibid.

opponents in general for the purpose of eliminating them."[8] Laughland's definition of political trials also includes "criminal trials of heads of state (and heads of government) for acts of state…, but the political ideology behind these trials is generally the same: that the law should be the same for everyone."[9] In this context, the concept of the rule of law helps differentiate between politicized partisan trials that have a direct political goal to eliminate regime's opponents and trials against political figures such as politicians, former dictators and perpetrators of state-induced crimes. Unlike the former category of partisan trials, whose legal proceedings are compromised by their political agenda, the rule of law has a chance to prevail only in the latter category.

When Laughland refers to the rule of law, he quotes Dicey's words, "We mean [by the Rule of Law], in the first place, that no man is punishable or can be made to suffer in body or goods except for a distinct breach of law established in the ordinary legal manner before the ordinary courts of the land."[10] The modern concept of the rule of law is present in national and international law, which reflects to a varying degree the principle that everybody should be equally accountable to clearly formulated, well-established and fair laws that are effectively and timely enforced by an independent judiciary. The rule of law is incorporated in the statute of the Council of Europe (CoE),[11] whose members are signatories to the European Convention on Human Rights (ECHR) based on "a common [European] heritage of the Rule of Law."[12] The Convention and the case law by the European Court of Human Rights (ECtHR) can, therefore, be used as a common denominator in finding out whether Western democracies and the former Soviet republics follow the rule of law principle in national trials against politicians. Any politically motivated justice in such trials would be incompatible with the rule of law, which all members of the Council of Europe pledged to maintain regardless of their different economic, political and social conditions.

The modern concept of the rule of law is well developed. There are various methodologies that are used to assess and measure the rule of law in the world. In particular, the World Justice Project (WJP) Rule of Law Index provides a comparative analysis of the current situation with the rule of law in more than one hundred countries and jurisdictions.[13] The WJP Index presupposes that the rule of law has the following four universal principles: (1) governments and private individuals are equally accountable under the law; (2) stable, clear and publicized laws are applied evenly to protect fundamental rights and freedoms; (3) laws are enacted, enforced

[8] Laughland 2008, p. 17.

[9] Laughland 2008, p. 16.

[10] Ibid., p. 7.

[11] See the Statute of the Council of Europe, opened for signature 5 May 1949 (entered into force 3 August 1949) https://conventions.coe.int/Treaty/EN/Treaties/Html/001.htm. Accessed 22 August 2020.

[12] See the European Convention on Human Rights (ECHR), opened for signature 4 November 1950 (entered into force 3 September 1953) (the Preamble). https://www.hri.org/docs/ECHR50.html. Accessed 22 August 2020.

[13] The WJP Rule of Law Index methodology is available at https://worldjusticeproject.org/methodology. Accessed 22 August 2020.

and administered in an accessible and fair manner; (4) independent, neutral and representative judiciary is provided with sufficient resources to deliver justice.[14] The 2015 WJP Index measures the rule of law progress in the Western European countries and in the transitional post-Soviet states selected for this research.[15] In this context, Miguel Schor persuasively argues that the modern concept of the rule of law includes constitutional review as its newest component and due process of law as the traditional component.[16] This book focuses only on the traditional component of the due process, which is essential in any criminal proceedings. Therefore, this research will rely on Schor's theory about the rule of law to analyze the lack of due process guarantees that are characteristic of the communist legacy of politically motivated justice in transitional post-Soviet states.

Christenson explains that the rule of law was missing in Soviet show trials due to the duality of the communist legal system. In particular, he effectively demonstrates that the Soviet duality of law incorporates a prerogative state with its arbitrary prosecution in political cases and a nominal state, whose "formalism of the ordinary courts provides a quasi-rule of law for daily [non-political] conflicts and regular crimes."[17] Most importantly, Christenson is right to point out that this exclusion of political cases from the rule of law and ordinary justice can be a weak point of all authoritarian regimes in the end. In other words, by blatantly disregarding any dissenting opinion, "such regimes shut their eyes to anything they might learn from those who challenge them."[18] Soviet show trials are a perfect example how the USSR failed to learn from its dissidents, who identified causes of the communist totalitarian collapse long before it actually happened.

There are various classifications of political trials in the academic literature. Christenson classifies political trials according to different issues and questions raised by these trials: "(1) Trials of public responsibility…[The main question in all trials from this group: What is public and what is private? Political trials within the rule of law: What is the nature of public responsibility? Partisan trials: Is this a political revenge?;] (2) Trials of dissenters…[The main question in all trials from this group: Is the dissent appropriate? Political trials within the rule of law: Is the policy immoral? Partisan trials: Is the trial designed to eliminate opposition?;] (3) Trials of nationalists…[The main question in all trials from this group: Is the government representing one people yet ruling another? Political trials within the rule of law: Does the nationalist group represent a distinct people? Partisan trials: Is the trial designed to further the domination over one ethnic group?;] (4) Trials of regimes…[The main question in all trials from this group: Was the former government legitimate? Political trials within the

[14] See the World Justice Project (WJP) What is the Rule of Law? https://worldjusticeproject.org/what-rule-law. Accessed 22 August 2020.

[15] In particular, Austria and Germany scored 0.82 and 0.81 points that correspond to the 7th and 8th places in the 2015 Global Rule of Law ranking respectively. Belarus and Ukraine scored 0.53 and 0.48 points with the correspondent 50th and 70th global ranking, available at https://data.worldjusticeproject.org/. Accessed 22 August 2020.

[16] Schor 2006.

[17] Christenson 1999, p. 29.

[18] Ibid.

rule of law: Is the court legitimate? Partisan trials: Is this a victor's justice?.]"[19] The split of Christenson's categories into political trials within the rule of law and partisan trials also highlights the differences in handling political cases in democracies and transitional post-Soviet countries.

Laughland divides political trials into the following categories: "(1) Regime trials; (2) War trials; (3) Purge trials; (4) Treachery trials; (5) Ethnic cleansing trials; (6) Conspiracy trials; (7) People's justice trials."[20] Kirchheimer defines three main categories of political trials: "(A) The trial involving a common crime committed for political purposes and conducted with a view to the political benefits which might ultimately accrue from successful prosecution; (B) The classic political trial: a regime's attempt to incriminate its foe's public behavior with a view to evicting him from the political scene; and (C) The derivative political trial, where the weapons of defamation, perjury, and contempt are manipulated in an effort to bring disrepute upon a political foe."[21] The three types of trials are subdivided according to various categories of offences invoked in political trials: (1) Homicide as 'a political weapon'; (2) Treason; (3) Libel; (4) Legal Repression of Political Organizations; (5) Trial by a successor regime.[22] Kirchheimer also uses the rule of law as a criteria to determine whether each category of political trials represents arbitrary justice, which highlights the difference between cases related to politics and politicized persecution.

I argue that the Soviet legacy of show trials belongs mainly to the category of classic politically motivated trials. Show trials occupy a special role among all other political trials. For the purposes of this research, I will adopt George Hodos' definition of a show trial, which "is a propaganda arm of political terror…[, whose] aim is to personalize an abstract political enemy, to place it in the dock in flesh and blood and, with the aid of a perverted system of justice, to transform abstract political-ideological differences into easily intelligible common crimes. It both incites the masses against the evil embodied by the defendants and frightens them away from supporting any potential opposition."[23] Communist show trials described in this book illustrate that this type of politicized partisan trials can be characterized by construed facts, wide publicity, invented facts and fiction, theatricality and judgments prepared in advance.

Posner observes that "[p]olitical trials can be contrasted with show trials such as those conducted by Nazi Germany, the Soviet Union, and many Soviet satellites."[24] According to Posner, show trials as such would be impossible in democratic societies, "because they would require the collaboration of people with different political views and goals – prosecutors, judges, lawyers, juries – or else the wholesale

---

[19]Ibid., p. 11.

[20]Laughland 2008, pp. 13–19.

[21]Kirchheimer 1961, p. 46.

[22]Ibid.

[23]Hodos 1987, p. xiii.

[24]Posner 2005, p. 106.

destruction of existing institutions, which itself would alert people to the government's intentions."[25] Most importantly, show trials help authoritarian states "cut the Gordian knot: governments eliminate partisan opponents as well as public threats without losing public support through the simple expedient of only pretending that they grant process protection."[26] Christenson describes the same propagandistic goal of Nazi Peoples' Courts to "operate at the center of propaganda...[and] more against the entire population than against the accused on trial."[27] Lynn Viola also mentions show trials turned against those who organized them.[28] Similar to Nazi Germany, Soviet "[p]artisan justice does not teach, only propagandize."[29] In other words, the main goal of this propaganda was to mobilize masses rather than determine the guilt or innocence of defendants in such partisan trials. Thus, the 'instrumentalization' of justice will be one of the key characteristics of Soviet politically motivated trials this text will focus on.

Based on the above-mentioned general theories of politically motivated justice proposed by various scholars, my research introduces its own definition of politicized justice to analyze a more narrow issue of the Soviet legacy of politically motivate trials. This definition offers a novel approach to the subject by emphasizing that Soviet political show trials pursued both direct and indirect goals. Soviet politically motivated justice, in general, included various types of political trials such as trials against class enemies (trials against representatives of bourgeoisie, independent farmers etc.), the Communist Party Purge against political competitors (Moscow show trials), rural (raion) trials, anti-Semitic trials (the so-called 'Doctors' Plot' and the 'Jewish Antifascist Committee'), military trials and criminal prosecution of dissidents in the late Soviet period. Although all of these trials were politically motivated in the sense that they pursued various political, rather than legal goals, it is possible to divide them into two categories of trials with direct and indirect goals of politicized justice. I would argue that trials against class enemies, rural (raion) trials, anti-Semitic trials, military trials and trials against Soviet dissidents belonged to the category, which had indirect political goals, because these trials pursued a broader political and social mission of reorganizing the structure of Soviet society by eliminating or excluding from politics entire social classes and groups. This research focuses rather on the second narrow category of Soviet trials against political competitors, whose goal was directly political, namely to use the system of criminal justice against any actual or potential opposition.

On the one hand, my definition of a political trial adopts a broad approach, which includes all trials that are related to politicians and political matters such as elections, regime change, activities of parties and other political organizations etc. On the other hand, this book discerns a separate group of partisan trials that are politicized (i.e. politically motivated) and used by governments against all forms of opposition.

[25] Ibid., p. 107.

[26] Ibid., p. 106.

[27] Christenson 1999, p. 27.

[28] Viola 2017.

[29] Christenson 1999, p. 29.

My research will provide analysis of the Soviet legacy of show trials, which, in my opinion, is the most vivid example of politicized partisan justice in the former USSR. Thus, for the purposes of this research I will discern between the two general groups of trials depending on the degree of their involvement in politics: (1) political trials that operate within a framework of the rule of law despite the political nature of a case under review; (2) politically motivated or politicized partisan trials, whose goal is political rather than legal. In the next chapter, I will refer back to these definitions of the Soviet politicized justice and political trials.

By analyzing various categories of politically motivated trials conducted during the Soviet times, in the subsequent chapter I elaborate on my own classification of politically motivated trials in the USSR. In particular, this research identifies the following subtypes of Soviet politicized trials: (1) Moscow trials used in the Communist Party Purge; (2) Rural (*raion*) trials; (3) Military Tribunals; (4) Secret summary trials; (5) Anti-Semitic trials, as well as persecution against various ethnic groups; (6) Repressions against independent peasantry (*kulaks*); (7) Trials against dissidents during the late Soviet period. Unwritten practices and rules of politically motivated justice applied in the course of these trials, in turn, are analyzed in Chap. 3, which highlights the different roles played by political trials in Western democracies and transitional post-Soviet states.

1.3 Relevant Theories of Constitutional Law

The purpose of this section is to analyze relevant theories that illustrate deficiencies of constitutionalism in the former Soviet republics and contrast these theories with my concept of 'Twofold Constitutionalism'. This book argues that the phenomenon of politically motivated justice is interconnected with the ongoing crisis of constitutionalism in transitional post-Soviet states. The crisis is demonstrated by several constitutional law theories. For instance, Alexei Trochev's *Theory of 'Non-linear Development'* characterizes the ups and downs of the post-Soviet constitutionalism.[30] Trochev identifies three main puzzles of post-Soviet constitutionalism in Russia: (1) the nonlinear development of the Russian Constitutional Court, which loses and regains its authority in circles; (2) the growing power of the Constitutional Court together with the simultaneous weakening of democratic institutions in Russia; (3) the non-implementation of decisions of the Constitutional Court by the executive and judiciary branches as well as the application of norms that had been already recognized as unconstitutional. This non-linear development is explained by constantly shifting priorities of key decision makers, the lack of legal awareness in the general population as well as drastic social and political changes after the collapse of the Soviet Union. The phenomenon of non-linear constitutionalism described by Trochev

[30]Trochev 2008.

illustrates how the unpredictability and arbitrariness of post-Soviet justice undermined the reputation of legal profession and the public trust in law after the collapse of the Soviet Union.

Andrey Medushevsky developed a theory of '*Nominal Constitutionalism*' to explain the Soviet tradition of written declaratory laws that remained only on paper. According to Medushevsky, with whom I fully agree, although Soviet Constitutions envisaged various rights and freedoms, they were rarely implemented in practice. The nominal constitutionalism of the Soviet Union was used by the Communist Party to hide numerous human rights violations as well as to secure internal and external legitimization of the communist regime. Medushevsky effectively argues that the nominal authority of Soviet written laws was exposed by the dissident movement, whose demonstrative implementation (Russian: v yavochnom poriadke) of the written constitution, though occasionally successful,[31] was persecuted in the Soviet Union as a crime or a social deviation.[32] The ultimate purpose of the demonstrative implementation by dissidents was, therefore, to show the declaratory nature of the written constitution, whose norms could always be trumped by arbitrary and formalistic application of criminal statutes or unwritten political rules.

Armen Mazmanyan coined the terms '*Failing Constitutionalism*' and '*Constitutionalization of Politics*' to describe the Soviet legacy of legal nihilism, political legalism and embedded formalism. Mazmanyan asserts that there is a danger that the 'wave of democratization' in the post-Soviet states "will evolve through undemocratic and unconstitutional channels."[33] Many former Soviet republics display various 'constitutional perversions' such as "the pathologic formalism of the post-Soviet judiciary…[,] [d]efective design of constitutional courts… [as well as] irresponsible political leaders who abuse constitutions and exploit the prevalent patterns of legal formalism to reach their political goals."[34] According to Mazmanyan, such irregularities are rooted in political culture of many post-Soviet states. Constitutionalization of politics is, in turn, necessary to "change the overall logic of constitutional structure from one based on rules and procedures to one based on concepts and principles."[35] Mazmanyan concludes that Constitutional courts can dismantle the Soviet

---

[31] For instance, *Article 125* of the 1936 Constitution guaranteed the "freedom of assembly, including the holding of mass meetings". The text of the 1936 Constitution in English language is available at https://www.departments.bucknell.edu/russian/const/36cons04.html#chap10. Accessed 25 December 2020. Although Soviet dissidents could occasionally organize peaceful assemblies, they were more often arrested for violating public order protected under Article *190.3* of the RSFSR Criminal Code. In particular, "Article 190-3…was a response to group demonstrations that took place after the [dissidents] Sinyavsky-Daniel trial in support of the defendants." In: Berman 1972, p. 82.

[32] Andrei Medushevsky (2011) Stalinizm kak model. Obozreniye izdatelskogo proekta ROSSPEN. Istoriya stalinizma, *Vestnik Evropy*, no. 30. https://magazines.gorky.media/vestnik/2011/30/stalinizm-kak-model-obozrenie-izdatelskogo-proekta-rosspen-istoriya-stalinizma.html. Accessed 24 December 2020.

[33] Mazmanyan 2012, p. 313.

[34] Ibid., p. 319.

[35] Ibid., p. 322.

legacy by going beyond the text of written laws and promoting democratic principles enshrined in written post-Soviet constitutions.

In light of Mazmanyan's theory of 'failing constitutionalism', the Soviet legacy of embedded formalism is fully compatible with Lenin's 'flexibility of law' "guided by a 'revolutionary consciousness' which always had to uphold the regime's interests as top priority…[without] restrain[ing] the leadership's freedom to maneuver."[36] Mazmanyan notes that the Soviet legal tradition was based on "the extremely positivist and legalistic vision of constitution and law in general in post-Communist environments."[37] Furthermore, in the former Soviet Union "law has never been perceived as an objective virtue – *jus*, but solely as a man-made – *lex*."[38] In other words, law is instrumentalized to the level of a procedure applied to reach specific political goals.[39] In constitutional terms, in the socialist legal tradition, for example, "the provision on the freedom of expression and assemblies of the written constitution acquire [only] a procedural shape: demonstrations and rallies can be held in this or that time, in this or that place...and so on….Constitutional law of freedom of expression is often substituted by administrative law."[40] The practice of embedded formalism then means that law is applied literally as a procedure, while completely missing the spirit and the concept of rights and freedoms guaranteed in it. Therefore, democratic principles enshrined in written constitutions can be violated by ruling elites to uphold their interests on the pretext that it is necessary to follow a formal procedure prescribed by law.

1.4 The Phenomenon of 'Twofold Constitutionalism' and Its Legal Orders

My research will offer a separate theory, which can explain the phenomena of 'nominal constitutionalism', 'sham constitutions', 'failing constitutionalism', 'non-linear development' of constitutional courts and 'constitutions without constitutionalism' in criminal justice of transitional post-Soviet states. Although there is much more to constitutionalism than just criminal law, I believe that a specific focus on politicized criminal justice can help reveal the absence of the rule of law in relation to such key values of any constitutional democracy as freedom of political speech and opinion, independent and professional judiciary, principle of legality or no punishment without law, right to counsel, presumption of innocence and the equality of all before the law. My theory of "*Twofold Constitutionalism*" emphasizes the duality of the Soviet legal system rooted in the traditional division of the tsarist legal system into formal law usually borrowed from abroad and informal, mostly unwritten, common

[36] Argenbright 2002, p. 252.
[37] Mazmanyan 2012, p. 319.
[38] Mazmanyan 2012.
[39] Rubenstein 1980.
[40] Mazmanyan 2012, p. 319.

law. I use the previous research on the Soviet system of criminal justice to show that the Soviet constitutions were twofold. The first written and official part of the Soviet Constitutions played only a nominal role by legitimizing the communist regime in the Soviet Union and abroad. The second informal and mostly unwritten part included customary law and other conventionalities of political justice that were superior to all written laws.

In particular, based on my research on the Red Terror and the Communist Party Purge I have found the following conventionalities and practices of Soviet politically motivated justice: (1) *Ex Parte Communication* between prosecutors, judges and organizers of show trials; (2) '*Judicial Prerogativism*', which disfavored actual and potential opponents of the ruling elites; (3) '*Prosecutorial or Accusatorial bias*', according to which a defendant was presumed guilty; (4) '*Confessions and Self-indictment*' that replaced any objective evidence of defendant's guilt or innocence; (5) *Accelerated and simplified 'summary' criminal proceedings* conducted by extra-legal bodies; (6) A doctrine of '*Crime by Analogy*', which in transitional former Soviet republics transformed into arbitrary recharacterization of criminal offences in violation of the principle *nullum crimen*; (7) A '*political amnesty*' or a 'pardon' granted in some political cases. All these informal practices of politicized justice represented the core of the Soviet unwritten constitution.

I further argue that the above-mentioned mostly unwritten practices of Soviet 'Twofold Constitutionalism' were so entrenched that they have survived the collapse of the Soviet Union. This Soviet legacy of two separate legal orders of written (formal) and unwritten (informal) constitutions can be still found in trials conducted against politicians in selected former Soviet republics. I believe that the Soviet legacy of 'Twofold Constitutionalism' is the narrow version of the 'law and order' concept. Although legal systems of the former Soviet republics formally belong to the European civil law family, many of these countries embraced the Soviet dual socialist legality doctrine rather than the Western concepts of the British *Rule of Law* and German *Rechtsstaat*. Therefore, the key difference here is that, unlike the *Rule of Law* and *Rechtsstaat*, under which written and unwritten norms are compatible with the same constitutional principles, the socialist legality is composed of written and unwritten provisions that not only contradict each other, but also pursue opposite values.

This research identified three significant similarities between the Soviet system of political justice discussed in Chap. 2 and recent politicized trials in some former Soviet republics covered in Chap. 3. The first significant similarity to the communist past is that in the chosen post-Soviet states politically motivated justice contributed to the creation of shadow extra-legal bodies that duplicate all branches of government and deal exclusively with political cases. According to Peter Solomon, this phenomenon can be described as 'compartmentalization'[41] of political justice, under which specialized extra-legal bodies are established separately from regular courts to process only political cases. Furthermore, similar to the Soviet Union, transitional post-Soviet republics do not have the true separation of powers between different

[41] Solomon 1996, p. 467.

branches of government, but rather a measurable separation of work between formal institutions and their 'para-constitutional' politically-charged shadow counterparts. In particular, in his research on the duality of law in modern Russia, Richard Sakwa refers to Eugene Huskey who found that "[f]rom the very first days of post-Soviet governance, the problem of duplication of administrative structures was apparent, initially focused on the structure of the dual executive as both the cabinet and the presidency created agencies with overlapping functions (Huskey 1995)."[42] The 'duumvirate' of Putin and Medvedev, who exchanged their presidential and prime-ministerial roles, became the best illustration of the Soviet duality of state in modern Russia. For instance, Medvedev and Putin presided over several para-constitutional bodies such as the State Council, the Legislative Council and the Presidential Council for National Projects that "worked in parallel to the government and [the Parliament]."[43] Sakwa concludes that "[b]y bringing together the various executive and legislative agencies in this way, the…[para-constitutional bodies] also undermined the separation of powers."[44] Similar to Russia, governments of many post-Soviet states include formal branches of government and para-constitutional organs with the real power of political decision-making.

The second feature of the Soviet legacy of politically motivated justice in post-Soviet states nowadays is the transformation of the maxims of criminal law and procedure into their complete opposites. For instance, the presumption of innocence is turned into the presumption of guilt, the principle of no punishment without law is replaced with the doctrine of analogy and arbitrary recharacterization, the judicial duty of care is transformed into judicial prerogativism and the principle of the equality of arms is substituted with the accusatorial bias. Finally, similar to the Soviet Union, in many former Soviet republics conventional goals of criminal punishment are also distorted in favor of the ruling elites. Deterrence, restitution, retribution, education and rehabilitation are replaced with such goals as political retribution and monopolization of power, regime's self-rehabilitation and restitution of political status quo, legitimization of existing regime and deterrence of disobedience, political education and enforcement of the regime's ideology.

Finally, I argue that unwritten customs, conventionalities and practices of politically motivated justice constitute the enforceable unwritten constitution of the former Soviet republics within the timeframe selected for my research. To show the constitutionalization of political justice in these countries, I rely on Joseph Raz' characterization of a constitution, which "in a thick sense of the word is (1) constitutive of the legal and political structure, (2) stable, (3) written [or partially unwritten], (4) superior to other law, (5) justiciable, (6) entrenched, and (7) express common ideology."[45] I believe that only by analyzing ongoing politicized trials in the former Soviet Union, it would be possible to reveal the Soviet legacy of 'Twofold Constitutionalism', which virtually divided many post-Soviet legal systems into two parallel

[42] Sakwa 2010, p. 192.

[43] Sakwa 2010, p. 194.

[44] Ibid.

[45] Sadurski 2012, p. 45.

legal orders. The first 'formal legal order' includes written democratic constitutions that remain only on paper and play a ceremonial role necessary for the legitimization of the ruling elites at home and abroad. The second legal order is represented by mostly unwritten authoritarian practices that despite their informal extra-legal character have a supra-constitutional rank, which can trump any law and prevent the transition of these countries from the duplicity of the socialist legality to the rule of law. A more detailed analysis of the two coexisting legal orders inherited from the USSR and the Russian Empire as well as the roles played by constitutions in democratic and non-democratic states represent the core of my theoretical concept of 'Twofold Constitutionalism' developed in this text.

The *first legal order* of a formal written constitution and its functions in transitional post-Soviet states is a key piece of the puzzle mentioned above. The special role played by written constitutions in authoritarian or transitional societies has been already addressed in the previous research.[46] Scholars who researched this topic before assert that such formal constitutions still matter even in authoritarian or transforming regimes. For instance, "Stalin, along with many Soviet elites, played a direct role in drafting the 1936 Constitution…Why would they bother if the document…[is] meaningless? The standard answer that the constitution is a legitimating device begs a question: How can an obvious sham document generate any legitimacy?"[47] Roles performed by formal constitutions can further clarify their role in transitional post-Soviet states.

Indeed, if the process of developing and adopting written constitutions is time-consuming and challenging,[48] why is it necessary for the leadership of transitional or authoritarian states, where the power of governments is not limited by democratic institutions, to keep a constitution, whose provisions remain only on paper? One answer to this question would be that even in non-democratic states formal constitutions can legitimize the ruling elites by performing various roles. Tom Ginsburg and Alberto Simpser confirm this hypothesis by finding in their study on authoritarian regimes that constitutions of these regimes "perform a variety of functions that can be grouped into four categories that we designate as an operating manual, a billboard, and window dressing."[49] It is true that written constitutions often perform the role, which Adam Przeworski described as the 'operating manual'.[50] In both democratic and non-democratic states "[c]oordination, precommitment, and agency control are all essential governmental functions that can be played by various institutions, but constitutions are particularly good solutions that have become standard in the modern era…[In other words,] [t]he constitutional text describes how government is to function, allowing various players to cooperate by following its instructions."[51] The role

[46]See (1) Ginsburg and Simpser 2013; (2) Barros 2002; (3) Murphy 2006; (4) Myerson 2008; (5) Brown 2011.

[47]Ginsburg and Simpser 2013, p. 1.

[48]Hale 2011.

[49]Ginsburg and Simpser 2013, p. 2.

[50]Przeworski 2013, pp. 21–35.

[51]Ginsburg and Simpser 2013, p. 6.

of a constitutional text as a guideline or instruction for the state apparatus is quite common for Western democracies and developing former Soviet republics.

The coordination role, which is common for all constitutions regardless of the political regime in place,[52] provides also a room for comparison between established democracies and transitional post-Soviet states covered in this research. It means that, while researching these countries, one should expect that "[a]ll regimes need institutions and need to coordinate on what institutions will play what role. Laying out the structures of government facilitates their operation because it prevents continuous renegotiation."[53] Moreover, in both democratic and non-democratic regimes constitutions play a political role by resolving present and potential conflicts among ruling elites. Although it is true that "[a] written constitutional text can thus minimize conflict over basic institutions for any regime", such conflicts over institutional power are more likely to lead to politicized partisan trials in authoritarian or transforming regimes, where even such a basic role of formal constitutions as the coordination role is often disregarded by elites in favor of political expediency.[54] The role of a constitution as an 'operating manual' also attains special significance in non-democratic or transitional societies.

In the Soviet model of government, which presupposes no real separation of powers, but rather a measurable separation of work between government institutions, formal written constitutions outline 'spheres of influence' for different government agencies that often compete with each other for power and, thus, need a formal document to define their mandate and competencies. The role of a 'constitutional operating manual' becomes especially important in the times of democratic transition, given that "[a]uthoritarian constitutions can also facilitate coordination by democrats at crucial moments of transition…The simple coordination function can become extremely important at the end of authoritarian regimes, preventing conflict from spiraling out of control over basic institutions."[55] Even in strong authoritarian states, the operating manual of a formal written constitution can be used to coordinate work of various state agencies.

Hilton Root supports this arguments by pointing out to the fact that "[a]ll [democratic and non-democratic] regimes need mechanisms to control agents, and the problem of gathering information on the activities of agents is an enduring one…Constitutional solutions to the agency problems also include institutions whereby a ruler ties his own hands. Doing so can be a means for enabling the powerful to enter into credible commitments."[56] Though a democratic constitution is supposed to be more than an 'operating manual', in transitional states the coordination achieved thanks to written constitutions can potentially increase the importance of constitutional provisions over time.

---

[52]Rotunda 1998.

[53]Ginsburg and Simpser 2013, p. 3.

[54]Hale 2011.

[55]Ginsburg and Simpser 2013, p. 3.

[56]Root 1989. See also Ginsburg and Simpser 2013.

Ginsburg and Simpser also note the positive role played by formal written constitutions in post-communist oligarchies in the long perspective. In particular, even formal constitutions, whose provisions have only nominal power in many post-Soviet states, "can help oligarchic actors to work together by establishing focal points, procedures, and institutions, thereby addressing problems of coordination and problems of commitment…[This coordination function of formal constitutions] becomes especially important during moments of intra-elite conflict or of regime crisis. Authoritarian constitutions also influence the contours of permissible and impermissible discourse. Finally, as Albert Hirschmann[57]…suggested about the law in general, constitutions can influence the values of citizens over time."[58] Another function of formal constitutions common both for democratic and non-democratic regimes is a 'billboard role'. A written constitution presents a desirable image of a country both to internal and external audiences.[59] With this idea in mind, one can argue that "[c]onstitutions are advertisements; they seek to provide information to potential and actual users of their provisions."[60] Internal audiences can deduce intentions and policy priorities of ruling elites by reading the text of written constitutions. Besides confirming the status of ruling elites as legitimate power brokers and constitution makers at home, constitutional provisions also grant legitimacy abroad, given that "from the very beginning, written constitutions have been adopted in part to signal capacity to engage on the international plane."[61] The 'billboard role' of constitutions is closely connected with their role as carriers of information.

While the information properties of written constitutions are present in both democratic and non-democratic states, authoritarian regimes tend to send different information messages with their constitutional provisions. In particular, in democratic countries, "by establishing procedures to divulge information that could potentially be used against them, [democratically elected] rulers make themselves vulnerable and, in consequence, enhance their credibility."[62] In non-democratic regimes, on the contrary, "authoritarian constitutions may serve to obscure information about true intentions of a ruler or about actual practices [of politically motivated justice] of a regime."[63] Another peculiarity of information messages from authoritarian constitutions is that non-democratic regimes often disregard constitutional rights and freedoms on purpose to show their complete impunity. For instance, Hollyer and Rosendorff effectively assert that authoritarian rulers openly violate election procedures or other constitutional rights and freedoms in order to demoralize an opposition and demonstrate their intentions to persecute their opponents in spite of existing law. The best example would be the increase in the level of torture after the accession to the Convention against Torture in certain authoritarian states, whose ruling elites are

---

[57]Hirschman 1992. See also Ginsburg and Simpser 2013.

[58]Ginsburg and Simpser 2013, p. 2.

[59]Hale 2011.

[60]Ginsburg and Simpser 2013, p. 6.

[61]Golove and Hulsebosch 2010.

[62]Ginsburg and Simpser 2013, p. 10.

[63]Ibid.

determined to show they are powerful enough to violate human rights even with an additional risk of international condemnation or sanctions.[64] Therefore, by manipulating their own constitutions, authoritarian regimes can send a strong message that only they have the legitimate power to decide when and how to implement or disregard the supreme law of the land.

Another role of authoritarian constitution is '*window dressing*', which is characteristic for many transitional former Soviet republics. This function means that the text of a constitution with all its democratic rights and freedoms is just a façade to cover real mechanics of day-to-day political repressions and domination by one group of political elites. In such regimes, "the promises in constitutions are not accurate signals of policy, but pure fictions… The point is that the extensive list of rights found in many totalitarian constitutions is hardly meant to provide for meaningful constraint on the state, or to signal government intents, but is instead a kind of 'cheap talk' that adopts the mere language of rights without any corresponding institutions." [65] There are two goals of this 'constitutional cheap talk'. The first goal is to cover shameful practices of politically motivated justice by presenting an illusionary world of rights and democratic institutions described in the formal and yet nominal written constitutions.[66] In their study of authoritarian constitutions, Ginsburg and Simpser also find that "[the cheap talk] might be taken to imply hiding actual practices [of politicized justice] from external scrutiny. At the margin, it might be that gullible outsiders believe that the…[constitution] is actually implemented."[67] The second goal of the 'cheap talk' is to present an image of a 'decent legal system' compatible with the universal standards of justice.[68] Authoritarian leaders legitimize and whitewash themselves through a democratic constitution "to fit the global scripts that define the basic formal elements, but without risk of costly constraints. Cheap talk is window dressing."[69] The discrepancy between written constitutions and actual practices can also be found in democratic states.

It would be naïve to suggest that constitutions are implemented literally in democratic states. Most constitutions are formulated in very general terms that would be hard to enforce, word by word, in every single case. Many constitutional provisions are rather promises. However, the gap between the general text of the constitution and its actual implementation does not mean that constitutions are meaningless in democratic societies. As David Law and Mila Versteeg suggest,[70] "[g]aps between promises and their actual observance are ubiquitous in law…This is in part because constitutions also operate as a kind of blueprint, describing things not as they are but

64 Hollyer and Rosendorff 2011.

65 Ginsburg and Simpser 2013, p. 7.

66 Gravina 2017.

67 Ginsburg and Simpser 2013, p. 7.

68 Popov and Uporov 2017.

69 Ginsburg and Simpser 2013, p. 7.

70 Law and Versteeg 2013, p. 8.

as they might be. Constitutions are aspirational documents that can serve to motivate people to build a future society."[71] Therefore, in democracies, law and practice attempt to follow the aspirational goals set in constitutions, as opposed to authoritarian or transitional states, where constitutional aspirations are meaningless,[72] as they are routinely disregarded and incompatible with actual legal practices. The main difference between authoritarian and democratic constitutions is, thus, that the former become the so-called 'hollow vessels'[73] described by Ginsburg and Simpser.

Joseph Stalin's Constitution of 1936 aspired to provide rights and freedoms such as universal suffrage, minorities and labor rights previously unknown in the Russian empire.[74] If implemented in practice, these constitutional provisions could have turned the constitutional aspirations into reality. However, "[w]hen Stalin included his list of rights in the 1936 constitutional text, he was debasing the very currency of rights and suggesting to his information-starved citizens that rights *everywhere* were meaningless promises."[75] Former military dictatorships (for instance, Myanmar[76] or Argentina) can be transformed into democracies, when "a constitution that protects free speech might, over time, foster an attitude or norm of tolerance for diversity of opinion. Of course, this need not always be the case: as the idea of constitutions as window dressing suggests, constitutions can also ring hollow to the public, especially when the regime practices are sharply at odds with them."[77] Although it is possible that a constitution can be potentially turned into a hollow vessel and fail even in established democracies like the United States nowadays,[78] authoritarian regimes are more likely to persuade their citizens that constitutions are just meaningless promises that have nothing to do with real life and unwritten political practices that have the actual power to trump any constitutional provision or written law.

The above-mentioned roles of written authoritarian constitutions such as an 'operating guide', a 'billboard' and 'window dressing' make constitutions useful for authoritarian regimes that want to obtain legitimacy at home and abroad. This explains why non-democratic countries keep their written constitutions, although constitutional provisions can be trumped by unwritten political practices any time for the sake of political expediency.[79] However, the extent to which these roles can influence the enforcement of constitutions depends on the specific country setting, given that "the particular mix of roles – operating manual, billboard, blueprint, or window dressing – will vary across time and space, and even across different provisions

---

[71] Ibid.

[72] Ludwikowski 1996.

[73] Ginsburg and Simpser 2013.

[74] Repressii i Konstitutsia SSSR 1936 goda 2002.

[75] Ginsburg and Simpser 2013, p. 8.

[76] Croissant and Kamerling 2013, pp. 105–125.

[77] Ginsburg and Simpser 2013, p. 12.

[78] Schweber 2013.

[79] Hale 2011.

of the same constitution."[80] Some properties of written constitutions are, nevertheless, useful for all non-democratic regimes regardless of the varying role, status and importance of constitutional law there. First, the presence of written constitutions appears to prolong the existence of non-democratic regimes.[81] Michael Albertus and Victor Menaldo found in their study[82] on electoral authoritarian regimes that "those that hold regular, multiparty elections but on a notoriously uneven playing field – have noted that their democratic-like constitutions may in fact help extend regime survival…[Furthermore, their] constitutions contribute to regime endurance by facilitating consolidation of political power and the international coordination of the governing coalition. Constitutional commitments can also facilitate investment and growth, which in turn may extend the lives of [non-democratic] regimes."[83] Therefore, written constitutions create in such authoritarian or transforming regimes an appearance of 'democratic processes', essentially an *imitated democracy*, that may attract foreign investors and prolong the regime's life-span.

Constitution writing as such can also be beneficial for all types of non-democratic regimes. By creating formal but yet fake mechanisms of self-constraint, authoritarian leaders try to appeal to other groups of ruling elites and win the popular support needed to legitimize their continuous stay in power. In his work on autocrats' credibility problem Roger Myerson effectively argues that any authoritarian leader may be potentially interested in creating a 'court of equals' that could potentially remove him or her from power. "Without such an institutionalized check on the leader…[an autocrat] could not credibly raise the support he needs to compete for power."[84] Another role of written constitutions that can be useful for all non-democratic regimes is that constitutions can provide foundations for elections that, at least on paper, could hold such an authoritarian leader accountable to the public. For instance, James Fearon notes that "[a]utocrats face the problem that the public cannot trust them to refrain from shrinking or stealing, and therefore will periodically choose to rebel against the ruler. One way to address this problem is to adopt a constitution that provides for [formally] fair elections to be held regularly. Because the results of such elections aggregate and make public the citizens' private information about the ruler's performance, they make it possible for the ruler to be rewarded by the citizenry for governing well."[85] Therefore, elections, even if they are mostly manipulated by those in power, create an appearance of an authoritarian leader being accountable to the public.

Another side of regular elections outlined by written constitutions useful for non-democratic regimes is that manipulated elections results present such regimes as popular and supported by the majority of the population. This, according to Simpser, helps an authoritarian leader "appear powerful to the public and enhance his control

[80] Ginsburg and Simpser 2013, p. 8.

[81] Gravina 2017.

[82] Albertus and Menaldo 2013, pp. 53–83.

[83] Ginsburg and Simpser 2013, p. 9.

[84] Myerson 2008.

[85] Fearon 2011, p. 5.

over allies and rivals."[86] Constitution making can also promote long-term plans of various non-democratic regimes that try to keep their influence even in case of inevitable democratic transition. For instance, Gabriel Negretto found out in his study of authoritarian constitution making "that [authoritarian regimes of] militaries choose to facilitate their long-term objectives of political, social, and economic transformation and to enhance their influence over post-transition democratic governments...and Negretto [also] argues that the key variable is whether they can mobilize partisan support for their institutional innovations. The point is that dictators, like democrats, do not have perfect foresight as institutional designers."[87] Constitution making can also help collect information important for authoritarian leaders. Such information gathering was present when Stalin drafted the 1936 Constitution[88] and "[m]any [citizens'] comments complained about the constitutional guarantee of free social benefits to workers but not to peasants...The regime was able to gauge what issues were important to the public, even if it chose to ignore them in the final analysis."[89] Thus, writing a constitution can be useful for non-democratic regimes even before the constitution is adopted.

Overall, both constitution writing and the text of a constitution may provide advantages to authoritarian leaders who often want to show that they are powerful enough to develop and introduce a new constitution. At the same time, "authoritarians, as compared with leaders in democracies, may be more insulated from social forces in choosing the timing and process of constitution making."[90] The symbolic significance of written constitutions[91] both for constitution makers and their target audiences explains why authoritarian leaders still develop and keep written constitutions despite the nominal status of such documents in non-democratic regimes. Given the importance of the 'constitutional project' for such regimes, "constitutional production can also be a 'consumption activity' for [authoritarian] rulers."[92] All these considerations explain how formal constitutions and the process of their development facilitate the legitimization of non-democratic regimes and their longevity.[93] Based on the previous research mentioned above it is, thus, possible to conclude that in non-democratic countries formal rules matter "even when there is a lot of [political] discretion at the top...[because n]o single person rules absolutely, and therefore there is a need for intra-elite coordination, as well as for devices to control subordinates."[94] Most importantly, despite their weak status in the legal hierarchy,[95] "[a]uthoritarian constitutions – and the process of making them – also provide important clues into

[86]Simpser 2013. See also Ginsburg and Simpser 2013, p. 5.
[87]Ginsburg and Simpser 2013, p. 13.
[88]Repressii i Konstitutsia SSSR 1936 goda 2002.
[89]Ginsburg and Simpser 2013, p. 13.
[90]Ibid., p. 13.
[91]Hale 2011.
[92]Ginsburg and Simpser 2013, p. 14.
[93]Croissant and Kamerling 2013, pp. 105–125.
[94]Ginsburg and Simpser 2013, p. 14.
[95]Gravina 2017.

regime [unwritten] practices."[96] Although informal conventionalities of politicized justice often relegate the conventional status of a constitution as the supreme law of the land to a mere decoration, even nominal authoritarian constitutions continue to perform roles of the 'operating guide', the 'billboard' and 'window-dressing' that are essential for the legitimization and longevity of non-democratic regimes.

Another piece of the "Twofold Constitutionalism" puzzle is ***the Second Legal Order*** of unwritten political practices and conventionalities inherited by transitional former Soviet republics from the USSR.[97] The parallel informal legal world complements and underlies the formal written constitution, which can be fully understood and studied only in combination with unwritten practices of politicized justice. It is true that formal rules are also not applied literally in democracies. However, in non-democratic, hybrid or transitional regimes informal political practices appear to play a more significant role than in established democratic states. Before explaining the inner mechanics of the informal legal order in transitional former Soviet republics, it would be useful to outline a general definition of formal and informal norms.

According to Helmke and Levitsky, informal norms are "social rules, usually unwritten, that are created, communicated, and enforced outside of officially sanctioned channels…[, while formal norms are] rules and procedures that are created, communicated, and enforced through channels widely accepted as official."[98] Given that written rules can be openly disregarded in transitional former Soviet republics, one can assert that "[w]hat matters [there] instead is said to be informal politics, the "real" workings of politics, those unwritten officially uncodified norms, habits, and practices that actually guide political behavior."[99] In this vein, the concept of "Twofold Constitutionalism" proposed in this book argues that informal rules of politically motivated justice play a key role in transitional states, as these rules can trump at any moment all formal laws including constitutional provisions. Therefore, this second code of informal rules deserves special consideration.

Numerous authors have already written about the existence of the second set of informal rules in totalitarian and authoritarian states. *Ernst Fraenkel* was the first to notice the duality of the legal system in Nazi Germany with its normative and prerogative states.[100] According to Fraenkel, the normative state was capable of regulating economic relations exclusively through law, while in the prerogative state politics could always trump law to prosecute opponents and to promote the ideology of National Socialism. *Robert Sharlet* developed the concept of the dual state by using the Soviet Union as an example of such a state.[101] In particular, Sharlet referred to the split of the Soviet system of justice into the socialist legality (Russian: *sotcialisticheskaya zakonnost*) and the 'Communist Party law'. Similar to Scharlet, *Richard*

[96] Ginsburg and Simpser 2013, p 14.
[97] Ludwikowski 1996.
[98] Helmke and Levitsky 2004.
[99] Ginsburg and Simpser 2013, p. 218.
[100] Fraenkel 1969.
[101] Sharlet 1998.

Sakwa found a dual state of the same kind in Russia after the fall of Communism.[102] In Sakwa's model Fraenkel's prerogative state became an administrative state, which disregards the written law and coexists with the constitutional state, where the public is supposed to follow the formal constitution. In her recent study on everyday law in Russia Kathryn Hendley observes that, similar to many other former Soviet states,[103] "Russia consistently languishes near the bottom of indexes that aim to measure the rule of law…Given the cornerstone of any definition of the Rule of Law is the equal treatment of all before the law, Russia's law stature within these indexes is almost certainly a result of its willingness to use the law as an instrument to punish its enemies."[104] This book argues that the unwritten practices of politicized justice[105] are rooted in the tsarist and communist legacies.

I fully agree with Hendley's research findings that the roots of this legal dualism in Russia and in other former Soviet republics are "at the heart of Russia's attitude toward law and legal institutions dating back to the Great Judicial Reforms of 1864 and perhaps further. But this dualism has rarely been acknowledged….A look back at Russian law in the tsarist and Communist periods reveals the long standing role of dualism, a syndrome that undergirds present-day attitudes."[106] In his recent article on the Russian Constitutional Court, Alexei Trochev agrees with Kathryn Hendley when he concludes that various dynamics of constitutionalism in Russia "have one feature in common: the duality of the Russian state and its legal system."[107] One element of this duality is traditional legal nihilism and disregard of law in Russian culture, which spread to the territories that used to belong to the Russian empire. Russian legal philosopher of the nineteenth century Bogdan Kistiakovsky wrote that "[t]he Russian intelligentsia never respected law and never saw any value in it. Of all the cultural values, law was the most suppressed. Given such circumstances,…[Russian] intelligentsia could not have hoped to develop a sound legal consciousness, which, on the contrary, remains at the lowest possible level of development."[108] Similar to Kistiakovsky, Russian writer Alexander Herzen observed that "[w]hatever his station, the Russian evades or violates the law wherever he can do so with impunity: the government does exactly the same thing."[109] The beginning of the legal dualism can also be traced back to the Great Judicial Reforms of 1864 that introduced a dual system of justice of urban (Russian: *mirovye sudy*) and rural (Russian: *volost'*) courts. "On

---

[102] Sakwa 2013.

[103] "And Russia is not alone…It is part of a surprisingly large group of authoritarian or quasi-authoritarian countries in which the courts mostly function within the law, but in which the political leadership feels entitled to use the courts to serve its goals and turns a blind eye to others with power or influence who are doing the same." In: Hendley 2017, p. 3. See also Melville and Mironyuk 2016, pp. 132–51.

[104] Hendley 2017, p. 2.

[105] Hale 2011.

[106] Hendley 2017, p. 5.

[107] Trochev 2017.

[108] Shragin and Todd 1977; Hendley 2017, p. 5.

[109] Ibid.

paper, the courts seemed quite different because the former were governed by statutory law, whereas the latter took local customs into account as well when resolving disputes."[110] Such a division of the legal system into customary and statutory law caused mixed reactions among legal scholars and inhabitants of the Russian Empire at that time.

I tend to agree with proponents of the *volost'* courts who argued that these rural courts gave an opportunity to maintain legal consciousness based on national customs and traditions, as opposed to urban courts that used statutory law often borrowed from abroad and, thus, alien to the legal culture in the vast territories of the empire. Cathy Frierson, in particular, mentioned in her study of this subject that "[s]upporters of the [*volost'*] court argued that customary law was a manifestation of rural legal consciousness and that this form of legal consciousness was legitimate." [111] Furthermore, Frierson explains that for many residents of rural areas in the Russian empire *volost'* courts were the only solution, as they "went to [the] court when the rules were uncertain and resorted to self-help when the communal norms were well-established."[112] Hendley also argues that *volost'* courts played a positive role by strengthening national legal consciousness and community norms, when she points out to the fact that "[, i]n contradiction of the common wisdom of peasants' lack of legal consciousness, those who have dug into the archival records have found that peasants saw the *volost* courts as a viable alternative and understood how to use them. Slowly but surely, these courts were unearthing community norms and holding litigants accountable to them."[113] It appears that *volost'* courts contributed to many positive social and legal developments in various regions and national communities of the Russian empire.

The system of justice based on local traditions, values, customs and conventionalities acceptable and comprehensible for residents of the Russian empire indeed helped address social and other issues pertinent for the society during that time. For instance, Beatrice Farnsworth's study of family law in the Russian empire reveals that *volost'* courts strengthened "the propensity of less powerful family members – daughters-in-law – to invoke the law to protect themselves. [Customary] Law became an equalizing force in an unequal society…, 'township [*volost'*] courts enabled gradual changes in the patriarchical order of the countryside."[114] Most importantly, the case law and procedures of *volost'* courts assisted in formulating, documenting and systematizing customary norms that, due to their previously unwritten and fragmented nature, could not occupy a proper place in the national legal hierarchy of the Russian empire. Frierson confirms this point of view by asserting that in the Russian empire "[p]easants took petty, primarily financial, disputes to the cantonal [*volost*] court…The large numbers of financial disputes signified that economic relations and agreements in the village no longer functioned according to rules that were tacit,

[110] Ibid., p. 6.

[111] Frierson 1986, pp. 526–545. See also Hendley 2017.

[112] Hendley 2017, p. 6.

[113] Hendley 2017, pp. 7–8.

[114] Ibid. See also Feifer 1964 and Farnsworth 1986.

informal, and intuitively perceived."[115] Ironically, this legal empowerment of peasants by *volost'* courts was terminated by the communist regime, which allegedly 'protected' the working class.

Karl Marx' theory of 'withering away with law' in an ideal communist society was later used by Ulianov-Lenin, the leader of Bolsheviks to dismantle the tsarist system of justice along with its urban and cantonal *volost'* courts after the October Revolution and the adoption of the first constitution of the Russian socialist republic in 1918.[116] This also marked the politicization of the entire system of justice, because, as Richard Pipes found in his research of Soviet revolutionary justice, "once Lenin came to power he promptly transformed justice into the handmaiden of politics."[117] Hendley concurs with Pipes on this matter, when she observes that "[t]he use of law by the political elite as a crude instrument for achieving their goals was certainly a key feature of socialist legality as it developed following the October Revolution. The use of highly scripted show trials to rid society of real and perceived enemies was only the most obvious example. This tactic reached a fevered pitch during the Great Terror of the 1930s, but never entirely disappeared [even in post-Soviet times]."[118] Thanks to greater access to historical archives of the early Soviet Union, "a more nuanced picture of the Rule of Law in the early decades of Communist Party power that recognizes its dualistic character has come into focus that is remarkably consistent…with Sharlet's larger dualism thesis [on the communist totalitarian system of justice]."[119] The division of Soviet justice into regular written norms mandatory for the general public and unwritten Communist Party norms applicable only to senior party members completed the establishment of the dual state in the Soviet Union. Compartmentalization of political justice in the USSR,[120] where separate agencies were established to deal exclusively with political cases, made it possible that "[i]n the Soviet political system the prerogatives of power included the use of agencies of justice against persons deemed enemies of the state…The involvement of the KGB in a case rendered it political and subject to [the unwritten practice of] telephone law."[121] I argues that these practices of politicized justice still constitute an unwritten constitution of many former Soviet republics.

The dual state with its legal nihilism and unwritten practices of politicized justice can be found in Russia as well as many other former Soviet republics even after the collapse of the Soviet Union. For instance, "Dmitrii Medvedev's comments in 2008 on the eve of his entry into the presidential race are illustrative: 'Without exaggeration, Russia is a country of legal nihilism…No other European country can boast of such a level of disregard for [formal] law'."[122] The still existing gap between formal

[115] Frierson 1986, pp. 526–545.
[116] Yanin 1996.
[117] Hendley 2017, p. 9. See also Pipes 1986.
[118] Ibid., p. 9.
[119] Ibid.
[120] Solomon 1996, p. 467.
[121] Hendley 2017, p. 10.
[122] Hendley 2017, p. 13.

written norms and routinely applied informal practices demonstrates the persistent duality of legal and social consciousness in the aftermath of the fall of Communism. The ability to navigate in the twofold world of legal fiction and political reality is the communist legacy in many former Soviet republics. Stephen Kotkin found in his study of Stalinism that "Russians' tendency to censor themselves is nothing new, but is an unfortunate carryover from the Soviet era, during which people learned to censor their public speech and to share their true thoughts with a small circle of family and close friends (if at all)…[Furthermore, i]t was not necessary to believe. It was necessary, however, to participate as if one believed – a stricture that appears to have been well understood, since what could be construed as direct, openly disloyal behavior became rare."[123] This Soviet phenomenon of social hypocrisy makes, in turn, possible the existence of "Twofold Constitutionalism" with its two parallel worlds of formal and informal norms. Jochem Hellbeck observes the same phenomenon when he notes that during the Soviet times "the private self often remained obscure, even in personal diaries, giving rise to a kind of 'split consciousness' or a 'dual soul' (*dvoedushie*)…Individuals possessed multiple identities."[124] Other researchers of modern Russia and other former Soviet republics concur that the phenomenon of multiple identities persists even after the collapse of the Soviet Union.

The fact that the split of social and legal consciousness is present in many former Soviet republics demonstrates that the legacy of "Twofold Constitutionalism" still occupies an important place in these countries. For instance, Kathryn Hendley notes that "[a] version of this sort of political correctness lingers on in present-day Russia. Perhaps it could be redefined as a need to 'speak Putinism', given that the current expectation is to appear to toe the line on Putin's policy. Many Russians, especially those socialized in the Soviet Union, are unwilling to speak openly except with trusted family members and friends."[125] In the same vein, Svetlana Boym "comments that 'saying what you mean' could be interpreted as being stupid, naïve, or not street-wise [in the post-Soviet context]."[126] In his description of Putin's Russia, British writer Peter Pomerantsev also "reflects that all cultures have differences between 'public' and 'private' selves, but in Russia, the contradictions can be quite extreme."[127] In this regard, Hendley draws conclusions regarding the Russian system of justice that can also be applicable to other former Soviet republics. She suggests that Fraenkel's model of the dual state can be applicable to "legal systems like Russia's, namely, that courts do not necessarily have a single institutional identity…The same court – even the same judge – can follow the law to the letter or openly disregard it, depending on the context."[128] These multiple institutional and individual identities make "Twofold Constitutionalism" possible.

---

[123] Kotkin 1997; Hendley 2017, p. 14.

[124] Hellbeck 2000; Engelstein and Sandler 2000.

[125] Hendley 2017, p. 14.

[126] Boym 1995; Hendley 2017, p. 14.

[127] Pomerantsev 2014; Hendley 2017, p. 14.

[128] Hendley 2017, p. 4.

The Soviet legacy of 'Homo Sovieticus' or a person able to navigate in multiple social and legal 'realities' raises the question whether the above-mentioned two coexisting legal orders of formal constitutional provisions and informal practices can be compared with the regular system of justice in established democracies. At the same time, democracies like the United Kingdom also have practices that occupy a high rank in the British legal hierarchy.[129] Considering this, what theoretical basis can be used to differentiate between state-sanctioned politically motivated justice of "Twofold Constitutionalism" in the former Soviet republics and the conventional administration of justice by independent judiciary in democratic states? I argue that *labeling theories*,[130] developed in the twentieth century to describe how a person can be labeled as a criminal in different societies, provide a useful theoretical framework for the comparison of transitional post-Soviet republics and established democracies. Macnaughton-Smith's concept of the '*Second Code*'[131] is one of such labeling theories that can help locate the place of the Soviet legacy of "Twofold Constitutionalism" within the current theories of criminology. In particular, Macnaughton-Smith made a proposition that every society develops and enforces law by its actual actions and routine practices rather than by written legal statutes. In practical terms, it means that a criminal liability is assigned to a specific suspect not only based on written rules of criminal law and procedure, but also in line with subjective judgments, unwritten conventionalities, principles and moral values maintained in the given society. The phenomenon of the 'Second Code' coined by Macnaughton-Smith is present in any complex society regardless of its political regime.

Similar to the concept of "Twofold Constitutionalism" offered in this text, Macnaughton-Smith's 'Second Code' presupposes the existence of two sets of rules. Unlike the set of official norms outlined in written laws, "[t]he second set of rules is not explicit. It has to be inferred from what actually happens, and so it can never be known with certainty, but only probabilistically."[132] For instance, according to this theory, a suspect could be labeled as a perpetrator based on subjective 'halo judgments' or 'subjective guesses' that are related to the suspect's age, social status, education etc. Macnaughton-Smith compares a legal system with the work at a factory, which has a number of rules, whose violation could lead to a penalty (dismissal) of those factory employees who violated them. Similar to formal written laws, factory rules are always broken, "and, in fact, the [factory] management does not want them kept."[133] The theory of the 'Second Code' presumes that it is impossible to follow and apply all official rules literally. Some form of interpretation of the official set of rules will be necessary to evaluate their relevance in each particular case. In this regard, Macnaughton-Smith speculates that those who apply official rules will do this in line with the second set of unofficial rules that "will be

[129] Raz 2009, p. 325.

[130] Several authors developed the labelling theories, i.e. (1) Gove 1980; (2) Paternoster and Iovanni 1989; (3) Becker 1963; (4) Braithwaite 1989.

[131] Macnaughton-Smith 1968.

[132] Ibid., p. 193.

[133] Macnaughton-Smith 1968, p. 193.

unwritten, [and] sometimes unknown."[134] Exactly this second set of unofficial rules becomes the 'Second Code', by which people actually live and are labeled by others as perpetrators.

In this dual system, it is not the first set of official rules, but the second set or code of unofficial rules is more important in resolving conflicts, assigning liability and punishing alleged perpetrators. Macnaughton-Smith accordingly asserts that "[w]hen you infringe the second set of rules you run a high risk of being punished for an offence against the first, official set. If you keep the second set your transgressions against the (universally broken) first set will probably be ignored or even rewarded."[135] The issue is that the existence of the 'Second Code' of informal norms and their prevalence over formal ones is often ignored or not openly recognized in many societies. It is also difficult to analyze the second set of unofficial rules, given that "[a]lthough the law abiding citizen keeps well within the second set [of rules], its contents are not known with any precision."[136] Macnaughton-Smith concludes his analysis by saying that it is possible to determine the content of the 'Second Code' by focusing more on how a given society labels a person as a perpetrator rather than on some 'universal concept' of a violation against formal written norms, which may differ from one country to another.

This book argues that the content of the 'Second Code' described by Macnaughton-Smith could be determined by studying legal practices, conventionalities, traditions and customs that are the result of historical and social development in each particular state. I argue that, as opposed to established democracies, where the 'Second Code' of informal practices usually complements and fills in the 'gaps' in the first set of official norms, in post-Soviet non-democratic or transitional states, the 'Second Code' includes politically charged practices that are in direct conflict with the first set of official, but only nominal constitutional provisions. Furthermore, the analysis of political trials in the transitional former Soviet republics and in established Western democracies shows that in the former group of countries the 'Second Code' of informal practices is completely detached from the official legal provisions that are often borrowed from abroad. Therefore, in transitional post-Soviet states informal practices of political justice rather undermine formal constitutions than complement them like in Western democracies. The probable root causes of this discrepancy between the two sets of official norms and unofficial practices could be explained by the longevity of the communist regime, which managed to replace the 'Second Code' of national legal traditions and customs of many former Soviet republics with the 'Second Code' of politically charged practices based on the communist ideology and quasi-legal concepts such as socialist legality, the doctrine of analogy, revolutionary consciousness or vigilance. Generations of legal professionals that study and practice law under the influence of these 'politically charged customs' continue to carry on with the Soviet legacy of 'Twofold Constitutionalism', which was not dismantled due to the lack of necessary judicial reforms and transitional justice measures. Recent

[134] Ibid.

[135] Ibid.

[136] Ibid., p. 194.

politically motivated trials against opposition leaders further reveal this duality of post-Soviet justice and the supremacy of the 'Second Code' of unwritten political practices over democratic constitutions adopted shortly after the collapse of the Soviet Union.

The labelling theory of the 'Second Code' described above provides a credible explanation of the difference between politics and administration of justice in transitional post-Soviet states and in Western democracies. It appears that in established democratic states both the first and the second 'codes' proscribe a clear line between political and judicial matters even in 'criminal proceedings' against politicians. Both official written norms of the first code and unofficial practices of the second code of democratic societies give all defendants in such political cases a fair opportunity to present their cases in court. In transitional post-Soviet societies, on the contrary, the division between the administration of justice and politics is blurred or absent in cases related to political matters. Politically charged unwritten practices of the 'Second Code' can trump all provisions of the first set of formal norms, thus creating a system of politicized justice run by politicians for the sake of political expediency. It also appears that politics and the administration of criminal justice often pursue different goals in the former USSR and in established democracies.

In Western democracies, the system of justice is supposed to ensure that everyone abides the law and perpetrators are prosecuted in accordance with law. The administration of justice in transitional former Soviet republics has the role usually performed by politics, in the sense that it helps attain and consolidate political power.[137] The system of justice performs political functions in transitional former Soviet republics, because, similar to politics, judiciary in these countries is dependent on fluctuating political interests and competing political elites. Similar to politics, the post-Soviet system of justice often attempts to 'please' the public by organizing show trials that are supposed to demonstrate the efficacy of government in 'fighting crime'.[138] In Western democracies, on the contrary, the administration of justice is usually independent from the influence of individual politicians and relies rather on career legal professionals who are supposed to administer justice regardless of political preferences or affiliations. Furthermore, unlike established democracies, in many former Soviet republics both politics and actual administration of justice are not governed by a written set of rules. In the post-Soviet context, both justice and politics are rather administered through the unwritten 'Second Code' of practices, whose influence and frequency of application depend on the "distribution of [political] forces (rasstanovka sil)."[139] Finally, taking into account that, similar to the Soviet Union, many former Soviet republics do not have a true separation of powers, but rather a measurable separation of work among state institutions, politicians from the executive branch are still often involved in appointment and promotion of judges. The dependence of judges on political forces turns the administration of justice into a mere extension of politics in these post-Soviet states.

[137] Solomon 2016.

[138] Kovalev 2004.

[139] Solomon 1992, p. 37.

The above-mentioned model of two codes with formal and informal rules can also clarify the role of show trials in transitional former Soviet republics. Taking into account that the administration of justice becomes in these countries just a surrogate and an extension of politics,[140] post-Soviet ruling elites use show trials to communicate the official ideology and the supreme status of informal practices of the 'Second Code' to the public.[141] Show trials become a useful political tool to undermine credibility of the opposition and belittle its criticism of government by branding opposition leaders as common criminals or foreign agents that do not have the moral standing to represent the popular dissent and organize protests against those in power. A role of 'appointed opposition' will be then delegated only to those who do not have significant popular support or depend on the ruling elites. Given that in the post-Soviet politics the winner often 'takes it all', the 'Second Code' of politicized practices provides an opportunity to get rid of potential and actual competitors after the change of ruling elites.[142] Once a political opponent is removed from politics and publicly humiliated in the course of his or her show trial, he or she may be released on amnesty to show the public that the 'system of justice' can be both strict and lenient with political opposition. In reality, the quasi-legal political amnesty is aimed at expelling strong opposition figures from the country and preventing the opposition from becoming popular martyrs that could question the moral legitimacy of the existing political regime. Finally, politically charged administration of justice utilizes informal practices of the 'Second Code' to legitimize those in power through political show trials. As opposed to simple extra-legal executions or assassinations of political opponents, which can compromise the 'moral image' of the ruling elites, pseudo-trials give the appearance of legality and legitimate use of state power against representatives of opposition. Therefore, the 'Second Code' of Soviet informal practices proved to be useful in organizing show trials, eliminating opposition and legitimizing post-Soviet elites.

The theory of a trial as a degradation ceremony[143] developed by Harold Garfinkel could further explain why post-Soviet authoritarian regimes find it more politically advantageous to organize politicized show trials instead of simply using non-legal means to remove opposition leaders from politics. Garfinkel effectively argues that any complex society has various degradation ceremonies aimed at lowering a social status of those who allegedly perpetrated offences against moral values, principles, norms and laws of these societies. By punishing the deviant behavior of a perpetrator, participants of degradation ceremonies confirm the importance of the above-mentioned norms and values. According to Garfinkel, "[t]he court and its officers have something like a fair monopoly over such [degradation] ceremonies, and there they have become an occupation routine."[144] Goals and mechanisms of a degradation

[140]Carothers 1999.

[141]Current Digest of the Post-Soviet Press 2010.

[142]Ergun 2010, pp. 67–85.

[143]Garfinkel 1956, pp. 420–24.

[144]Ibid., p. 424.

ceremony are virtually identical to those of a politicized show trial in many former Soviet republics.

One of the goals of the degradation ceremony is to cause the moral indignation by publicly denouncing an alleged perpetrator. Harold Garfinkel asserts that, by using a public denunciation against someone, "we publicly deliver the curse: 'I call upon all men to bear witness that he is not as he appears but is otherwise and in essence...of a lower species."[145] I argue that the Soviet tradition of a politically motivated show trial pursues the same goal and is by itself a form of a degradation ceremony. As opposed to a non-politicized criminal trial, which denounces an offender who violated written provisions of law, the Soviet show trial is supposed to cause the moral indignation against political opponents by publicly denouncing them for their violation of unwritten political norms and practices.[146] Another similarity of the Soviet-type show trial and the degradation ceremony is that they both serve "to effect the ritual destruction of the person denounced."[147] Garfinkel also notices the political implications of the degradation ceremony given that "in politics, a degradation ceremony must be countered as a secular form of communion...[, which binds persons to the collectivity...[and] may reinforce group solidarity.]"[148] In the same vein, a show trial binds the community together by demonstrating that 'self-proclaimed' political opponents are in fact common criminals that do not belong to the collectivity and must be publicly denounced due to their 'deviant behavior'.

The alteration in the public perception of political opposition appears to be the major outcome of the Soviet-type show trial as a degradation ceremony. As a result of the politicized show trial, an opposition politician is supposed to lose his or her moral standing and legitimacy, which would undermine opposition's criticism of those who are in power. By organizing a show trial, a repressive regime demonstrates the public its power and the 'weakness' of a certain opposition leader, who appears to be helpless in his or her confrontation with the state apparatus. Moreover, with the help of the show trial the repressive regime labels representatives of political opposition as 'common criminals' that allegedly tried to disguise their 'true criminal identity' under a 'false identity' of political opponents.

In line with Garfinkel's theory, the politicized show trial reconstitutes the identity of an opposition politician in the aftermath of the trial "when the former identity [of a government opponent] stands as accidental...[and] the new identity [of a common criminal becomes] the basic reality."[149] Thus, when an opposition leader is denounced as a criminal in a show trial, in the eyes of the target audience, "[w]hat he is now is what 'after all,' he was all along."[150] Instead of eliminating political opponents and turning them into martyrs, repressive post-Soviet regimes use the old

[145]Ibid., p. 421.

[146]Hodos 1987.

[147]Garfinkel 1956, p. 424.

[148]Ibid.

[149]Garfinkel 1956, p. 422.

[150]Ibid.

Soviet practice of show trials to convert political opposition into easily intelligible crimes and, thus, undermine the ability of opposition to lead the popular dissent.

1.5 Interplay Between Written (Formal) and Unwritten (Informal) Constitutions

The interaction between formal and informal norms plays a key role in understanding the Soviet phenomenon of 'Twofold Constitutionalism'. The purpose of this section is to elaborate on the meaning of informal practices, their interplay with formal norms and the constitutional nature of unwritten rules in the Soviet legal culture. Unwritten practices and their role in non-democratic states have been already analyzed in the works of such authors as Stiglitz,[151] Merkel and Croissant[152] and Wilson.[153] The most comprehensive account of informal practices in the former Soviet Union, in my opinion, was given by Alena Ledeneva, who researched the impact of such practices on the post-communist economic transition in Russia and other former Soviet republics.[154] For the purpose of this research, it is essential to establish the difference between informal and formal norms. According to Ledeneva, "the ideal type of formal rules include juridical or quasi-juridical rules that are consciously produced and enforced by mechanisms created for purposes of such enforcement."[155] Unlike formal rules, "the ideal types of informal norms include customs, codes and ethics that are byproducts of various forms of social organization (for example, family, personal network, neighborhood, community, club membership)."[156] The interplay between both categories of norms is of major importance for this research on unwritten practices of politicized justice in the former Soviet Union.

The central issue to be addressed within this book is how formal (written) and informal (unwritten) norms interact with each other and which set of norms prevails over the other. Based on the previous analysis of post-Soviet unwritten practices,[157] it appears that informal norms compensate for inconsistencies or contradictions of existing formal laws. As the famous Russian proverb goes, "the imperfection of our laws is compensated for by their non-observance (nesovershenstvo nashikh zakonov kompensiruetsya ikh nevypolneniem)."[158] In many post-Soviet states, frequently changing, unenforceable and self-contradicting written laws lead to the systemic violation of the very same laws by virtually everyone. Ledeneva observes that in post-Soviet transitional societies troubled with economic hardships "nearly everybody is

[151] Stiglitz 2003.
[152] Merkel and Croissant 2000.
[153] Wilson 2005.
[154] Ledeneva and Kurkchiyan 2000.
[155] Ibid., p. 17.
[156] Ledeneva and Kurkchiyan 2000.
[157] Gravina 2017.
[158] Ledeneva and Kurkchiyan 2000, p. 2.

compelled to earn in the informal economy in order to survive – a practice that is punishable, or could be made so…[For instance, b]usinesses are taxed at a rate that forces them to evade taxes in order to do well."[159] The wide-scale disregard of written norms makes it impossible to impose sanctions on such a big group of offenders. Therefore, virtually everyone is guilty of violating formal norms and can find oneself under the threat of punishment, which is "'suspended' but can be enforced at any time."[160] The arbitrariness of such selective punishment, in turn, undermines the credibility of any legal system.

For the purposes of this research, it must be noted that the issue of selective prosecution in the context of post-communist criminal justice usually happens at the pretrial stage and, thus, should be treated separately from the phenomenon of dependent post-Soviet judiciary, whose credibility is undermined by political pressure and interventions in the course of a trial. Maria Popova corroborates this opinion in her research on politicized justice in emerging democracies, when she finds that "Khodorkovsky…[,] who defied the Putin's administration's informal ban on meddling in politics [,]…bec[a]me Russia's most visible…political prisoner…[whose] selective prosecution…generated talk about Russia's catastrophic failure at building a rule-of-law-based post-communist state."[161] While the political leadership of Russia selectively initiated a pre-trial investigation against Khodorkovsky for his involvement in politics, the issue of a politically dependent judiciary manifested itself later during and even after the trial in his case. For instance, Popova observes that, although "[o]nce [already] imprisoned, Khodorkovsky saw a series of court decisions dismember his multibillion-dollar company, Yukos,…his defense, human rights advocates, opposition figures, and even former Russian judges have claimed that the numerous criminal cases against Khodorkovsky…and other Yukos employees were decided in the Kremlin rather than in court."[162] In this regard, I will analyze selective justice through judicial prerogativism, which targets victims of politicized justice at the pre-trial stage, while the lack of independent judiciary will be scrutinized through prosecutorial bias, which occurs already in court.

According to Ledeneva's concept of post-Soviet informal practices, "[b]ecause of the pervasiveness of [formal] rule violation, punishment is bound to occur selectively on the basis of criteria developed outside the legal domain."[163] In other words, the above-mentioned arbitrariness of criminal sanctions triggers the application of unwritten rules that determine who becomes the next victim of selective punishment. In the context of this research on politicized criminal justice, it is necessary to note that victims of a politically motivated trial need not be guilty of violating formal provisions of written criminal statutes. The described mechanism of selective persecution can also target a completely innocent person to send a 'message' to the public about the alleged 'effectiveness' of the criminal justice system and to remove

[159] Ledeneva 2006, p. 13.

[160] Ibid.

[161] Popova 2012, p. 10.

[162] Ibid., p. 9.

[163] Ledeneva 2006, p. 13.

inconvenient opponents of ruling elites. Ledeneva notes that the practice of arbitrary punishment is the legacy of the Soviet Union, where "a certain freedom and flexibility did exist [under written law] but could be restricted at any moment…[and] it became a routine practice for the authorities to switch to the written code only 'when necessary'."[164] Alternatively, a person may be selectively prosecuted for violating formal laws when the real reason for prosecution is in fact non-compliance with unwritten political rules. Though oligarch Mikhail Khodorkovsky was formally convicted for economic crimes, "what most…interpretations have in common, however, is that Khodorkovskii [and his Yukos company] violated the unwritten rules announced in June 2000 at the meeting between Putin and oligarchs, who were told to stay out of politics."[165] Thus, the violation of unwritten political rules appears to be the real reason behind Khodorkovskii's prosecution.

Solomon notes that during the Soviet times the scope of interventions by the Communist Party into the work of the judiciary fluctuated depending on the current political situation and the interpretation of socialist legality by various state agencies. For instance, "some legal officials who were especially principled, courageous, or stubborn took the risk of disregarding or opposing…[unwritten political practices and i]n such battles victory could go to either side depending upon the 'distribution of [political] forces' (rasstanovka sil)."[166] Ledeneva echoes this assessment by asserting that the ineffectiveness of formal norms leads to volatility and flexibility of informal unwritten norms that are "introduced and [continuously] negotiated outside formal institutions."[167] Immo Rebitschek reaches the same conclusion in his research on the Soviet Procuracy in the Molotov region in 1943–1950. In particular, Rebitschek observes that Soviet regional prosecutors, who were responsible for the practical application of socialist legality, tried to enforce written rules of criminal procedure and limit political interventions "by means of conflict and negotiations."[168] To describe the phenomenon of continuously changing balance between formal and informal rules, Rebitschek coined the term "Steered Justice System", which seeks to "reconcile the function [of formal written norms] and political means [of unwritten informal practices]."[169] The main feature of the steered system is that informal practices prevail over formal norms when legal officials are unable or unwilling to resist political interventions.

The key proposition of this book is that the unwritten informal practices and rules described above became an unwritten constitution of many transitional post-Soviet states. There are three arguments in support of this claim. First, informal practices and rules have a ***radiating effect*** in the sense that at any moment they can prevail over formal rules including constitutional provisions in all spheres of social and political life. Ledeneva asserts that unwritten rules are ubiquitous, because

---

164 Ledeneva 2006.

165 Ibid., p. 194.

166 Solomon 1992, p. 37.

167 Ledeneva 2006, p. 13.

168 Rebitschek 2015.

169 Ibid.

"[i]nformal practices are often justified as a rational response to perceived defects in formal rules and their enforcement, but they are also indicative of defects in informal norms, both producing and resulting from patterns of distrust in public institutions and disregard for formal rules."[170] Furthermore, the phenomenon of unwritten norms can prevail everywhere given that "practices that have come to be known as extra-legal or informal…[are present in such key areas of life as] elections,…, the media,…industry and business,…legal and security spheres."[171] In other words, these informal norms underlie the entire legal system.

Second, the above-mentioned unwritten norms subvert values of written democratic constitutions replacing them with an opposite set of principles and standards that undermine all post-Soviet reforms. Sakwa also refers to the constitutional nature of such unwritten practices by calling them 'para-constitutional', because the parallel informal legal system "do[es] not repudiate the formal constitutional framework but operate[s] within its institutional constraints while subverting its spirit."[172] Thirdly, informal rules have a constitutional character, because they are recognized and routinely applied by everyone including public officials, representatives of judiciary and legal enforcement agencies. In this regard, Ledeneva points out that informal rules are used by virtually everyone, because they are "based on shared expectations about formal rules…and on mutual understanding about informal norms of friendship or other relationship."[173] All above mentioned characteristics of informal norms contribute to the establishment of a parallel constitutional order.

To summarize, the Soviet tradition of 'Twofold Constitutionalism' presupposes a continuous interaction of formal (written) and informal (unwritten) norms that create two coexisting legal orders. The widespread use of informal norms is often triggered by contradictions, legal loopholes and inefficiency of formal norms. In many transitional post-Soviet societies, virtually everyone has to violate some formal norms in order to operate in the changing political, economic and legal environment. Due to the widespread violation of formal norms, law enforcement agencies often use arbitrary punishment by selectively targeting those whose prosecution would be exemplary for supporting at least the appearance of justice and useful for eliminating opponents of ruling elites. Similar to the Soviet times, formal legal provisions are applied only when it is necessary and advantageous to achieve immediate political goals and priorities. Such arbitrary application of written and unwritten norms creates two coexisting orders, where informal norms can prevail over formal ones at any moment, depending on political expediency and the interpretation of these norms by legal officials. The set of informal norms can be called a constitution, because these norms become pervasive by having a radiating effect on the entire legal system, undermine the democratic spirit of written constitutions by sustaining old Soviet authoritarian practices and represent common legal culture by perpetuating themselves in routine practices shared by the majority of people in transitional post-Soviet societies. This

---

[170] Ledeneva 2006, p. 27.

[171] Ibid., p. 189.

[172] Sakwa 2010.

[173] Ledeneva 2006, p. 16.

book argues that the removal of this dual constitutionalism is essential for ensuring the post-Soviet transition to a democratic society.

1.6 Steps to Be Taken to Dismantle the System of 'Twofold Constitutionalism'

This research will offer three ways to deal with the Soviet legacy of politically motivated justice in the former Soviet Union. ***First***, the political nature of criminal justice can be removed by enforcing legal provisions and principles of national written constitutions that are blatantly violated in politically motivated trials against opposition leaders in many former Soviet republics. However, given the absence of necessary legislative reforms, the lack of judicial independence and pervasive corruption in these countries, the national legal avenue is not looking very promising now. ***Second***, if a former Soviet republic joined the Council of Europe, strategic litigation in the European Court of Human Rights (ECtHR) combined with the international pressure can be an effective instrument for protecting rights of political prisoners. In a number of landmark decisions in '*Ilgar Mammadov v. Azerbaijan*' (no. 15172/13), '*Tymoshenko v. Ukraine*' (no. 49872/11) and '*Lutsenko v. Ukraine*' (no. 6492/11) the ECtHR supported defendants' complaints about the arbitrariness of criminal proceedings initiated against them. Nevertheless, it should also be taken into account that only a few complaints about politically motivated justice have actually met a very high standard of proof required under *Article 18* ECHR invoked by the Court in such cases.[174] ***Third***, in the long run, only a true decommunization process combined with restorative and reparatory justice could rehabilitate victims of political persecutions as well as prevent politicized trials in the former Soviet Union in the future. Richard Sakwa, in his research on the Soviet duality of the legal system in modern Russia, also supports the enforcement of written constitutions and democratic principles enshrined in them in order to counter unofficial political rules of 'paraconstitutionalism'.[175] Sakwa asserts that "[t]he normative state [of formal written norms] remains the source of constitutional renewal."[176] In particular, in Russia and in other transitional former Soviet republics independent opposition politicians could not come to power by default, because their "route…was increasingly blocked by the suffocating regulations imposed on the electoral process by

---

[174] *Article 18* ECHR—Limitation on use of restrictions on rights. The violation of this article can be found only in conjunction with another article of the Convention. Moreover, to meet the burden of proof required under *Article 18*, an applicant must prove "that the whole legal machinery of the respondent State…was ab initio misused, that from the beginning to the end the authorities were acting with bad faith and in blatant disregard of the Convention." See the ECtHR, the final judgment in the case '*Khodorkovskiy v. Russia*', 31 May 2011, Case No. 5829/04, p. 64, para 255. https://hudoc.echr.coe.int/sites/eng/pages/search.aspx#{%22appno%22:[%225829/04%22],%22itemid%22:[%22001-104983%22]}. Accessed 22 December 2020.

[175] Sakwa 2010.

[176] Ibid., p. 203.

the [political] administrative regime."[177] The removal of informal political practices and restrictive rules would effectively enable free and fair elections guaranteed by post-Soviet constitutions.

Another example is the presence of the informal practice of 'telephone law' or ex-parte communication, which subverts the constitutional right to a fair trial guaranteed in all post-Soviet states. Sakwa refers to Kathryn Hendley's research on 'telephone justice' in Russia to demonstrate that it is so persistent that "when powerful business or political interests are involved, courts are...[subverted]; and...'the Kremlin has been able to dictate [judges] the outcome of cases in which it takes a strong interest,' with the Yukos affair only the best-known example."[178] The elimination of 'telephone justice' would, therefore, pave the way for a society where the rule of law and democratic constitutional norms could have a chance to prevail. Sakwa concludes that "[h]owever imperfect the...[written] constitution may be, it provides the framework for the development of a pluralistic political society and open public sphere...In other words the fundamental challenge is to ensure that political practices are brought into greater conformity with constitutional norms, above all by limiting the prerogative powers of the regime and thus reducing the duality of the system."[179] Therefore, written formal constitutions remain in the former Soviet Union the most likely catalyst of transition from the Soviet legacy of arbitrary extra-legal dualism to a democratic society governed by the rule of law.

1.7 Research Methodology

In the framework of my research design, I will seek to answer the following ***Question***: What is the role of politically motivated trials in the context of the transition from state repressions to the rule of law in the former Soviet Union? A case study helps test my ***Hypothesis*** that, as opposed to Western European democracies where trials against politicians usually lead to the constitutional dialogue and reconciliation, trials against politicians in transitional former Soviet republics reveal a parallel system of justice, whose mostly unwritten rules, judicial and prosecutorial practices inherited from the Soviet times hinder the successful post-communist transition. In order to answer my research question, I use both qualitative and quantitative data. In particular, I rely on secondary use of quantitative data and legal rankings compiled by the *Judicial Framework and Independence* by Freedom House, which can help clarify whether lack of independent judiciary can contribute to the politicization of the system of justice in criminal cases against opposition in the former USSR. The *Rule of Law Index* of the World Justice Project is used in my research to assess the situation with the rule of law and its correlation with criminal prosecution against politicians in Western democracies and in transitional post-Soviet states.

---

[177] Ibid., p. 198.

[178] Hendley 2009, p. 201.

[179] Sakwa 2010, pp. 199, 202.

I further complement this quantitative data with qualitative analysis of eight cases against politicians from two former Soviet republics and two Western European countries (two cases from each country). Because this research also aims at finding out whether membership in the Council of Europe could play a significant role in preventing a relapse into politically motivated justice, only one of the two selected former Soviet republics (Ukraine) is a signatory to the *European Convention on Human Rights* (ECHR). Cases selected in the non-signatory state (Belarus) are analyzed using the legal approach of the European Court of Human Rights as if this country joined the Council of Europe. Taking into account that politically motivated justice is also a social phenomenon, my research is based on a classical approach to social enquiry.[180] In particular, I make the following *assumptions*: (1) Politically motivated trials hinder the post-communist transition to the rule of law; (2) Soviet "show trials" are an example of politically motivated justice; (3) Criminal prosecution is selective when it targets exclusively opposition while granting immunity to members of a ruling party. An *independent variable* that can influence the level of politically motivated justice is independent judiciary and the rule of law that are absent in transitional former Soviet republics due to the lack of reforms after the collapse of the Soviet Union. Arbitrary prosecution of popular politicians is *a dependent variable*, which can be changed, under the influence of the independent variable.

All of the above-mentioned variables can be measured through rankings and evaluation reports that are prepared by independent expert organizations. For instance, the role of the membership in the Council of Europe can be assessed through the European Court of Human Rights' official statistical reports[181] on reviewed cases and implemented judgments that can reveal persistent systemic problems inherited by the former Soviet republics after the collapse of the USSR. Openness and fairness of the election process can be evaluated with the use of independent reports prepared by the Organization for Security and Cooperation in Europe (OSCE),[182] the European Network of Election Monitoring Organizations (ENEMO)[183] and other national and international independent election observation missions. The progress in the post-communist judicial reforms can be quantified with the help of the WJP Rule of Law Index that can demonstrate whether the absence of reforms and the rule of law deficiencies correlate with criminal prosecution against opposition leaders. This quantitative data will be combined with the qualitative legal analysis of jurisdictions chosen for this research.

[180] King et al. 1994.

[181] The official statistics of the European Court of Human Rights are available at https://www.echr.coe.int/pages/home.aspx?p=reports&c. Accessed 25 December 2020.

[182] OSCE/ODIHR election observation reports. https://www.osce.org/odihr/elections. Accessed 25 December 2020.

[183] ENEMO election observation reports available at https://www.enemo.eu/en/home. Accessed 25 December 2020.

1.8 Jurisdictions Chosen for My Research

This doctoral research will cover the following *four countries: Austria, Belarus, Germany and Ukraine.* The selection of the Western European countries was based on their experiences of dictatorships in the past as well as present independent judiciary and availability of recent cases against politicians. While selecting the former Soviet republics, the preference was given to countries with high level of corruption, which can be a pretext for politically motivated justice, and geopolitical characteristics. Furthermore, during the selected time Belarus and Ukraine have chosen a remarkably similar path vis-a-vis the (former) imperial center. The ex-president of Ukraine Yanukovych did not sign an Association Agreement with the EU at the Eastern Partnership Summit in Vilnius in November 2013. Following a request from Moscow to stall the EU-Ukraine negotiations, Yanukovych's government has then postponed the signing of the agreement with the EU and proclaimed stronger cooperation with the Russian Federation and its Customs Union. The EU officials have criticized Yanukovych for the political persecutions. Like Lukashenka in Belarus, Yanukovych cooperated closely with the ruling elites of the Russian Federation and staged trials against his opponents such as the former Prime Minister Yulia Tymoshenko and other opposition politicians. Moreover, Tymoshenko's medical treatment and politicized trial proceedings in her case became the subject of negotiations between the EU and Ukraine.[184] Because this research also aims at finding out whether the membership in the Council of Europe could play a significant role in preventing a relapse into politically motivated justice, one of the former Soviet republics (Belarus) is not a signatory to the European Convention on Human Rights.

Austria and Germany have been selected from among Western European states, because these countries have a high level of judicial independence,[185] which is an important safeguard against politically motivated justice. Both countries had dictatorial regimes in the past. Germany experienced the National Socialism or Nazism in 1933–1945 as well as the communist regime in East Germany in 1949–1990. Austria lived under the dictatorship of Engelbert Dollfuss in 1933–1934 and the Nazi regime after the Anschluss (German: annexation) in 1938–1945. In particular, this research will analyze the recent criminal proceedings against a former senior government official from the Austrian government.[186] In Germany rigorous investigations even led to the president's resignation.[187] Therefore, Germany and Austria with their own history of dictatorial regimes can provide useful lessons of transitional justice.

---

[184] EU-Ukraine association deal might hit ratification problems if Tymoshenko situation remains unchanged. https://www.kyivpost.com/article/content/ukraine-politics/eu-ukraine-association-deal-might-hit-ratification-112197.html?cn-reloaded=1. Accessed 25 December 2020.

[185] According to the Global Competiveness Report 2014–2015, Germany occupies the 15th place with 5.9 points, while Austria is on the 28th place with 5.2 points. https://reports.weforum.org/global-competitiveness-report-2014-2015/rankings/. Accessed 25 December 2020.

[186] Mayr 2011.

[187] See more about President Wulff's resignation at https://www.bbc.co.uk/news/world-europe-17072479. Accessed 25 December 2020.

Ukraine was selected, because, according to the 2015 Corruption Perceptions Index (CPI), it remains one of the most corrupt countries in Europe.[188] Belarus, which also has significant corruption,[189] has been selected as the only state in Europe (besides Vatican) yet to join the Council of Europe (CoE).[190] In terms of culture, religion and history Belarus has a lot in common with Ukraine. Similar to Ukraine, cases selected in Belarus will be analyzed using the legal approach of the European Court of Human Rights as if Belarus joined the Council of Europe. Besides significant problems with corruption, the two countries have low protection of political freedom, which in combination with the Soviet past can provide a very fertile ground for politically motivated justice. The British ambassador in Minsk from 2003–2007, Brian Bennett, in his book described Belarus as the last dictatorship in Europe.[191] While Belarus remains the last dictatorship in Europe, it has also been rated in 2015 as "non-free" in terms of political rights and civil liberties.[192] The 2018 rating of Ukraine was "partly free".[193] Therefore, it is very likely that both Ukraine and Belarus have politically motivated trails against politicians in the recent past.

In this context, in order to assess the legacy of the communist totalitarian regime, it is useful to differentiate between definitions of dictatorships, authoritarian regimes and totalitarianism that can help us better understand various forms of politicized justice that are currently utilized in transitional former Soviet republics. For instance, according to Juan Linz, "authoritarian regimes are political systems with limited, not responsible political pluralism, without intensive nor extensive political mobilization, and in which a leader or a small group exercises power within formally ill-defined limits but actually quite predictable ones."[194] A similar concept is also offered by Samuel Huntington, "who writes that authoritarian regimes are characterized by a single leader or group of leaders with either no party or a weak party, little mass mobilization, and limited political pluralism."[195] There are various approaches to defining dictatorships in academic literature. In particular, the definition of a dictatorship is given by Acemoglu and Robinson, who, "emphasize representation…[and] argue

[188]According to the 2015 Corruption Perception Index, Ukraine had 130th place with a score of 27 points among 168 countries. https://www.transparency.org/cpi2015. Accessed 25 December 2020.

[189]In 2015, Belarus occupied 107th place and scored 32 points, at https://www.transparency.org/cpi2015. Accessed 25 December 2020.

[190]See the Recommendation 1441 (2000) on the situation in Belarus. https://assembly.coe.int/nw/xml/XRef/Xref-XML2HTML-en.asp?fileid=16771&lang=en. Accessed 25 December 2020.

[191]Bennett 2012.

[192]Since the launch of Freedom House's annual "*Freedom in the World*" *rating* in 1972 Belarus has been consistently rated as "non-free" or "partially free" for its low level of political rights and civil liberties protection. https://www.freedomhouse.org/report-types/freedom-world#.VBcDDxYyKSo. Accessed 25 December 2020.

[193]According to the Freedom House, Ukraine had a "free" status from 2005 until 2010. https://www.freedomhouse.org/report-types/freedom-world#.VBcDDxYyKSo. Accessed 25 December 2020.The 2018 'Freedom in the World' Score ranked Ukraine as 'Partly Free'. https://freedomhouse.org/report/freedom-world/freedom-world-2018. Accessed 25 December 2020.

[194]Linz 2000; Ezrow and Frantz 2011, p. 2.

[195]Huntington 1968; Ezrow and Frantz 2011, p. 2.

that dictatorships are regimes in which the government represents solely 'the preferences of a sub-group of population…decisions are made either by a single individual, the elite, a junta, or an oligarchy."[196] A different approach is used by Paul Brooker, whose "definition focuses on the electoral process, with dictatorship defined as the 'theft of public office and powers."[197] The difference between authoritarian regimes and dictatorships is that the latter have a stricter form of control over state power by an individual or a group of people.

The notion of a dictatorship is, in turn, closely related to the phenomenon of totalitarianism, which is well researched in the context of the communist and Nazi regimes. For instance, Huntington generally characterizes "totalitarian regimes as rule by a single party led by an individual with a powerful secret police and a highly developed ideology. In totalitarian regimes the government has total control of mass communication and social and economic organizations … [that] aim to create an ideal society through the use of government propaganda."[198] Hannah Arendt, who researched the origins of totalitarianism in the Soviet Union and Nazi Germany, effectively argues that "ideology plays a prominent role in totalitarian regimes…[, under which] the leadership wants to transform *human nature*, by providing a complete road map for the organization of human life…exert full control over society, subject citizens to omnipresent terror as a means of ensuring compliance."[199] The difference between totalitarian and authoritarian or dictatorial regimes appears critical for this research. According to Linz' classification of political regimes, unlike "[a]uthoritarian [or dictatorial] regimes [that] do not seek to homogenize society and instead allow for some degree of pluralism…[,] totalitarian regimes place great emphasis on political mobilization and use ideology as a main source of their legitimacy."[200] Thus, for the purposes of this research, I differentiate between the Soviet totalitarian state, which exercised total control over society, and authoritarian or dictatorial regimes of transitional former Soviet republics that still allow some degree of pluralism in relatively non-homogenous societies.

1.9 Overview of Selected Jurisdictions

The goal of this section is to highlight differences that exist between criminal justice systems in established democracies in Western Europe and transitional former Soviet republics. In particular, I will argue that, similar to the former Soviet countries, Western democracies also have unwritten legal traditions and practices that are deeply rooted in their constitutional history. However, in Germany and Austria such unwritten practices complement and reinforce provisions of written constitutions, as

[196] Ibid.
[197] Ibid.
[198] Ibid.
[199] Arendt 1973; Ezrow and Frantz 2011, p. 3.
[200] Linz 2000; Ezrow and Frantz 2011, p. 4.

opposed to Ukraine and Belarus, where such informal practices create a parallel legal world, which is incompatible with written democratic constitutions drafted shortly after the collapse of the Soviet Union. This phenomenon of "Twofold Constitutionalism" manifests itself in the former Soviet republics during modern show trials against opposition leaders, whose arbitrary prosecution demonstrates not only the politicized nature of such criminal proceedings, but also the supremacy of informal political practices over formal laws of these countries. The strong patronage politics exercised by governments of transitional states leads to the politicization of law and judiciary that become just an instrument in the power struggle among representatives of post-Soviet ruling elites.

I would like to emphasize that this book does not attempt to idealize the West European countries and present them as 'perfect role models' for the former Soviet republics. As this chapter demonstrates, the European democracies selected for my research had their own, at times thorny and difficult, path towards the present democracy and the rule of law. Given the numerous cultural, historical, and existential differences, it is impossible to merely transplant constitutional practices from Western European countries to develop Western-like democratic institutions and judiciary in the transitional or authoritarian states of the former Soviet Union. The task is rather to demonstrate different approaches to trials related to politics in consolidated democracies and in the countries that are experiencing democratization.

There are indeed many differences, in terms of economic development, politics and law, between selected Western countries (Germany and Austria) and post-Soviet states (Belarus and Ukraine). The book uses examples of trials from Western Europe to show the key differences in judicial proceedings against politicians and political parties in consolidated democracies, authoritarian and transitional-hybrid regimes. The demonstration of such divergences between Western European countries and some post-Soviet states could also discharge the claim of many authoritarian leaders that the persecution of their political opponents is 'similar' to prosecution of corruption and organized crime in established democracies. The present research compares the procedural differences between 'political trials' conducted in the West and in the former USSR to highlight a contrast between such Western and Soviet juridical concepts as positive and negative application of material unlawfulness, social dangerousness and legal consciousness. The book also provides an overview of roles traditionally played by political trials in established democracies and in the post-Soviet societies that are still in transition from the authoritarian 'dual state' to the genuine, rather than the declaratory rule of law.

1.9.1 Austria

Although historically Austria had several documents that can be called a constitution, this research will focus on the constitutional developments after the dissolution of the Austro-Hungarian Empire in 1918 and the establishment of the Austrian state in the aftermath of WWI. The Constitution of Austria, which was drafted by the prominent legal scholar Hans Kelsen,[201] became a prototype for other European constitutions and "may be addressed as one of the eldest constitutions in Europe…[, whose] core elements are still in force today."[202] With regard to the broader goal of this research to analyze a phenomenon of an unwritten constitution in the former USSR, it is worthy of note that Austria has its "written as well as its efficient constitution."[203] In particular, Herbert Hausmaninger effectively argues that Austria's efficient constitution is influenced by the dominant political parties and a great number of the so-called constitutional laws (German: *Bundesverfassungsgesetze*) that can be adopted by two-thirds of the members of parliament (German: *Nationalrat*) and do not have to be necessarily included into the original text of the constitution.[204] This division into written and efficient constitutions reflects legal traditions and the history of constitution-making in Austria.

The history of the Austrian constitution shows its path to a democratic society. As opposed to Kelsen's Constitution of 1920,[205] which gave substantial powers to the parliament, the constitution adopted by the authoritarian Christian-Social Patriotic Front (German: *Vaterländische Front*) abolished the parliamentary democracy and promoted in its stead the dictatorial regime of Engelbert Dollfuss in 1933.[206] The subsequent assassination of Dollfuss was followed by the annexation (German: *Anschluß*) of Austria by Nazi Germany in 1938. Only after the liberation of Austria by the allied forces in 1945 did the provisional government adopt a provisional constitution and "a Constitutional Law on the Re-establishment of Rule of Law in Austria."[207] After the popular elections, the same year the Austrian parliament reintroduced the Constitution of 1920 in the version amended in 1929. However, only by signing the State Treaty of 1955 (German: *Staatsvertrag*) could Austria receive its sovereignty back from the allied forces.[208] Furthermore, regaining sovereignty became a constitutional matter, as the Austrian parliament had to pass the federal constitutional law on the neutrality of Austria (German: *Bundesverfassungsgesetz*).

The return to the democratic constitution included certain transitional justice measures in the country. For instance, the so-called denazification (German: *Entnazifizierung*) covered former Nazis, who "were…forced to register, were deprived of political rights (above all the right to vote) and were excluded from the civil service and some other professional activities."[209] Similar to other European countries, Austria established its own people's courts to prosecute Nazi war criminals in

---

[201] Schwartz 2006, pp. 175–176.

[202] Stelzer et al. 2011, p. 2.

[203] Stelzer et al. 2011, p. 1.

[204] "Thus, aside from more than 40 amendments inserted into the text of the constitutional document, there exist approximately 600 constitutional provisions 'floating' outside the Constitution". In: Hausmaninger 1998, p. 18.

[205] Kelsen's Constitution was amended in 1929 to strengthen the presidential powers.

[206] Zurcher 1934, p. 664.

[207] Hausmaninger 1998, p. 8.

[208] Liebhart et al. 1991, pp. 375–382.

[209] Hausmaninger 1998, p. 9.

a summary manner. However, the outbreak of the cold war between the West and the communist bloc facilitated the reintegration of former Nazi officials as well as their subsequent amnesty in 1948.[210] As opposed to Germany, where the post-war transition included the new constitution (the *Bonner Grundgesetz*) in order to avoid the mistakes of the Weimar Constitution, "Austrians did not blame the constitution for the demise of democracy and the establishment of an authoritarian regime."[211] Therefore, Austria preserved its old constitution and complemented it with democratic practices of the unwritten efficient constitution.

The core of the Austrian efficient constitution manifests itself in its principles. The Federal Constitutional Court of Austria recognizes three basic principles, i.e. the democratic state, the federal state and the Rule of Law (*Rechtsstaat*) .[212] It is necessary to note that Rechtsstaat is not explicitly mentioned in the written constitution, as it is assumed "that the principle of Rechtsstaat silently underlay the constitution."[213] Manfred Stelzer also points out that after WWII the Austrian constitutional law incorporated many other principles like the separation of powers,[214] the liberal principle and the separation of state and church.[215] Although these additional principles have never become effective,[216] they outline the limits for constitutional amendments that can be initiated by a parliamentary majority through the adoption of *Bundesverfassungsgesetze.* The scope of such constitutional revisions is addressed in *Article 44* of the Constitution, which envisages "a mandatory referendum…in the case of a 'total revision' of the Federal Constitution."[217] The meaning of the 'total revision' is connected with the three basic principles mentioned above. Thus, as long as constitutional amendments do not encroach on the basic principles, they would respect the limits set by the Constitutional Court in its case law.

The constitutional jurisprudence related to political parties would be the most relevant for this research. *Article 1* of the Political Parties Act says that there should be no restrictions for the establishment of a party unless a federal constitutional law restricts the founding of such a party.[218] The Constitutional Court has affirmed the fee regime for the founding of parties by ruling that "the Minister of Interior does not have the power to prohibit the founding of a political party nor should he or she confirm that a political party has been founded."[219] The only federal constitutional law restricting the establishment of a party is the National Socialism Prohibition Act of 1945 (German: *Wiederbestätigungsgesetz*), which prohibits any national socialist organization. If a party does not meet legal requirements, it simply does not acquire

[210]Ibid.

[211]Stelzer et al. 2011, p. 15.

[212]Liebhart et al. 1991.

[213]Stelzer et al. 2011, p. 32.

[214]Walter et al, Bundesverfassungsrecht, n 53, 88f. In: Stelzer et al. 2011, p. 33.

[215]Gampl 1971; Stelzer et al. 2011, p. 33.

[216]Stelzer et al. 2011, p. 33.

[217]Stelzer et al. 2011, p. 33.

[218]Liebhart et al. 1991.

[219]Cf VfSlg 9648/1983. In: Stelzer et al. 2011, p. 49.

a legal personality. However, in practice the failure to acquire the legal personality can be disputed in courts and administrative bodies that may have a different interpretation whether a political party in question complied with the existing legislation. In this regard, Stelzer is of the opinion that, according to the current constitutional jurisprudence, the strict prohibition of a party with national socialist aims "results in a violation of the principle of certainty of justice and thus the principle of the *Rechtsstaat*."[220] This constitutional jurisprudence should be interpreted in connection with the concept of social partnership in Austria.

The system of social partnership is probably the most peculiar feature of Austrian politics. Social partners are associations that represent interests of various professions. On the one hand, the role of social partners was not mentioned in the written constitution for a long time. A constitutional amendment of 2008, which integrated social partnership into the constitutional framework, has stated that the Austrian "republic now appreciates the role of social partners, respects their autonomy and supports their dialogue by establishing self-governing bodies."[221] On the other hand, in practical terms of the efficient constitution, social partners always played a key political role by advising the main parties, evaluating draft legislation and nominating candidates to key government positions. For decades, these associations, whose membership is compulsory for some professions,[222] were the driving force for constitutional compromises[223] reached by the two main parties.[224] Even though the influence of social partners was diminished by newly established parties, it remains an indispensable tool for resolving political conflicts in Austria.

Protection of human or fundamental rights (*Grundrechte*) is another interesting aspect of Austrian Constitutional Law, as the Constitution does not include a separate catalog of rights and freedoms. Austria relies in this respect on the 1867 Basic State Law on the General Rights of Citizens (German: *Staatsgrundgesetz über die allgemeinen Rechte der Staatsbürger*)[225] incorporated into the modern constitutional doctrine. Another peculiarity of the human rights framework is that, when Austria joined the European Convention on Human Rights in 1958, the Convention obtained the rank of constitutional law in the country. As a result of this, any complaint lodged with the Constitutional Court of Austria can invoke rights envisaged by the Convention. In terms of criminal justice, *Article 83(2)* of the Constitution[226] stipulates the right not to be deprived of one's lawful judge. This right is complemented with

---

[220] Stelzer et al. 2011, p. 15.

[221] Stelzer et al. 2011, p. 58.

[222] For instance, "[b]y law all employees (civil servants are the exception) are members of the Chamber of Labour and are obliged to pay fees which are deducted from their wages by the employer and transferred to the chamber." In: Stelzer et al. 2011, p. 56.

[223] Schwartz 2006, pp. 175–176.

[224] The Social Democratic Party (SPÖ) and the People's Party (ÖVP).

[225] Besides the law on the general rights of citizens, rights relevant for this research could be found in *Article 90* of the Constitution, which guarantees principles of criminal procedure, the 1988 federal constitutional law on personal freedom and the Political Parties Act of 1975.

[226] See the English version of the Austrian Constitution at https://www.servat.unibe.ch/icl/au00000_.html. Accessed 25 December 2020.

the equality clause envisaged by *Article 7* of the Constitution, which guarantees equality of all citizens regardless of race, gender, faith, estate or birth. Taking into account that equality is considered by the Constitutional Court to be a part of the principle of democracy, "core elements [of the equality principle] could therefore not be abolished but in the process of a 'total revision' could trigger a mandatory referendum."[227] The above-mentioned human rights framework is, thus, sufficient to prevent politicized justice in court.

There have been several trials against senior public officials in Austria. Cases of these politicians could be called political, because they influenced the socio-political discourse in the country. However, criminal charges brought against these officials have been confirmed in the course of independent investigation proceedings. Some of these politicians have even received an imprisonment sentence or had to pay a fine. For instance, former Interior Minister of Austria, Mr. Ernst Strasser of the People's Party (ÖVP), was exposed by the media when he as the European Parliament MP asked for a bribe of 100,000 EUR in exchange for passing amendments in the European Union legislation.[228] Although Strasser was found guilty as charged and initially sentenced to four years of imprisonment, in 2013 the Supreme Court of Austria (*Oberster Gerichtshof*) reduced on appeal his sentence to three years in jail.[229] In a different case Susanne Winter, a far-right member of Parliament for the Freedom Party of Austria (FPÖ), was convicted of hate speech for making anti-Islamic statements. An appellate court upheld her conviction in 2009 and sentenced her to a fine of 24,000 euros and a suspended imprisonment of three months.[230] Ernst Strasser, who used to be the Minister of Interior of Austria, became a librarian in a prison library and served his sentence after the judgment of the Austrian court went into force.[231] Both Strasser and Winter resigned from all positions in their parties after their trials.

1.9.2 Germany

Germany has a rich history of constitutionalism, which includes the Frankfurt Constitution of 1849 (German: *die Paulskirchenverfassung*), the Imperial Constitution of 1871 (*die Verfassung des Deutschen Reiches*), the Weimar Constitution of 1919 (*die Weimarer Verfassung*) and the German Basic Law of 1949 (*das Grundgesetz*). This research will focus only on the Basic Law, which drew on the lessons learned from the

[227] VfSlg 15373/1988. In: Stelzer et al. 2011, p. 210.

[228] See more information about Strasse's corruption affair at https://www.bbc.com/news/world-europe-21017914. Accessed 25 December 2020.

[229] See the reasoning of the Supreme Court of Austria in Ernst Strasser's case, available in German at https://www.ris.bka.gv.at/Dokument.wxe?Abfrage=Justiz&Dokumentnummer=JJT_20141013_OGH0002_0170OS00030_14M0000_000. Accessed 25 December 2020.

[230] Urteil Gegen Susanne Winter Bestätigt. https://stmv1.orf.at/stories/369117. Accessed 25 December 2020.

[231] Former Minister Now a Prison Librarian, 18 November 2014. https://www.thelocal.at/20141118/former-minister-now-a-prison-librarian. Accessed 25 December 2020.

tragic events of National Socialism in 1933–1945 as well as the communist regime in East Germany in 1949–1990. Similar to the post-Soviet states Germany experienced transitional justice. In this regard, the country also had its history of politicized the Nazi people's court (*Volksgerichtshof*) and communist show trials in East Germany. However, unlike Ukraine and Belarus, Germany overcame the communist and Nazi legacy of politicized justice and completed its democratic transition after reunification in 1990.

Similar to other countries of the communist bloc, the German Democratic Republic (GDR) replicated the Soviet duality of formal and informal norms. The European Court of Human Rights (ECtHR) found this duality of law in its landmark judgment in '*Streletz, Kessler and Krenz v. Germany*', which dealt with GDR's practice of protecting "the border between the two German States 'at all costs'.... [and] annihilate...[ing] border violators [*Grenzverletzer*]...in order to preserve the GDR's existence, which was threatened by the massive exodus of its own population."[232] When after the reunification of Germany in 1990, German courts sentenced three former senior GDR's officials to various terms of imprisonment for giving the orders to shoot border violators, the former officials appealed to the ECtHR and argued that they had been sentenced for actions that "did not constitute offences, at the time when they were committed, according to the law of the GDR or international law...[in violation of *Article 7 § 1 ECHR*]."[233] The Court in Strasbourg disagreed with the applicants and observed that, although Article 7 § 1 ECHR includes both written and unwritten law, the unwritten informal practice of protecting border 'at all costs' cannot be protected under the Convention.

The ECtHR used several arguments to substantiate its opinion. First, the Court noticed that the practice of protecting the state border 'at all costs' contradicted both GDR's own written law on the statute book as well as GDR's obligations under international law. In particular, the court reasoned that the practice of annihilating border violators cannot be described as 'law' under Article 7 ECHR, because the practice in question "emptied of its substance the [written] legislation on which it was supposed to be based, and which was imposed on all organs of the GDR, including its judicial bodies."[234] The given informal practice of killing border violators also violated the right to life protected by international law under *Article 3* of the Universal Declaration of Human Rights as well as by *Article 6* of the International Covenant on Civil and Political Rights, which was ratified by GDR in 1974. Furthermore, everyone's right to life, which enjoys the supreme rank in the international human

232 See ECtHR, *Streletz, Kessler and Krenz v. Germany*, 22 March 2001, Case Nos. 34044/96, 35532/97 and 44801/98 (*Streletz, Kessler and Krenz* 2001), paras 71–73. https://hudoc.echr.coe.int/app/conversion/pdf/?library=ECHR&id=001-59353&filename=001-59353.pdf. Accessed 25 December 2020.

233 In particular, Article 7 § 1 of the Convention...provides: "No one shall be held guilty of any criminal offence on account of any act or omission which did not constitute a criminal offence under national or international law at the time when it was committed. Nor shall a heavier penalty be imposed than the one that was applicable at the time the criminal offence was committed." See para 46 of the ECtHR's judgment in *Streletz, Kessler and Krenz* 2001.

234 See *Streletz, Kessler and Krenz* 2001, above n 232 para 87.

rights hierarchy, is also protected by *Article 2 ECHR*. Therefore, the Court cannot help but conclude that the practice and its informal orders of protecting the state border 'at all costs' were "superimposed on the rules of written law at the material time."[235] This essentially created two coexisting legal orders of formal and informal norms where the latter could prevail.

In his concurring opinion in the case, Judge Zupančič described this duality of law and practice that contradicted each other as the "schizophrenic interpretation…[which dispensed] the positive law on the statute book…[and] prevail[ed] over the objective significance of the relevant definitions of offences in the GDR's own criminal law."[236] The Federal Constitutional Court of Germany also identified the contradictions between GDR's written law on the statute book and informal unwritten practices of border protection. In particular, the Federal Court observed that GDR's written law on the use of firearms at the state border was comparable with legal provisions on the use of force (German: *unmittelbarer Zwang*) in the German Federal Republic (FRG).[237] However, in GDR informal orders to protect the state border 'at any cost' were "superimposed on…[written] legal provisions…[and, thus,] left no room for limitation of the use of firearms."[238] Thus, the Federal Court concluded that GDR's border guards followed informal orders of their political leadership when they 'annihilated' border violators, which meant that in GDR "the written law was eclipsed by the requirements of political expediency…[and] constituted extreme injustice."[239] The supreme rank of informal practices that prevailed over written law essentially recreated in GDR the Soviet co-existing legal orders of formal and informal norms.

The purpose of this section is to show that the written Constitution of Germany is complemented by constitutional jurisprudence and traditions that effectively prevent informal practices of politically motivated justice. The objective system of values is a good example of such constitutional traditions that cannot be found anywhere in the text of the Basic Law. Instead, the system of values is "one that derives from the gloss the Constitutional Court has put on the constitutional text."[240] According to the case law of the Constitutional Court, the objective system of values includes, in particular, individual inviolability, physical integrity, liberty, equality and dignity as the top objective value.[241] Donald Kommers and Russel Miller persuasively argue that this open-endedness of the constitutional jurisprudence helps not to "exclude considerations of political reality in the construction and application of the constitution."[242]

[235] See *Streletz, Kessler and Krenz* 2001, above n 232, para 67.

[236] *Streletz, Kessler and Krenz* 2001, the Concurring Opinion by Judge Zupančič.

[237] *Streletz, Kessler and Krenz* 2001, above n 232, p. 13.

[238] *Streletz, Kessler and Krenz* 2001, above n 232.

[239] *Streletz, Kessler and Krenz* 2001, above n 232.

[240] Kommers and Miller 2012, p. 57.

[241] Lüth Case, 7 BVerfGE 198, 205 (1958). See also Annette Guckelberger, "Die Drittwirkung der Grundrechte," Juristische Schulung 12 (2003): 1151–57; and Christoph Möllers, "Wandel der Grundrechtsjudikatur: Eine Analyse der Rechtsprechung des Ersten Senats des BVerfG,"Neue Juristische Wochenschrift" 28 (2005): 1973–79." In: Kommers and Miller 2012, p. 57.

[242] Kommers and Miller 2012, p. 58.

Werner Heun concurs with this assessment by pointing out that "constitutions are political law…[which is] not narrowly tailored but leave above all broad discretion for the legislature and are open to new developments and interpretations."[243] Therefore, the objective system of values highlights the division between the formal constitutional law, which repeats the formal text of the Basic Law, and the substantial constitutional law, which complements the text of the German Constitution.

The so-called militant democracy (*streitbare or wehrhafte Demokratie*) is yet another legal tradition derived from the jurisprudence of the Constitutional Court of Germany. The concept was initially introduced by Karl Löwenstein in 1933 in response to the weaknesses of the Weimer democracy, which was unable to prevent the rise of National Socialism into power in Germany. The militant democracy is not explicitly mentioned in the constitutional text. However, in post-war Germany the Constitutional Court "developed 'militant democracy' into an 'all purpose' principle and uncompromisingly used it as an argument, criterion and reasoning in a couple of its decisions."[244] According to this constitutional jurisprudence, militant democracy is supposed to protect the free and democratic basic order mentioned in *Article 18* (forfeiture of fundamental rights—sentence 1), *Article 21* (prohibition of political parties—Section 2) and *Article 91* (internal emergency—Section 1) of the German Basic Law.[245] Although the militant democracy concept "has been ridiculed as a 'fossil of democratic theory',"[246] this concept is still relevant in Germany in light of the currently pending case on the prohibition of the National Democratic Party (NPD) under *Article 21(2)* of the German Basic Law.

Unlike the transitional former Soviet republics, where political matters are not openly addressed in the legal context, German judiciary recognizes the political nature of some disputes. In particular, Kommers and Miller point out that the second senate of the Constitutional Court was established to "decide political disputes between branches and levels of government, settle contested elections, rule on constitutionality of political parties…[,] preside over impeachment proceedings and decide abstract questions of constitutional law."[247] Heun agrees with this assessment by observing that "[p]olitical disputes are…quite often discussed in constitutional terms…[and] Constitutional Court decisions can often be read like political tracts."[248] In this regard, the judicial discretion of the Constitutional Court is of paramount importance, because "its comprehensive interpretative powers transform almost all political questions into constitutional questions which may be or are decided by

---

243 Heun et al. 2011, p. 6.

244 Thiel 2009, p. 112.

245 The principle of militant democracy is also connected with *Article 20* (right to resist—Section 4), *Article 79* (Ewigkeitsklausel—Section 3), *Article 33* (principles of public service—Section 5) and other constitutional and sub-constitutional provisions.

246 Fromme speaks of an 'ageing process' and an 'erosion' of the militant democracy. In: Thiel 2009, p. 139.

247 Kommers and Miller 2012, p. 18.

248 Heun et al. 2011, p. 7.

the Court."[249] Therefore, the decisions made by the Constitutional Court play a paramount role in cases related to political issues.

Values and principles of Constitutional Law are also reflected in German Criminal Law. In particular, the rule of law principle (*Rechtsstaat*) is stipulated in the so-called eternity clause of *Article 79(3)* of the German Basic Law,[250] which essentially means that "constitutional amendments reducing the Rule of Law in a significant manner would be inadmissible."[251] Several constitutional provisions guarantee civil rights in criminal proceedings and protect against arbitrary prosecution. In particular, *Article 101(1)* prohibits ad-hoc tribunals and protects the right to a lawful judge (the right to a predetermined judge). *Article 103* provides for the right to have a lawful court hearing (the right to be heard) and envisages that a person should not be punished more than once for the same offence according to the general laws. Krey Volker observes that the same constitutional provision prohibits the punishment without statute law (*nulla poena sine lege*), the retroactive effect and customary law aggravating punishment, the analogy of law as well as unclear criminal statutes that undermine the principle of certainty.[252] Moreover, according to *Article 104*, deprivation of liberty must be sanctioned by an order of a judge in accordance with formal law requirements. Judicial independence is further envisaged in *Article 97* of the Basic Law, which stipulates that judges abide only by law and have permanent full-time positions. These norms that safeguard against politicized justice are complemented with constitutional provisions.

The Basic Law contains some safeguards against arbitrary prosecution of elected politicians. *Article 46*, Sections 2 and 4 guarantee the immunity for members of the German Federal Parliament (Bundestag). In the same vein, *Article 47* stipulates the right of the members of Parliament to refuse to give evidence. Political opposition or minority in the Parliament also has substantial rights under the Basic Law, "where parliamentary rights to control the executive are often formulated as minority rights."[253] Kommers and Miller refer to Volker Röben who mentions in his assessment of *Article 44(1)*, which requires only one fourth of MPs to establish an investigative committee, that this article "is the most litigated constitutional provision of the constitution…[because t]he obvious interest of the parliamentary majority will…be…to protect its [g]overnment against the opposition."[254] Heun mentions that the minority can also exercise its control over government through "a major question (*Große Anfrage*) which…implies that a parliamentary group of five per cent of the members back the question…[and a] minor question (*Kleine Anfrage*) that any political group of Parliament may pose will be answered only in a written form."[255]

[249] Ibid., p. 7.

[250] See the Basic Law of the Federal Republic of Germany, available in English at https://www.gesetze-im-internet.de/englisch_gg/. Accessed 25 December 2020.

[251] Krey and Stenger 2008, p. 5.

[252] Krey 2002, pp. 41–99.

[253] Kommers and Miller 2012, p. 217.

[254] Kommers and Miller 2012, p. 218.

[255] Heun et al. 2011, p. 119.

Furthermore, according to *Article 44* of the Basic Law,[256] the parliamentary group can establish a committee of enquiry, which is "mostly used by the opposition."[257] An abstract judicial review of a statute already passed by the majority under *Article 93(1)* is also "[o]ne of the most effective weapons of the opposition."[258] Thus, the Basic Law provides opposition with broad rights as well as protects the political minority from arbitrary criminal prosecution.

There were trials related to political cases in Germany. For instance, Mr. Christian Wulff, a member of the ruling Christian Democratic Union (CDU), resigned in 2012 as the President of Germany due to allegations of his corruption. One of the charges in the criminal proceedings against him was that Wulff during his tenure as a governor of Lower Saxony allegedly provided political favors to a German businessman who paid around 720 EUR for accommodation of Wulff's family during the beer festival 'Oktoberfest' in 2008.[259] In 2014, two years after his resignation, Wulff was acquitted by a court of all corruption charges.[260] Mr. Marcel Zech, the far-right politician and a member of the National Democratic Party (NPD), was charged for appearing in a public place with a tattoo of the Auschwitz concentration camp, which also had a slogan "*Jedem das Seine*" (to each his own) of the Buchenwald death camp's gate.[261] Although Zech was found guilty of incitement, he received only a suspended six-month sentence.[262] Speculations about the political character of these trials deserve consideration in the next chapters of this book.

1.9.3 Ukraine

The Supreme Council of then Ukrainian Soviet Socialist Republic declared Ukraine an independent state by adopting the Act of Independence on August 24, 1991. Over ninety per cent of Ukraine's electorate supported the independence in a state referendum conducted on December 1, 1991.[263] The proclamation of Ukraine's independence was preceded by a failed coup d'état of conservative communists who tried to remove from power the leader of the Soviet Union, Mikhail Gorbachev. Similar declarations of independence proclaimed by other former Soviet republics led to the ultimate dissolution of the Soviet Union, agreement on which was reached by

---

[256] The Basic Law of Germany at https://www.gesetze-im-internet.de/englisch_gg/. Accessed 25 December 2020.

[257] Ibid.

[258] Heun et al. 2011, p. 119.

[259] See more information about Wulff's trial at https://www.bbc.com/news/world-europe-26365262. Accessed 25 December 2020.

[260] Vasagar 2014.

[261] Corcoran and Hall 2015.

[262] Macias 2015.

[263] Lalpychak 1991.

leaders of the newly independent states in early 1991. Five years later, the Parliament of Ukraine passed a Constitution, which replaced the 1978 Constitution of the Ukrainian Soviet Socialist Republic. The constitutional debate was so lengthy that the Constitution was literally passed overnight on July 28, 1996. The new Constitution established the semi-presidential-parliamentary republic, which was supposed to prevent the confrontation between Parliament and the President.

The 'Orange Revolution', which was a public response towards wide-scale electoral fraud during the 2004 presidential campaign,[264] revealed the ongoing constitutional crisis. Independent election observation reports showed vote rigging organized in favor of Viktor Yanukovytch, who was then the official candidate and the Prime Minister of Ukraine, and against Viktor Yushchenko, who represented the united opposition.[265] Given the numerous instances of electoral fraud, the Supreme Court of Ukraine ordered a rerun of the disputed second round of the Presidential elections,[266] which was eventually won by Yushchenko. The political compromise reached after the revolution envisaged a constitutional reform "that the team of outgoing President Leonid Kuchma forced Yushchenko to accept in return for a peaceful transition to the presidency in early 2005: the presidency Yushchenko inherited would be weakened as of January 2006, with the prime minister gaining direct control over key ministries…and…becoming exclusively beholden to Parliament rather than being nominated or removed at the whim of the president."[267] The reform was, thus, a result of a political consensus, which was not discussed beforehand with the public.

The strengthening of the prime minister and weakening of the president led to a conflict within the executive branch. In particular, "Yushchenko did use his formal power to try to subordinate the prime minister [Tymoshenko] after they clashed publicly, replacing Tymoshenko in September 2005 with the more pliable Yury Yekhanurov."[268] Viktor Yanukovytch again became Prime Minister as a result of the 2006 parliamentary elections. The constitutional crisis became evident when all sides openly disregarded formal laws in favor of informal political practices. For instance, President Yushchenko "issued and enforced a decree of extremely dubious constitutionality in April 2007 to dissolve the parliament…[which] was not simply 'followed' according to formal legal procedures but enforced through the extensive coordination of informal networks around the president."[269] Viktor Yanukovytch won the 2010 presidential elections with a small margin of 3.48%.[270] Yanukovytch's

---

[264] See the chronology of the Orange Revolution by Deutsche Welle. https://www.dw.de/chronology-of-the-orange-revolution/a-2804808. Accessed 25 December 2020.

[265] See the OSCE/ODIHR Election Observation Mission Final Report on Presidential Election, 31 October, 21 November and 26 December 2004, which showed the scale of electoral fraud during the 2004 presidential campaign. https://www.osce.org/odihr/elections/ukraine/14674. Accessed 25 December 2020.

[266] Bredies et al. 2007, pp. 121–122.

[267] Ginsburg and Simpser 2013, p. 231.

[268] Ibid., p. 231.

[269] Ibid., p. 233.

[270] In the 2010 presidential elections Yulia Tymoshenko received the support of *45.47% of the voters (11,593,357 votes)*, while Yanukovytch received *48.95% (12,480,335 votes)*, see the

presidency also resulted in the redistribution of competences within the executive power and new constitutional changes.

Shortly after the elections, the Supreme Court decided to nullify the 2004 constitutional reforms and return broad presidential powers to Yanukovytch. When President Yanukovytch appointed four new judges to the Constitutional Court, the Court "suddenly realized—almost six years after the 2004 constitutional reforms—...[that] the reforms...[were] unconstitutional and thus repealed the constitutional amendments."[271] Ekaterina Mishina persuasively shows that "the concentration of power in...Yanukovytch's hands ...and the manipulation of courts for political purposes upset the system of checks and balances...[which] has created a real threat to the Ukrainian political model that was once characterized by pluralism."[272] Furthermore, Yanukovytch's refusal to sign an association agreement with the European Union in autumn 2013 exacerbated the situation and led to the popular social uprising also known as the 'EuroMaidan', which ousted Yanukovytch from power in 2014.[273] Similar to the 'Orange Revolution', the latest uprising also led to the changes in the Constitution as the Ukrainian Parliament restored the constitutional amendments of 2004.

Henry Hale explains such frequent changes in the Constitution and the political system of Ukraine by showing the gap between formal institutions and informal politics. Formal laws rarely function as assumed also in other hybrid post-communist regimes that combine both democratic and authoritarian characteristics. Hale persuasively shows that "[w]hat matters instead is said to be informal politics, the 'real' workings of politics, those unwritten and officially uncodified norms, habits, and practices that actually guide political behavior."[274] Furthermore, Hale acknowledges that "an emerging body of research is now focusing on how formal rules and informal institutions interact...and recent theoretical work suggests that one of the ways that formal institutions can have political effects is by inducing change in informal rules."[275] In other words, formal constitutions play a role in the former Soviet republics, but this role does not always correspond with the traditional theory of constitutionalism in Western democracies.

It appears that the key difference between transitional countries like Ukraine and established democracies is the social and cultural context. Ukraine and other transitional former Soviet states are "characterized by high degrees of *patronalism*, a

OSCE/ODIHR Election Observation Mission Final Report. www.osce.org/odihr/elections/ukraine/67844. Accessed 25 December 2020.

[271] Mishina 2014.

[272] Ibid.

[273] Malkin and Raziye 2015.

[274] Informal institutions are 'socially shared rules, usually unwritten, that are created, communicated, and enforced outside of officially sanctioned channels' and formal institutions are 'rules and procedures that are created, communicated, and enforced through channels widely accepted as official'. Helmke and Levitsky 2004; Hale 2011; Ginsburg and Simpser 2013, p. 219.

[275] Hale 2011; Ginsburg and Simpser 2013, p. 219.

syndrome typically manifesting itself in the weak Rule of Law, high levels of corruption, strong patronage politics, and low levels of social capital."[276] What separates Ukraine from other 'hybrid' post-communist regimes, however, is that the country reformed its formal constitution by dividing executive power between the president and the prime-minister, while many post-Soviet republics retained constitutions giving broad powers to presidents that represent the most powerful office in their countries. Hale concludes his analysis of reforms in Ukraine by hypothesizing that changes in formal constitutional provisions can eventually improve "the prospects for nondemocratic regimes to develop more democratic features."[277] Indeed, in the former Soviet Union formal written laws contain various safeguards against politically motivated criminal justice.

The Ukrainian Constitution contains several provisions that could prevent cases of politically motivated justice. In particular, *Article 80* of the Constitution guarantees immunity of the members of the Ukrainian Parliament (Ukrainian: *Verkhovna Rada*).[278] *Article 129* envisages the equality of arms principle through "equality before the law and the court of all participants in a trial…[,] adversarial procedure and freedom of the parties to present their evidence to the court and to prove the weight of evidence before the court."[279] Moreover, the same provision stipulates legality of court proceedings, the right of an accused person to counsel as well as "openness of a trial and its complete recording by technical means."[280] *Articles 126* and *127* further provide for independent judiciary. According to these provisions, judges have personal immunity,[281] while "influencing judges in any manner is prohibited".[282] *Article 7* of the Criminal Procedure Code stipulates such principles of criminal proceedings as the rule of law, equality before law and court, presumption of innocence and no punishment without law.[283] Nevertheless, all these provisions did not prevent politically motivated justice in Ukraine.

I also argue that the application of Soviet informal practices after the collapse of the USSR became possible in Ukraine, because the country consistently failed to implement the reform of its system of criminal justice. For instance, in 2013, only

[276] Ibid.

[277] Ibid.

[278] According to *Article 80*, para 3, "People's Deputies of Ukraine shall not be held criminally liable, detained or arrested without the consent of the Verkhovna Rada of Ukraine." The English version of the Ukrainian Constitution: https://www.refworld.org/cgi-bin/texis/vtx/rwmain/opendocpdf.pdf?reldoc=y&docid=5d63a1ed4. Accessed 25 December 2020.

[279] The English version of the Ukrainian Constitution: https://www.refworld.org/cgi-bin/texis/vtx/rwmain/opendocpdf.pdf?reldoc=y&docid=5d63a1ed4. Accessed 25 December 2020.

[280] *Article 129* of the Constitution.

[281] *Article 126* of the Constitution says that "a judge shall not be detained or arrested without the consent of the Verkhovna Rada of Ukraine, until a verdict of guilty is rendered by a court". The English version of the Ukrainian Constitution: https://www.refworld.org/cgi-bin/texis/vtx/rwmain/opendocpdf.pdf?reldoc=y&docid=5d63a1ed4. Accessed 25 December 2020.

[282] *Article 126* of the Constitution.

[283] The Criminal Code of Procedure available in Ukrainian at https://zakon0.rada.gov.ua/laws/show/4651-17. Accessed 25 December 2020.

seven years after its accession to the Council of Europe (CoE), Ukraine managed to adopt a new Code of Criminal Procedure (CPC), which replaced the old Soviet CPC dating back to 1960.[284] Although during 2010–2014 covered by this research the Venice Commission provided Ukraine with a number of recommendations[285] on the reform of the Prosecutor's Office, Constitutional reform, the reform of the Judicial System and the Status of Judges of Ukraine, the Government of Ukraine failed to introduce necessary reforms.

The issue of show trials in Ukraine came into the international spotlight with politicized criminal justice used by the former President Yanukovytch and his government against "politicians belonging to potential powerful political opposition groups,"[286] including "12 former high-ranking officials from the Tymoshenko government."[287] Although several complaints were submitted in this regard to the European Court of Human Rights,[288] the cases of the former Prime Minister Tymoshenko and the former Interior Minister Lutsenko deserve special consideration within this research. Yuri Lutsenko, a popular opposition leader at that time, was charged with multiple offences including embezzlement and abuse of office, as a result of which he was sentenced to confiscation of property and four years in prison.[289] Yulia Tymoshenko also faced numerous criminal charges, the main of which was exceeding her official powers as the Prime Minister of Ukraine when she signed an allegedly unfavorable gas deal with Russia. Ms. Tymoshenko was found guilty as charged and sentenced to seven years imprisonment and a three-year ban on holding public office.[290] The ECtHR recognized Lutsenko and Tymoshenko's pretrial detention as arbitrary.[291] Although

[284] See the new Code of Criminal Procedure, a Ukrainian version is available at https://zakon4.rada.gov.ua/laws/show/4651-17. Accessed 25 December 2020.

[285] See recommendations provided by the European Commission for Democracy through Law (the Venice Commission) to Ukraine, available at https://www.venice.coe.int/webforms/documents/?country=47&year=all. Accessed 25 December 2020.

[286] See the Danish Helsinki Committee for Human Rights, Legal Monitoring in Ukraine II, available at https://khpg.org/en/index.php?id=1313446474. Accessed 25 December 2020.

[287] See the European Parliament resolution on Ukraine d.d. 9 June 2011, available at https://www.europarl.europa.eu/document/activities/cont/201106/20110620ATT21953/20110620ATT21953EN.pdf. Accessed 25 December 2020. In particular, criminal cases were opened against the following members of Tymoshenko's government: Mr. Didenko former First Deputy Chairman of the state oil and gas company "Naftogaz", Mr. Filipchuk, the former Environment Minister, Ms. Gritsoun, the first deputy chairman of the Treasury, Mr. Ivashchenko, the Acting Minister of Defense, Mr. Korniychuk, First Deputy Minister of Justice, Ms. Kushnir, deputy chief accountant «Naftogaz», Mr. Lutsenko, the former Interior Minister, Mr. Makarenko and the former Head of the State Customs Administration of Ukraine.

[288] '*Korniychuk v. Ukraine*' (no. 10042/11), '*Ivashchenko v. Ukraine*' (no. 41303/11) and '*Makarenko v. Ukraine*' (no. 622/11).

[289] See RFE/RL, "Ukraine's Jailed Former Interior Minister Sentenced In Second Case," *RadioFreeEurope/RadioLiberty*, August 17, 2012, sec. Ukraine. https://www.rferl.org/content/ukraine-lutsenko/24679808.html. Accessed 25 December 2020.

[290] Polityuk and Balmforth 2011.

[291] See ECtHR, '*Tymoshenko v Ukraine*', 30 April 2013, Case No.49872/11; ECtHR, '*Lutsenko v Ukraine*', 3 July 2012, Case No.6492/11. Furthermore, the Government of Ukraine later recognized that Ms. Tymoshenko's imprisonment was politically motivated.

both politicians have been already released from prison, the issue of arbitrary justice is still present in political discourse of Ukraine.

1.9.4 Belarus

Similar to other post-Soviet republics that adopted their democratic constitutions within several years of the collapse of the USSR, the Supreme Council (then the legislative body of Belarus) adopted in 1994 a democratic constitution, which envisaged broad individual rights and freedoms, the independence of judicial organs and the separation of powers. Although at that time Belarus made a progress towards the democratic transition, the reforms were interrupted shortly afterwards with the 1994 presidential elections won by Aleksandr Lukashenka who "has clearly sought to subordinate and control all aspects of public life, both in government and in civil society."[292] In particular, Lukashenka organized two referenda in 1996 and 2004 to amend the Constitution and significantly expand his presidential powers. The history of these referenda helps understand ongoing politicized trials against the opposition in Belarus.

The 1996 referendum led to substantial constitutional changes. President Lukashenka's attempts to take away powers from other branches led to a conflict with Parliament. When the Parliament refused to prolong his term in office from five to seven years, limit the role of the Constitutional Court and create the second chamber of Parliament, whose members could be chosen by the President, Lukashenka unilaterally organized a referendum on the constitutional changes suggested by him. Although the official results were in favor of Lukashenka's proposals, neither the international community nor independent observers recognized the results of the referendum.[293] Human Rights Watch made an observation that the referendum gave Lukashenka "quasi-dictatorial powers…[under which] the president…can often bypass the legislature altogether and rule on his own …and [t]he judiciary, including both the Constitutional Court and the courts of general jurisdiction, are subject to strong presidential pressure and the judiciary does not exercise control over the actions and decisions of the executive."[294] Therefore, the first referendum was a turning point for the democratic transition in Belarus.

The second referendum of 2004 further broadened presidential powers. It was conducted simultaneously with the parliamentary elections and brought even more significant constitutional changes as voters had to agree whether the president could

---

[292] See Haman Rights Watch Background Information "Republic of Belarus", available at https://www.hrw.org/reports/1997/belarus/Belarus-03.htm. Accessed 25 December 2020.

[293] According to Alex Danilovich, while only Russia and some other former Soviet republics recognized the referendum, "[t]he French Embassy on Minsk, for instance, circulated a statement on behalf of the EU saying the 20th July was the last day of Lukashenka's legitimate mandate." In: Danilovich 2006.

[294] See Human Rights Watch Background Information "Republic of Belarus", available at https://www.hrw.org/reports/1997/belarus/Belarus-03.htm. Accessed 25 December 2020.

stay in office for an unlimited number of terms. The 1994 version of the Constitution envisaged maximum two terms of holding the presidential office. Though the 'overwhelming majority' of people allegedly supported the unlimited number of presidential terms in 2004, the validity of the referendum outcome was questioned by the Organization for Security and Cooperation in Europe (OSCE) due to numerous voting irregularities.[295] Furthermore, Lukashenka has stated that he intends to run for presidency as many times as his health allows.[296] Despite these changes, the current Constitution at the same time contains various safeguards against arbitrary justice.

Even in its amended version, the Constitution of Belarus contains due process guarantees that are supposed to protect anyone from arbitrary prosecution. For instance, according to *Article 23*, "[r]estriction of personal rights and liberties shall be permitted only in the instances specified in law... [Furthermore, n]o one may enjoy advantages and privileges that are contrary to the law."[297] The principle of legality is stipulated in *Article 25* of the Constitution, which says that "[t]he restriction or denial of personal liberty is possible in the instances and under the procedure specified by law."[298] The same provision guarantees the right of a detained person to a judicial review of the detention and the arrest. *Article 26* envisages the presumption of innocence, under which "[n]o one may be found guilty of crime unless his guilt is proven under the procedure specified by law and established by a court sentence that has come into legal force."[299] The same constitutional norm outlines that a person accused of committing a crime is relieved from an obligation to prove one's innocence before a court. *Article 27* protects against self-incrimination, as it guarantees that "[n]o one shall be compelled to be a witness against oneself, members of his family or close relatives."[300] Finally, *Article 102* is supposed to protect representatives of the political minority in the two-chamber parliament, where "[t]he deputies of the House of Representatives and members of the Council of the Republic shall enjoy immunity in expressing their opinions and exercising their powers."[301] These written

---

[295]For instance, "[l]imitations on candidates' ability to campaign were particularly egregious in light of the massive, nationwide, and apparently State-funded campaign in support of a "yes" vote on the referendum." See the OSCE/ODIHR Election Observation Mission Final Report on Parliamentary Elections of 17 October 2004. https://www.osce.org/odihr/elections/belarus/38658?download=true. Accessed 25 December 2020. See also the European Commission for Democracy through Law (Venice Commission) Opinion no. 314/2004 on the Referendum of 17 October 2004 in Belarus Adopted by the Venice Commission at its 60th Plenary Session (Venice, 8-9 October 2004). https://www.venice.coe.int/webforms/documents/default.aspx?pdffile=CDL-AD(2004)029-e. Accessed 25 December 2020.

[296]See the statement made President Alexander Lukashenka during his press conference on 17 October 2014, available in English: https://eng.belta.by/president/view/lukashenko-no-reasons-not-to-run-for-the-presidential-office-if-i-stay-healthy-7516-2014. Accessed 25 December 2020.

[297]See the English version of the Constitution of Belarus: https://law.by/main.aspx?guid=3871&p0=V19402875e. Accessed 25 December 2020.

[298]Ibid.

[299]Ibid.

[300]Ibid.

[301]Ibid.

formal norms could be understood only in conjunction with unwritten practices of politicized justice applied in Belarus.

The case of the opposition leader and the former presidential candidate Mikalai Statkevitch is illustrative of the unwritten politicized justice practices[302] used against the opposition in Belarus.[303] In 2011, Mr. Statkevich was sentenced to six years imprisonment in Belarus for "organizing mass disorder"[304] shortly after his presidential election campaign against Alexander Lukashenka, who is considered to be one of the most corrupt leaders in the world.[305] After spending four years in prison, Statkevich was amnestied in 2015 by president Lukashenka together with several other opposition politicians, whose release from prison was just a pretext to obtain the foreign financial support and the international recognition of Lukashenka's fifth presidential term.[306] Another former presidential candidate, Andrei Sannikov, was recognized as a prisoner of conscience by Amnesty International.[307] In 2010, after a ten-day trial the court in Belarus sentenced Sannikov to five years in prison for allegedly organizing riots in December 2010 shortly after rigged presidential elections in Belarus.[308] The Government of Belarus ignored Sannikov's claims that he became a victim of police brutality when during his detention "[p]olice assaulted Mr. Sannikov by pinning him down with a riot shield and repeatedly jumping on it, severely injuring his legs."[309] Similar to Statkevich,[310] Andrei Sannikov was pardoned by President Lukashenka and released from prison in April 2012. Such

[302] See the Human Rights Watch UPR Submission to UNHRC on the situation with human rights violations in Belarus, 13 April 2015: https://www.hrw.org/news/2015/04/13/human-rights-watch-upr-submission-unhrc-belarus. Accessed 25 December 2020.

[303] Vadzim Smok. "Political Prisoners – No Longer a Sticking Point in Belarus-EU Relations?" Belarus Digest: News and Analytics on Belarusian Politics, Economy, Human Rights and More, 10 June 2015. https://belarusdigest.com/story/political-prisoners-no-longer-a-sticking-point-in-belarus-eu-relations/. Accessed 25 December 2020.

[304] See Mikalai Statkevich's profile on the website founded by the US NGO "Freedom Now" to support prisoners of conscience: https://www.freedom-now.org/campaign/cases-in-belarus/ (link no longer active).

[305] Fletcher 2014.

[306] Deutsche Welle 2015.

[307] See the Statement by the Amnesty International on Sannikov's case 'Oppositioneller gefoltert', available in German: https://www.amnesty.de/urgent-action/ua-264-2010-1/oppositioneller-gefoltert?destination=node%2F5309. Accessed 25 December 2020.

[308] See the OSCE/ODHIR Election Observation Mission Final Report, 4, (Feb. 22, 2011), the Office for Democratic Inst. and Human Rights, Org. for Security and Cooperation in Europe, Republic of Belarus Presidential Election, 19 December 2010. https://www.osce.org/odihr/elections/75713. Accessed 25 December 2020.

[309] Petition To: United Nations Working Group On Arbitrary Detention, Human Rights Council United Nations General Assembly, In the Matter of Andrei Sannikov, Citizen of Belarus v. Government of Belarus, available at https://www.freedom-now.org/wp-content/uploads/2011/11/Petition-re-Andrei-Sannikov-15.09.11.pdf (link no longer active).

[310] See a statement made by Miklós Haraszti, the United Nations Special Rapporteur on the situation of human rights in Belarus, Belarus: UN expert hails release of political opponents, points to further steps ahead of presidential polls. https://www.ohchr.org/en/NewsEvents/Pages/DisplayNews.aspx?NewsID=16347&LangID=E. Accessed 25 December 2020.

obvious discrepancies between formal norms of the written Constitution of Belarus and its informal political practices have attracted international attention. For instance, the UN Special Rapporteur on the Independence of Judges and Lawyers, Dato' Param Cumaraswamy, noted in his report on Belarus that temporary "decrees issued under the 'necessity' power, not being issued under a law, prevail over existing laws"[311] even if these decrees are no longer in force or are incompatible with the Constitution of Belarus.

Furthermore, in Belarus everyone understands the incompatibility of formal constitutional provisions with routine political practices that override all written laws. Alexander Lukashuk, who researched Lukashenka's rise to power in Belarus, found an interesting explanation of this "Twofold Constitutionalism" proposed by pro-governmental 'experts'. According to Lukashuk, "[i]n order to circumvent the [written] Constitution and various laws adopted during the first years of independence, Belarusian legal scholars introduced a novel twist into jurisprudential theory: the distinction between 'legal' and 'nonlegal' laws. If a law corresponds to the public's intentions, they reasoned, it should be deemed a 'legal' law; if, on the other hand, it contradicts the public's mood and the president's intentions, it should be considered a 'nonlegal' law and may be ignored altogether."[312] In other words, supporters of Lukashenka's regime openly recognized that the country's written constitution and laws could altogether be trumped by unofficial political practices that have a supra-constitutional standing. Therefore, as the above-mentioned analysis of the four constitutions shows, both Western democracies and transitional former Soviet republics have formal written laws and informal practices. However, in the transitional post-Soviet states such informal practices (i.e. ex-parte communication, judicial prerogativism, prosecutorial or accusatorial bias, confessions and self-indictment of accused, the arbitrary recharacterization of offences, simplified extra-legal procedures and occasional political amnesties) not only contradict written law, but can also trump all formal legal norms including constitutional provisions for the sake of political interests of ruling elites. Moreover, the population of transitional states is aware of this legal duality because of politicized trials against opposition leaders, whose exemplary punishment shows that a written constitution is only subsidiary to unwritten political practices inherited from the Soviet Union.

1.10 Conclusions

To summarize the concept of politically motivated justice presented in this book, I argue that the phenomenon of 'Twofold Constitutionalism' includes two parallel legal

[311]See the Report of the Special Rapporteur on the Independence of Judges and Lawyers, Submitted in Accordance with the Commission Resolution 2000/42, 8 February 2001 (E/CN.4/2001/65/Add.1), Addendum: Report on the Mission to Belarus. https://www.refworld.org/docid/45377abb0.html. Accessed 25 December 2020.

[312]Lukashuk 1998, p. 46.

orders of written formal constitutions and unwritten political practices. Both legal orders play their own roles in authoritarian or transitional post-Soviet states. The first legal order of written nominal constitutions serves as a legitimating device for the post-Soviet elites both at home and abroad by performing the roles of the 'operating manual', the 'billboard' and the 'window dressing'. Furthermore, representatives of non-democratic regimes, in general, tend to engage in constitution writing to receive information important for the public, prolong their stay in office, guarantee themselves a 'secure place' after a possible transition, obscure information about their true intentions and raise the support they need to compete for power. Nevertheless, despite the nominal power of democratic principles enshrined in many post-Soviet written constitutions, they can still influence citizens' values and raise the significance of constitutional provisions over time. Therefore, regardless of a great political discretion in non-democratic or transitional states, political elites of these countries still benefit from their written, yet nominal, constitutions.

The second legal order of unwritten political practices stems from the tsarist and communist times. The duality of the system of justice began with urban courts that used written statutory law and cantonal *volost'* courts that decided on the basis of customary law of the Russian empire. This legal duality was reinforced by traditional for Russia culture of low legal consciousness and nihilism towards written statutory law. The system of urban and *volost'* courts was abolished altogether after the Bolshevik revolution by the communist regime, which replaced the customary law and legal traditions accumulated by the *volost'* courts with politically charged practices based on political expediency and the Marxist-Leninist ideology. Nevertheless, the communist system of justice was also dual, as it included written formal norms of socialist legality mandatory for the general public and unwritten Communist Party rules applied only to senior party members. Routine repressions against actual or potential political opponents as well as the supremacy of the communist political ideology over law relegated the status of the Soviet constitutions to a mere decoration. The Soviet phenomenon of social hypocrisy, or hiding one's true intentions, also known as a 'dual soul' (Russian: *dvoedushie*) cemented the duality of the state and its institutions that had multiple identities.

The same phenomenon of the Soviet legal duality can be still found in Russia and many other transitional former Soviet republics, where informal political practices have more power than constitutional provisions. Although it is also possible to observe a certain gap between constitutional promises and their actual implementation in established democracies, the legal system can hardly be called dual in democratic states. As opposed to non-democratic societies, where constitutions are just 'hollow vessels' and empty promises, in democratic societies law and practice tend to follow constitutional aspirations. At the same time, practices and traditions can also have power, which is no less than that of written law, in democracies like the UK, where there is no single written constitution. In order to analyze different roles played by unwritten practices in the administration of justice in democratic and transitional societies, this book relies on the labelling theories developed by criminologists in the twentieth century to explain how a suspect is labelled as an offender in different social settings. In particular, Macnaughton-Smith's labelling theory of the 'Second Code' describes the two sets of rules of formal written and informal unwritten norms that are present in any complex society regardless of its political regime. Macnaughton-Smith effectively argues that, while the first official set of norms is supposed to be frequently violated, those who apply the first set cannot avoid using some form of subjective interpretation and judgment that constitute the core of the second set of informal rules. This 'Second Code' does not have a clear list of informal unwritten rules and practices. Its content can be rather determined by principles, believes and social attitudes widespread in a given society.

Soviet political show trials and their 'degradation ceremonies' analyzed in the subsequent chapter demonstrate that in many former-Soviet republics the 'Second Code' of customary law and national legal traditions was replaced during the Soviet times with politically charged practices and conventionalities of the communist ideology. Therefore, unlike democratic societies, where the unwritten 'Second Code' of customs and traditions complements and fills in the gaps in the official written set of norms, in transitional former Soviet republics the 'Second Code' of politically motivated practices undermines and contradicts democratic constitutions adopted shortly after the fall of the Soviet Union. Given the longevity of the communist regime in the Soviet Union and its influence on legal practitioners and ruling elites in transitional post-Soviet states, one can claim that the 'Second Code' of communist politically charged customs and practices still retains its supra-constitutional status and reveals itself through politicized show trials as a 'degradation ceremony' aimed at discrediting any opposition. The actual influence of these political practices could differ from one former Soviet republic to another due to differences in the scope of transitional justice measures and reforms undertaken by these countries. It appears, thus, the greater the influence of the 'Second Code' of informal political practices, the stronger would be persecution against opposition politicians in a given post-Soviet society.

One of the preliminary conclusions of my research is that trials against politicians perform different roles in the selected Western democracies and transitional former Soviet republics. In Western Europe, such trials address important questions of politics and social life as well as contribute to the public discourse in the framework of the rule of law. In the former Soviet Union, trials against politicians often pursue purely political goals and use law as a decoration or an alibi to get rid of influential opponents. Politicized trials in the post-Soviet states reveal a parallel legal world of mostly unwritten practices and conventionalities inherited from the communist repressive system of criminal justice, which is illustrated in the next chapter with various types of politically motivated trials conducted throughout the entire history of the Soviet Union.

References

Albertus M, Menaldo V (2013) The Political Economy of Autocratic Constitutions. In: Simpser A, Ginsburg T (eds) Constitutions in Authoritarian Regimes. Cambridge University Press, Cambridge (Comparative Constitutional Law and Policy), pp. 53–82. doi: https://doi.org/10.1017/CBO9781107252523.006

Arendt H (1973) The Origins of Totalitarianism, 1st edn. Mariner Books, New York

Argenbright R (2002) Marking NEP's Slippery Path: The Krasnoshchekov Show Trial. The Russian Review, 61(2), pp. 249–275

Barna I, Pető A (2015) Political Justice in Budapest after World War II. Central European University Press

Barros R (2002) Constitutionalism and Dictatorship: Pinochet, the Junta, and the 1980 Constitution. Cambridge University Press, Cambridge, UK/New York

Becker H (1963) Outsiders; Studies in the Sociology of Deviance. The Free Press

Bennett B (2012) Last Dictatorship in Europe: Belarus Under Lukashenko, 1st edn. Oxford University Press

Berman H (1972) Soviet Criminal Law and Procedure: The R.S.F.S.R. Codes, 2nd new edn. Harvard University Press, Cambridge, MA

Boym S (1995) Common Places: Mythologies of Everyday Life in Russia, 60599th edn. Harvard University Press, Cambridge, MA

Braithwaite J (1989) Crime, Shame and Reintegration, 9th edn. Cambridge University Press, Cambridge, UK/New York

Bredies I, Umland A, Yakushik V (eds) (2007) Aspects of the Orange Revolution III: The Context and Dynamics of the 2004 Ukrainian Presidential Elections. ibidem Press, Stuttgart

Brown N (2011) Reason, Interest, Rationality, and Passion in Constitution Drafting. PS: Political Science & Politics 6(4): 675–89

Carothers T (1999) Western Civil-Society Aid to Eastern Europe and the Former Soviet Union [notes]. East European Constitutional Review no. 4: 54

Christenson R (1999) Political Trials: Gordian Knots in the Law, revised, expanded, subsequent edn. Routledge, New Brunswick, NJ

Corcoran K, Hall A (2015) German Politician Marcel Zech Faces Prison for Nazi Auschwitz Tattoo, Daily Mail Online. https://www.dailymail.co.uk/news/article-3362648/German-far-right-politician-faces-five-years-prison-seen-Auschwitz-tattoo-swimming-pool.html. Accessed 25 December 2020

Croissant A, Kamerling J (2013) Why Do Military Regimes Institutionalize? Constitution-making and Elections as Political Survival Strategy in Myanmar. Asian Journal of Political Science, 21(2), pp. 105–125. doi: https://doi.org/10.1080/02185377.2013.823797

Current Digest of the Post-Soviet Press (2010) Bakiyev's Trial Becomes Anti-Russian Show. 62, no. 46/47 (November 15): 17

Danilovich A (2006) Russian-Belarusian Integration: Playing Games Behind the Kremlin Walls. Ashgate Publ Co, Aldershot, UK/Burlington, VT

Deutsche Welle (2015) Freed Belarus Opposition Figure Delivers Warning about Lukashenko, https://www.dw.com/en/freed-belarus-opposition-figure-delivers-warning-about-lukashenko/a-18669993. Accessed 25 December 2020

Engelstein L, Sandler S (eds) (2000) Self and Story in Russian History, illustrated edn. Cornell University Press, Ithaca

Ergun A (2010) Post-Soviet Political Transformation in Azerbaijan: Political Elite, Civil Society and the Trials of Democratization. Uluslararası İlişkiler, Volume 7, No 26, p. 67-85

Ezrow N, Frantz E (2011) Dictators and Dictatorships: Understanding Authoritarian Regimes and Their Leaders. Continuum, New York

Farnsworth B (1986) The Litigious Daughter-in-Law: Family Relations in Rural Russia in the Second Half of the Nineteenth Century. Slavic Review, 45(1), pp. 49–64. doi: https://doi.org/10.2307/2497921

Fearon J (2011) Self-Enforcing Democracy. The Quarterly Journal of Economics, 126(4), pp. 1661–1708

Feifer G (1964) Justice in Moscow - First-hand account of the functions of Soviet courts; from Worker's Tribunals to the Supreme Court, 1st edn. Simon and Schuster, New York, NY

Fletcher M (2014) Belarus: Europe's secret state, GQ, 2014. https://www.martinanthonyfletcher.com/europes-secret-state-gq-magazine/. Accessed 25 December 2020

Fraenkel E (1969) The Dual State: A Contribution to the Theory of Dictatorship, Lawbook Exchange edn. (translation Shils EA, Lowenstein E). The Lawbook Exchange, Ltd, Clark, NJ

Freedom House (2020) The Report, Nations in Transit 2020 - Dropping the democratic facade in Europe and Eurasia. https://freedomhouse.org/report/nations-transit/2020/dropping-democratic-facade. Accessed 22 December 2020

Frierson C (1986) History: Rural Justice in Public Opinion: The Volost Court Debate 1861-1912. Slavonic and East European Review, 64.4, 526–45

Gampl I (1971) Österreichisches Staatskirchenrecht. Springer, Vienna/New York

Garfinkel H (1956) Conditions of Successful Degradation Ceremonies. American Journal of Sociology, 61(5), pp. 420–424. doi: https://doi.org/10.1086/221800

Ginsburg T, Simpser A (eds) (2013) Constitutions in Authoritarian Regimes. Cambridge University Press, Cambridge, UK. doi: https://doi.org/10.1017/CBO9781107252523

Golove D, Hulsebosch D (2010) A Civilized Nation: The Early American Constitution, the Law of Nations, and the Pursuit of International Recognition. 85 New York University Law Review 932

Gove W (1980) The Labelling of Deviance: Evaluating A Perspective, 2nd edn. SAGE Publications, Inc, Beverly Hills, CA

Gravina R (2017) Theories and practices of Soviet constitutions and of the 1993's post-Soviet constitution: from the USSR to the Russian Federation [Teorie e prassi delle costituzioni sovietiche e della costituzione post-sovietica del 1993: dall'URSS alla Federazione Russa]. Journal of Constitutional History [Giornale di Storia Costituzionale], (33), pp. 49–69

Hale H (2011) Formal Constitutions in Informal Politics: Institutions and Democratization in Post-Soviet Eurasia. World Politics, 63(4), pp. 581–617. doi: https://doi.org/10.1017/S0043887111000189

Hausmaninger H (1998) The Austrian Legal System, 1st edn. Springer Netherlands, Boston/The Hague

Hellbeck J (2000) Writing the Self in the Time of Terror: Alexander Afinogenov's Diary of 1937, Self and Story in Russian History. Cornell University Press, pp. 69–93. doi: https://doi.org/10.7591/9781501723933-006

Helmke G, Levitsky S (2004) Informal Institutions and Comparative Politics: A Research Agenda. Perspectives on Politics, 2(4), pp. 725–740

Hendley K (2009) "Telephone Law" and the "Rule of Law": The Russian Case. Hague Journal on the Rule of Law, 1(2), pp. 241–262. doi: https://doi.org/10.1017/S1876404509002413

Hendley K (2017) Everyday Law in Russia, illustrated edn. Cornell University Press, Ithaca/London

Heun W et al. (2011) The Constitution of Germany: A Contextual Analysis. Hart Publishing, Oxford, UK/Portland, OR

Hirschman A (1992) Rival Views of Market Society and Other Recent Essays, Harvard University PR edn. Harvard University Press, Cambridge, MA

Hodos G (1987) Show Trials: Stalinist Purges in Eastern Europe, 1948-1954, 1st edn. Praeger, New York

Hollyer J, Rosendorff B (2011) Why Do Authoritarian Regimes Sign the Convention Against Torture? Signaling, Domestic Politics and Non-Compliance. Quarterly Journal of Political Science, 6(3–4), pp. 275–327. doi: https://doi.org/10.1561/100.00010059

Huntington S (1968) Political Order in Changing Societies. The Henry L. Stimson Lectures Series Edition. Yale University Press, New Haven, CT

Huskey E (1995) The State-Legal Administration and the Politics of Redundancy. Post-Soviet Affairs 11: 2, 115-143

King G, Keohane R, Verba S (1994) Designing Social Inquiry: Scientific Inference in Qualitative Research. Princeton University Press, Princeton, NJ

Kirchheimer O (1961) Political Justice: The Use of Legal Procedure for Political Ends, new edn. Princeton University Press, Princeton, NJ

Kommers D, Miller R (2012) The Constitutional Jurisprudence of the Federal Republic of Germany, 3rd revised and expanded edn. Duke University Press Books, Durham, NC

Kotkin S (1997) Magnetic Mountain: Stalinism as a Civilization, 1st edn. University of California Press, Berkeley, CA

Kovalev K (2004) Lay Participation in Adjudication in NIS: An Independent Jury or a Court of 'Nodders'? Conference Papers - Law & Society (May 27): N.PAG

Krey V (2002) German Criminal Law, General Part: Textbook. Kohlhammer Studienbücher. Kohlhammer, Stuttgart

Krey V, Stenger J (2008) The rule of law in German criminal proceedings: German Constitutional Law and the European Convention on Human Rights. Institut für Rechtspolitik an der Universität Trier (Rechtspolitisches Forum), Trier

Lalpychak C (1991) Independence: Over 90% Vote Yes in Referendum; Kravchuk Elected President of Ukraine (12/08/91), Kyiv Press Bureau, available at https://www.ukrweekly.com/old/archive/1991/499101.shtml. Accessed 25 December 2020

Laughland J (2008) A History of Political Trials: From Charles I to Saddam Hussein, new edn. Peter Lang Oxford, Oxford

Law D, Versteeg M (2013) Constitutional Variation among Strains of Authoritarianism. In: Simpser A, Ginsburg T (eds) Constitutions in Authoritarian Regimes. Cambridge University Press (Comparative Constitutional Law and Policy), Cambridge, UK, pp. 165–196. doi: https://doi.org/10.1017/CBO9781107252523.011

Ledeneva A (2006) How Russia Really Works, 1st edn. Cornell University Press, Ithaca

Ledeneva A, Kurkchiyan M (eds) (2000) Economic Crime in Russia, 1st edn. Kluwer Law International, London/Boston, MA

Liebhart K, Pelinka A, Pribersky A (1991) National Identity in Austria: Towards an Analysis of its Constitution (In German). Österreichische Zeitschrift für Politikwissenschaft, 20(4), pp. 375–382

Linz J (2000) Totalitarian and Authoritarian Regimes, UK edn. Lynne Rienner Publishers, Boulder, CO

Ludwikowski R (1996) Constitution-Making in the Region of Former Soviet Dominance. Duke University Press Books, Durham, NC

Lukashuk A (1998) Yesterday as Tomorrow: Why It Works in Belarus. East European Constitutional Review, 7, p. 43

Macias A (2015) German Politician Gets 6 Months of Probation for Sporting a Nazi Tattoo, Business Insider. https://www.businessinsider.com/marcel-zech-gets-probation-for-having-a-nazi-tattoo-2015-12. Accessed 25 December 2020

Macnaughton-Smith P (1968) The Second Code: Toward (or Away from) an Empiric Theory of Crime and Delinquency. Journal of Research in Crime and Delinquency, 5(2), pp. 189–197. doi: https://doi.org/10.1177/002242786800500208

Malkin B, Raziye A (2015) Vladimir Putin Saved My Life, Says Ousted Ukrainian President Viktor Yanukovych, Telegraph. https://www.telegraph.co.uk/news/worldnews/europe/russia/11692593/Vladimir-Putin-saved-my-life-says-ousted-Ukrainian-president-Viktor-Yanukovych.html. Accessed 25 December 2020

Mälksoo L, Benedek W (eds) (2017) Russia and the European Court of Human Rights: The Strasbourg Effect. Cambridge University Press (European Inter-University Centre for Human Rights and Democratisation), Cambridge, UK. doi: https://doi.org/10.1017/9781108235075

Mayr W (2011) Corruption Scandals in Austria: A Web of Sleaze in Elegant Vienna. https://www.spiegel.de/international/europe/corruption-scandals-in-austria-a-web-of-sleaze-in-elegant-vienna-a-791113.html. Accessed 25 December 2020

Mazmanyan A (2012) Failing constitutionalism: From political legalism to defective empowerment. Global Constitutionalism, 1(2), pp. 313–333. doi: https://doi.org/10.1017/S2045381711000128

Melville A, Mironyuk M (2016) "Bad enough governance": state capacity and quality of institutions in post-Soviet autocracies. Post-Soviet Affairs, 32(2), pp. 132–151. doi: https://doi.org/10.1080/1060586X.2015.1052215

Merkel W, Croissant A (2000) Formale und informale Institutionen in defekten Demokratien. Politische Vierteljahresschrift, 41(1), pp. 3–30. doi: https://doi.org/10.1007/s11615-000-0002-9

Millar J (1992) Cracks in the Monolith: Party Power in the Brezhnev Era: Party Power in the Brezhnev Era, 1st edn. Routledge, Armonk, NY

Mishina E (2014) The Difficult Destiny of the Ukrainian Constitution, Institute of Modern Russia, 24 March. https://imrussia.org/en/rule-of-law/698-the-difficult-destiny-of-the-ukrainian-constitution. Accessed 25 December 2020

Murphy W (2006) Constitutional Democracy: Creating and Maintaining a Just Political Order. Johns Hopkins University Press, Baltimore, MD

Myerson R (2008) The Autocrat's Credibility Problem and Foundations of the Constitutional State. American Political Science Review, 102(1), pp. 125–139. doi: https://doi.org/10.1017/S0003055408080076

Paternoster R, Iovanni L (1989) The Labeling perspective and delinquency: An elaboration of the theory and an assessment of the evidence. Justice Quarterly, 6(3), pp. 359–394. doi: https://doi.org/10.1080/07418828900090261

Pipes R (1986) Legalized Lawlessness: Soviet Revolutionary Justice. Hyperion Books, London

Polityuk P, Balmforth R (2011) Ukraine Jails Tymoshenko for 7 Years, Irks EU, Russia. Reuters, 11 October. Available at https://www.reuters.com/article/us-ukraine-tymoshenko-idUSL5E7LB0OQ20111011. Accessed 25 December 2020

Pomerantsev P (2014) Nothing Is True and Everything Is Possible: The Surreal Heart of the New Russia, reprint edn. PublicAffairs

Popov M, Uporov I (2017) Local Councils of the Soviet State Between the Constitution of The USSR In 1924 And 1936 (Legal Aspect). Historical and social-educational ideas, 9, pp. 60–64. doi: https://doi.org/10.17748/2075-9908-2017-9-1/2-60-64

Popova M (2012) Politicized Justice in Emerging Democracies: A Study of Courts in Russia and Ukraine, illustrated edn. Cambridge University Press, New York

Posner E (2005) Political Trials in Domestic and International Law. Duke Law Journal, 55(1), pp. 75–152

Przeworski A (2013) Ruling against Rules. In: Simpser A, Ginsburg T (eds) Constitutions in Authoritarian Regimes. Cambridge University Press (Comparative Constitutional Law and Policy), Cambridge, UK, pp. 21–35. doi: https://doi.org/10.1017/CBO9781107252523.003

Raz J (2009) Between Authority and Interpretation: On the Theory of Law and Practical Reason. Oxford University Press, Oxford

Rebitschek I (2015) Vortrag zum Panel: "Building Socialist Legality: the Judiciary in the Postwar Soviet Union". In: Rahmen des Jahreskongresses der "Association for Slavic, East European, & Eurasian Studies" (ASEEES) in Philadelphia (PA)

Repressii i Konstitutsia SSSR 1936 goda (2002) Voprosy Istorii No. 1: 3–26

Rotunda RD (1998) Eastern European Diary: Constitution-Building in the Former Soviet Union. The Green Bag. An Entertaining Journal of Law 1, 163

Root H (1989) Tying the King's Hands: Credible Commitments and Royal Fiscal Policy During the Old Regime. Rationality and Society 1 (2):240–58

Rubenstein J (1980) Soviet dissidents: Their struggle for human rights, 1st edn. Beacon Press, Boston, MA

Sadurski W (2012) Constitutionalism and the Enlargement of Europe, 1st edn. Oxford University Press, Oxford, UK

Sakwa R (2010) The Dual State in Russia. Post-Soviet Affairs, 26(3), pp. 185–206. doi: https://doi.org/10.2747/1060-586X.26.3.185

Sakwa R (2013) Systemic Stalemate: Reiderstvo and the Dual State. In: Robinson N (ed) The political economy of Russia. Rowman & Littlefield, Lanham, MD

Schor M (2006) The Rule of Law. Suffolk University Law School Faculty Publications. Paper 30

Schwartz W (2006) Austria—Structure, Objectives, and Results of the Austrian Constitution Convention—Or: How Not to Change a Constitution [Notes]. European Public Law, no. 2 (2006): 167, pp 175–176

Schweber H (2013) Constitutional Failure, *Huffington Post* (blog), 18 September. https://www.huffingtonpost.com/howard-schweber/constitutional-failure_b_3949657.html. Accessed 25 December 2020

Shragin B, Todd A (1977) Landmarks: A Collection of Essays on the Russian Intelligentsia—1909, 1st edn. Howard, NY

Simpser A (2013) Why Governments and Parties Manipulate Elections: Theory, Practice, and Implications. Cambridge University Press, Cambridge, UK; New York

Solomon P (1992) Soviet Politicians and Criminal Prosecutions. The Logic of Party Intervention. In: Millar J (ed) Cracks in the Monolith: Party Power in the Brezhnev Era: Party Power in the Brezhnev Era, 1st edn. Routledge, Armonk, NY

Solomon P (1996) Soviet Criminal Justice Under Stalin. Cambridge University Press, Cambridge, UK/New York

Solomon P (2016) The Effectiveness of the Administration of Justice. Review of Central And East European Law 2: 211

Stelzer M et al. (2011) The Constitution of the Republic of Austria: A Contextual Analysis. Hart Publishing, Oxford, UK/Portland, OR

Stiglitz J (2003) Globalization and Its Discontents, 1st edn. W. W. Norton & Company, New York

Sharlet R (1998) Stalinism and Soviet Legal Culture, Stalinism. In: Tucker R (ed) Stalinism: Essays in Historical Interpretation, new edn. Routledge, New Brunswick, NJ, pp 155–179

Thiel M (ed) (2009) The 'Militant Democracy' Principle in Modern Democracies, 1st edn. Routledge

Trochev A (2008) Judging Russia: The Role of the Constitutional Court in Russian Politics 1990–2006, reissue edn. Cambridge University Press, Cambridge, UK

Trochev A (2017) The Russian Constitutional Court and the Strasbourg Court: judicial pragmatism in a dual state. In: Mälksoo L, Benedek W (eds) Russia and the European Court of Human Rights: The Strasbourg Effect. Cambridge University Press (European Inter-University Centre for Human Rights and Democratisation), Cambridge, UK, pp. 125–149. doi: https://doi.org/10.1017/9781108235075.007

Vasagar J (2014) Former German President Christian Wulff Cleared over Bribery Claim, Financial Times. https://www.ft.com/cms/s/0/c9901e9e-9f9b-11e3-b6c7-00144feab7de.html#axzz4FmoKTxBo. Accessed 25 December 2020

Viola L (2017) Stalinist Perpetrators on Trial: Scenes from the Great Terror in Soviet Ukraine, illustrated edn. Oxford University Press, New York, NY

Wilson A (2005) Virtual Politics: Faking Democracy In The Post-Soviet World. Yale University Press, New Haven, CT

Yanin V (1996) Otechestvennaya Istoriya. Istoriya Rossii s drevneishikh vremen do 1917 goda: Entsiklopediya v 5-ti tomakh. Volume 5: D-K, 1st edn. Nauchnoe izd-vo 'Bol'shaya Rossiiskaya entsiklopediya, Moscow

Zurcher A (1934) Austria's Corporative Constitution. American Political Science Review, 28(4), pp. 664–670. doi: https://doi.org/10.2307/1947197

Chapter 2
Origins of Communist Politically Motivated Criminal Justice

Contents

Abstract This chapter presents detailed analysis of communist show trials, their categorization and the Soviet legacy of 'Twofold Constitutionalism'. It offers a critical assessment of the Soviet system of criminal justice and its trials. My analysis of these trials is made in chronological order—from the earliest Soviet 'agitation trials' and show trials against 'people's enemies' to a regional 'model show trial' in communist Hungary and persecution of political dissidents in the late Soviet period of "Brezhnev's Stagnation" and "Perestroika". One of the aims of the chapter is to demonstrate that the communist traditions of politicized justice became an unwritten Constitution of the USSR, dividing its legal system into two coexisting legal orders of formal and informal norms. To achieve this aim, the chapter provides two outcomes. *First*, it makes a categorization of the communist trials with a special emphasis on victims of arbitrary justice and goals pursued by these trials. *Second*, the chapter analyses major legal characteristics of political justice during the communist regime. Categorization of political trials under Communism and their features helps me scrutinize my hypothesis that, unlike in established democracies, trials against politicians in selected former Soviet republics can reveal a split into a nominal written Constitution and its informal unwritten counterpart.

Keywords Communist show trials · Agitation trials · People's enemies · Class struggle · Soviet dissidents · Soviet constitutions · Communist Hungary

© T.M.C. ASSER PRESS and the author 2021

A. Galushko, *Politically Motivated Justice*,
https://doi.org/10.1007/978-94-6265-459-4_2

2.1 Introduction

This chapter offers a critical assessment of the Soviet system of criminal justice and its origins. This historical overview is necessary to understand the general context, in which various 'political trials' were conducted initially in the USSR and then replicated in its allies in Eastern Europe. My analysis of these trials will be made in chronological order—from the most representative early Soviet 'show trials' against 'people's enemies' to a 'regional show trial' in communist Hungary and the persecution of political dissidents in the late Soviet period of "Brezhnev's Stagnation". For the purpose of this research, I use Ron Christenson's characterization of politicized trials that "are attempts by regimes to control opponents by using legal procedure for political ends."[1] Christenson's conceptual framework also covers the Soviet tradition of politicized justice, whose "aim was not only legal but also political in a direct sense …[, because] the law was being used merely as an alibi."[2] One of the aims of the book is to demonstrate that the Soviet system of political justice became an unwritten Constitution of the USSR. To achieve this aim, the chapter provides two outcomes. *First*, it makes a categorization of the above-mentioned political trials with a special emphasis on victims of politically motivated justice and goals pursued by these trials. *Second*, this chapter analyzes major legal features that were peculiar to political justice during the communist regime. Categorization of political trials under Communism and their features help me confirm or reject in the next chapters my hypothesis that, unlike in Western European states, trials against politicians in selected former Soviet republics can reveal a split into a nominal written Constitution and its informal unwritten counterpart.

2.2 Origins of the Soviet System of Criminal Justice

The goal of this section is to outline origins of the Soviet system of justice, whose main features can be fully explained only through an analysis of legal traditions and institutions that preceded the USSR. The origins of the Soviet repressive system of criminal justice under Joseph Stalin can be traced back to the Russian empire and Lenin's theory about crime and punishment in a communist society.[3] In my opinion, Stalin's policies on criminal justice not only inherited some weaknesses of preceding models of criminal justice, but also represented an attempt to remove those elements that could threaten or limit his personal power. In this context, it is unsurprising that after coming to power thanks to the 1917 Revolution, Bolsheviks wanted to dismantle the Tsarist system of justice, which prosecuted them once in the Russian empire.

---

[1]Christenson 1999, p. xiii.

[2]Ibid., p. xiii.

[3]Solomon 1996, pp. 2–5.

The system of criminal justice, which preceded the Bolshevik revolution, had three key characteristics that would later influence formation of the communist model of criminal law and procedure. First, prosecutors occupied a very powerful position within the structure of criminal justice in the Russian Empire. Todd Foglesong and Peter Solomon note in their review of Soviet criminal justice that in the Russian Empire the Procuracy was "[o]riginally created by Peter the Great as the "eye of the Czar"...[to] ensure ... compliance with the edicts of the autocrat."[4] Interestingly, strong Prosecutor's Office with wide competences was preserved both in the USSR and many former Soviet republics, whose territories once belonged to the Russian empire.

The institute of the Procuracy was created by the Russian tsar Peter I,[5] who introduced numerous legal and administrative reforms that transformed the medieval Russian empire into a modern European state. Initially the tsar established a supervisory institution of so-called 'Fiscals' that were supposed to oversee the work of courts, central and local administrations as well as collect secret reports among the population about possible violations of law.[6] Fiscals, who were not accountable to anyone except the tsar, quickly received a reputation of corrupt officials and racketeers.[7] Therefore, in 1722 Peter I issued an order to establish an institution of Procuracy, whose main role was to represent interests of the tsar by exercising control over decisions and activities of all state organs in the entire Russian empire.[8] Peter formulated the future mission of the newly created Procuracy by stating that this institution will serve as his 'eye'.[9] The Procuracy was reformed on numerous occasions by the next Russian emperors. For instance, after the judicial reform of 1864,[10] besides their traditional task of legal supervision, Russian Prosecutors General also performed the additional functions of ministers of interior and justice. Although after the Bolshevik 1918 Revolution the tsarist Procuracy was abolished by the 'Decree on Courts', it was soon reestablished in 1922 as a supervisory body, whose main task was to oversee the enforcement of laws and the fight against crime in the Soviet Union.

The Procuracy became the cornerstone of Soviet justice, where the "Socialist legal theory emphasized the key role of the *Prokuratura* in the administration of justice."[11] Sajó observes the continuity of the Russian traditions of the tsarist Procuracy in the Soviet times when "[t]he organizational design of the Soviet *Prokuratura* was inherited from the czarist administration. It was a select, centralized body; prosecutors

[4] Foglesong and Solomon 2001, p. 58.

[5] Zviagintsev and Orlov 1997.

[6] Zviagintsev and Orlov 1994.

[7] Ibid., p. 6.

[8] Zviagintsev and Orlov 1997.

[9] Zviagintsev and Orlov 1994.

[10] Zviagintsev and Orlov 1996.

[11] Sajó 2001.

served in total subordination to their superiors, in what was a quasimilitary organization."[12] Unlike prosecutors from Western Europe who traditionally represented criminal prosecution in court, the Soviet Procuracy enjoyed a special status,[13] as Soviet prosecutors earned more money than judges as well as could directly supervise and intervene into activities of all state organs. Lenin allocated a special mission to the Procuracy, which was supposed to become "the bulwark of socialist legality ...Thus the task of the *Prokuratura* was to 'see the establishment of a truly uniform understanding of [this] legality."[14] Such an extensive mandate turned the Procuracy into a ubiquitous institution with broad powers that "included the authority to ask for ordinary and extraordinary review of court decisions, even when it was not a party in the case it sought to review."[15] Therefore, the tsarist roots and further development of the Procuracy created an institution, which was different from Prosecutor's Offices in other countries. The second important feature of the tsarist system of justice was low legal awareness. Andrei Medushevsky in his research on Russian constitutionalism refers to traditional for Russia legal dualism of written positive law often borrowed from other countries and "unwritten peasant law...., which was only partially reflected in the effective legislation but constituted a real base of legal awareness of the overwhelming segment of the population [in the Russian empire]."[16] Furthermore, George Yaney effectively argues that "as of 1917...legal institutions reached only a minority of the population [in the Russian empire]".[17] Taking into account that the empire had vast territories, courts were located mostly in cities, while residents of rural areas were not aware of written legal procedures transplanted by Russian monarchs from other legal systems. The third and the most important weakness of the Russian empire was disrespect of law. For instance, Solomon describes "the low status ...[of] law ... in Russian political culture...[, where, as] in other autocracies [,]...the ruler stood above the law."[18] No wonder that the population of the Russian empire had a negative attitude towards legal institutions they knew very little about and whose main purpose was to maintain unlimited power of the monarch.

These and other weaknesses of the Russian empire led to its ultimate collapse and the communist October Revolution in 1917. The very survival of the newly formed communist state demanded some significant changes in its system of justice. Researchers of early Soviet criminology observe that Vladimir Lenin, a leader of the revolution and a professional lawyer, was behind the new Soviet model of criminal justice. For instance, Inga Markovits describes a naive and 'nightmarish model'

[12]Ibid.

[13]Zviagintsev and Orlov 2001.

[14]Sajó 2001.

[15]Ibid.

[16]Medushevsky 2006, p. 99.

[17]Solomon 1996, p. 3.

[18]Ibid.

of the new communist system of criminal justice designed by Lenin, who thought that crimes will be just "a rare exception, and will probably be accompanied by … swift and severe punishment (for the armed workers are men of practical life, not sentimental intellectuals, and they will scarcely allow anyone to trifle with them)."[19] Such a profane vision of criminal justice was implemented by an equally amateurish group of new Bolshevik legal officials.

Inga Markovits' analysis of Mirjan Damaška's comparative approach to the legal process in different systems of justice could explain why Lenin thought that crimes would be a rare exception in the utopian communist society accompanied by the 'swift and severe punishment'. Markovits uses the comparative model proposed by Damaška to describe the Soviet criminal system of justice as an example of hierarchical policy-implementing judicial processes due to "its stress on societal interests, its judicial activism, and its powerful role for the procuracy."[20] As opposed to other Damaška's judicial models of hierarchical conflict resolution, coordinate conflict resolution and coordinate policy implementation, the Soviet system of criminal justice "involve[d] forms of decision-making that no longer manifest any respect for the possible objections, and thus the rights, of those immediately affected."[21] In this policy-implementing model, the only goal of the highly hierarchical Soviet judicial bureaucracy was to use justice merely as an instrument to achieve public goals proclaimed by the Communist Party rather than to protect individual rights and freedoms. Markovits finds that it was unsustainable, because the Soviet model disrespected rights and objections of defendants, which "could, indeed, no longer be defined as judicial conflict resolution."[22] Therefore, the ultimate utopian public goal of the Soviet hierarchical policy-implementing model was the eradication of crime as a social phenomenon, which was supposed to be achieved by the swift and severe punishment and complete disregard of individual rights.

There were three reasons why Lenin's approach to criminal law was revolutionary for Russia and required new legal officials who proved their absolute loyalty to the Communist Party. First, taking into account that previous legal officials belonged to the Tsarist bourgeoisie, they could not possibly retain their positions in the Soviet state. The reason for this was simple: only new proletariat legal officials could participate in the class struggle "discriminating against 'former people' who had done well under the previous regime and promoting 'proletarians' and 'poor peasants' in their stead."[23] Second, similar to Nazi judges that preferred their "healthy folk sentiment"[24] or '*gesundes Volksempfinden*' to written law, Soviet judges and prosecutors were also obliged to follow their revolutionary conscience "rather than the letter of the

[19] Markovits 1989, p. 1333.

[20] Ibid., p. 1319.

[21] Ibid.

[22] Markovits 1989, p. 1319.

[23] Edele 2011, p. 64.

[24] See Law and Justice in the Third Reich in the Holocaust Encyclopedia. https://www.ushmm.org/wlc/en/article.php?ModuleId=10005467. Accessed 23 December 2020.

law".[25] Revolutionary consciousness (Russian: *revolutsionnoe pravosoznaniye*) and socialist legality (Russian: *sotsilalisticheskaya zakonnost*) are yet another example of how written and unwritten norms were interchangeably used in the Soviet legal system.

The normative distinction of socialist legality from the Western Rule of Law was the addition of the word 'socialist' to the communist concept of legal order. In the communist bloc legality was called 'socialist', because various "socialist (socialistic) theories of law have emphasized the importance of law in class domination…and envisioned a normative system that reflected social equality and solidarity, that is a theory of law based on social justice."[26] Legality was officially pronounced 'socialist' to emphasize that it was "the most developed form of law in history as it served the most developed social formation (communism)."[27] András Sajó notes that the Communist Party used the formal 'socialist addendum' to present the communist concept of legality as "a qualitatively superior alternative to bourgeois Rule of Law."[28] However, the reality of socialist legality presupposed a regular disregard of existing written laws,[29] as "it often served show-trial and other propaganda purposes only, as exemplified by the [declaratory] Stalin constitution."[30] Furthermore, Sajó points out that within the socialist camp the concept of legality also varied to a certain degree, "not only because of modifications in the forms of domination but also because Soviet legal solutions were imposed on diverse cultures and societies."[31] Thus, the Communist Party denoted the concept of legality as 'socialist' to present it as the morally superior form of law and emphasize that legality could be limited by political goals of the socialist ideology.

The communist leadership emphasized the uniqueness of its socialist legality to show that it was different from and superior to the western concept of the Rule of Law. The 'moral superiority' of the socialist legality ultimately justified the existence of the communist regime as such. At the same time, the main concepts of the socialist legality were transplanted, often under different names, from Western European countries. The Soviet doctrine of analogy was taken from "Tsarist law, [which,] like the law of many European autocracies, has contained the principle of analogy and left no place for its opposite, *nullum crimen sine lege*."[32] The notion of a socially dangerous act is most similar to the concepts of *Straftat Begriff* (definition of a crime)

---

[25] Solomon 1996, p. 64.

[26] Sajó 2001.

[27] Sajó 2001.

[28] Ibid.

[29] Rebitschek 2015.

[30] Sajó 2001.

[31] Ibid.

[32] Solomon 1996, p. 31.

and *Materielle Rechtswidrigkeit* (material unlawfulness) proposed by German criminologist Franz von Liszt.[33] Similar to the Soviet Union, "in Germany…the prosecutor became the main figure, both directing the police and assuming responsibility for screening cases, including after confessions."[34] However, the concepts transplanted by the Soviet scholars from the western legal systems did not bring to the Soviet Union the western standard of a fair trial due to judicial bias, prerogativism, arbitrary recharacterization of an offence and other informal rules of politicized justice. The new democratic constitutions introduced after the collapse of the USSR faced the same fate of being subverted by the Soviet legacy of unwritten political practices.

There are several important characteristics of socialist legality that distinguish it from the Western concept of legality. As opposed to Western law, socialist legality was not supposed to limit the government in its interventions. Sajó observes that "[i]n the 1930s, law (not only criminal law) was structured as an unrestrained authorization, and even a command to intervene in anything and everything."[35] Zweigert and Kötz point out that the most important difference between Western legality and socialist legality is that under the latter "law is politically and socially functional."[36] In other words, while socialist legality is subordinated to political considerations, in the West "Law always has the additional function of setting limits to politics…[especially in matters of criminal justice, where] the 'Rule of Law'…is to protect the zones of freedom of the citizen from invasion by the authorities."[37] Thus, the Western concept of legality is different from socialist legality in the sense that the latter promotes unrestricted state intervention in all social areas, disregards privacy in favor of state interests and completely subordinates law to politics.

On the one hand, the concept of socialist legality required from all Soviet citizens and institutions strict adherence to Soviet written laws. Vladimir Lenin, who followed Karl Marx and Friedrich Engels' anti-law sentiments,[38] argued that law would be necessary only during the initial period of transition to the ideal communist society, which would not need any legal norms.[39] On the other hand, Lenin, who developed the concept of socialist legality, demanded strict implementation of Soviet laws "without forgetting the limits of legality in the revolution".[40] Revolutionary consciousness or vigilance was, in turn, used by early Soviet courts as an official excuse for imperfect legislation, which could not possibly cover all forms of legal relations in the brand new socialist society. Unofficially, however, it set the

[33]Liszt and Schmidt 1932.

[34]Solomon 2015, p. 162.

[35]Sajó 2001.

[36]Zweigert et al. 1987, p. 302.

[37]Ibid.

[38]Bloom 1946.

[39]Lenin V.I.Polnoye sobranie sochineniy, tom 33, Gosudarstvo i Revolutsia s. 95.

[40]Ibid., tom 44, s. 465.

limits of legality through unwritten practices of the communist leadership that did not want to constrain itself with law. According to a Decree on Court from 22 November 1917, revolutionary consciousness became a source of law in the Soviet system of justice and with the adoption of the 1922 RSFSR Criminal Code it was renamed into 'socialist conscience', which then played a role of the official legal ideology used by Soviet courts.[41] The third feature of Lenin's revolutionary model was that two previous points were necessary preconditions for massive political repressions and even state-sanctioned physical terror, which could be done only by people completely loyal to the Communist Party leadership.

Therefore, Lenin and other "Bolsheviks decided to staff their legal agencies with their own people, politically trustworthy amateurs...who lacked not only higher legal education, but even general secondary education."[42] Most importantly, old Bolshevik ideology further relegated the status of law, because they practiced the 'nihilistic anti-law approach', which "treated the law as wholly instrumental, a tool in the hands of rulers rather than a good in itself."[43] Lenin himself supported 'flexibility of law', "guided by a 'revolutionary consciousness' which always had to uphold the regime's interests as top priority...[without] restrain[ing] the leadership's freedom to maneuver."[44] Some of these drastic changes in criminal justice, however, did not serve Joseph Stalin, who became Lenin's official successor, and was not so much devoted to the Leninist Bolshevik ideology,[45] but rather to the goal of concentrating state power in his hands.

2.3 The System of Criminal Justice Under Stalin

After Lenin's death in 1924 Stalin competed for ultimate power over the Political Bureau[46] (Russian: *Politburo*) with various factions within the Communist Party. The key ingredient of Stalin's success in this power struggle was his control over the system of political repressions carried out by the Soviet secret police, also known as the *Joint State Political Directorate* (OGPU),[47] which was later reorganized into NKVD and then KGB. Taking into account that "[t]he posts that Stalin occupied in the

[41] Maksimova 2014.

[42] Solomon 1996, p. 4.

[43] Ibid., p. 3.

[44] Argenbright 2002, p. 252.

[45] For instance, Lenin criticized negative aspects of Stalin, who, "[h]aving become General Secretary,...has unlimited authority concentrated in his hands." In: Buranov 1994, p. 180.

[46] The Political Bureau (Russian: Политбюро) was the chief decision making body of the Soviet leadership established by the Communist Party during the October Revolution of 1917 and preserved until the collapse of the USSR in 1991.

[47] Joint State Political Directorate under the Council of People's Commissars of the USSR (Russian: *Obyedinyonnoye gosudarstvennoye politicheskoye upravleniye* pri Sovnarkome SSSR).

party and the government let him determine who went where to serve the state",[48] he managed to outvote his opponents at party meetings. While understanding the special power of the secret political police, "he assured OGPU of a prominent future role in government."[49] This was the 'Joker' played by Stalin later to annihilate his rivals during the show trials or secret repressions.

Communist Party leaders like Trotsky, Zinoviev and others were too busy fighting with each other before they finally realized that the entire 'army' of the Red Terror was loyal only to Stalin. According to Donald Rayfield's research on Stalinism, this was the moment when Felix Dzierzynski and his "OGPU were now entirely Stalin's men—there was no other shepherd for the sheepdogs to follow."[50] The same assessment of Stalin's rise to power is given by James Harris and other researchers of Stalinism. In particular, Harris refers to the so-called circular flow of power in the early Soviet Union, when "Stalin used his control over appointments to build a personal following in the Party apparatus."[51] Stalin's propensity to micromanage his appointees is confirmed by Robert Service, who wrote that Stalin "wanted to be kept abreast of developments and relayed regular instructions to his subordinates."[52] Stalin's close involvement in state affairs also influenced the development of the Soviet system of criminal justice.

Although Stalin held the modest title of General Secretary of the Communist Party, the real wide scope of his powers revealed itself in his immense influence on the creation of the Soviet system of criminal justice. Researchers of Stalinism have no doubts that he was the sole creator of many criminal law provisions. Peter Solomon points out that "Stalin's predilection for personal decision making and his intolerance of direct criticism ...discouraged scholarly contributions to criminal policy."[53] The dictator's great interest in criminal law, where 'every change...bore the mark of his hand'",[54] is explained by his intention to keep power as Lenin's only successor and further legitimize terror against his actual and potential opponents. Thus, the Soviet system of criminal justice was significantly influenced by Stalin's personality and his struggle for power.

In his management style, Joseph Stalin acted like a classic dictator, who usually preferred individual decision-making and tried to project his 'vast knowledge' in various sciences. For instance, besides his involvement in criminal justice, Stalin tried to present himself as a wise 'father of nations' by authoring several scholarly works.[55] In this respect, Rayfield effectively argues that Stalin was influenced by his native Georgian culture, where "[t]he ideal ruler, for Georgian kings, was a universal

---

[48] Rayfield 2004, p. 136.

[49] Ibid.

[50] Ibid., page 137.

[51] Davies and Harris 2005, p. 63.

[52] Service 2005, p. 247.

[53] Solomon 1978, p. 19.

[54] Solomon 1996, p. 462.

[55] For instance, Stalin published books on various topics such as '*The new Russian policy*' (1931), '*Dialectical and Historical Materialism*' (1938), '*The History of the Communist Party of the Soviet*

genius—a scholar and an artist as well as a strategist."[56] Solomon also notes that "the leader Joseph Stalin emerges…as a classic dictator, capable of directing criminal policy and dominating decision-making about it."[57] Under these circumstances, influence of other decision makers on the Soviet system of criminal justice was limited due to "Stalin's predilection to personal decision-making and his intolerance of direct criticism of his policies."[58] For instance, "[d]uring the late 1940s Stalin introduced a series of changes in the criminal law without…[his judicial chiefs'] advice or consent. In abolishing (temporarily) the death penalty (1947) and in setting new penalties for rape (1949), Stalin reportedly did not even consult his judicial lieutenants."[59] Nevertheless, legal policies[60] designed by the dictator were not always enforced "[w]hen Stalin tried to use the criminal law for purposes and in ways not accepted by its enforcers (legal officials, police, and others) or call for penalties that struck them as too severe."[61] Thus, although Stalin played a major role in creating the Soviet system of criminal justice, the non-enforcement of its written norms undermined the status and authority of law in the Soviet society.

As opposed to his public legislative initiatives such as the Soviet Constitution of 1936, Stalin usually kept his supervision of politically motivated justice in secret from the Soviet society. Political show trials were supposed to give an impression of the 'independent' Soviet judiciary at work. Only recent research in the Soviet archives revealed "how thoroughly Stalin himself planned the key political show trials…how it was he who scripted the fictional confessions; how he directed the state security service in detail on the conduct of the trials; and how criminal cases against a multitude of arrested "wreckers"…were reviewed in advance by the special Politburo commission for political (criminal) cases before the final decision was made in the Politburo/inner circle around Stalin."[62] Similar to public show trials, secret extra-legal executions of political enemies took place in accordance with personal instructions given by Stalin[63] as well as clandestine Decrees such as the secret NKVD order # 00447 approved by the entire Politburo on July 30, 1937, which launched repressions and executions of uncooperative peasantry and other 'anti-Soviet elements'.

Union' (1938), '*Marxism and Problems of Linguistics*' (1950), '*Economic Problems of Socialism in the U.S.S.R.*' (1952) as well as articles and even personal poetry.

[56]In particular, "Stalin's obsession with literature and writers, with science and scientists, and his personal jealousies in these fields, mirror Georgian kings such as Teimuraz I, who like Nero, envied his rivals as much in poetry as in politics." In: Rayfield 2004, p. 17.

[57]Solomon 1996, pp. 461–462.

[58]Ibid., p.19.

[59]Ibid.

[60]Berman 1966.

[61]Solomon 1996, p. 463.

[62]Rosenfeldt 2009, p. 392.

[63]Oleg Khlevniuk found archive documents that corroborate Stalin's personal involvement in the Great Purge. *See* Khlevniuk 2008.

The practice of extra-legal executions was promoted due to several reasons during Stalin's times. First, penal labor colonies or GULAGS were already overcrowded in the peak of the Great Purge in 1938. Rayfield points out that "[i]n December 1938 the GULAG population passed the million mark, and there were nearly as many in the prison and other labor colonies…run by inexperienced and frightened administration...[Thus,] the camps could not keep up with the mass arrests; those detained in… grotesquely overcrowded prisons often died…before they could be executed."[64] The issue of overcrowded camps could be resolved only by increasing the number of summary proceedings and extrajudicial killings. At this time "Stalin and Ezhov therefore decided that the percentage of 'enemies' sentenced to death rather than forced labor must rise from 0.5 to 47%. In 1937 and 1938 the NKVD's own records show that 1,444,923 persons were 'convicted' of counterrevolutionary crimes, and of these 681,692 were shot."[65] The 'conviction' as such was just a farce to cover up the extra-legal nature of killings. Rayfield observes that during the Purge "most victims were sentenced by a troika or a joint commission of the Public Prosecutor and the NKVD, some received quasi-judicial sentences from the Military Collegium of the Supreme Court."[66] Thus, extra-judicial killings kept prisons from further overcrowding.

The Purge also targeted entire social classes, groups and ethnic minorities. It was virtually impossible to sentence in ordinary courts such a big number of people. For instance, "[c]ertain categories of the population were more vulnerable to arrest than others: 95 percent of those shot were men. Xenophobia was key: non-Russians, only 18 percent of the population, provided 37 percent of the victims. Poles, Finns, Estonians, and Latvians were singled out to the extent that the USSR in 1937 had half as many ethnic Poles and Balts as it had in 1926…[Moreover, s]ome minority peoples effectively faced genocide."[67] Thus, the conveyor of extra-judicial killings was the only method to eradicate such big groups of people without causing major social resistance.

Anti-Semitic sentiments were especially strong in Russia also prior to the communist regime. For instance, Arno Lustiger mentions that "[u]nder Ivan the Terrible, the Jews were considered to be the henchmen of the hostile Poles. During the First World War they were deported as supposedly being pro-German…[In the USSR] their aversion to all 'real Russian things' was building a fifth column of the West, led by the Americans."[68] In the early Soviet times, anti-Semitism was often presented as a form of tsarist and bourgeois oppression, as Lenin himself "condemned the pogroms…and acknowledge[d] at the same time that among the leaders of the Bolsheviks were quite

---

[64]Rayfield 2004, p. 309.

[65]Ibid., p. 310.

[66]Rayfield 2004, p. 311.

[67]Ibid.

[68]Lustiger and Brackman 2003, p. 200.

a number of Jews."[69] The role of national minorities became even more important during WWII, when the Soviet war "policy of 'Ukrainization', 'Belorusification', or… 'Yiddishization' (i.e. concessions to certain nationalities in the administrative, cultural and other areas) was aimed at mobilizing the sympathy of various national elements inside the USSR and of their counterparts abroad."[70] For instance, almost immediately after Hitler's invasion in the Soviet Union the Communist Party simultaneously initiated the so-called Slav and Jewish anti-fascist committees to exercise influence on public opinion among North Americans of Slavic and Jewish origin "(mainly in the USA)."[71] Thus, the 'nationality card' was played to mobilize support both within and outside the USSR.

Joseph Stalin, who used to be a commissar on nationalities,[72] supported similar initiatives even before WWII and "permitted Jewish settlements to flourish in the Crimea, supported the creation of a secular Yiddish culture, and established a Jewish autonomous region in Birobidzhan to rival Palestine for the allegiance of Jewish masses inside and outside the country."[73] Although Stalin had "personal animus against the Jews",[74] among his close associates were a number of Jews like Lazar Kaganovich or "[t]he Hungarian Jew Karl Pauker [who] commanded Stalin's personal security detail for a time in the 1930s and used to shave the dictator with an open razor, before his own execution during the Great Purge in 1937."[75] Therefore, despite general anti-Semitic sentiments in the USSR, the Communist Party either strengthened or weakened the national autonomy of Jews and other Soviet ethnic groups, depending on the current political situation. When support of national minorities was no longer needed towards the end of the war "between October 1943 and June 1944, several small nationalities were expelled from border areas to Central Asia or Siberia after being unjustly accused of treason and collaboration with the enemy: the Chechens, Ingush, Karachays, Balkars, Kalmyks, and Crimean Tatars among them."[76] Jewish communities previously supported by the communist regime faced the same fate after WWII.

In particular, the post-war campaign initiated by the Communist Party against 'rootless cosmopolitism' targeted mostly Soviet Jews. Lustiger observes that "Jewish pedagogues, journalists, artists, and scientists, even those who never dealt with Jewish affairs, were dismissed and prosecuted."[77] Although such dismissals and official

---

[69] Ibid., p. 47.

[70] Redlich 1982, p. xii.

[71] Redlich 1982, p. 12.

[72] Lustiger and Brackman 2003, p. 50.

[73] Rubenstein and Naumov 2005, p. 33.

[74] For instance, when Joseph Stalin's daughter Svetlana dated Alexei Kapler, a war correspondent and a Jew, Stalin said, "[s]he couldn't even find herself a Russian… Stalin [also] liked to tell Svetlana [, who married her Jewish classmate] that 'the Zionists put him over on you.'" In: Alliluyeva 1969, p. 152. In: Rubenstein and Naumov 2005, p. 35.

[75] Rubenstein and Naumov 2005, p. 33.

[76] Ibid.

[77] Rubenstein and Naumov 2005, p. 200.

Soviet propaganda were not openly anti-Semitic, at this particular time "[t]he navy newspaper Krasny flot attacked people personally, calling them 'the Jew Rudny', or the Jew Ivich."[78] In 1952 this anti-Jewish purge culminated in the trial against the Jewish Antifascist Committee, whose members were accused of turning the Committee "into an espionage and nationalist ring, directly controlled by reactionary forces in the United States…[while t]he main offence was the demand for a Jewish republic in the Crimea as a 'bridgehead' for the Americans."[79] Although, in a secret show trial, thirteen defendants claimed that they gave their confessions under torture and psychological pressure,[80] all of them were sentenced to death except Lina Stern, who was exiled to a remote area of the USSR to continue her scientific research, which "could prolong Stalin's life."[81] In 1953 the official newspaper Pravda informed about the so-called 'Doctors' plot', which involved a group of predominantly Jewish doctors who allegedly applied wrong medical treatment to assassinate Soviet leadership, "linking them to an American and Zionist plot…and the late Solomon Mikhoels, who…was exposed as a 'bourgeois Jewish nationalist'."[82] Only Stalin's death in 1953 saved the accused from prosecution under the destalinization campaign initiated by the next Soviet leader Khrushev.

Although Stalin practiced a clandestine approach to political justice mentioned above, he was undoubtedly behind the so-called Kirov Law, which introduced some drastic changes in the Soviet criminal procedure. The Resolution "On Amending the Present Union-Republic Codes of Criminal Procedure"[83] was adopted in 'response' to the assassination of Kirov, who was a popular leader of the Communist Party. Historians have no doubt that this "notorious resolution [was] issued in Stalin's own formulation immediately after the murder of Sergei Kirov on 1 December 1934".[84] Published in the main Soviet newspaper 'Pravda', this resolution established a summary judicial procedure in cases of 'terrorism', according to which "the investigation of such cases was to be concluded within a period of not more than ten days…the case was to be heard without…the defendant or his counsel…., and the death sentence to be carried out immediately upon rendering of the judgment."[85] By introducing such gruesome changes in the criminal procedure, Stalin used Kirov's murder as a political pretext for the Great Purge, as a result of which "[t]he number of NKVD [political] sentences rose from just under 79,000 in 1934 to approximately 267,000 a year later."[86] The Kirov law incorporated with some slight changes into

[78]Lustiger and Brackman 2003, p. 201.

[79]Ibid., page 222.

[80]Redlich 1982.

[81]Lustiger and Brackman 2003, p. 243.

[82]Rubenstein and Naumov 2005, p. 62.

[83]Sean's Russia Blog 2009.

[84]Rosenfeldt 2009, p. 392.

[85]SZ (1934), no. 64, item 459; cf. SU (1935), no. 2, item 8. In: Berman 1972, p. 55.

[86]Rosenfeldt 2009, p. 391.

the special section of the RSFSR Code of Criminal Procedure was repealed by the USSR Supreme Court only in 1956.[87]

The nature of Stalin's criminal law policies must be interpreted in close connection with social and economic challenges that in many cases threatened the very existence of the USSR. The dire economic situation of the population in the aftermath of the civil war was one such threat. The 'New Economic Policy' (NEP), which included some elements of capitalist market economy to mitigate negative consequence of the civil war, was discontinued by Stalin shortly after Lenin's death. Stalin's alternative model of collectivization and rapid industrialization led to further poverty, lack of basic goods, economic and other crimes as well as popular discontent. In order to hide its failure and shift the blame to someone else, the Communist Party organized 'exemplary trials' against mid-level factory specialists and representatives of stigmatized ethnic minorities "as if to placate the workers".[88] An alternative reason for organizing exemplary public show trials would be their effectiveness in communicating communist ideology and new social norms to a large number of people across the USSR. Simon Liberman, a victim of such a staged trial, "explained the wave of 'exemplary trials' of specialists in the 1920s as an indication of the psychological and political insecurity of Lenin's successors…[who] were desperate to attract support from workers."[89] In any case, such attempts of the Soviet ruling elites to find scapegoats as well as subsequent social uprisings exposed vulnerability of the communist regime at that time.

Stalin's policies of forced collectivization and rapid industrialization, which essentially presupposed the elimination of entire social classes and expropriation of individual property, could not but provoke social resistance both in rural and urban areas. There are many historical records[90] that urban workers, who suffered from food shortages, poor working and living conditions, felt extremely disillusioned with Stalin's economic and social policies. Aggressive collectivization measures "provoked the first major instances of rural unrest…[and] fears that disturbances might spread to the peasant dominated [Soviet] army".[91] According to David Shearer's research on crime in the 1930s, the USSR witnessed "an explosion of "social disobedience" that instilled fear into political and especially secret police elites."[92] The deplorable economic situation also led to proliferation of black market activities,[93]

[87] Vedomosti SSSR (1956), no. 8, item 193. In: Berman 1972, p. 50.

[88] Kuromiya 2003, p. 253.

[89] Ibid.

[90] For example, the Vichuga workers uprising of 1932, during which 16,000 textile workers temporarily took control of an entire town, see Harman 2007.

[91] Ward 1993, p. 41.

[92] Viola 2002, p. 33.

[93] Osokina 2002, pp. 170–200.

larceny of workers and collective farmers,[94] higher conviction rates,[95] increasing juvenile delinquency[96] as well as distrust of the ruling elites.

Elena Osokina, who researched the Soviet black market, describes a parallel world of unofficial economy, which "'in symbiosis' with state economic practices…[was] a hybrid structure 'shadowing' the official economy."[97] The illegal shadow market thrived during constant shortages of goods in the USSR and showed remarkable skills of mimicry. To avoid attention of Soviet authorities and criminal punishment for speculation,[98] "black marketeers disguised their illegal practices to resemble forms of legal socialist production and trade."[99] Despite criminal prosecution of black market activities, their scope was staggering. For instance, "during the hungry years of the First Five-Year Plan…practically every Soviet citizen was involved at some level in 'speculation'…Speculation surrounded and engulfed all legal forms of distribution and trade, and all forms of production in the USSR contributed to speculation."[100] The USSR punished as illegal activities not only the sale of stolen or counterfeit goods at the black market, but also barter, resale of goods, private production and distribution that were considered to be normal operations in free market economies. This, of course, only widened the gap between the illusory official picture of the 'prosperous' Soviet economy and the expanding parallel world of black market activities.

Gaps between social classes in the Russian empire created a subculture of deprived individuals and criminals known as *vorovskoy mir* (Thieves' World),[101] which had a range of principles and rules alternative to the official legal system. Growing population of the Soviet concentration camps or GULAGs[102] facilitated further dissemination of the criminal subculture. For instance, "[i]n December 1938 the GULAG population passed the million mark, and there were nearly as many in the prisons and other labor colonies."[103] Many Soviet families had friends or relatives that were arrested and imprisoned during various purges. Inevitably, those prisoners who managed to survive brought the prison subculture including the prison slang and a system of values to the Soviet society. Therefore, a closed group of high-ranking criminals known as "Thieves-by-Law" (Russian: *vory v zakone*) managed to expand their own

---

[94] Osokina 2002, pp. 170–200.

[95] "The annual numbers convicted in the Russian Federation (RSFSR) alone exceeded one million at that time", see Osokina 2002, p. 195.

[96] Edele 2011, pp. 64–65.

[97] Osokina 2002, p. 10.

[98] "The maximum penalties for speculation as a form of business or on a large scale…[were] seven years in the RSFSR, eight years in Latvian SSR, ten years in the Turkmen SSR, and ten years with resettlement and confiscation of property in Armenian SSR". See Berman 1966, p. 16.

[99] Viola 2002, p. 184.

[100] Ibid., p. 192.

[101] Serio and Razinkin 1995.

[102] The acronym GULAG stands for 'Principle Administration of Camps' (Russian: Glavnoye Upravleniye Lagerey).

[103] Rayfield 2005, p. 309.

parallel extra-legal system of norms and penalties beyond the penitentiary setting to the general Soviet population.

In his response to the social unrest and the rise of crime, Stalin followed Lenin's theory of 'swift and severe punishment' by introducing new 'draconian' criminal provisions, whose strict nature was unheard of even under Russian tsars. Although forced collectivization and expropriation of private property led to the great famines and even cannibalism in rural areas of the USSR,[104] criminal penalties were introduced to ensure complete extermination of independent peasantry (kulaks) as a class. To starve peasants to death, 'unauthorized consumption of food' was criminalized in 1932 by "a law 'On the Protection of the Property of State Enterprises, Kolkhozy and Co-operatives'".[105] Nicknamed the "Law of Three Spikelets", it envisaged punishment in the form of execution or confiscation of property, which was applied even to twelve-year-old children who took a few wheatears.[106] As a post-factum legitimization of this policy Stalin lowered in 1935 the age of criminal responsibility in the Criminal Code by making the death penalty applicable from the age of twelve. Furthermore, collectivization was legitimized through laws or directives that introduced new types of criminal offences such as 'killing one's own horse' ...[and] failure by a kolkhoz chairman to deliver grain".[107] From this time on excessive penalties against 'anti-Soviet elements' became one of the main features of the Soviet system of criminal justice.

The use of criminal justice as a tool in the fight against certain social classes manifested itself in the USSR in the form of judicial '*prerogativism*'. Christopher Osakwe, who analyzed the role of this legal phenomenon in Soviet criminal procedure, concludes that prerogativism is a unique feature of Soviet criminal law, which "operate[s] either in favor of the litigant, if he happens to be privileged, or to his detriment, if he is a member of a disfavored class."[108] Indeed the Soviet judiciary provided preferential treatment even to habitual criminals,[109] who, "as opposed to class enemies, were [considered as] 'socially friendly'."[110] For instance, such crimes as "kidnaping, rape, insult, defamation, theft, robbery, embezzlement, fraud...were subject, under the 1926 Code as originally enacted, to extremely mild penalties, judged in comparison with the penalties attached to crimes against the state under Soviet law, or judged in comparison with the penalties attached to crimes against the person or private property in many Western countries."[111] Politicization of Soviet criminal justice was one of the reasons why the Soviet 1926 Code originally envisaged milder penalties for crimes against property than for crimes against the state.

---

[104] Ibid., pp. 194–196.

[105] Ward 1993, p 50.

[106] Mishina 2013.

[107] Solomon 1996, p. 4.

[108] Osakwe 1985, p. 332.

[109] Ironically, Stalin was himself a bank robber and a convict in his youth.

[110] Ward 1993, p. 197.

[111] Berman 1966, p. 27.

Berman describes this political nature of Soviet law by pointing out that "[t]he special part of the 1926 Code…provided for more lenient penalties for non-political crimes than for political (By 'political crimes,' in this context, is meant crimes against the state and serious crimes against the administrative order.)"[112] Political cases were in general handled more strictly in the USSR given that "[t]he death penalty was reserved for the most serious political crimes and for certain military crimes."[113] Furthermore, milder sanctions were applied against those who committed crimes against private property rather than state (socialist) property. Here Soviet criminal justice simply followed the leader of Bolshevik Ulianov (Lenin), who acknowledged nothing as private.[114] As opposed to private property, "[b]y the law of August 7, 1932, 'social ownership'…or socialist ownership..., including state, collective farm and cooperative ownership, was declared to be 'sacred and inviolable,' and persons 'infringing' it were 'to be considered as enemies of the people."[115] Thus, the type of property mattered in the imposition of milder or stricter sanctions.

Initially the Code outlined milder punishment for property crimes. For instance, "[t]heft of personal property committed for the first time was punishable by deprivation of freedom up to three months, and if repeated, up to six months (Article 162). Even large-scale theft of state property was only punishable by deprivation of freedom up to five years (Article 162)."[116] However, with the end of the New Economic Policy (NEP)[117] and the launch of industrialization and collectivization campaigns, the law of 7 August 1932 introduced harsher penalties in relation to crimes committed against state property. Namely, "the law imposed the death penalty on persons guilty of stealing goods being transported by rail or water as well as persons guilty of stealing collective farm or cooperative property, unless the act was committed under mitigating circumstances, in which case the minimum penalty was deprivation of freedom for ten years with confiscation of entire property."[118] In this context, it is possible to claim that crimes against state property were recharacterized as political crimes that envisaged the strictest possible sanctions.

Furthermore, different categories of offenders could expect different treatment by the Soviet system of justice. Imprisoned common criminals were used by the Soviet penitentiary authorities to control their 'political inmates' and even conduct extrajudicial executions.[119] Sometimes Soviet law enforcers showed "that banditry was punished almost as severely as telling anti-Soviet jokes…[, as a result of which]

[112] Ibid.

[113] Berman 1966, p. 27.

[114] Sajó 2001, pp. 14493–96.

[115] Berman 1966, p. 27.

[116] Ibid.

[117] Argenbright 2002.

[118] Ibid.

[119] Forsythe 2009, p. 518.

some of the public regained confidence [in law]."[120] Such meticulous arbitrary application of criminal law provisions to receive politically desirable judicial outcomes obviously required a special kind of legal officialdom that Stalin had to establish after his rise to power. Stalin could not possibly be satisfied with the system of state administration inherited from Lenin. The main weakness of Lenin's government was non-professional, amateurish system of criminal justice. Judges, prosecutors and other legal officials who received their posts thanks to their commitment to the communist ideology were not motivated enough to perform their duties effectively. Not only did they lack necessary education, they also "left their posts quickly, to be replaced by new and equally unprepared colleagues."[121] Taking into account that these amateur legal officials were not committed to a long-term career in the Soviet system of justice, they could not be easily influenced through promotions or disciplinary measures. Furthermore, the Communist Party public image was at stake when "the performance of these officials fell to such a low level as to breed disrespect for Soviet justice."[122] Stalin's officialdom had to produce a new breed of Soviet career officials that would not only be ready to fight abundant common crimes, but also eradicate actual or potential 'political enemies' of the ruling elites. Such a split into common and politically motivated justice was formalized through the establishment of two layers of the Soviet system of criminal justice. The first layer included OGPU/NKVD, 'troikas' and 'dvoikas' that conducted 'fast-track' proceedings and even passed extrajudicial sentences in political cases. NKVD murderers were, in their turn, easily disposable through the 'purge of purgers' in the same extrajudicial proceedings.[123] The main task of the first layer was "to cover up extralegal coercion and to prevent diffusion of information that might embarrass the regime."[124] The second layer consisted of the traditionally powerful Procuracy, "the USSR Supreme Court and the new USSR Commission of Justice [that had] major powers over local courts and judges."[125] Even if ordinary judges dealt with some political cases, in such a centralized system of justice they had no choice but to follow their 'socialist consciousness' and maintain the socialist legality in the fight against class enemies.[126] The second layer promoted respect towards Soviet legal institutions by giving "the appearance of normal legality...demonstrating to the world that the...[USSR] operated an acceptable administration of justice."[127] Solomon concludes that thanks to the split of the system of justice "Stalin...foster[ed]...compliance of legal officials with central directives that would have made officials of the late tsarist ministry of

120 Rayfield 2005, p. 308.

121 Solomon 1996, p. 6.

122 Ibid., p. 447.

123 Viola 2017.

124 Solomon 1996, p. 458.

125 Ibid., p. 448.

126 Berman 1966.

127 Ibid., p. 458.

justice envious."[128] The extra-legal hierarchy and the involvement of government bodies were equally impressive.

The split of the system of criminal justice gets more obvious when we look at the structure of judicial bodies in the USSR. Soviet courts and courts from Western civil law countries had essentially a similar judicial hierarchy. On the one hand, there was the Supreme Court of the USSR along with republican Supreme Courts, military tribunals as well as local district courts that dealt with civil and criminal matters. On the other hand, under Stalin almost every Soviet law-enforcement agency had shadow extra-judicial bodies[129] to review and even adjudicate in a summary procedure political cases of the so-called people's enemies (Russian: *vragi naroda*). The OGPU and other state security agencies had special boards (Russian: *osoboiye soveshaniya*), collegiums (*kollegii*) and 'troikas' that were cooperating with 'dvoikas' represented by local NKVD chiefs and prosecutors.[130] Special collegiums were even introduced in the Soviet Supreme Court in the form of a military tribunal.[131] All these extra-legal courts[132] could "pass sentence extra-judicially (Russian: *vo vnesudebnom poriadke*) [, while] the top of this pyramid, the supreme 'dvoika' consisted of the head of the NKVD,... Yezhov and the Chief Prosecutor,... Vyshinskii."[133] Furthermore, any communication between the Politburo, formal judicial organs and informal extra-legal bodies was handled as top-secret information transmitted only through "the 'special' or 'secret' offices that both the Procuracy and the courts were equipped with".[134] Such abundance of extra-legal bodies led to their fierce competition, which, in turn, ensured that no single agency could challenge the Communist Party's monopoly to terror.

Judicial prerogativism further demonstrates the interplay of official written norms and unwritten practices in the USSR. Although the Soviet law never openly called to disfavor or privilege certain categories of defendants, the unwritten practice of

---

[128] Solomon 1996, p. 460.

[129] "V. M. Kuritsyn: "1937 god v istorii sovetskogo gosudarstva", Sovetskoe gosudarstvo i pravo, 2, 1988, pp. 109–19; Markus Wehner: "Stalinismus und Terror", Stalinismus. Neue Forschungen und Konzepte, pp. 365–390; Khlevyuk, "The Objectives of the Great Terror, 1937–38", pp. 161–69; McLoughlin: "Vernichtung der Fremden", pp. 66–69. In: Rosenfeldt 2009, p. 428.

[130] "On the development of the extra-judicial organs and their work in the 1920s and 1930s, see e.g. RGASPI (RTsKhIDNI)/Volkogonov papers, box 14, folder 6...Rolf Binner und Marc Junge: Wie der Terror 'gross' wurde. Massenmord und Lagerhaft nach Befehl 00447"...V. Kudryashov, A. Trusov: Politicheskaya yustitsiya v SSSR, Moscow 2000, pp. 73–81, 279–87; Barry McLoughlin: "'Vernichtung der Fremden'", Der grosse Terror in der UdSSR 1937–38 im Lichte neuerer Publikationen, "Jahrbuch für Historische Kommunismusforschung 2001, pp. 64–66." In: Rosenfeldt 2009, p. 428.

[131] Ibid., pp. 389–395.

[132] Kudryavtsev, Trusov: Politicheskaya yustitsiya v SSSR, p. 279, 281; McLoughlin: "'Vernichtung der Fremden'", pp. 64–67, 81; Suvenirov: Tragediya RKKA, pp. 229–31; Torchinov, Leonchuk: Vokrug Stalina, p. 510. In: Rosenfeldt 2009, p. 428.

[133] Ibid., p. 395.

[134] Ibid., p. 393.

judicial prerogativism manifested itself in the official Soviet doctrines of analogy, socialist legality and revolutionary consciousness. It can be presumed that the Soviet criminology inherited the analogy doctrine from the Russian Empire, because "Tsarist law, like the law of many European autocracies, has contained the principle of analogy and left no place for its opposite, *nullum crimen sine lege*, but the reformers who composed the 1903 draft code decided to eliminate analogy".[135] It was reintroduced in the USSR in the 1926 RSFSR Criminal Code.[136] The analogy doctrine was essentially based on a very broad concept of the socially dangerous act, which was defined by *Article 6* of the Code as "any act or omission that is directed against the Soviet system *or* that violates the legal order established by the worker-peasant power during the period of transition to the communist system."[137] The application of the analogy doctrine by Soviet courts further illustrates discrepancies between written law and legal practices.

Soviet official judicial guidelines required restrictive interpretation of the doctrine of analogy in the case law.[138] For instance, "[i]t was stressed that an act could not be punished by analogy unless it was proscribed by the General Part of the Criminal Code; that is, it must have been a socially dangerous act, committed intentionally or negligently."[139] Nevertheless, early Soviet courts often 'analogized' common crimes such as larceny or petty hooliganism that required mild punishments with 'counter-revolutionary crimes' subject to the death penalty even if the accused did not pursue a counter-revolutionary goal while committing the offence. This meant that in practice criminal punishment was assigned based on the court's case-by-case evaluation of the 'social dangerousness' of the offence rather than on offender's motives.[140] Furthermore, the abolishment of the written norm about the analogy doctrine did not prevent unofficial prerogativism. The USSR abolished the doctrine only in 1960 by introducing the new Fundamental Principles of Criminal Legislation of the USSR and the Union Republics. In 1975 Solomon argued that despite the abolishment of the analogy in the USSR, "there would always be room for analogizing by prosecutors and by judges wherever the definitions of criminal offences (*corpora delicti*) were broad, and the removal of analogy would not have affected administrative proceedings at all. The Special Boards of the NKVD would still be empowered to send to prison for five years 'persons recognized as socially dangerous'"[141] The doctrine

---

[135] Solomon 1996, p. 31.

[136] "Article 16 of the Criminal Code stated: "If any socially dangerous act is not directly provided for by the present Code, the basis and limits of responsibility for it shall be determined by application of those articles of the Code which provide for crimes most similar to it in nature". In: Berman 1966, p. 22.

[137] Berman 1966, p. 22.

[138] Cf. decrees of the Plenum of the Supreme Court of the USSR of 1937 and 1939 cited in V.M. Chkhivadze, ed., supra, note 30, p. 121. In: Berman 1966, p. 34.

[139] Ibid.

[140] Kuznetsova and Tiazhkova 2002, s. 41.

[141] Solomon 1978, p. 174.

of analogy was indeed used in the political trials against dissidents during the late Soviet period.

Analogy was not at all a novel concept introduced by the Communist Party, "as it was found in the codes of a number of nineteenth-century European states…[In the USSR, the doctrine of analogy was introduced] when after the Revolution legislators found it difficult to compose a list of specific offences comprehensive enough to protect the young state 'when class enemies were abundant and when…[Soviet] court experience was less developed'."[142] Soviet scholars often argued that the doctrine of analogy was fully compatible with Stalin's call for strict adherence to socialist laws known as 'stability of law', which represented a functional alternative to the western Rule of Law. For instance, "as V.M. Chkhivadze put it, analogy was incompatible…only with the slogan of Classical school, the 'bourgeois principle' of *nullum crimen sine lege*, which, Chkhivadze claimed, had no place in Soviet law…In other words, to achieve 'stability of law' it was not necessary to accept the 'Rule of Law'."[143] Furthermore, in the legal hierarchy of the Soviet system of justice the defense of the communist ideology and its doctrine of an 'ideal socialist society' prevailed over the protection of individual rights and freedoms. Given this politicized approach to law, "[t]he utilitarian principle of 'social defense' had in fact held sway in Soviet legal thinking, while the classical tenet 'Rule of Law' had been rejected as 'bourgeois'."[144] Therefore, analogy illustrated systemic differences that existed between the Rule of Law and socialist legality.

It is, thus, important to differentiate analogy and other Soviet practices that violated the principle of *nullum crimen sine lege*. First, the classical concept of the Soviet doctrine of analogy (Article 16 of the Criminal Code) presupposed that there was no statutory definition for a 'socially dangerous' act and a judge was expected to apply another statutory definition, which provided for crimes most similar to it in nature.[145] For instance, the exile of adult family members of 'people's enemies' to remote settlements in Siberia is an example of analogy, because the original legal basis of punishing families of deserters (Article 58 of the 1926 RSFSR Criminal Code) was extended by analogy to family members of 'people's enemies' through an additional secret order.[146] It must be noted that here the use of analogy was more 'civilized' than extra-judicial executions often conducted by Soviet repressive organs without making a reference to any legal provision.

---

[142] Ibid., page 23.

[143] Ibid., page 25.

[144] Ibid., page 26.

[145] "Article 16 of the Criminal Code stated: "If any socially dangerous act is not directly provided for by the present Code, the basis and limits of responsibility for it shall be determined by application of those articles of the Code which provide for crimes most similar to it in nature". In: Berman 1972, p. 22.

[146] In particular, the secret decision of the Politburo #P51/144 from 5 July 1937 ordered imprisonment and exile from five to eight years of the wives of 'traitors' and 'Trotskyists'. In: Gaidar 2012, p. 459.

Second, the violation of *Lex Certa* principle occurred due to vague definitions of criminal offences (corpora delicti) in the Soviet criminal statutes. For instance, Berman notes that in the early Soviet times, "[c]ounterrevolutionary crimes themselves were defined in the broadest terms."[147] In this context, almost any action could be arbitrarily defined as a counterrevolutionary crime in violation of *Lex Certa* and *nullum crimen sine lege* principles. Third, the Soviet system of justice also used the practice of arbitrary recharacterization of petty crimes such as larceny, theft and other property crimes into political offences. An example of this would be the recharacterization of "stealing of social property…[into a counterrevolutionary crime or] a crime against the state."[148] Thus, the three practices of analogy, broad definitions of offences and recharacterization violated the *nullum crimen* principle and gave grounds for political persecution.

It is worthy of note that the Soviet concept of socially dangerous act is very close in its meaning to the concepts of *Straftat Begriff* (definition of a crime) and 'material unlawfulness' or '*Materielle Rechtswidrigkeit*' (German) introduced by German criminologist Franz von Liszt. According to these concepts, the material definition of crime should be understood in the context of a particular social and legal order. Besides the formal unlawfulness, which presupposes that an act has to meet certain formal criteria to be qualified as a crime, material unlawfulness means that the given act is also in "opposition to the moral and social values."[149] According to Nina Persak, the concept of material unlawfulness is "perhaps best described by the German term of *Unrecht* (nepravo), which belongs more to the moral theory or philosophy of law, [than] to the criminal law theory…, namely, it is more about 'immorality' and 'antisocialness'…th..[a]n 'illegality', despite its name."[150] In this sense, the notion of material unlawfulness gives an opportunity to consider mitigating or exculpatory circumstances of an act, which, "regardless of the formal unlawfulness or the prescription of an act in the positive law, render the act 'not unlawful' (*nicht rechtswidrig*), if supported by justifying reasons (*Rechtsfertigungsgründe*)."[151] In this regard, material unlawfulness is usually applied in a negative meaning to remove criminal culpability from a person, who has formally breached the law by referring to customs or practices that render a criminal statute inapplicable. Material unlawfulness can also be applied in a 'positive way' to find a criminal offence in the absence of a formal breach of law.[152] In the Soviet Union, social dangerousness, as an analogue of Western material unlawfulness, was applied

[147] Under Article 58-1 of the 1926 RSFSR Criminal Code "an act was said to be counterrevolutionary if it was 'directed to the overthrow, subversion, or weakening of the power of the worker-peasant Soviets." In: Berman 1972, p. 23.

[148] Ibid., p. 29.

[149] Persak 2007, p. 97.

[150] Ibid.

[151] Ibid.

[152] For instance, in the newly established democracies like Indonesia material unlawfulness is also applied in a 'positive sense' to convict a person "for doing something that is reprehensible according

in both negative and positive ways with the only exception that social danger did not provide any legal reference to unwritten customs, practices or norms that were usually employed under material unlawfulness.

The concept of social dangerousness was especially important in ensuring that an act attained a certain level of social danger to qualify as a criminal offence in the USSR. In particular, Article 3 of the [1960 RSFSR] Criminal Code [envisaged] that "only a person guilty of committing a...socially dangerous act provided for by law [zakon] shall be subject to criminal responsibility and punishment ... [Furthermore,] there must also be a crime, that is, a violation of a specific provision of the Special Part of the Code."[153] Berman observes that, according to the 1926 Criminal Code, to impose a criminal sanction it was enough for a judge to find only social dangerousness, "and not violation of a specific provision of the Special Part of the Code."[154] Moreover, in the early Soviet times the concept of social dangerousness was applied more arbitrarily given that "in some cases punishment was based on the social danger of the person, rather than of the *act* he committed."[155] Besides eliminating the dominant role of social dangerousness in judicial sanctioning in the 1960 RSFSR Criminal Code, the late Soviet system of criminal justice used social dangerousness also to find exculpatory or mitigating circumstances for an act, whose level of danger was too low to qualify it as a criminal offence. In this regard, Berman describes the so-called minor antisocial acts that, "because of their insignificance or because of the character of the act committed, fall short of being crimes [and] may be brought before [informal nonprofessional] comrades' courts."[156] Such developments downplayed the arbitrary application of social danger by the Soviet judiciary.

It was obvious for Stalin that complete submission of judiciary would be impossible to achieve under Marx, Engels and Lenin's concept of 'withering away of the state'. Old Bolsheviks Pashukanis and Krylenko's theory of 'dying out criminal law' was officially branded as heresy and their "liquidation...as counterrevolutionaries perfectly symbolized the Stalinist duality of law and terror."[157] Stalin's task was to create a brand new system of justice that could be effectively applied in the vast Soviet territories to ensure complete obedience of all citizens to Soviet law as well as swift prosecution of all present and future political enemies of the communist regime in line with the very same law. Exactly due to the above-mentioned reasons, Stalin

---

to community standards even if that act did not constitute a crime under a statute or other law at the time it was committed (Sapar-djaja 2002: 67,210)." In: Butt 2009.

[153] Berman 1972, p. 11.

[154] Ibid.

[155] For instance, "Article 7 of the 1926 Code provided: With regard to persons who have committed socially dangerous acts or who represent a danger because of their connection with a criminal environment or because of their past activity, measures of social defense of a judicial-correctional, medical, or medical-education character shall be applied." In: Berman 1972, p. 21.

[156] Ibid., p. 9.

[157] Berman 1972, p. 32.

drafted in 1936 the new Soviet Constitution under the motto "we need stability of laws now more than ever".[158]

Uniformity and stability of laws were certainly more suitable for the communist totalitarian regime than "withering away" or "winding up" of law. Osakwe agrees with this hypothesis by pointing out that "[j]ust as Napoleon needed to regulate the power of the provinces, so too the Soviet political leaders sought uniformity throughout the country. Regularity and uniformity provide a basis for efficient manipulation."[159] Indeed, written uniform law was a basis for the obedient Soviet society, whose activities can be easily predicted and controlled within the official legal framework. The unofficial parallel legal system provided a much wider freedom of maneuver for the communist repressions that would be deemed illegal not only by international legal standards, but also under the existing Soviet laws. Criminal law policies developed by Stalin preserved Lenin's ideas about the 'flexibility of law' as well as the 'swift and severe punishment' that were useful for political repressions under the unofficial extra-legal limb of the Soviet system of justice. Stalin's official limb of criminal justice, which had to ensure the supremacy of the communist bureaucratic machine as well as its domestic and international legitimization, replaced Lenin's amateurish legal officialdom and the anti-law approach with long-term career legal officials loyal to the party leadership as well as uniformity and predictability of written law.

This new double-track approach was legitimized[160] through the adoption of the 1936 all-Union Constitution in order to project an appearance of legality in the course of staged show trials and rampant Great Purge repressions that took place at the very same time. Although Stalin's Constitution of 1936 stipulated some positive economic rights that were not included in Western Constitutions, the 1936 Constitution[161] also declared such traditional negative civil and political rights as freedom of religion (*Article 124*) as well as 'universal and direct suffrage by secret ballot' (*Article 134*). In terms of criminal justice *Article 14u* envisaged replacement of republican criminal codes and codes of criminal procedure with All-Union codes that were never adopted.[162] Stalin's Constitution also contained such important procedural rights as defendant's right to counsel (*Article 111*), to access case materials (*Article 110*) as well as prohibition of arrest not authorized by a court or a prosecutor (*Article 127*). Nevertheless, *Article 102* of the Constitution fails to stipulate that justice is administered only by courts, thus legitimizing the de-facto split of criminal justice into ordinary courts and special extrajudicial political tribunals.

---

[158] Berman 1972, p. 32.

[159] Osakwe 1985, p. 334.

[160] For instance, *Article 102* of the Constitution fails to stipulate that justice is administered only by courts, thus legitimizing the de-facto split of criminal justice into ordinary courts and special extrajudicial political tribunals.

[161] See the English version of the 1936 Constitution at https://www.departments.bucknell.edu/russian/const/36cons04.html#chap10. Accessed 23 December 2020.

[162] Republican codes still had to comply with the *all-union fundamental principles of criminal legislation* from 1924.

The duality of the Soviet state was already described by Osakwe's theory[163] about state law and party law and Solomon's 'compartmentalization'[164] of political justice. This book argues that Stalin established '*Twofold Constitutionalism*' in the USSR. On the one hand, Stalin's written Constitution was so much detached from reality that it was "treated merely as a piece of paper, with little legal effect".[165] It does not mean, however, that the USSR had no Constitution. According to Paul Magnarella, "[b]y definition, every state, even one with a dictatorship, has a constitution".[166] On the other hand, the unwritten Constitution of political justice reflected "a [real] set of legal norms and procedures that structure[d] its legal and governmental systems."[167] The 'Twofold Constitutionalism' was the Soviet narrow version of the 'rule according to law' concept.

Though formally Soviet law belonged to Western civil law, the '*socialist legality*'[168] concept was different from the British *Rule of Law* and German *Rechtsstaat*. *First*, equal rights guaranteed under Soviet law were in reality undermined by prerogativism, which disfavored actual or potential opponents of the regime. *Second*, predictability and uniformity of laws along with their flexible application let the communist party manipulate public opinion and get away with its failures. These key characteristics of the Soviet unwritten Constitution formed the basis of politically motivated justice enforced through conventional judicial practices and unpublished rules. The duplicity of the Soviet system of criminal justice was so instrumental in consolidating and legitimizing the Soviet regime that it was later replicated in the former communist bloc countries. While Stalin's written Constitution was repealed in 1977, his unwritten Constitution proved to be indispensable for the next political elites before and beyond the collapse of the USSR.

2.4 From 'Mock Educational Trials' to Stalin's Show Trials

This section will provide analysis of the most representative show trials conducted under Stalin. It would be unfair to assert that the phenomenon of show trials spontaneously appeared during the Soviet times. Soviet political trials stem from the legal culture and traditions of educational mock trials initially used in the Russian Empire and then copied by the communist revolutionaries. Elizabeth Wood conducted an extensive research on mock 'agitation trials' (Russian: *agitatsionnye sudy*) organized in the early USSR in the form of educational and theatrical performances.

---

[163] Osakwe 1985.

[164] Solomon 1996, p. 467.

[165] Waldron 2009.

[166] Ibid.

[167] Ibid.

[168] Russian: *sotsialisticheskaya zakonnost.*

Wood notes that although the Communist Party alleged the unique nature of Soviet agitation trials, "[i]n fact, however, the trials had their roots deep in the tsarist past. They drew from religious mystery plays that tried the Sinner…[in tsarist Russia]".[169] As opposed to show trials, Soviet authorities always presented 'agitation trials' as theatrical performances or mock trials that were performed by actors who brought into the public spotlight both criminal and non-criminal (common) matters. Though this text would not provide analysis of specific 'agitation trials' that had non-legal nature, brief description of the two functions performed by these trials can further shed light on their later transformation into true political show trials.

First, agitation trials educated the general population by raising awareness about the new legal regime established in the aftermath of the communist October Revolution. The Communist Party branches prepared detailed guidelines on how to conduct mock 'agitation trials' "that would teach 'revolutionary vigilance' and Soviet legal consciousness (pravosoznanie)."[170] The purpose of these trials was not to teach people the basics of the Soviet legislation, taking into account that "[t]he majority of trials did not even name articles of law in their indictments."[171] Officially, mock trials were staged in local peasants and workers' clubs to entertain, socialize and educate about such mostly non-criminal community matters as alcoholism, sexual life, malpractice and sponging. In reality, communist political instructors used mock trials to communicate to the general population a new set of social rules and policies of the Soviet Union. Furthermore, although such trials were fictional, they legitimized the newly created Soviet state in all regions of the USSR by "strengthening the hegemony of these new local authorities."[172] The 'customary ritual' of such 'trials' determined their effectiveness.

The second function of agitation trials was mobilizing the population through performances based on local customs and traditions. In other words, thanks to the staged mock trials the Soviet citizens "were learning not only to speak Bolshevik but also to act Bolshevik…[, which involved] whole practice of judging and being judged."[173] The central place occupied by customs in such trials proves that the Communist Party was well aware about the special role played by customary law in the legal culture of the Russian Empire.[174] For instance, fictional trials involved real names of local community members, traditions and daily routines known to the audience, because "local customs made the trials seem 'real' and engaging to the local community."[175] This theatrical customary justice was certainly appealing to

[169] Wood 2005, p. 7.

[170] "Politsud" (Instruksiia), RGVA 9/13/51/215-18; P.M. Vedernikov, "Sansudy I ikh postanovka na osnove kollektivizma ispolnitelei," Krasnyi put' 19 (November 1924): 97–122; L. Reinberg, Instsenirovannye proizvodstvennye sudy (Moscow, 1926), 10. In: Wood 2005, p. 6.

[171] Ibid.

[172] Ibid., p. 8.

[173] Ibid., p. 10.

[174] Hendley 2017.

[175] Wood 2005, page 4.

uneducated poor peasants and workers, whose devotion to the communist regime was indispensable for the implementation of the Red Terror.

Wood argues that such a wide scale theatricalization of justice led to the phenomenon of a "theatrical state" in the early USSR described by the social anthropologist Clifford Geertz.[176] An interesting procedural custom in such trials was prohibition of "[a] guilty plea [which] would have obligated the court to proceed directly to sentencing, thus bypassing the questioning of witnesses and obviating the entire dramatic interest of the play!"[177] Thanks to the mock trials, soldiers, peasants and workers were trained to conduct later real show trials of kulaks and other 'enemies' of the Soviet people. Thus, by their nature, seemingly innocuous agitation trials eventually turned to be more political than they initially appeared to be.

Such a strong emphasis on the customary ritualism and local community problems as opposed to normative law became the key feature of upcoming political trials in the USSR. The simplistic character of a fictional agitation trial set a very low standard for a criminal procedure in the Soviet society. In order to be credible in the eyes of the Soviet public, a trial had to entertain and educate, personify alleged internal and external threats as well as provide solutions to specific community issues in the framework of customary practices and traditions. Application of fictional agitation trials in practice happened in the so-called Shakhty case (Russian: *Shakhtinskoye delo*), which took place in the Ukrainian coal-mining region of Donbass in 1928.

Researchers of the Soviet history concur that the Shakhty case was the first show trial, which then became a 'prototype' for the numerous political trials that would follow shortly afterwards.[178] In order to understand the root-causes of the Shakhty affair, one has to look at the bigger picture of a socio-economic situation in the Soviet Union at that time. The Soviet leadership had announced the Stalin's policy of rapid industrialization, according to which the Soviet Union would have to reach the industrial level of Western countries in less than ten years. To fulfill such an ambitious public promise, the USSR committed enormous human resources to this cause as well as invited foreign engineers that could facilitate the development of the Soviet industrial sector. Despite such extensive efforts, "there has been a catastrophic decline in industrial production, aggravated by a poor harvest".[179] Furthermore, numerous industrial catastrophes and injuries were caused due to safety rules relaxed to achieve higher productivity in the shortest time.

Neither Stalin nor the Communist Party could possibly accept their responsibility for such a failure. Instead, the Soviet authorities announced that they uncovered an 'international plot' of Soviet and foreign engineers who sabotaged the rapid industrialization by destroying mining equipment in the entire Donbass region. The Central Committee of the Communist Party (*TsK KPSS*) gave this case the highest priority

---

[176]Ibid., p. 11.

[177]I.V. Rebel'skii, "Agit sud po likvidatsii negramotnosti," Prosveshchenie na transporte 9–10 (1923): 34–38; Klubnaya rabota. Prakticheskaia entsiklopediia dlia podgotovki klubnykh rabotnikov (Moscow: Proletkul't [1926]), 6:13.

[178]Wood 2005.

[179]Rosenbaum 1962, p. 239.

in the Soviet media, because "[i]n Stalin's mind the case linked the…'external' and 'internal' enemies."[180] The accused 'wreckers' (Russian: *vrediteli*), who supposedly followed orders from Paris and Berlin, became an embodiment of internal and external threats to the newly established Soviet state. One of the reasons why the international media widely covered the Shakhty trial was that a group of fifty-three defendants included three German engineers from the well-known German firms A.E.G. and Knapp. For foreign observers, "[i]t was obvious that the German and…[Soviet] specialists were to be used as scapegoats for Bolshevik failures."[181] "To every economic problem Stalin had a punitive response [-] reprisals for imaginary campaign of sabotage."[182] This was a "method of explaining economic failure which any Government might envy."[183] The subsequent trial proved to be a theatrical show.

Before going into the trial proceedings in the Shakhty case, it would be useful to explain briefly why specific Soviet officials were assigned to the case. A prosecutor during the trial was Nikolai Krylenko, an old Bolshevik and a co-organizer of the Red Terror, who was promoted after his participation in this and other trials to top positions of the Commissar of Justice and the Prosecutor General. To create an illusion of an impartial tribunal, "Stalin chose [as a trial judge] the rector of Moscow University, Andrey…Vyshinsky, a man of international stature whose reputation added further luster to both the trial and its verdict."[184] Besides being a renowned lawyer, Vyshinsky was Krylenko's personal rival and a man loyal to Stalin, with whom he "shared a cell in a czarist prison…during their revolutionary days".[185] Furthermore, Stalin could blackmail the trial judge Vyshinsky, who belonged to the beleaguered Menshevik minority of the Communist Party and "as a youthful prosecutor of the provisional government…had issued a warrant for Lenin's arrest."[186] Therefore, the trial could not be called impartial from the start, taking into account that both the prosecutor and the judge were 'motivated' enough to reach a guilty verdict.

The hallmark of the Shakhty case and subsequent show trials became the interchangeable use of formal law and extrajudicial practices. The Shakhty case was tried by the extra-legal "Special Judicial Presence, a judicial body whose powers and jurisdictions were not specified by any legal document."[187] The presumption of innocence was openly disregarded from the very beginning, when "[b]efore the trial Stalin declared all the defendants guilty of sabotaging industry at the behest of French intelligence."[188] However, if formal law was more useful than extralegal practices

[180]"Stalinskoe delo I prakticheskie zadachi c dele bor'by s nedostatkami khoziaistvennogo stroitel'stva," Pravda, 12 April 1928. In: Wood 2005, p. 195.

[181]Rosenbaum 1962, p. 239. See also Urban 1982.

[182]Rayfield 2005, p. 164.

[183]Conquest 1990, p. 391.

[184]Gorman 2007, p. 50.

[185]Ibid.

[186]Rayfield 2005, p. 162.

[187]Gorman 2007.

[188]Rayfield 2005, p. 163.

for achieving political aims, the Soviet justice was an example of legal formalism. When the German Embassy in the USSR requested to appoint a German lawyer to German defendants, the Soviet authorities rejected this request, because "there was no provision for such a contingency in any Russo-German treaty."[189] Vyshinsky and Krylenko's rivalry also created an impression of formal equality of arms in the sense that Vyshinsky enjoyed using "his authority as a presiding judge to discipline Krylenko when the latter became carried away with his attacks on the defendants."[190] The theatrical setting of the trial further emphasized its legal duplicity.

There is no doubt that the Shakhty trial drew on the theatricality of early agitation trials. It was not accidental that the trial was conducted "in the marble Hall of Columns in Moscow, a venue whose theater equipment made it ideal for show trials."[191] The trial atmosphere was also soaked with legal melodrama. Foreign journalists present during the trial reported that "defendants repeatedly retracted their previous confessions, and several indicated that their confessions had been extracted by blackmail or by outright brutality."[192] Lyons, an eyewitness of the trial, perfectly described it as "a spectacle of men confessing incredible crimes…a 'Roman circus'… - a crowd came to see a righteous hanging."[193] Wood argues that similar to agitation trials, the Shakhty trial was partially improvised, because "those very mistakes and retractions gave the trials more of a sense of events that were being lived and not just performed."[194] This might even confused some defendants who pleaded not guilty still believing in the impartiality of the formal Soviet justice.

Nonetheless, the legal masquerade organized by the Soviet authorities only reinforced foreign observers' conviction that the trial was not fair and impartial. Indeed the trial procedure left an impression of two parallel realities. In the first one, which represented the formal Soviet system of criminal justice, "[p]rocedural guarantees are ostensibly noted. The defense attorneys were allowed to state their objections to various proceedings (though admittedly not all the defendants even had lawyers)."[195] The second 'shadow' legal world hid in the backstage of proceedings, where "Efim Evdokimov, a former convict and OGPU chief…, had the physical work wringing confessions from the fifty three defendants and making them fit for public testimony".[196] Furthermore, violation of safety rules due to negligence at work were arbitrarily characterized as counter-revolutionary economic crimes and 'wrecking' that were punishable with death penalty. However, even without knowing all the truth about the 'false bottom' of the Soviet system of justice, the international community could clearly see that it was just a kangaroo trial.

---

189 Rosenbaum 1962, p. 250.

190 Gorman 2007.

191 Rayfield 2005, p. 162.

192 Gorman 2007.

193 Rayfield 2005, p. 194.

194 Wood 2005, p. 195.

195 Ibid., p. 195.

196 Rayfield 2005, p. 162.

Due to the Soviet officials' sloppiness, "[t]he six-week trial attracted mockery from the foreign press."[197] Mistakes made by the playwrights of the trial included not only contradictory and retracted 'confessions', but also procedural blunders that did not fit even the most basic concept of a fair trial. For instance, the fundamental right to defend oneself was undermined when the trial court "refused to accept witnesses for the defense on the grounds that the court already had sufficient evidence".[198] The indictment was not read to the defendants on the ground that "the Foreign Commissariat had declared eight pages secret because these involved the French and Polish governments in the plot."[199] Some theatrical scenes appeared to be bizarre even to "the Soviet public [which was not] yet ready to applaud such witnesses as the twelve-year-old boy who demanded that his accused father be shot." These 'defects' of the very first show trial were taken into account by the Soviet leadership when it organized the subsequent Moscow show trials.

Soviet repressive organs learned several lessons from the 'failures' of the Shakhty trial. First, to avoid similar embarrassment with retracted confessions, "if the accused became obstreperous in rehearsals, the trial, if held at all, was behind closed doors and the public saw only newspaper reports that saboteurs had been sentenced to death."[200] Second, the public opinion was prepared for the trial through a separate campaign and "from now on the [workers'] clubs would be called upon to 'prepare public opinion' for such trials."[201] Finally, the lack of credible evidence was compensated with 'facts' and 'case law' of the previous show trials. In other words, "[e]ach conviction helped to ensure that the next defendants would be found guilty *because the last ones had been.*"[202] Therefore, the unwritten 'customary law' of show trials contributed to the creation of an informal legal system, which existed in parallel with written formal laws of the USSR.

Most importantly, the first show trial demonstrated that even the communist totalitarian regime cared to a certain extent about the international response to the trial. Kurt Rosenbaum concludes in his research on the German involvement in the Shakhty trial that thanks to intensive diplomatic negotiations and concessions, "[t]he three German…[defendants] were acquitted, and the A.E.G., since it was not mentioned in the verdict, was *de-facto* exonerated."[203] Furthermore, the mockery in foreign media and the international criticism of the trial was so intense "that Stalin could only have five [out of eleven accused sentenced to death] actually executed."[204] Such occasional leniency would also be presented in the next trials as 'humanism' of the

[197] Ibid., p. 163.

[198] Rosenbaum 1962, p. 254.

[199] Rosenbaum 1962, p. 249.

[200] Rayfield 2005, p. 163.

[201] Wood 2005, p. 196.

[202] B. Shneerson, "Spetsialisty, kul'trabota i bor'ba s vreditel'stvom," klub i revolutsiia 21–22 (November 1930): 6–14; Vyshinsky's concluding speech in the Great Purge Trial, ed. Robert C. Tucker and Stephen F. Cohen (New York, 1965), 525–26. In: Wood 2005, p. 196.

[203] Rosenbaum 1962, p. 249.

[204] Wood 2005, p. 163.

Soviet system of criminal justice. To sum up, the Shakhty affair signaled that the Soviet authorities were determined to use theatrical techniques of agitation trials in actual criminal proceedings against political 'enemies' of the communist regime in the future.

2.5 Show Trials Scaled Up in the USSR

The experience of the Shakhty affair as well as other similar 'wreckers' show trials' was carefully collected and analyzed by the Soviet repressive organs.[205] The first show trials indicted engineers, technicians and representatives of other professions that allegedly conducted subversive activities against the Soviet state. All of them followed the general pattern of the Shakhty trial in terms of dramatic confessions, public condemnation and often a 'lenient conviction' to imprisonment instead of a death sentence. The so-called Moscow show trials opened the new chapter of criminal prosecution against political opposition and competing factions within the Communist Party. The defendants in these trials were top-brass old Bolsheviks that occupied senior government positions. However, neither their former revolutionary accomplishments nor friendship with Lenin saved them from multiple criminal charges and eventual execution.

This book argues that the Moscow trials further widened a gap between de-jure norms of criminal justice and parallel extra-legal practices that secured the de-facto relationships of political loyalty and domination. While senior party members loyal to Stalin could get away with various crimes committed in the name of the Revolution, any political opposition or its possible threat were swiftly prosecuted under the guise of the formal legal system and its written ceremonial laws, whose principle task was to enforce practices of the extra-legal system of political justice. The content of this formal legal system was de jure determined by decisions of Soviet judiciary and legislation passed by the Soviet authorities. The true meaning of these norms could be, however, interpreted only in conjunction with unwritten political practices. To use an allegory, we can compare the USSR with a human body and the Soviet system of criminal justice with its immune system. Then, accordingly, the Soviet informal system of politically motivated criminal justice acted exactly like an HIV virus, which usually tricks the immune system by pretending to be its part in order to destroy it from within. Taking into account that the Soviet system of criminal justice was already weakened and compromised by the Red Terror, it was quite easy for the virus of political justice to spread further and annihilate even those who advanced it in the first place.

Three Moscow show trials were the most representative among all political trials in the USSR in the sense that they included many elements utilized in the next show trials. The first Moscow trial was conducted in August 1936 against Zinoviev,

[205] For instance, the 'Industrial Party' trial in 1930, the 'Mensheviks trial' in 1931 and the 'Metropolitan-Vickers' trial in 1932.

Kamenev and other old Bolsheviks "who turned to…[Leon Trotsky] for support, forming 'the United Opposition'."[206] The second trial took place in January 1937 against new participants of Trotsky's 'conspiracy exposed' in the first trial. The third and final Moscow show trial of Trotskyist conspirators followed in March 1938. All Moscow trials incorporated the following eight elements that revealed the parallel legal system of politically motivated justice: (1) *Ex Parte Communication* between prosecutors, judges and organizers of show trials; (2) '*Judicial Prerogativism*', which disfavored those who were in opposition or could potentially be a threat to the ruling elites; (3) '*Prosecutorial or Accusatorial bias*', according to which a defendant was presumed guilty; (4) '*Confessions and Self-indictment*' that replaced any objective evidence of defendant's guilt or innocence; (5) *Accelerated and simplified 'summary' criminal proceedings* in response to a 'terrorist threat'; (6) '*Crime by Analogy*' and 'Arbitrary Recharacterization'; (7) *Extrajudicial character* of secret political trials; (8) A '*political amnesty*' or a 'pardon' granted to some defendants. These elements of politically motivated justice manifested themselves throughout various stages of criminal proceedings in all three Moscow show trials.

Ex parte Communication between judicial and political bodies preceded each Moscow show trial. Such communication played a key role during an 'investigation' aimed at framing up the defendants. First, Stalin appointed cadres suitable for the collection of 'incriminating evidence' in the 'investigation' of this kind. Prior to the first trial in 1936, he "withdr[ew]…many of the most experienced officers from all active departments of the Secret Police into what he knew to be an investigative farce."[207] Second, NKVD assigned the case to officers who were closely watching the 'opposition' within the Communist Party and had not found any conspiracy. Thus, investigators themselves were 'motivated' to forge the evidence for the previous years, because "if such a plot had come into being without their discovering it, they would clearly have been reprimanded at the very least."[208] Finally, to ensure effective communication of his orders to the investigators, Stalin relied on the parallel system of criminal justice represented by the NKVD Secret Political Department, which stood apart from ordinary organs of pre-trial investigation.

The information now available about the Moscow trials proves that Stalin personally micro-managed the trials, yet his communication with the court was kept in strict secrecy to maintain an impression of his 'neutrality' in the matter.[209] While hiding from others political justice at work, in response to those who criticized the trials "Stalin…had a simple answer: the matter was in the hands of the Prosecutor and the court…They must let justice take its course."[210] The court proceedings were supposed to hide a political agenda behind the trials and choreograph the routine work of 'fair justice' in the most subtle details. For instance, "Stalin…instructed the assistant to see to it that all the defendants were served with tea with lemon

[206] Conquest 2008, p. 11.
[207] Conquest 2008, p. 81.
[208] Ibid.
[209] Khlevniuk 2008.
[210] Conquest 2008, p. 90.

and cakes."[211] For an outside observer, "[i]n appearance the accused were well-groomed...men...They drank tea, and there were newspapers sticking out of their pockets...The impression created was that the accused, the prosecutor, and the judges were all inspired by the same single...objective, to explain all that had happened with the maximum precision."[212] In the parallel reality of political justice, however, "the sentences were [already] a part of the original [trial] script, and had been imposed by...[Stalin] himself."[213] Only by keeping the system of political justice entirely secret, could the formal Soviet system of justice save at the very least the appearance of its 'independence'.

If we consider the phenomenon of *Judicial Prerogativism* in the framework of the Moscow show trials, it should be noted that many of the defendants could hardly be called innocent people. Among those accused were Bolsheviks like Ivan Bakaev, the head of *Cheka* in Leningrad, who was complicit in the Red Terror, or Ivan Smirnov, who violently suppressed peasant revolts and became "[k]nown as the 'Lenin of Siberia'".[214] Ironically, some of the accused in the Moscow trials contributed to the previous show trials. For instance, Georgy Pyatakov acted as a witness during the first Moscow trial, Genrih Yagoda as the head of NKVD 'obtained confessions' from the defendants and "Bukharin...demanded death for all...[accused in Shakty trial]."[215] Despite their controversial past, all defendants of the Moscow trials were charged of multiple crimes that had very little to do with their actual role in the Communist Party. Their real crimes such as secret extra-legal executions and implementation of ill-conceived policies could implicate the entire regime, thus, "[t]he state and party offices previously held by the accused were not mentioned".[216] Instead, the defendants were charged with treason, espionage, terrorism, plans to assassinate Stalin and other leaders and even "mixing glass and nails with foodstuffs, butter in particular."[217] In reality, the only reason why these Bolsheviks stood trial was that they criticized Stalin or could be a threat to his growing political domination after Lenin's death in 1924.

The main criterion which united all defendants in one group disfavored by the Soviet judiciary was that they had failed to prove their unconditional loyalty to Stalin or were his personal political enemies. In an act of political vendetta, "Stalin...personally insisted, for example, on the inclusion of Smirnov",[218] although Smirnov was in jail already during the alleged Trotskyist conspiracy. The reason was that Smirnov "had spoken approvingly of the proposal to remove Stalin and...Stalin thus

[211] Heilbrunn 1991, p. 88.
[212] Feuchtwanger 1937.
[213] Conquest 2008, p. 92.
[214] Ibid., p. 84.
[215] Rayfield 2005, p. 163.
[216] McLoughlin and McDermott 2003, p. 47.
[217] Conquest 2008, p. 390.
[218] Ibid., p. 107.

had a particular grudge against him."[219] It seemed improbable that the Soviet judicial prerogativism, which was usually directed against bourgeoisie, could also be applied against old Bolsheviks, most of whom came from workers and peasants' families. Nevertheless, even here legally indoctrinated principle of 'class struggle' was used in light of an informal political system of justice, when "parents of those in the dock were transformed into capitalists or Orthodox priests."[220] In an attempt to dehumanize defendants in the third trial, an indictment dismissed any possibility of a non-guilty verdict by "[p]ortray...[ing the defendants] as 'reptiles', 'mangy curs' and other unprepossessing representatives of the animal world."[221] Therefore, it is not surprising that none of the accused Bolsheviks managed to escape death.

The phenomenon of judicial prerogativism was, in turn, closely connected with *Prosecutorial/Accusatorial Bias* displayed by both a prosecutor and a trial judge. It is important to note that Andrey Vyshinsky, who acted as a judge in the Shakhty trial, became a public prosecutor in the Moscow trials. Unlike his predecessor Krylenko, Vyshinsky understood "Stalin's tactics: to introduce and publicize democratic institutions of law while doing completely the opposite under their cover, pulling the wool over gullible people's eyes, both in the West and at home."[222] Vasiliy Ulrikh, who presided over the three trials, "was a lackluster figure with no real legal training—the judge was useful primarily because he could be depended upon to hand down guilty verdicts and death sentences."[223] There are several vivid examples of Vyshinsky and Ulrikh's 'double allegiance' to a system of political justice. Vyshinsky, who mercilessly humiliated the defendants, notoriously burst with the biased attitude towards them in one of his Moscow trial speeches, "I demand that these dogs gone mad should be shot—every one of them!"[224] The prosecutor grew so much into his 'role' that he "sometimes infringed on established court procedure, and [even] Ulrikh cautioned Vyshinskii to address the accused as defendants and not as political enemies."[225] Finally, Prosecutor Vyshinsky "not only dictated to the defendants how they should 'periodise' confessions before the court, but also determined personally the gravity of the 'crimes'."[226] The presiding judge actively supported the biased attitude towards defendants.

Though, unlike Vyshinsky, the presiding judge Ulrikh did not openly attack the defendants during the trial, he was more involved in a 'backstage' work of the parallel political system of justice. For instance, "[e]ach time the court recessed, Ulrikh and his staff read the stenographers' record...[and] excised passages which might have cast doubt on the defendant's guilt and ensured that all references made by the accused

[219] Ibid., p. 84.

[220] McLoughlin and McDermott 2003, p. 46.

[221] Ibid., p. 44.

[222] Vaksberg 1990, p. 64.

[223] Gorman 2007.

[224] Conquest 2008, p. 103.

[225] McLoughlin and McDermott 2003, p. 48.

[226] Ibid., p. 47.

to the policies of the USSR and the VKP(b) were omitted".[227] Historians assert that Ulrikh personally "telephoned Stalin…during the trial and visited…[him] to find out what sentence to pass."[228] Once reprimanded by Stalin for trying to send the Kirov's murder case for further investigation, Ulrikh "never demurred again."[229] All these examples show that the trial judge's complete dependence and subordination to the secret system of political justice left him no choice but to exercise the accusatorial bias in court.

Besides the accusatorial bias in court, public bias was also supposed to create an impression of fair justice. Similar to the Shakhty affair, the presumption of innocence was publicly disregarded and turned into 'presumption of guilt', according to which a defendant was presumed guilty until (if) proven otherwise. In the Soviet public discourse, "reporters and…writers described the accused as cynical, deceitful, bloodthirsty and criminal, a gang of unprincipled murderers, poisoners, thieves, wreckers and saboteurs."[230] The public smear campaign against the defendants included "the usual hack verses by the poetaster Demian Bedny, with the title 'No Mercy'."[231] Moreover, 'condemnation manifestos' "headed 'No Pity'"[232] from other old Bolsheviks, open letters from workers and even schoolchildren "demanding that the court order the shooting of all fascist reptiles and hirelings"[233] revealed the political system of justice, which was oriented more towards the public relations effect of the trials rather than formal law.

It must be noted that the standard concept of the presumption of innocence was inapplicable in the context of Stalinist show trials both in terms of the traditional rule of evidence[234] and testimonies given by defendants in such 'court proceedings'. Although the presumption of innocence could be found in the written 1936 Soviet Constitution (Article 111—the right to defense)[235] and various norms of the 1926 Criminal procedure code,[236] these written norms were overridden by the practices of state propaganda[237] and official statements that incriminated defendants even before

---

[227] Ibid., p. 46. Here VKP(b)—the All-Union Communist Party of Bolsheviks.

[228] Rayfield 2005, p. 255.

[229] Ibid., p. 256.

[230] Russian State Archive of Socio-Political History (RGASPI), f. 495, op. 175, d. 101, l. 105. In: McLoughlin and McDermott 2003, p. 44.

[231] Conquest 2008, p. 98.

[232] Ibid., p. 98.

[233] Heilbrunn 1991, p. 92.

[234] *Ei incumbit probatio qui dicit, non qui negat* (Latin: Proof lies on the person who asserts, not on the person who denies).

[235] In particular, Article 111 of the 1936 Constitution envisaged that "in all courts of the U.S.S.R. cases are heard in public, unless otherwise. provided for by law, and the accused is guaranteed the right to be defended by Counsel", The 1936 Constitution is available in English at https://www.departments.bucknell.edu/russian/const/36cons04.html#chap10. Accessed 23 December 2020.

[236] Fletcher 1968.

[237] Ebon 1987.

a show trial took place. Self-indictment and forced confessions given by defendants could not be called in-court testimonies in the conventional sense. Furthermore, in the early Soviet times the presumption of innocence as such was not recognized in the Soviet Union. For instance, John Quigley asserts in his research on the presumption of innocence in the USSR that "[d]uring the period immediately following the 1917 Russian revolution, the doctrine of dictatorship of the proletariat prevailed and some jurists viewed the presumption of innocence as weighing too strongly in favor of the accused and against the state."[238] Tadevosian, who was among Soviet scholars[239] that stood against the presumption of innocence, argued that "in the laws in force in the U.S.S.R. there are no previously established presumptions of guilt and innocence and there is no need of any previously determined presuppositions or presumptions."[240] Thus, Soviet legal practitioners had rather dismissive attitude towards the presumption of innocence, making it useless for defendants of show trials to rely on the written provisions that guaranteed it.

The guilt of defendants was presumed by organizers of show trials. However, this did not formally switch the burden of proof from the defense to the Prosecutor's Office. In this context, Berman notes that although "[t]he 1923 Code contained no provision concerning the burden of proof…, [m]any Soviet jurists, however, in commenting on the Code, stated that it is presupposed by the entire system of Soviet criminal procedure that the burden of proof of the guilt of the accused rests on the prosecution and that the accused is not required to prove his innocence."[241] Though the 1960 RSFSR Code explicitly stated that "the obligation of proof may not be transferred to the accused (Article 20) [,]…it does not say from whom it may not be transferred."[242] In the late Soviet period the 1977 Constitution also contained written provisions that were supposed to guarantee the presumption of innocence. For instance, the USSR Supreme Court "found the presumption…in Article 158,

[238]"While the East European socialist states have followed the presumption of innocence…China did not do so during the period in which class struggle figured more prominently than in the East European states." V. Lukashevich, "Garantii Prav Obviniaemogo v Sovetskom Ugolovnom Protsesse [Guarantees of the Rights of the Accused in Soviet Criminal Procedure." In: Quigley 1989, p. 303.

[239]"Other Soviet jurists of that period objected to a presumption of innocence on the grounds that it was excessively formal and abstract, linking it to the medieval system of formal proofs that had been used in Europe. They feared that it would allow a court an easy solution if proof gathering in a case proved difficult. In such a case the court could avoid difficult issues of fact by simply declaring that there was doubt and pronouncing a judgment of not guilty. They said, moreover, that its meaning was unclear…A prime desideratum in early Soviet legal thought was to make the law understandable to the public. Further in light of its abstractness, the presumption of innocence was seen as conflicting with the Marxist concept of truth." M. Strogoich, Obvinenie i Obviniaemyi Na Predvaritel'nom Sledstvii i Na Sude [The Accusation and the Accused at the Preliminary Investigation and at Trial]. In: Quigley 1989, p. 304.

[240]Ibid.

[241]Berman 1974, p. 57.

[242]Ibid., p. 60.

which guarantees a 'right to defense'."[243] Besides the right to defense, Soviet jurists found the presumption in "the Article 160 right not to be presumed guilty without a court judgement of guilt."[244] Soviet authorities were also obliged to protect the presumption under its international obligations such as the International Covenant on Civil and Political Rights ratified by the USSR in 1973.[245] However, these written provisions were routinely disregarded when Soviet 'political offenders' from show trials described in this text were presumed guilty by a verdict, which was prepared long before their trial.

The Soviet authorities learned a lesson from the Shakhty affair criticized by the West and invited international journalists-apologists of Stalinism to attend the Moscow trials. For example, the New York Times (NYT) correspondent Walter "Duranty was brandishing the fascist threat in order to justify the ruthless Soviet measures…[and] assured his readers of the enlightened nature of the [O]GPU".[246] Another NYT journalist Harold Denny reported during the trials that "conversations with individuals indicate a general feeling that justice has been done."[247] Jacob Heilbrunn concludes in his analysis of Duranty's fake reporting that "[Duranty] was instrumental in furthering the [USSR] recognition that followed Roosevelt's election in 1932."[248] Shortly before the second trial the Soviet Comintern headquarters instructed "foreign communist leaders… to organize [a campaign] to refute the arguments of…democratic press, who will try to discredit the trial."[249] Unlike the Shakhty trial, the Moscow show trials had an intricate public relations agenda, which was used to convince both national and international audiences of the trials legitimacy.

To make the Soviet system of criminal justice credible, the Communist Party widely publicized defendants' *Confessions and Self-indictment* that were yet other mysterious and vivid features of the Moscow show trials. Denny himself was puzzled that many defendants pleading guilty as charged looked like "men…marching toward

[243]"The Court formulation is: In order to ensure the accused (or defendant) the right to defense, courts must strictly observe the constitutional principle that the accused (or defendant) is presumed innocent until his guilt is proved in the manner provided by statutory law and is established by a court judgement that has entered into force." Decree No. 5, Plenum of the USSR Supreme Court, O Praktike Primeneniia Sudami Zakonov, "Obespechivaiushchikh Obviniaemomu Pravo na Zashchitu [On Court Practice in Applying Statutes Protecting the Right of the Accused to Defense], para 2, BULL. Verkh Suda SSR [Bulletin of the USSR Supreme Court] 8 (No. 4, 1978)." In: Quigley 1989, pp. 307–308.

[244]Ibid., p. 308.

[245]The International Covenant on Civil and Political Rights, adopted 16 December 1966 (entered into force 23 March 1976) (Article 14-2). This Treaty states: "Everyone charged with a criminal offence shall have the right to be presumed innocent until proved guilty according to law." In: Quigley 1989, p. 310.

[246]Heilbrunn 1991, p. 92.

[247]Ibid., p. 89.

[248]Heilbrunn 1991, p. 99.

[249]McLoughlin and McDermott 2002, p. 60.

the firing squad amid gales of laughter."[250] Sidney Hook, a former Marxist, who followed the trials at that time, noted, "defendants all confessed to everything with eagerness and at times went beyond the excoriations of the prosecutor in defaming themselves. Equally mystifying was the absence of any significant material evidence."[251] Western legal practice showed that "[p]eople, especially on capital charges, plead not guilty even if there is a great deal of evidence against them."[252] Furthermore, "it was not only confession which was so strange, but also repentance—the acceptance of the prosecutor's view that the acts confessed to were appalling crimes."[253] It was so bizarre that even "the average Soviet citizen who had not been in jail found them as puzzling as foreigners did."[254] The inner mechanics of Soviet political justice can shed the light on the 'mystery' of numerous confessions.

Confessions made in the course of the Moscow trials make sense when we take into account that the prosecutor Vyshinsky "developed a theory of law in which confession is the queen of evidence."[255] Recent research into the history of the second Moscow trial also reveals that "[f]or a whole year, the defendants had been tortured by Stalin's jailers by means of 'the conveyor system' (depriving prisoners of sleep, subjecting them to endless interrogation)."[256] It also took a while to 'obtain' confessions from the defendants of the first trial who initially denied their guilt. Trotskyist Mrachkovsky's confession was especially difficult to obtain, because his "key interrogation is said to have lasted ninety hours, without result, though Stalin rang up at intervals to inquire how things were going."[257] Another feature of a parallel system of political justice was that it used the formal legal system merely as an instrument of pressure. When old Bolsheviks refused incriminating themselves under torture, "the decree of 7 April 1935 extend…[ed] all penalties, including death, down to twelve-year-old children…[,thus, Stalin] could now threaten oppositionists quite 'legally' with the death of their children as accomplices if they did not carry out his wishes."[258] Nevertheless, the trials did not go as smoothly as it was planned by Stalin.

Various historical sources point to judicial abnormalities that could have been noticed by a careful observer of the Moscow trials. A journalist, Maria Gresshoener, and the writer, Lion Feuchtwanger, wrote at the time of the Moscow trials that they "cannot understand why no evidence was produced other than the defendants'

---

[250] Heilbrunn 1991, p. 88.

[251] Hook 1984.

[252] Conquest 2008, p. 110.

[253] Ibid., p. 110.

[254] Conquest 2008, p. 110.

[255] Rayfield 2005, p. 162.

[256] Heilbrunn 1991, p. 89.

[257] Conquest 2008, p. 84.

[258] Ibid., p. 75.

confessions."[259] Despite its ruthless methods, the secret system of political justice occasionally malfunctioned and embarrassed its managers. When Pyatakov claimed in his false confession that he had a flight from Berlin to Oslo in 1935 to meet Trotsky, the Norwegian media reported that "no German aircraft landed on the alleged date…near Oslo…[which] caused embarrassment in court."[260] Similar to the Shakhty trial, some defendants retracted their confessions already in the courtroom. When a former Soviet diplomat Krestinsky unexpectedly pleaded not guilty at the beginning of the trial, "the court recessed for twenty minutes…to give time to put a little pressure on…[him]."[261] The accused Bukharin defiantly noted in his trial speech, "The confession of the accused is a medieval principle of jurisprudence."[262] Soviet authorities tried various procedural tricks to avoid such public embarrassments in court.

The first "practice of calling short court recesses deserves further investigation."[263] When Krestinsky pleaded not guilty, a recesses was called, during which, according to various witness accounts, "[t]he investigators dislocated his left shoulder, so that outwardly there was nothing to be seen."[264] Other eyewitnesses of the trial claimed that after the recess "Krestinsky was replaced in the dock by a double or an actor."[265] Second, court clerks rewrote the original trial protocol, because "remarks and confessions made by the accused had to be given an unequivocal tone."[266] For instance, "infrequent meetings noted in the original protocol became 'stable and constant links'".[267] Third, additional 'witnesses' were found to corroborate the prosecution line of argumentation and implicate defendants in additional crimes they did not 'confess' to.

For instance, an old Bolshevik Mantsev already sentenced to death by the Military Collegium of the Soviet Supreme Court "was granted a stay on execution, in order to play the role of a useful witness".[268] Furthermore, NKVD agents provocateurs present among the accused were supposed to provide testimony and be executed later similar to Danton's trial where "he and his followers were mingled in with men accused as thieves and common spies, and each was carefully linked with the others by joint accusations."[269] Finally, a snowball of 'case law'[270] from the previous political trials proved to be another key element of the informal political system of justice.

---

[259] McLoughlin and McDermott 2002, p. 59.
[260] Ibid., p. 61.
[261] Conquest 2008, p. 344.
[262] Ibid., p. 394.
[263] McLoughlin and McDermott 2002, p. 48.
[264] Conquest 2008, p. 352.
[265] Ibid., p. 353.
[266] McLoughlin and McDermott 2002, p. 46.
[267] McLoughlin and McDermott 2002, p. 46.
[268] Conquest 2008, p. 43.
[269] Ibid., p. 93.
[270] Vaksberg 1990.

"When Vyshinskii was short of arguments, he mentioned the links, allegedly established as fact during the NKVD pre-trial investigation, between the defendants and those condemned in the previous show trials".[271] These methods eventually helped establish a web of trials interconnected with each other through false testimonies, forged evidence and confessions obtained under torture.

Stalin also used the de-jure justice system to give the defendants hope that they and their families would not be arbitrarily prosecuted. A decree of 11 August 1936 "reestablished public hearings and the use of lawyers, and allowed appeals from the accused for three days after the sentence."[272] It is also significant that the beginning of the Moscow show trials coincided with the adoption of the 1936 Constitution, which "(on paper) had to be the most democratic in the world."[273] The Constitution guaranteed among other procedural rights the defendant's right to counsel (*Article 111*)[274] and the freedom from arbitrary arrest (*Article 127*) blatantly disregarded in all three trials. In the same vein, though Article 17 of the Constitution guaranteed that each Soviet republic could leave the Soviet Union, "the right to secede was only nominal."[275] While Stalin's Constitution created a virtual legal reality, the real unwritten Soviet Constitution envisaged doctored evidence, confessions under torture and other sinister practices applied during the Moscow show trials. The gap between these two systems was insurmountable. The trials showed the Soviet repressive organs that their mandate to torture was unlimited in the parallel system of political justice. Stanislav Kosior, who co-organized the Soviet artificial famine in Ukraine (Holodomor) in 1932–33,[276] endured torture only to sign his 'confession' when NKVD men "brought his sixteen-year old daughter into the room where the investigation was taking place and raped her before her father's eyes."[277] In the de facto justice system of Moscow show trials, "the historian Nevskii and Bukharin's old friend Sokolnikov…refused to make incriminatory depositions and were shot."[278] After all, in Stalin's parallel system of politically motivated justice the only alternative to confession was an immediate extra-legal execution without a 'trial'.

The above-mentioned forced confessions were often obtained by using the *Doctrine of Analogy* in cases against defendants' families. The 'system of hostages'

[271] McLoughlin and McDermott 2002, p. 46.

[272] Conquest 2008, p. 90.

[273] Vaksberg 1990, p. 64.

[274] The first Moscow trials defendants supposedly refused to have defense councils. During the third trial, defense councils "had to proceed under [prosecutor] Vyshinskii's direction, and they began…by expressing agreement with the indictment…After their remarks had been 'doctored'…the contributions from the defence team read like variations of Vyshinskii's main arguments." In: McLoughlin and McDermott 2002, p. 47.

[275] Sakwa 2012, p. 239.

[276] Applebaum 2017. *See also* Levchuk et al. 2020.

[277] According to historian Roy Medvedev, Kosior's daughter, "having been released from prison, committed suicide by throwing herself under a train." In: Chirot 1996, p. 155.

[278] McLoughlin and McDermott 2002, p. 43.

established by Stalin included not only the death sentence which could be potentially applied to children from the age of twelve, but also an official exile of adult 'family members of people's enemies'[279] to the remote areas of Siberia. In other words, family members of people's enemies were punished due to their 'social dangerousness' in violation of the principles of *nullum crimen sine lege* (no punishment without law) and personal liability. The original legal basis of punishing families of people's enemies was Article 58 of the 1926 RSFSR Criminal Code, which envisaged an exile to Siberia from five to ten years "in respect of the adult members of the family of a servicemen traitor in the event of the latter's flight or escape across the frontier."[280] Additional secret orders and decrees extended application of this norm to families of non-servicemen. For instance, exactly at the time of the Moscow show trials against the so-called Trotskyist conspiracy a secret decision of the Politburo #P51/144 from 5 July 1937 ordered imprisonment from five to eight years of the wives of traitors and Trotskyists.[281] Therefore, the secret Politburo decree extended the scope of the existing discriminatory criminal norm and allowed Soviet judges to draw a legal analogy between wives of the Moscow trials defendants and family members of military deserters explicitly mentioned in the law. For instance, "Bukharin's wife, Anna Larina, was arrested soon after the trial…but survived to serve eighteen years in labor camp and exile."[282] By targeting defendants' families, the regime swiftly got rid of its opponents and potential witnesses.

The concept of a socially dangerous act envisaged by Article 16 of the 1926 RSFSR Criminal Code could be applied in favor or to the detriment of defendants. For instance, if a defendant was a representative of the 'working class', his or her offence would be considered by a Soviet court as less 'socially dangerous' than an offence committed by a 'class enemy'. Offences committed by members of the Communist Party were rarely recognized as socially dangerous, because such member usually stood before extralegal interparty 'courts', rather than general Soviet courts. For instance, Osakwe differentiates between state law and the so-called Party law of criminal procedure, according to which the "[Communist] Party court [arrogated] to itself the right to try the offender before affording the opportunity to the state system."[283] While a senior Party member who committed an offence was usually acquitted by the Party court due to the absence of 'social danger', a low rank Party official could be scapegoated by the Party court and then subjected to double jeopardy in the state court, which would already presume that actions of this party member were socially dangerous.[284] Markovits describes the same 'double track system of justice' in East Germany, which had "rules governing the characterization of an issue either as a matter for the Party or the court. Party issues were preferably *not*

[279]Russian: *Semyi vragov naroda.*

[280]Conquest 2008, p. 75.

[281]Gaidar 2012, p. 459.

[282]Conquest 2008, p. 395.

[283]Osakwe 1985, p. 351.

[284]Ibid., pp. 346–350.

decided by the judiciary."[285] Moscow show trials were the most vivid example of 'prosecuting' former Party members.

The majority of the Moscow trial defendants were promptly sentenced to death and executed. The main 'target' of the trials "Trotsky, *in absentia*, received the death penalty [too]."[286] The parallel system of politically motivated justice again prevailed over the formal criminal law, according to which "seventy-two hours' grace was allowed for the accused to put in their petitions for pardon."[287] None of the defendants were pardoned, while "the announcement of their execution was made only twenty-four hours after the verdict."[288] Very few people like Radek, Sokolnikov, Bessonov and Pletnev were sentenced to lengthy prison sentences, in a gesture of ostentatious leniency, only to be re-sentenced to death or extra-judicially executed later. Even the hope of the pardon was based on an informal political promise made by Stalin allegedly on behalf of the Politburo, "which guaranteed [the accused] their lives...and the liberty of their families."[289] However, this verbal promise had no enforcement guarantees both in the formal and informal (political) systems of justice once the defendants pleaded guilty and were sentenced to death.

At the same time, the Moscow trials were conducted in parallel with a secret purge of the Red Army.[290] The main reason for the purge was "[t]he...vulnerability to a military coup...[in the occasion of which] the type of machine Stalin built can crack very easily."[291] As opposed to the public Moscow trials, "[t]he court martial was held behind closed doors...and no 'materials' from the military trials were produced."[292] Characterized by accelerated and extremely simplified procedures, the military tribunal against popular in the Soviet society the Red Army commanders Tukhachevsky, Uborevitch, Yakir and others, who were allegedly recruited by Nazi intelligence, "took two to two and a half hours for the whole group."[293] The Moscow show trials and expedited secret military tribunals set an 'example' for local show trials conducted later. The Moscow trials were replicated in 1953 when an anti-Semitic campaign was launched in the USSR with a show trial nicknamed a 'Doctor's plot'. The plot involved several doctors accused of conspiring with an international Jewish organization to assassinate the Soviet leadership.

Using the Soviet terminology, the Moscow trials were exemplary court proceedings.[294] "This was, in fact, the political preparation of the Party branches throughout the country for the campaign...against all the enemies of the General Secretary

[285] Markovits 2006, p. 292.

[286] Heilbrunn 1991, p. 90.

[287] Conquest 2008, p. 104.

[288] Ibid.

[289] Ibid., p. 87.

[290] Alexandrov 1963.

[291] Conquest 2008, p. 186.

[292] Ibid., pp. 202–203.

[293] Ibid., p. 202.

[294] Russian: *pokazatenlniye sudebniye protzesy*.

[Stalin]."[295] The Moscow trial death verdicts legitimized a general narrative about wreckers among old Bolsheviks, which instilled fear, promoted paranoia and boosted readiness of local authorities to prosecute as many people as possible in order to prove their loyalty to the central leadership in Moscow. Furthermore, the line between political and criminal responsibility completely disappeared when numerous 'deviationists' (Russian: *uklonisty*) were expelled from the Communist Party and "VKP(b) district officers were directed to hand over lists of members to be expelled to NKVD."[296] This must have certainly motivated regional communist leadership to implement fully Joseph Stalin's *NKVD order # 00447*, which concluded in 1937 a collectivization campaign with wide repressions against independent peasantry (kulaks) and other 'anti-Soviet elements', whose persecution was launched with the abolishment of the new economic policy (NEP) in 1927–28. In his letter to the republican party branches Stalin ordered "to organise 'two to three open show trials' in each district [raion] to destroy the 'wreckers in the rural economy', and to mobilize the peasantry for the campaign."[297] The Moscow trials set a 'judicial standard' that would ultimately become a part of the communist legacy in the USSR and beyond its borders.

Unlike the Shakhty affair, the Moscow trials "had on the whole been a success for Stalin."[298] Thanks to an international media campaign, the trials were mostly recognized as legitimate in the public opinion abroad. For instance, "on 4 September 1937…'the English jurist Pritt'…[commended]…[in] the London *News Chronicle*…the complete propriety and authenticity of the trial. And this was one case among many."[299] Even in the diplomatic community "Joseph E. Davies, the U.S. ambassador to Moscow from 1936 to 1938,…lent his support to the show trials."[300] The foreign tacit recognition of the show trials were complemented with other Joseph Stalin's 'accomplishments' such as the silencing of all dissenting voices in the Communist Party, the revelation of 'wreckers' allegedly responsible for all economic failures as well as stronger obedience of local officials that were now eager to implement the collectivization and other Stalin's plans. Most importantly, the Moscow trials exposed the system of political justice that existed in parallel and sometimes completely replaced the formal system of criminal law.

The replacement of formal laws with informal rules of politically motivated justice became evident through egregious violations of the Soviet criminal law and procedure that were in force at that time. For instance, during the pretrial investigation preceding Moscow trials, in order to make sure that the accused would stay in pretrial detention, "applications to have the investigative custody prolonged were not made on a regular

[295] Conquest 2008, p. 88.

[296] McLoughlin and McDermott 2002, p. 38.

[297] Ibid., p. 42.

[298] Conquest 2008, p. 105.

[299] Ibid., p. 107.

[300] Heilbrunn 1991, p. 98.

basis."[301] To put defendants under pressure, "the right of the defendants to defend themselves was hampered by the fact that the time allowed them to familiarize themselves with the masses of material collated since arrest was far too short."[302] The defendants were further disadvantaged during the trial,[303] because "the court employed 'evidence' that the defendants could not have known about, charges which had never been made during the countless bouts of nocturnal questioning."[304] Finally, the trial protocol unintentionally proves the violation of the formal procedure by demonstrating that "the actual verdict contains allegations which were not included in the indictment."[305] Such procedural perversions effectively show the superiority of informal rules of political justice over all formal Soviet laws that were simply disregarded by the communist leadership for the sake of its immediate political interests.

Taking into account the above-mentioned defects of the Soviet show trials, it is possible to discern several characteristics of the parallel system of political justice established by Stalin. *First*, the Soviet authorities kept the existence of the system of political justice in secret by making it operational mostly through clandestine directives, unwritten rules and practices. *Second*, the parallel system of justice turned the major maxims of criminal law into their complete opposites.[306] *Third*, the political system of justice was implemented through parallel secret state bodies that duplicated all three branches of government. *Fourth*, official criminal law became a mere extension of the parallel system of political justice, which had a higher supra-constitutional rank than any other legal provision. Finally, as opposed to the conventional criminal punishment, whose goals are deterrence, restitution, retribution, education and rehabilitation,[307] Soviet politically motivated punishment scapegoated a defendant and shifted the blame for ineffective policies to imaginary external and internal enemies, eliminated political competitors, actual and potential opponents as well as concentrated state power in the hands of a few people. This Soviet totalitarian 'know-how' of political justice was eventually replicated by the USSR allies in Eastern Europe.

[301] McLoughlin and McDermott 2002, p. 49.

[302] Ibid.

[303] Vaksberg 1990.

[304] McLoughlin and McDermott 2002.

[305] Ibid.

[306] For instance, in the Soviet system of political justice the presumption of innocence was turned into presumption of guilt, the principle 'No punishment without Law' was replaced with the doctrine of analogy, the 'Judicial Duty of Care' was transformed into judicial prerogativism and the principle of the "Equality of Arms" was substituted with the accusatorial bias.

[307] Shizhou 2010.

2.6 Soviet Show Trials Replicated in Hungary

The victory of the Allied Forces in WW II changed the political map of the post-war Europe. Many European countries such as Albania, Bulgaria, the Czechoslovak Republic, East Germany (later GDR), Hungary, Poland, Romania and the newly created republic of Yugoslavia saw the rise of pro-Soviet forces. Feeble communist governments established in these countries received full political, financial and military support of the USSR. Besides its money and weapons, the Soviet Union brought to the new communist allies its advisors and 'expertise' in organizing massive political repressions that would ensure the entrenchment of the communist ideology in Europe. Not all newly proclaimed communist states, however, wanted to be relegated to the status of a Soviet satellite. The Socialist Federal Republic of Yugoslavia (SFRY) was the first to disobey orders from Kremlin, due to which SRFY was expelled from the Communist Inform-Bureau (Cominform). The Yugoslav Prime Minister Josip Broz Tito's open confrontation with the USSR at that time "appeared as a serious threat to the whole structure of Communist domination in the area, and hence resort was…to measures designed to prevent anybody else from seeking his own 'road to socialism'."[308] Tito "was now denounced by Moscow as a traitor to Communism and a tool of the imperialists. 'Titoite' and 'Titoism' now became [Soviet] terms of abuse, to be linked with that…category of enemies, the "Trotskyites."[309] Taking into account that Trotskyites were the target of the Moscow show trials, it did not take long before the first show trial took place in the new communist allies of the USSR in Eastern Europe.

Communist Hungary was chosen by the Kremlin leadership to be a place of the first genuine Soviet-type show trial. In fact, the first Hungarian show trial "served as a model for all satellite countries…[after r]epresentatives of Poland, Czechoslovakia, and East Germany came to Budapest to study its organization and procedure."[310] There were several reasons why Hungary became the place of the first post-war show trial. *Mátyás Rákosi*, then a Secretary-General of the Hungarian Working People's Party, "considered himself to be the Stalin of Hungary…[and] was well and often tested [by the USSR]."[311] The Hungarian Politburo at that time included Ernő Gerő and Mihály Farkas, whose "connection…to the Soviet security services reaches back to the time of their exile in the USSR [before WW II]."[312] Furthermore, the Hungarian communist leadership saw a show trial as an opportunity to get rid of competitors among its own party ranks.

Negotiations between the Hungarian communist authorities and the USSR represent the most significant historical proof of ex-parte communicationin the first show trial to be conducted in Hungary. After unsuccessful attempts to replace Tito in

---

[308] G L 1956, p. 249.

[309] Sakmyster 2011, p. 46.

[310] Hodos 1987, p. 25.

[311] Ibid., p. 36.

[312] Ibid., p. 170.

1948, the USSR planned to conduct "show trials…to unmask Tito and all potential Titos within the leadership of the satellite countries".[313] The plan of the future trial was discussed at the highest level when "[i]n the early summer 1948, Rákosi was summoned to Moscow to receive his orders from Beria for the preparation of a show trial."[314] Similar to the Soviet model,[315] the secret parallel system of political justice produced the 'indictment', which "was drawn up by Rákosi, edited by the legal experts of the Soviet and Hungarian secret police, and submitted to Stalin and Beria."[316] Only after their secret 'approval', did the president of the prosecutor's office Gyula Alapi receive the final indictment "shortly before the beginning of the trial".[317] An active involvement of the Soviet side in the matter is confirmed by the many similarities of the Hungarian trial with the Moscow show trials.

Similar to the Moscow trials, the chain of clandestine communication between political and judicial organs was maintained through various secret extra-judicial bodies that worked under the umbrella of the official state security service (ÁVH).[318] To manage preparations for the upcoming trial, "within the ÁVH, a secret special branch had been formed."[319] The peculiarity of the Hungarian trial was the additional involvement of Soviet 'advisors', which initially "swelled to twelve and reached forty at the peak of the purges."[320] Exactly like in the USSR, these secret groups stayed in the shadow of the official system of justice to create an illusion of a fair trial in the most intricate details. For example, in order to 'groom' before the trial the defendants that already confessed under torture or other 'darkness-at-noon techniques',[321] ÁVH chambers "had been transformed as if by magic into a cosy, intimate pastry-shop where the Soviet and Hungarian security men plied their selected victims with pastry, fruit and even alcoholic beverages."[322] When the accused signed their 'confessions', "[d]octors appeared to heal the wounds of torture and to distribute vitamins and medicines."[323] Thus, the formal system of justice and its secret politically motivated counterpart worked hand in hand to prepare the first trial.

The Hungarian show trial was supposed to demonstrate a connection between internal and external threats to the communist regimes in Eastern Europe. László Rajk, an old-guard Hungarian communist, became a 'perfect victim' of judicial prerogativism in the planned show trial. On the one hand, Rajk had power and access to information, which can be potentially useful for 'enemies of the communist regime'. As the Minister of Interior, Rajk "smashed one bourgeois opposition

---

313 Ibid., p. 35.
314 Hodos 1987, p. 36.
315 Vaksberg 1990.
316 Hodos 1987, p. 50.
317 Ibid.
318 ÁVH—Communist State Security of Hungary (Hungarian: Államvédelmi Hatóság).
319 Hodos 1987, p. 39.
320 Ibid.
321 Koestler 1994.
322 Szasz 1971, p. 165.
323 Hodos 1987, p. 49.

party after another…organized the trial against Cardinal Mindszenty, and, with it, destroyed the power of the Catholic Church in Hungary."[324] Rajk occupied a high position in the party and "[t]o Farkas, he represented a dangerous opponent in his drive to attain absolute power over tools of repression."[325] Furthermore, "in contrast to Mátyás Rákosi,...[Rajk] did not come in the train of the Red Army to the homeland…[a]nd rumor had it that there also was personal rivalry between the two men in the implementation of policy."[326] Furthermore, Rákosi "regarded Rajk as a political rival and for some time had been seeking to diminish his importance in the Party and the government."[327] If *László Rajk* was exposed as a traitor, this would ultimately implicate all of his supporters in the party and lead to his eventual elimination.

On the other hand, Rajk was an international figure, which could theoretically be a cover of his alleged collaboration with 'capitalist spies'. Rajk had extensive international contacts, because "[d]uring the Spanish Civil War, he fought in the ranks of the International Brigade…[, afterwards] fled to France and spent three years in internment camps."[328] Furthermore, as a member of the Hungarian antifascist resistance he was caught by Gestapo and "[in 1945] was liberated from a prison near Munich."[329] In a prospective show trial, Rajk's international activities could easily be 'connected' with various foreign intelligence services. Most importantly, using his international contacts, Rajk could be 'linked' with a mythical Tito's 'conspiracy' against the communist regimes in Eastern Europe. In reality, Rajk most probably fell out of grace when in summer 1948 "he was summoned to Moscow to defend his 'national' approach to Communism, and failed to restore [Soviets'] confidence."[330]All of this was enough to relegate Rajk from his high status of a communist to a member of the judicially disfavored class of political enemies.

After the expulsion of Yugoslavia from the Cominform (the Information Bureau of the Communist and Workers' Parties), the national approach to Communism illustrated the disagreement between the Soviet leadership in Moscow and "East European Communist leaders who, in the late 1940s, represented (or might represent) a national or, to be more correct, a local implementation of Communism disagreeing with the Party line imposed by Moscow."[331] Rajk, who "was the most popular person in the party [in Hungary]…in part because, of the entire top party leadership, he was the only non-Jew", could be viewed as one of the representatives of the 'national approach', because he "approached Communism in a different, more romantic, idealist fashion, believing that its moral and human aspect was of major importance."[332] This disagreement in the communist bloc also revealed the clash among Hungarian communists

[324]Ibid., p. 37.
[325]Ibid.
[326]G L 1956, p. 250.
[327]Sakmyster 2011, p. 46.
[328]Hodos 1987, p. 36.
[329]Hodos 1987, p. 37.
[330]G L 1956, p. 250.
[331]Ibid., p. 248.
[332]Ibid., p. 250.

that stayed in exile in Moscow and those who remained in Hungary and joined the resistance during WWII.

Rajk clearly belonged to the second group, as he "spent the war years in Hungary, and fought in the underground."[333] As opposed to Rajk, *Mátyás Rákosi, József Révai, Mihály Farkas* and *Ernő Gerő* "came from Moscow, had been functionaries of the Comintern, and with the possible exception of Révai, the cultural 'pope' of Hungarian Stalinism, were also trusted agents of the Soviet State Security."[334] Thus, Rajk's only 'fault' was that he could not be fully trusted by the Soviet leadership, because he "was a more native product, unschooled in the Kremlin."[335] Exactly due to this reason, Rajk "was treated as an outsider by the Muscovites, who accepted him with deep misgivings only because they needed at least one Hungarian native in the inner sanctum."[336] This, was used against Rajk by Rákosi, Révai, Farkas and Gerő, who wanted to get rid of a political competitor and prove their full allegiance to the Soviet leadership in Moscow.

The judicially disfavored group of potential conspirators, thus, included "former refugees..., 'internationalist' veterans of the Spanish civil war...in sum all of the leading party functionaries...who had not been recruited, or at least approved, by the Soviet security services."[337] From the moment of Rajk's sudden arrest in May 1949 and during the pre-trial 'investigation' Rajk's interrogators kept on insisting that he no longer had a privileged status of a communist but was instead "a Trotskyite,...a nationalist, an anti-Soviet element...[and] anti-Party."[338] Such a sudden change of status was enough for "[n]aked physical and psychological torture...to be applied in order to turn him into a fascist police informer, a spy of the Deuxième Bureau, and an agent of the Gestapo."[339] Seven other accused also fit the 'conspirators' profile'. For instance, Dr. Tibor Szőnyi, who was implicated as a spy by an anonymous informer, "had to escape from Hungary to Austria after the suppression of the revolution of 1919."[340] General György Pálfi had a conflict with the security police Chief Gábor Péter, for whom the show trial gave "his long awaited opportunity to rid himself of his rival."[341] Like in the USSR, each show trial in communist Hungary targeted a large group of 'deviationists' such as Browderists,[342] Rajkists, cosmopolitans and later Zionists. Therefore, Rajk and others were prosecuted not because they committed

[333] Ibid.

[334] Hodos 1987, p. 34.

[335] G L 1956, p. 250.

[336] Ibid., p. 250.

[337] Hodos 1987, p. 35.

[338] Hajdú 1996, pp. 82–86.

[339] Hodos 1987, p. 45.

[340] Ibid., p. 38.

[341] Hodos 1987.

[342] This term was named after Earl Browder, who as the general secretary of the US Communist Party saw the 1943 Tehran conference between Roosevelt, Churchill and Stalin as a sign of the peaceful coexistence between Communism and capitalism. Browder's approach was later denounced as heresy and a deviation from the 'true Communism'.

the crimes they were accused of, but due to their belonging to a group, which was disfavored under informal rules of political loyalty and domination.

The accusatorial bias exercised against the accused in court manifested itself in the multiple criminal charges they faced. According to the propagandistic 'Blue Book' about László Rajk's trial published in 1949, which also served as a guideline for subsequent show trials in Eastern Europe, Rajk was charged with "war crimes directed against people…the crime of sedition…[and] the crime of having once and continuously been the leader of an organization aiming at the overthrow of the democratic state order."[343] Similar to Soviet show trials, the prosecutor Gyula Alapi tried to emphasize the gravity of committed 'crimes' by dehumanizing the defendants when he spoke about them in his speech, "We are confronted with crawling sneaking snakes…instruments and puppets…of the foreign imperialist enemies."[344] In the spirit of the Moscow trials, the presiding judge Péter Jankó, who committed a suicide after Rajk's rehabilitation in 1956,[345] collaborated closely with the prosecution to organize the show trial. For instance, "[a] few days before the trial began, the state prosecutor summoned *Jankó…and handed…[him] the script of the trial, complete with…questions* and the well-rehearsed answers of the defendants."[346] The show in the courtroom was also magnified by a parallel reality of communist propaganda.

In the best traditions of the Soviet agitation trials, all official media outlets already passed their 'guilty verdict' on the defendants and Joseph Tito that were publicly stigmatized as criminals and traitors. Once the indictment was published, the public was informed about "the murderous plans of Rajk and Tito' which were 'thwarted by the vigilance of the Hungarian Worker's Party…(*Független Magyarország*, 12 September 1949) and similar slogans: 'He who attacks the people's fatherland will pay dearly' (*Szabad Nép*, 13 September 1949)."[347] Following the Soviet tradition of public condemnations at workers meetings, "Mrs. Gellérthegy [said] at the blitz meeting of the fitting shop…-"I send the Tito-clique, the imperialists and their agents the burning hatred of all mothers' (*Szabad Nép*, September 13th, 1949)"."[348] As a clear Déjà vu of the Moscow trials, the presumption of innocence was completely ignored when just a day before the trial "[a]t one meeting, a Communist was recorded as declaring: 'A rope for all traitors like Rajk'."[349] Similar to Soviet show trials, the accused fully confessed their 'guilt' at the trial.

As expected, confessions made by the defendants during the trial corroborated each other and created an impression of lawfulness. The prosecutor unintentionally revealed the duplicity of the formal system of criminal justice when he stated that "the material of the whole trial is contained in this confession."[350] In the hidden world of

---

[343] Koltai 1949, p. 5.

[344] Ibid., pp. 253–254.

[345] Klajn 2007, p. 140.

[346] Hodos 1987, p. 50.

[347] Szasz 1971, p. 165.

[348] Ibid., p. 165.

[349] Daily Worker, 15 September 1949. In: G L 1956, p. 251.

[350] Koltai 1949, p. 270.

political justice, such confessions were "achieved with rubber truncheons, rifle butts, electric shocks, sleeplessness, hunger and cold—a mixture of the most advanced and archaically barbaric methods of physical and psychological tortures."[351] Like in the USSR, those few who did not confess "were not put on trial, but simply disappeared in one of the many secret camps of the *ÁVH*."[352] Some interrogators could not overcome a cognitive dissonance between incredible criminal charges against the accused and a parallel reality of extrajudicial practices used to confirm these charges. For instance, "Colonel László Angyal, one of Rajk's interrogators, committed suicide; he could not bear the pressure of torturing a comrade he was convinced was innocent."[353] Like in the Soviet trials, a minor lapse happened when accused Dr. Szőnyi, who was supposedly recruited by the CIA director Allen Dulles, "failed to recognize a photograph of…Dulles."[354] The Soviet practice of 'witnesses' complemented the 'confessions' to compensate the absence of credible evidence.

The practice of engaging agent provocateurs as 'witnesses' was fully replicated in Rajk's trial. On the one hand, they strengthened an illusion of impartial court proceedings by presenting 'evidence' which entirely confirmed confessions given by the defendants. On the other hand, witnesses' statements help us better understand the internal mechanics of the parallel system of political justice. A careful observer of the trial could not help but notice that "[t]here were no witnesses for the defense, only for the prosecution—twenty in all."[355] Furthermore, the prosecution could easily obtain any 'testimony' from these 'witnesses', who "were without exception detainees of the *ÁVH*…[im]prison[ed] for having committed genuine [nonpolitical] crimes."[356] Once the 'witnesses' played the roles assigned to them by the informal political justice, the formal system of justice was then used to get rid of them. "After the trial, they were all sentenced, in secret trials, to new and longer prison sentences for having prosecuted and tortured communists during the fascist era."[357] Therefore, the parallel system of political justice and its official counterpart complemented each other forming a symbiosis of formal law and extra-legal practices.

As opposed to the USSR, Hungarian criminal statutes never envisaged the doctrine of analogy. The initial legal basis for people's trials was the Act VII of 1945, "which supplemented the provisions of numerous government decrees."[358] The Act consisted of the previous Prime Ministerial Decree no. 1440/1945 ME, which violated the principle of *nullum crimen, nulla poena sine lege*,[359] The original purpose of the Act and the decrees was to punish war crimes perpetrated during WW II. However, the

---

[351] Hodos 1987, p. 46.

[352] Ibid., p. 46.

[353] Kopacsi 1981, p. 39. In: Hodos 1987, p. 47.

[354] Hodos 1987, p. 62.

[355] Ibid., p. 50.

[356] Ibid.

[357] Ibid.

[358] Barna and Pető 2015, p. 25.

[359] Retroactive norms of the Act stipulated that "the crimes described in this decree shall be punishable where the criminal act has [already] been perpetrated on entry into force of this decree, and

Act VII of 1946 established special councils for 'political trials' at people's tribunals to deal with crimes committed after the war. Thus, people's tribunals originally created to punish war criminals "increasingly became a device for the Hungarian Communist Party (*Magyar Communista Párt*) to engage and suppress...political opponents' (Papp 2011, 38–39)."[360] Taking into account peculiarities of the legal system in communist Hungary, instead of the analogy doctrine a similar practice was used by the Communist Party to achieve essentially the same purposes of politically motivated justice.

Similar to the Moscow show trials, Rajk and the principle co-defendants were sentenced to death. To give an impression of judicial leniency, secondary defendants like Brankov and Justus received life imprisonment "while Ognjenovic, an official of the Yugoslav minority organization, was given a nine-year sentence."[361] The formal legal system was used to achieve the goals of politically motivated justice by denying the defendants' right to appeal. The Act XXXXIV of 1947 "replaced the institution of appeal with a 'complaint of annulity'...[which] could only be submitted in cases where there had been a significant breach of the provisions of the law...[but not] on a point of fact."[362] Moreover, the principle of equality of arms was violated, because "public prosecutors could launch appeals whenever they wanted—whether to get the sentence reduced or increased."[363] The true political nature of these violations was confirmed when in March 1956 Rákosi rehabilitated Rajk and, although denying his personal involvement, "admitted that the defendants at the 1949 trial had been innocent 'victims of a frame-up'."[364] The 'post-mortal' political amnesty was a convenient way to hide a still functioning parallel system of politically motivated justice under the guise of communist-style 'pseudo-restorative justice'.

The Rajk trial was just a prelude to a range of political trials held afterwards in Hungary. On the one hand, the communist authorities used formal criminal justice to conduct "the secret trials of hundreds of Rajkists."[365] On the other hand, in the informal system of political justice "[h]undreds of other Rajkists were deemed to be too unimportant or too unpredictable to be brought into court; they were sent without trial to secret internment camps of the AHV in Kistarcsa and Recsk."[366] Similar to the USSR, secret trials initially targeted other 'deviationists' and people who were implicated under torture by defendants in the previous trials. Even János Kádár, who would later become a leader of communist Hungary, was arrested and allegedly tortured by ÁVH people. Then, like in the case of Soviet generals, "[a]nother purge swept into prison the top ranks of the army, trained and educated in the prewar

---

was not punishable under the legal provisions in force at the time of the perpetration of the criminal act." In: Barna and Pető 2015, p. 23.

360 Ibid., p. 17.

361 Hodos 1987, p. 62.

362 Barna and Pető 2015, p. 25.

363 Ibid., p. 24.

364 Sakmyster 2011, pp. 57–58.

365 Hodos 1987, p. 62.

366 Ibid., p. 64.

period."[367] Complying with the Stalinist approach, the political and military leadership purge overlapped with the beginning of the forced collectivization and persecution of Hungarian *kulaks* or independent farmers (*nagygazdák*).[368] The resemblance with the Soviet 'Great Purge' became complete when in 1952 the Hungarian communist authorities organized an anti-Zionist campaign, which "peaked with the arrest of Jewish doctors working in exclusive party and *ÁVH* hospitals..., thus mirroring the 'doctors' plot' in the Soviet Union."[369] Thus, post-war political trials in communist Hungary fully replicated the Soviet method of splitting the system of justice into its formal and informal (political) components.

There are several conclusions that can be drawn from the Rajk trial and the subsequent purges in communist Hungary. *First*, the Soviet model of show trials was not a unique 'phenomenon' inherent only to the USSR under Stalin, but rather a set of practices that could be shared between similar totalitarian regimes. The Rajk trial demonstrated that the Soviet show trials could be replicated in Hungary and later in other Soviet satellite countries. *Second*, close involvement of Soviet 'advisors' in the organization of post-war political trials in Hungary proved that the USSR actively promoted its model of politically motivated justice to consolidate the communist regimes in Eastern Europe. *Third*, the major characteristic of the Soviet model was the split of criminal justice into two parallel systems. The Rajk trial and the Moscow trials revealed an official decorative system of justice used to maintain the appearance of legality as well as an informal system of political justice, which included mostly unwritten norms and extra-judicial practices that allowed achieving political domination unconstrained by norms of formal law.

2.7 Trials Against Dissidents of the Late Soviet Period

Shortly after Joseph Stalin's death in 1953, the next leader of the USSR Nikita Khrushchev declared at a secret Communist Party meeting a policy of 'destalinization' in his speech 'On the Cult of Personality and Its Consequences'.[370] The new policy, which was later communicated to the Soviet society and the international community, denounced Stalin for creating a cult of his personality, unlashing mass terror and repressions and making mistakes that caused numerous deaths during WW II. The policy of destalinization encompassed unprecedented rehabilitation of political prisoners, return to the socialist legality and various reforms that would lead to temporary liberalization of the Soviet system of government also known as

367 Ibid., p. 66.

368 Balassa 1960, pp. 35–51.

369 Hodos 1987, p. 66.

370 Khrushchev 1956.

Khrushev's 'Thaw' (Russian: *ottepel*).[371] The policy of destalinization did not put, however, an end to the parallel system of politically motivated justice in the USSR, which was eventually exposed by the movement of dissidents in the late Soviet period.

Taking into account that Khrushev was a member of Stalin's 'close circle' of confidants, *the 'Thaw'* was merely a half-hearted policy, which did not lead to any serious attempts to investigate, let alone criminally prosecute those responsible for the crimes of Stalinism. Once Khrushev was himself removed from power by Leonid Brezhnev through an inter-party coup in 1964, the period of Brezhnev's 'Stagnation' was accompanied with reversal of previous political reforms and economic decline. The new wave of political liberalization under the brand of 'Restructuring' or 'Perestroika' introduced in 1985 by the last Soviet leader Mikhail Gorbachev did not prevent, however, the ultimate collapse of the Soviet Union in 1991. Throughout these stages of post-Stalinist transformations more and more people started questioning the communist regime and noticing a gap between the fictional character of Soviet formal laws that stipulated various rights and the reality of informal unwritten rules that ensured the unlimited power of the Communist Party. Though these critics of the regime belonged to various ideologies and groups, in the Western literature they became known under the collective name of dissidents. In the USSR, where dissidents were stigmatized by the Communist Party, they belonged to a judicially disfavored group of 'anti-Soviet elements' or renegades (Russian: otshepentsy).

The dissidents' movement was non-violent and included various activities such as 'Samizdat' or reproducing prohibited literature in the USSR, 'Tamizdat' or printing abroad materials about the repressive nature of Communism as well as organizing unauthorized peaceful assemblies, distributing petitions and calling for hunger strikes in support of people persecuted for their criticism of the communist doctrine. In the book, I will on the most distinctive goal of the dissidents' movement, namely "to pull down the 'façade of legality' of communist power, which blurred its repressive character."[372] In the USSR, dissidents tried to achieve this goal by demanding *in person and without prior arrangement (Russian: v yavochnom poriadke)* practical implementation of civil and political rights that were de-jure envisaged in the Soviet legislation, but de-facto remained simply declaratory. Andrei Medushevsky notices in his analysis of Stalinist legacy that dissidents' demonstrative implementation of the declaratory norms of Soviet law was inadvertently prosecuted by the communist regime as a deviation or a crime.[373] This text offers an analysis of several key trials against dissidents that fully exposed the division into the two separate systems of formal and political justice in the USSR.

An overview of changes that took place in the Soviet legislation could help us understand whether 'destalinization' addressed the judicial defects of political justice discussed in the previous sections. There is no doubt that Stalin's death was a trigger for many reforms in the Soviet system of criminal justice. Harold Berman argues, for

---

[371] Nathans 2011.

[372] Přibáň 2002, p. 2.

[373] Medushevsky 2011.

example, that "the 1958 and 1960 reforms in the fields of criminal law and procedure are, at many points, specifically directed against abuses which were characteristic of the Stalin era."[374] In particular, the new Fundamental Principles of Criminal Law and Legislation of the USSR and the Union Republics of 1958, the new Statute on Crimes against the State of 1958 and the new RSFSR Criminal Code of 1960 introduced several liberalizations of norms related to the so-called political cases.[375] In terms of corpus delicti, "crimes formerly denominated as counterrevolutionary were classified either as 'Especially Dangerous Crimes Against the State' or as 'Other Crimes Against the State'."[376] Criminal sanctions no longer included "(a) deprivation of political and civil rights, (b) banishment from the USSR, (c) being declared an enemy of the working people".[377] These and other reforms were introduced by legal experts who "consciously looked to pre-revolutionary Russian and Western models."[378] The new 1977 Soviet Constitution, at least on paper, seemed to be a sign of moderate 'democratization' too.

Brezhnev's Constitution of 1977 was proclaimed in the USSR as the Constitution of 'developed socialism'. The new Constitution reinforced rights of Soviet citizens. In terms of due process guarantees, *Articles 157-162* "provide that court proceedings must be open to members of the general public, …that the defendant has a right to counsel…as well as the right to an appointed interpreter if he does not have full command of the language in which the proceedings are conducted…and that the defendant is presumed innocent until his guilt has been established by a court of competent jurisdiction."[379] *Moreover, Article 48 stipulated* "the right to take part in the management and administration of state and public affairs",[380]*Article 49* further envisaged that "[p]ersecution for criticism is prohibited. Persons guilty of such persecution shall be called to account",[381] *Article 52* guaranteed the right to association and *Article 58* even provided for "the right to lodge a complaint against the actions of officials, state bodies and public bodies."[382] The analysis of dissidents' trials below shows that all these 'progressive' constitutional standards belonged to a fictional world of the socialist legality.

Various pseudo-liberal reforms conducted in the USSR after Stalin's death were usually taken with a grain of salt abroad. When the Western public was asked about the state of Soviet justice, "[t]he answer seem[ed] to be: much better than in the days of Stalin, when enemies of the state would be shot or sent off to labor camps with or without summary trials. But while the forms of legality are more closely

[374] Berman 1974, p. 32.
[375] Millar 1992.
[376] Berman 1974, p. 38.
[377] Berman 1974, p. 37.
[378] Ibid., p. 20.
[379] Osakwe 1979.
[380] See the English version of the 1977 USSR Constitution. https://www.departments.bucknell.edu/russian/const/77cons02.html#chap07. Accessed 24 December 2020.
[381] Ibid.
[382] Ibid.

observed…, political repression persists."[383] Soviet political trials were often an important indicator, because they revealed the general situation with the system of justice, its main defects and the split of the Soviet legal system into formal and informal (political) norms. Although majority of trials against dissidents were closed for the general public, similar to Stalin's show trials, various witnesses' accounts and subsequent research expose the ex-parte communication between the judiciary and Communist Party officials.

Similar to the Moscow trials, KGB, which was an NKVD's successor agency, played a crucial role in the ex-parte communication to influence court proceedings and even to determine an outcome of a trial in advance. The parallel world of political justice as usually revealed itself in a Politburo's decision to prosecute a certain dissident. For instance, in 1969 the Head of KGB Yuri Andropov reported at a Politburo meeting about the Soviet Major General Piotr Grigorenko, a Ukrainian born dissident, who allegedly planned to establish the first Soviet human rights organization. According to the KGB files, Andropov "concluded with a recommendation that criminal charges be laid against Grigorenko…Three weeks later, the general was arrested in Tashkent, where he had intended to monitor the trial of ten Crimean Tatar activists."[384] In 1978, a potential trial against the spokesman of the Soviet Jewish dissident community Anatoliy Shcharansky accused of espionage was also discussed at Politburo. Andropov reported to Politburo members: "The trial will [be]…[in] a good place, a club, and the audience, properly prepared, will therefore be small".[385] The Politburo members further decided on Shcharansky's sentence prior to the trial: "Of course, Shcharansky will not receive the death penalty, but the court will give him a severe sentence, say, for example, fifteen years."[386] Therefore, a 'political trial' against any 'uncooperative' dissident had no risk of acquittal in court.

Shcharansky's trial became an example of the Soviet judicial prerogativism against vocal ethnic groups. The Soviet authorities rejected Mr. Shcharansky's multiple requests to immigrate to Israel under a pretext that his scientific work constituted a state secret. Shcharansky and representatives of other Soviet ethnic minorities belonged to a group of so-called 'rejected applicants' (Russian: *otkazniki*), who were denied an opportunity to emigrate from the USSR. Shcharansky, who was born in a multiethnic community of the Ukrainian city of Donetsk, "was simultaneously an advocate of the Jewish struggle for free emigration and of various ethnic groups that seek to reform Soviet society from the inside."[387] Shcharansky, like other *otkazniki*, was fired by his research institute and as a dissident had contacts with foreign journalists, which was a formal legal pretext of accusing him of committing high treason and passing secret scientific information to the CIA. In the parallel system of the

[383] Time Magazine 1978a.

[384] Yurii Andropov, No. 887–A, (16 Apr. 1969). https://psi.ece.jhu.edu/kaplan1/IRUSS/BUK/GBARC/pdfs/dis60/kgb-69-1.pdf. Accessed 24 December 2020. *See also* Horvath 2014, pp. 147–175.

[385] Beckerman 2011, p. 75.

[386] Beckerman 2011.

[387] Time Magazine 1978b.

Soviet political justice, however, Shcharansky was actually persecuted because of a government plan "to put down Jewish dissidence and of the persistence of traditional anti-Semitism."[388] A dissident academician Andrei Sakharov said in particular that "[t]he Shcharansky trial…had been an attempt to stir up anti-Semitic feelings within the country. "The Soviet authorities are trying to break up the movement for Jewish emigration".[389] Ukrainian, Georgian or Lithuanian dissidents, who sought greater national autonomy for their republics, were also persecuted as members of a judicially disfavored group of 'nationalists'.

When Shcharansky stood before the Soviet court in 1978, he also faced the accusatorial bias. While his mother was denied to attend the trial, his brother Leonid was admitted to the courtroom and could report on some procedural irregularities that disadvantaged Shcharansky's position during the trial. The court's bias towards Anatoliy Shcharansky became obvious at the very beginning when the trial judge rejected "the defendant's first action…to dismiss the lawyer who had been assigned to him by the KGB in place of the attorney he had requested."[390] Moreover, according to Leonid Shcharansky, his brother "was frequently interrupted by the judge, prohibited from calling defense witnesses and forbidden to question government witnesses."[391] In the best traditions of the Moscow show trials, "[o]ne of the prosecution witnesses was Dr. Sanya Lipavsky, a KGB agent provocateur".[392] Lipavsky argued that Shcharansky had a number of meetings with CIA agents allegedly to discuss the implementation of the Helsinki Treaty in the USSR, "but the dates of the meetings that Lipavsky reported were before the treaty had even been signed."[393] The court, however, was too biased in favor of the prosecution to notice this and other inconsistencies in Lipavsky's testimony that eventually led to Shcharansky's thirteen-year prison sentence.[394]

A trial against Georgian dissident and writer Zviad Gamsakhurdia was an example of the 'show trial' confession. Gamsakhurdia, who would become the first president of Georgia after the collapse of the USSR, was charged in 1977 with conducting 'anti-Soviet activities' that included his work on distribution of prohibited *samizdat* literature and participation in the Georgian Helsinki Group, which criticized human rights violations in the USSR. Shortly after a three-year prison sentence pronounced by the court, Soviet central television channels broadcast Gamsakhurdia's 'confession', in which he allegedly admitted his guilt and condemned Western propaganda against the Soviet Union. Furthermore, two foreign journalists were tried *in absentia* and "formally accused in a Moscow court of libeling [Soviet] television employees by suggesting…that the televised confession of Zviad Gamsakhurdia may have

---

[388] Ibid.

[389] Ibid.

[390] Time Magazine 1978b.

[391] Ibid.

[392] Ibid.

[393] Beckerman 2011.

[394] In 1986, the USSR exchanged Shcharansky for two Soviet spies, Karl Koecher and Hana Koecher, detained in West Germany.

been fabricated."[395] The political performance completely replaced formal justice when already convicted Gamsakhurdia "duly appeared in court, accompanied by two guards, viewed the film of his confession, and pronounced it undoctored."[396] Naturally, this did not add much credibility to his 'confession' in the West.

I believe the Soviet practice of violating Lex Certa took place in the trial against Vladimir Bukovsky, who in 1967 organized a demonstration with the slogans for a release of previously arrested fellow dissidents and against the newly introduced *Article 190.3* of the RSFSR Criminal Code. Even the Stalin's Constitution of 1936, which was still in force at that time, guaranteed the freedom of street processions and demonstrations.[397] Nevertheless, Bukovsky was charged with the very same *Article 190.3*, which punished "Organization of, or Active Participation in, Group Actions Which Violate Public Order."[398] The criminal offence formulated by this repressive norm was so broad that any peaceful rally or demonstration could be characterized as a crime against the public order. Furthermore, at the trial many testimonies showed that Bukovsky's actions did not fall within the scope of the criminal law provision. "One policemen testified there had been no disturbance. Numerous witnesses confirmed that Bukovsky had instructed the demonstrators to behave properly."[399] To qualify Bukovsky's actions as an offence, the trial court relied on prosecutor's assertion that "basically, public order was violated by the slogans."[400] Bukovsky, who did not plead guilty, received the maximum penalty of three years in prison.

An example of simplified procedures was a case of a world-famous nuclear physicist Andrei Sakharov, who used his scientific fame to criticize the Soviet authorities at the international arena. Without any trial and in flagrant disregard of the presumption of innocence,[401] in 1978 the KGB chief Andropov called Sakharov the 'enemy number one' of the USSR.[402] When in 1979 Sakharov criticized the Soviet invasion in Afghanistan, the Politburo decided in an extra-judicial fashion to send Sakharov into exile to the city of Gorky, where he and his wife were essentially isolated from the rest of the world. Simplified procedures of the parallel system of political justice

---

[395] Rubenstein 1980, p. 244.

[396] Time Magazine 1978b.

[397] *Article 125* of the 1936 Constitution. https://www.departments.bucknell.edu/russian/const/36cons04.html#chap10. Accessed 24 December 2020.

[398] According to *Article 190.3*, "The organization of, and, likewise, the active participation in, group actions which violate public order in a coarse manner or which are attended by clear disobedience of the legal demands of representatives of authority or which entail the violation of the work of transport or of state and social institutions or enterprises shall be punished by deprivation of freedom for a term not exceeding three years, or by correctional tasks for a term not exceeding one year, for a term not exceeding one year, or by a fine not exceeding 100 rubles". In: Berman 1974, p. 181.

[399] Rubenstein 1980, p. 65.

[400] Ibid.

[401] The 1960 Code of Criminal Procedure "studiously omit to state *express verbis* that 'the burden of proof of the guilt of accused shall rest on the prosecution,' and that 'the accused shall be presumed to be innocent until proven guilty'". In: Berman 1974, p. 59.

[402] Kalugin 2008, s. 276.

also contributed to the creation of a parallel system of 'punitive medicine' for dissidents. The Soviet legislation in force envisaged compulsory treatment in a psychiatric hospital for a person charged with a crime "on the basis of a psychiatric opinion."[403] Dr. Ian Spencer, who researched the extensive political abuse of the Soviet psychiatry, concluded that a Soviet "judge was no more independent than a psychiatrist, especially given that senior psychiatrists were also officers in the KGB."[404] The price of disobedience was high for the Ukrainian human rights activist "Dr. Semyon Gluzman, who refused to diagnose a dissident as mentally ill, [and] was sentenced to a lengthy period in prison and exile (Gluzman 1989)."[405] Those dissidents who could not be indicted in an open trial were swiftly confined as mentally ill patients by a system of punitive psychiatry.

As opposed to the trials described above, the affair of 'young specialists' had an unexpected 'happy ending'.[406] In 1982 KGB arrested several young scholars, who organized a secret dissident network to copy and distribute prohibited in the USSR literature, which was critical of the communist socio-economic system and advocated for a stronger role of civil society. All participants of the network were charged with anti-Soviet activities and propaganda. In 1983 some of the accused, who signed a 'letter of repentance', were released in accordance with an amnesty decree adopted by the Supreme Council of the USSR under Andropov's chairmanship, who became a leader of the USSR.[407] As usually, international criticism played an important role in this and other Soviet 'political cases'. Another decisive factor in the out-of-court resolution of this case through the informal system of political justice was that Andropov did not want to start his 'reign' with a big show trial.[408] Nevertheless, the individual pardon granted by the Soviet political leadership before a trial was quite extraordinary even for the Soviet legal practice. The fact that the pardon was granted in such a way confirmed once again the supremacy of the shadow system of political justice over its official counterpart, which served only a decorative purpose.

The very existence of the parallel system of political justice and its superiority over its formal counterpart is confirmed by the legal nihilism among senior Soviet officials at that time. Rights guaranteed by the Soviet Constitution were never treated seriously and dissidents' demands to observe the Constitution were often considered as infantile. For instance, before being arrested, a dissident told a KGB officer that the Soviet Constitution protected freedom of speech. "Please, the KGB man is said to have responded, 'we're having a serious conversation'."[409] Higher informal norms of political justice trumped not only the Constitution, but also the international law.

---

[403] Articles 58 and 59 of the 1960 RSFSR Criminal Code, Articles 188, 403–414 of the 1960 RSFSR Code of Criminal Procedure. In: Berman 1974, p. 11.

[404] Spencer 2000, p. 359.

[405] Ibid.

[406] Out of the whole group of 'young specialists' only Mikhail Rivkin refused to sign a letter of repentance and was sentenced to seven years in prison and five years of exile.

[407] Shubin 2008, s. 280.

[408] Delo Kagarlitskogo // Solidarnost'. 1991 # 12. S. 13. In: Shubin 2008, s. 280.

[409] Time Magazine 1978b.

In 1975, the USSR signed the Final Act of the Conference on Security and Cooperation also known as Final Helsinki Act, which was supposed to guarantee the respect towards basic human rights in all signatory states.[410] Though Soviet dissidents established republican 'Helsinki Unions' to ensure implementation of the Act in the USSR, the nihilistic attitude of the Soviet authorities was more than dismissive. For instance, "[a]t the Office of Visas and Registration…dissident Andrei Feder was told: "All the Helsinki Accords are only promises to us—for us they are not law"."[411] Moreover, the Soviet authorities punished "a blue-collar worker, Mikhail Kukobaka, [who] was placed in psychiatric hospital for distributing the Universal Declaration among Mogilev plant workers."[412]

Thus, by disregarding formal law, the USSR de-facto recognized the primacy of political justice.

In light of the above-mentioned political repressions conducted in the late Soviet period, it is possible to make three conclusions. *First*, the so-called policy of destalinization as well as various legal reforms introduced after Stalin's death did not prevent politically motivated prosecution of those who opposed the Soviet socio-economic model. *Second*, the analysis of trials against Soviet dissidents confirm the presence, though in the more moderate form, of such main features of the Stalinist model of politically motivated justice as ex-parte communication, judicial prerogativism, prosecutorial or accusatorial bias, confessions and self-indictment of accused, analogy, arbitrary recharacterization, simplified procedures and political amnesties. *Third*, all these legal defects of trials against dissidents revealed the split of criminal justice into the official system of merely declarative legislation and the parallel system of mostly unwritten rules and practices that had a supra-constitutional rank in the USSR. This book argues that in the Soviet state, where the written Constitution and other formal legislation were only nominal, judicially operative norms and practices of the shadow system of politically motivated criminal justice constituted the only true Constitution and the supreme 'law' of the USSR until its collapse in 1991.

2.8 The Soviet System of Political Justice and Its 'Twofold Constitutionalism'

Various authors have already noticed the duality of the communist socialist legality. Jiří Přibáň, who analyzed the phenomenon of 'legalist fictions' in communist societies, argues that "dissidents used the concept of socialist legality to expose the repressive character of the communist regime and its ignorance of both national laws and international legal obligations."[413] In the previous sections, I have also discussed

[410] The Helsinki Final Act, signed on 30 July–1 August 1975. https://www.osce.org/mc/39501. Accessed 24 December 2020.

[411] Kowalewski 1980, pp. 5–29.

[412] Ibid.

[413] Přibáň 2002, p. 2.

Osakwe's theory[414] about the split of the Soviet legal system into state law and party law and Solomon's 'compartmentalization'[415] of political justice in the USSR. Their ideas formulated during the Soviet times have been confirmed in Medushevsky's more recent research on the Stalinist legacy. According to Medushevsky, the Soviet duality of formal and informal norms could be explained through the phenomenon of '*Nominal Constitutionalism*', which provided legal 'camouflage' for the communist political repressions, centralized administrative power as well as legitimized the communist regime both at home and abroad.[416] The split into actual and formal Constitutions is most similar to *Honne* and *Tatemae* that show the difference between true feelings and public behavior in Japanese society. This split is also well illustrated by George Orwell's '*doublethink*',[417] according to which members of a totalitarian society, though formally following declarative norms, strictly obey unwritten rules of the political regime at the same time. This book further argues that the system of political justice was a part of the Soviet 'Twofold Constitutionalism'.

To test my hypothesis about the constitutional nature of the Soviet system of political justice, I will use Joseph Raz' characterization of a Constitution, which "in a thick sense of the word is (1) constitutive of the legal and political structure, (2) stable, (3) written, (4) superior to other law, (5) justiciable, (6) entrenched, and (7) express common ideology."[418] In terms of the legal and political structure of the USSR, informal rules of politically motivated justice were constitutive in the broadest sense. The parallel world of political justice played an important role in defining "powers of the main organs of the different branches of government"[419] by giving extraordinary powers to repressive organs like KGB/NKVD, whose omnipotence could often trump almost any state authority. The Soviet political structure as such was established based on politically motivated 'class struggle' against representatives of bourgeoisie. The Red Terror and the Great Purge ultimately led to the domination of one-party, which did not tolerate dissenting voices even among its own ranks. The socialist legality was also born from the spirit of repressions based on the quasi-legal theories of 'revolutionary vigilance' and 'Soviet legal conscience', 'flexibility of laws' as well as swift and severe punishment of 'people's enemies'. Such instruments of political justice as analogy and recharacterization were initially incorporated into Soviet legislation and later into judicial practices and legal traditions of the USSR.

---

414 Osakwe 1985.

415 Solomon 1996, p. 467.

416 Medushevsky 2011.

417 "DOUBLETHINK means the power of holding two contradictory beliefs in one's mind simultaneously, and accepting both of them...To tell deliberate lies while genuinely believing in them, to forget any fact that has become inconvenient, and then, when it becomes necessary again, to draw it back from oblivion for just so long as it is needed, to deny the existence of objective reality and all the while to take account of the reality which one denies...Even in using the word DOUBLETHINK it is necessary to exercise DOUBLETHINK. For by using the word one admits that one is tampering with reality; by a fresh act of DOUBLETHINK one erases this knowledge; and so on indefinitely, with the lie always one leap ahead of the truth." In: Orwell 1961.

418 Sadurski 2012, p. 45.

419 Alexander 2001, p. 153.

The system of politically motivated justice was extremely stable and durable throughout all stages of the Soviet history. The practice of 'assigning verdicts' to political cases at Politburo meetings preserved well beyond Stalin's death at the times of moderate liberalization during the so-called Khruschev's thaw, Brezhnev's stagnation and Gorbachev's perestroika. Furthermore, the analysis of political trials made in the previous sections proves that such core characteristics of Soviet political justice as ex-parte communication, judicial prerogativism, prosecutorial or accusatorial bias, defendants' confessions and self-indictment, analogy, recharacterization, simplified summary procedures and political amnesties were always present in the Soviet legal culture. Though the severity of political repressions varied over time, they preserved the continuity of the communist totalitarian regime and its principles until the very collapse of the USSR.

The norms and practices of the Soviet politically motivated justice were mostly unwritten. The written provisions that were used to initiate politically motivated prosecution were usually classified as secret. Nevertheless, norms of the so-called Kirov law, the secret NKVD order # 00447 on the forced collectivization and other clandestine decrees were later incorporated into the Soviet legislation or superimposed through judicial and extra-legal governmental practices on formal written laws that had only a declarative character. Joseph Raz himself admits that a Constitution in a thick sense is a vague concept and the mere fact that a country has a written Constitution does not necessarily mean "that there cannot be an 'unwritten' part of the constitution—for example, a part that is 'customary law'".[420] He gives an example of the UK, whose Constitution is composed of unwritten common law and the written documents like "the Bill of Rights of 1689, the Act of Union between England and Scotland of 1706…[and] the European Communities Act of 1971."[421] Thus, the mostly unwritten form of the Soviet system of political justice does not preclude it from being a Constitution in a thick sense of this word.

The analysis of several Soviet show trials in the previous sections demonstrates that the norms of political justice had a supra-constitutional rank in the sense that they had more weight than the nominal written Constitutions of the USSR. The Soviet dissident movement eventually exposed the decorative function of Soviet constitutional rights and freedoms that were always trumped by informal rules of political domination and repressions imposed by the Soviet leadership. The primacy of informal political norms over the formal law manifested itself in the Soviet legal nihilism, which questioned enforceability of any written law, as well as occasional political amnesties and individual pardons that elevated political discourse above written laws and previous jurisprudence. In the every-day life of the Soviet society, it meant that all written laws, bylaws and international documents ratified by the USSR were unenforceable if they endangered the interests of the Communist Party. Taking into account that the power of the regime was at stake during show trials, the Soviet leadership could not let ordinary laws and even the written Constitution meddle in the affairs of political justice, whose legal status was supreme.

---

[420] Raz 2009, p. 325.

[421] Ibid.

The Soviet unwritten Constitution of political justice was justiciable thanks to Soviet judicial practices and customary law. Like in the '*Kingdom of Crooked Mirrors*',[422] these practices represented an antipode of the due process, where the presumption of innocence turned into the presumption of guilt, the principle of no punishment without law was replaced by Soviet courts with analogy and recharacterization, the duty of judicial care became the prerogativism and the equality of arms principle was transformed into the prosecutorial bias. All these quasi-judicial procedures and conventionalities became the core of the Soviet unwritten Constitution, which was thoroughly protected by all Soviet courts. When major political shifts happened, Soviet courts used the logic of the unwritten political Constitution to declare as incompatible Lenin's New Economic Policy (NEP), Stalin's Great Purge or Khrushev's Thaw, while the declarative character of the Soviet written Constitutions was left untouched by fictitious reforms of the communist system.

This book argues that, unlike other written Soviet Constitutions,[423] Stalin's Constitution of 1936 was the most entrenched both in terms of its longevity and influence on the Soviet legal culture. Stalin's nominal written Constitution was in force for more than forty years. Despite the policy of destalinization and a new constitution project proposed by Khrushev in 1962, the Soviet leadership did not rush to get rid of the Constitution personally developed and approved by Stalin. Although Stalin's written Constitution was previously declared as "the most democratic in the world",[424] it was used in tandem with his unwritten Constitution of well-entrenched practices of political repressions and terror. The nominal Constitution written by Stalin would be useless for the next Soviet leaders if it did not have a useful 'addendum' of unwritten rules that solidified the power of the Communist Party. It was virtually impossible to secure 'amendments' in the unwritten Constitution without overhauling the entire communist regime. Therefore, taking into account that the Soviet Union existed for almost seventy years, the Soviet system of political justice was one of the most entrenched constitutional systems, in terms of its longevity, in the world.

Stalin's unwritten Constitution of political justice expressed a common ideology of the Soviet people. Soviet dissidents acknowledged that they were in minority and did not represent an average Soviet citizen, who found the communist regime quite 'tolerable 'despite its weaknesses that were not 'catastrophic' for individual comfort and conscience.[425] In fact, even some dissidents believed that reforms could bring the USSR back to the true 'Leninist model' of socialism.[426] Medushevsky agrees that the duality of the Soviet legal system was aimed at creating a new Soviet man (*Homo Sovieticus*), who will be loyal to the regime, adaptive to current challenges and unable

---

[422] The Soviet movie "Kingdom of Crooked Mirrors" Review (1963). https://www.thespinningimage.co.uk/cultfilms/displaycultfilm.asp?reviewid=3267. Accessed 24 December 2020.

[423] The USSR had three Constitutions, drawn up respectively in 1924, 1936 and 1977.

[424] Getty 1987, p. 112.

[425] Shubin 2008, s. 217.

[426] Ibid., s. 11-26.

to act independently from the state.[427] The Soviet anthropological experiment of social engineering was quite successful, because many generations of Soviet citizens sincerely believed in the communist propaganda[428] and were indifferent or too scared to publicly question political repressions. Therefore, the mostly unwritten norms of political justice gradually became the common ideology of the prevailing part of the Soviet society.

Taking into account the above-mentioned considerations, it is possible to argue that the Soviet Constitutions were twofold. The first part, which was written and official, played only a nominal role by legitimizing the communist regime in the USSR and abroad. The second part, which was informal and mostly unwritten, included customary law and other conventionalities of political justice, which was justiciable in Soviet courts and superior to other written laws. The culture of political repressions conceived by Stalin was so much interweaved with the Soviet legal and political structure that it constituted one of the most stable and entrenched constitutional systems in the world. Though the Soviet leadership occasionally changed some wording of the declarative written Constitutions, the next political elites kept the unwritten Constitution of political justice untouched to preserve and expand their power monopoly. While the previous academic research acknowledges the split of the Soviet legal system into formal and informal parts, this text makes the next step to argue that this split survived the collapse of the USSR and can still be revealed via political trials selected for this research from criminal cases that have recently taken place in transitional former Soviet republics.

2.9 Conclusions

Any analysis of the Soviet system of criminal justice requires a careful consideration of legal culture, traditions and practices that can be traced back either to the Russian empire or radical social changes that took place in the aftermath of the 1917 Bolshevik revolution. Among legal traditions that stemmed from the Russian tsarist past and survived in the USSR one can discern traditional for Russia 'legal dualism' of written positive law often transplanted by Russian monarchs from abroad and unwritten peasant common law. While the former was usually used by Russian tsars to maintain 'Potiomkin villages'[429] of pseudo legal liberalism, the latter was actually supposed

[427]In the USSR *Homo Sovieticus* was given the derogative name of '*Sovok*' (a scoop in English) to emphasize instrumentalization of a human being by the Communist Party. Also in Medushevsky 2011.

[428]Ebon 1987.

[429]The term 'Potiomkin villages' (Russian: *Potiomkinskiye derevni)* appeared after the Russian nobleman Grigoriy Potiomkin allegedly ordered the construction of fake villages in Ukraine in order to deceive the Russian Empress Catherine II who went on an inspection trip to the Crimean peninsula.

to ensure the law and order in the most remote areas of the vast Russian empire. The Soviet Union also preserved the tsarist institution of Procuracy with its omnipresent and powerful prosecutors that were supposed to be the 'eyes' of Russian autocrats. The violent October revolution of 1917 resulted in the collapse of the weakened Russian empire, which marked the creation of the new communist legal order known as the socialist legality.

In order to survive the dire consequences of the civil war and its own failed policies as well as to maintain control over numerous territories, the newly established communist regime set several goals for its system of justice. *First*, to create a brand new society of Soviet people that would strictly follow new Socialist laws and become obedient tools in the implementation of communist policies. *Second*, to institutionalize state-sanctioned persecution against bourgeoisie and others simply due to their belonging to 'class enemies'. *Third*, to have flexible laws that would ensure the freedom of maneuver for the communist leadership, which must not be constrained by any formal legislation. *Fourth*, to legitimize the new Soviet state in the eyes of the international community and at home. To achieve these goals, the Bolshevik leader Vladimir Lenin naively planned to set up an interim legal system administered by amateurish but politically trustworthy legal officials. Lenin's approach was based on Marx and Engels' theory about 'withering away' of the state and law that would be unnecessary in an 'ideal communist society'. However, Lenin failed to achieve the above-mentioned goals within a single legal system, because even a totalitarian government cannot expect that its citizens willfully abide laws that are only 'flexible' for the very same government. Furthermore, openly arbitrary persecution against 'enemies' of the communist regime could not possibly secure a long-term international and domestic legitimation.

It is also important to note that, despite the supreme rank of informal political norms in the Soviet legal tradition, the communist regime needed the existence of a formal legal order for the legitimization of its status at home and abroad, international cooperation and trade as a legitimate partner for the rest of the 'civilized world'. For instance, the Soviet dependence on international trade prevailed over political interests of the Communist Party during one of the first show trials in the so-called Shakhty case of 1928, which involved a group of Soviet and German engineers employed by German firms A.E.G. and Knapp that were accused of sabotage and espionage.[430] Thanks to the firm position of the Weimar Republic, which actively protected its citizens arrested in the USSR, "[in July 1928 t]he…[arrested] Germans were acquitted, and the A.E.G., since it was not named in the verdict [of the show trial], was de facto exonerated."[431] Furthermore, taking into account "that the Germans desired to restore good relations with the [resources-rich] Soviet Union…[, n]egotiations for the extension of the Commercial Treaty of October, 1925, were resumed on November 22, and the new [trade] Treaty was signed a month later."[432] Moreover, the criticism of the Shakhty trial in foreign press forced Stalin to display 'humanism' of the

---

[430] Rosenbaum 1962, pp. 238–60.

[431] Ibid., p. 257.

[432] Ibid., p. 260.

Soviet system of justice to the international community, given "that..[he] could only have five [out of eleven accused sentenced to death] actually executed."[433] Similar considerations of internal and international legitimacy prompted the newly appointed leader of the USSR Andropov not to prosecute young scholars accused of 'anti-Soviet propaganda' in the affair of 'young specialists' of 1982, because he did not want to start his 'reign' with a big show trial.[434] Thus, such internal and international factors motivated the Soviet leadership to maintain the 'façade' of the formal constitution, which camouflaged repressions and arbitrary political trials.

Lenin's official successor Joseph Stalin realized that it would be impossible to achieve the above-mentioned goals of the socialist legality in the framework of a singular official legal system. After defeating Lenin's associates in the inter-party struggle, Stalin rejected the previous nihilistic law approach and preferred instead the establishment of a permanent legal system, which would formally belong to the continental law tradition and include the informal political language of the 'class struggle' at the same time. In this regard, he fell back on the tsarist tradition of 'legal duality' to create a twofold system of justice. The first part was supposed to provide an official legal framework that would be recognized abroad and formally followed by ordinary citizens in the USSR. The second unofficial component of the system included mostly unwritten judicial traditions and totalitarian practices that would secure the most intimate political interests of the communist leadership in spite of any law. To support this double-track system of justice, Stalin established the whole new officialdom, which consisted of long-term career officials devoted to the communist regime and its quasi-legal concepts such as 'revolutionary vigilance' and the 'crime by analogy'. The twofold system was maintained by the tsarist-like powerful Procuracy and puppet judiciary, which recognized the supremacy of the Soviet 'legal conscience' over written law.

There are several reasons to believe that the legal system conceived by Stalin was twofold. The most significant sign of the split was the creation of shadow extra-legal bodies that duplicated all branches of government. To deal with political cases, the USSR established secret political departments, *troikas* and *dvoikas* in already repressive government agencies like OGPU, NKVD and KGB. Special boards and collegiums often adjudicated political trials instead of ordinary courts. The notorious Politburo of the Soviet leadership became a shadow quasi-legislative body, which issued secret guidelines on political repressions and even delivered verdicts before any 'trial'. Another proof of the Soviet legal dualism is the classified communication between extra-judicial bodies and their official counterparts in judiciary, Procuracy and law-enforcement agencies. This secret communication was supposed to create an illusion of a pseudo-independent singular system of justice, which was actually divided into two parallel legal orders.

The duplicity of the socialist legality was finalized with the adoption of the 1936 Constitution approved by Stalin. Though the constitution provided for numerous rights in criminal justice including the rights to counsel, to access case materials

---

433 Wood 2005, p. 163.

434 Delo Kagarlitskogo // Solidarnost'. 1991 # 12. S. 13. In: Shubin 2008, s. 280.

as well as prohibition of arbitrary arrest, the subsequent Great Purge of massive political repressions relegated the constitutional provisions to the strictly nominal status. Mostly unwritten norms and customs of political justice, in turn, filled in the existing legal void and became the real constitution, which determined the actual authority of legal and governmental systems in the USSR. Such a split into separate realities was not a unique phenomenon in the Soviet society. The alternative realities of *vorovskoy mir* (thieves' world), the black market, the communist propaganda and the Soviet punitive psychiatry demonstrated the duplicity of the Soviet society and its ability to navigate in a 'twofold world'. Thus, unlike the British *Rule of Law* and German *Rechtsstaat* that promote the adherence of both written and unwritten norms to the same principles, the socialist legality is composed of formal and informal parts that not only contradict each other, but also have an opposite set of values.

The adoption of the 1936 Constitution symbolically coincided with the Moscow trials that like other political trials revealed the duality of the Soviet system. Soviet show trials drew on the tsarist tradition of mock trials later enhanced by Bolshevik agitation trials aimed at educating the population about Communism. The Moscow trials had several characteristics that disclosed their affiliation with a parallel system of political justice. There was no risk of acquittal in these trials, because a guilty verdict was in advance delivered by the political leadership through the ex-parte communication with all trial participants. Proceedings were saturated with theatrical practices such as extensive confessions and repentance of accused that usually 'confessed' under torture or other 'darkness-at-noon' interrogation techniques such as a system of 'family hostages'. The trials did not target single individuals, but entire social classes, whose members were disfavored through judicial prerogativism in court and sometimes even tried *in absentia.* Judges and prosecutors exercised accusatorial bias towards defendants charged with multiple crimes who were already presumed guilty in a pretrial public smear campaign. Finally, the broad *corpora delicti* allowed judges arbitrarily characterize defendants' non-criminal actions as grave crimes such as terrorism or treason allegedly 'plotted' by external and internal enemies of the Soviet Union.

Besides the Moscow trials used in the Communist Party purge, this book also identified other categories of Soviet political justice such as rural (*raion*) trials, military tribunals, anti-Semitic trials, repressions against independent peasantry (*kulaks*) and trials against dissidents during the late Soviet period. Similar to the Moscow trials, they also targeted actual and potential opponents of the regime, boosted the inter-party discipline of local communist officials as well as scapegoated random victims for policy failures made by the Communist Party. Unlike the widely publicized Moscow show trials, other categories of political persecution were often clandestine as well as involved accelerated and simplified criminal procedures. Alternatively, extra-judicial bodies simply executed those who did not 'confess' or were too insignificant and unpredictable to be 'presented' in a show trial. In exceptional cases, however, victims of Soviet political trials were rehabilitated or pardoned, sometimes *post-mortem*, to display ostentatious leniency of communist justice. The above-mentioned categories of political trials were in line with the informal 'customary law' of political justice superimposed on Soviet formal written legislation.

Another peculiar feature of Soviet political trials, which also confirms the dual nature of the communist system of justice, was the inversion of the fair trial principles. Like in the Soviet fairytale the '*Kingdom of Crooked Mirrors*',[435] the parallel world of Soviet political justice transformed the maxims of criminal law and procedure into their complete opposites. For instance, in the Soviet system of political justice the presumption of innocence was turned into presumption of guilt, the principle of no punishment without law was replaced with the doctrine of analogy and arbitrary recharacterization, the judicial duty of care was transformed into judicial prerogativism and the principle of the equality of arms was substituted with the accusatorial bias. Furthermore, in the Soviet system of political justice, conventional goals of criminal punishment were also distorted in favor of the ruling elites. Deterrence, restitution, retribution, education and rehabilitation were replaced with such goals of political justice as political retribution and monopolization of power, regime's self-rehabilitation and restitution of political status quo, legitimization of existing regime and deterrence of disobedience, political education and enforcement of regime's ideology.

The duality of the Soviet system of criminal justice was so instrumental in consolidating the communist regime in the USSR that it was also replicated after WW II in the Soviet satellite states in Eastern Europe. László Rajk's show trial in communist Hungary became a 'blueprint' for a range of Soviet-like show trials in Bulgaria, Poland, Czechoslovakia and East Germany. The main goal of these trials was to strengthen new feeble communist regimes and remove those local communist leaders, who like Yugoslav leader Josip Broz Tito, would not be satisfied with a status of a Soviet satellite. Most importantly, the show trials conducted by the communist states in Eastern Europe proved that the Soviet split into formal and politically motivated justice could be 'exported' to other totalitarian countries that formally had their own legal systems. The policy of destalinization introduced by Soviet leaders after Stalin's death in 1953 and the 1977 Constitution of 'developed Socialism' were only half-hearted measures that neither removed the duality of the Soviet legal system nor prevented new political trials against Soviet dissidents. The Soviet dissident movement exposed, in turn, the nominal character of the Soviet legislation subordinated to mostly unwritten political rules, which contributed to the ultimate collapse of the USSR in 1991.

Taking into account that the Soviet constitutions played only a nominal role, could the Soviet omnipotent system of political justice be called an unwritten constitution? To test this hypothesis, I have used Joseph Raz' description of what a constitution means in a 'thick sense' of the word. I believe that, according to Raz' criteria,

[435]The Soviet movie 'Kingdom of Crooked Mirrors' "is fairly explicit in its commentary, attacking a society's ability to manufacture a false reality, which here translates as American capitalism…The core idea [of the fairytale]…[is] a society enslaved by a self-manufactured false reality, carries a powerful message regardless of time or place." In the Kingdom of Crooked Mirrors Review (1963). https://www.thespinningimage.co.uk/cultfilms/displaycultfilm.asp?reviewid=3267. Accessed 24 December 2020.

Soviet practices of political justice could be in fact called a constitution. *First*, the mostly unwritten customary norms of political justice were indispensable for both the Soviet one-party political system and the system of socialist legality based on such quasi-legal concepts as the legal conscience, analogy and arbitrary recharacterization. *Second*, the analysis of show trials proves that the system of political justice was extremely stable throughout all stages of the Soviet history. *Third*, though norms of Soviet political justice were mostly unwritten, according to Raz, its customary law could still be an unwritten part of the constitution. *Fourth*, the Soviet constitutions and laws disregarded in show trials demonstrate that political justice had a supra-constitutional rank in the USSR. *Fifth*, norms of political justice were justiciable thanks to such Soviet court practices as the ex-parte communication, the judicial prerogativism, the accusatorial bias and the presumption of guilt. *Sixth*, given the mostly unwritten character of Soviet political justice and longevity of the communist regime in the Soviet Union (69 years), it was one of the most entrenched systems in the world. Finally, Soviet political justice expressed the common ideology of a new Soviet men or *Homo Sovieticus* created in the course of the communist social engineering experiment.

It is not a new idea that in some societies the reality is split into formal (ceremonial) part and the informal but actual state of things. The Soviet duality of justice is perhaps rooted in the Asian culture of formal and informal norms of behavior. A good example would be the ancient Japanese concepts of *Honne* (meaning person's true intentions and feelings) and *Tatemae*[436] (meaning opinions and actions displayed only in public).[437] For instance, the period between the two World Wars was marked for Japan with the outward compliance *(Tatemae)* with legal standards borrowed from Europe and the customary devotion *(Honne)* to godlike Emperors, which eventually led to the militarization of Japan. In a legal analysis of this phenomenon, Matthias Zachmann notes that, while the imperial army committed numerous atrocities during the Asia-Pacific War, "Japanese international lawyers tried to keep up the preten[s]es that Japan was still fighting by the book of humanitarian law, and became increasingly dissociated from reality."[438] The socialist legality is another example how law can be split into two coexisting legal orders.

The critical assessment of the Soviet system of criminal justice and show trials that took place under Communism effectively demonstrates that the USSR had a 'Twofold Constitution', which is rooted in traditional for Russia legal dualism of written positive law and unwritten common law. The first formal part of the constitution included written provisions that played only a nominal role necessary for the legitimization of the communist regime both at home and abroad. The second informal part consisted of mostly unwritten norms of political justice, which shaped the true legal and political structure conceived by Joseph Stalin. In the next chapter, I will argue that the Soviet 'Twofold Constitutionalism' was so entrenched that it has survived the collapse of the USSR and can be still exposed through trials conducted

[436] *Tatemae* literally means *façade* in Japanese.

[437] The Japan Times 2011.

[438] Zachmann 2014.

against politicians in selected former Soviet republics that are now sovereign states and have their own legal systems.

The next and concluding chapter also provides an analysis of two cases from each of the four jurisdictions within my research (Ukraine, Belarus, Germany and Austria). These case studies help determine whether 'political trials' in transitional former Soviet republics are qualitatively different from those in established democracies. The chapter further examines whether the Soviet legacy may be responsible for any potential differences between the Western and post-Soviet administration of justice. Furthermore, based on the case studies of trials from Western Europe and the former Soviet Union, I identify the role, which could be played by the Council of Europe and the European Court of Human Rights in preventing a relapse into politically motivated justice in post-Soviet states. This qualitative legal analysis of cases and trial proceedings is complemented with the secondary use of quantitative data such as official statistics of applications submitted to the European Court of Human Rights as well as international legal ratings. Most importantly, by using the relevant case law of the Strasburg Court, the final chapter offers a list of general legal criteria that can be applied to analyze future allegations about politically motivated justice.

References

Alexander L (2001) Constitutionalism: Philosophical Foundations, 1st edn. Cambridge University Press, Cambridge, UK/New York

Alexandrov V (1963) The Tukhachevsky Affair, 1st edn. MacDonald

Alliluyeva S (1969) Only One Year (translated by Chavchavadze P), 1st edn. Harper & Row Publishers

Applebaum A (2017) Red Famine: Stalin's War on Ukraine. Doubleday, New York

Argenbright R (2002) Marking NEP's Slippery Path: The Krasnoshchekov Show Trial. The Russian Review, 61(2), pp. 249–275

Balassa B (1960) Collectivization in Hungarian Agriculture. Journal of Farm Economics, 42(1), pp. 35–51. https://doi.org/10.2307/1235320

Barna I, Pető A (2015) Political Justice in Budapest after World War II. Central European University Press

Beckerman G (2011) When They Come for Us, We'll Be Gone: The Epic Struggle to Save Soviet Jewry, illustrated edn. Mariner Books, Boston, MA, US/Godalming, UK

Berman H (ed) (1966) Soviet Criminal Law and Procedure: The RSFSR Codes, 1st edn. (translation Spindler JW). Harvard University Press

Berman H (1972) Soviet Criminal Law and Procedure: The R.S.F.S.R. Codes, 2nd new edn. Harvard University Press, Cambridge, MA

Bloom S (1946) The "Withering Away" of the State. Journal of the History of Ideas, 7(1), pp. 113–121. https://doi.org/10.2307/2707273

Buranov I (1994) Lenin's will: falsified and forbidden. Prometheus Books, Amherst, NY

Butt S (2009) "Unlawfulness" and corruption under Indonesian law. Bulletin of Indonesian Economic Studies, 45(2), pp. 179–198. https://doi.org/10.1080/00074910903040328

Chirot D (1996) Modern Tyrants: The Power and Prevalence of Evil in Our Age. Princeton University Press

Christenson R (1999) Political Trials: Gordian Knots in the Law, revised, expanded, subsequent edn. Routledge, New Brunswick, NJ

Conquest R (1990) The Great Terror: A Reassessment. University of Alberta Press, Edmonton, Canada

Conquest R (2008) The Great Terror: A Reassessment, 1st edn. Pimlico, London

Davies S, Harris J (eds) (2005) Stalin: A New History. Cambridge University Press, Cambridge, UK/New York

Ebon M (1987) The Soviet Propaganda Machine, 1st edn. McGraw-Hill, New York

Edele M (2011) Stalinist Society: 1928–1953, illustrated edn. Oxford University Press, Oxford

Feuchtwanger L (1937) Moscow, 1937: My Visit Described for My Friends, 1st American edn. Viking Press. https://www.revolutionarydemocracy.org/archive/feucht.htm. Accessed 23 December 2020

Fletcher G (1968) The Presumption of Innocence in the Soviet Union. UCLA L. Rev., 15, p. 1203

Foglesong T, Solomon P (2001) National Institute of Justice (U.S.), Crime, Criminal Justice and Criminology in Post-Soviet Ukraine (U.S. Dept. of Justice, Office of Justice Programs, National Institute of Justice)

Forsythe D (2009) Encyclopedia of Human Rights, 1st edn. Oxford University Press, Oxford/New York

G L (1956) The Case of László Rajk. The World Today 12, no. 6 (June 1): 247–56

Gaidar Y (2012) Russia: A Long View, illustrated edn. (translation Bouis AW). The MIT Press, Cambridge, MA

Getty J (1987) Origins of the Great Purges: The Soviet Communist Party Reconsidered, 1933–1938. Cambridge University Press

Gorman R (2007) Great Events from History: The 20th Century 1901–1940, Vol.1, illustrated edn. Salem Press, Pasadena, CA

Hajdú T (1996) The party did everything for you: the interrogation of László Rajk, 7 June 1949. A transcript of the secret recording. The New Hungarian Quarterly, Vol. 37 (Spring): pp. 82–86

Harman M (2007) 1932: The Vichuga Uprising. https://libcom.org/history/1932-vichuga-uprising. Accessed 8 May 2018

Heilbrunn J (1991) The New York Times and the Moscow Show Trials. World Affairs, 153(3), pp. 87–101

Hendley K (2017) Everyday Law in Russia. Illustrated Edition. Cornell University Press, Ithaca/London

Hodos G (1987) Show Trials: Stalinist Purges in Eastern Europe, 1948–1954, 1st edn. Praeger, New York

Hook S (1984) Memories of the Moscow Trials. https://www.commentarymagazine.com/article/memories-of-the-moscow-trials/. Accessed 23 December 2020

Horvath R (2014) Breaking the Totalitarian Ice: The Initiative Group for the Defense of Human Rights in the USSR. Human Rights Quarterly, 36(1), pp. 147–175. https://doi.org/10.1353/hrq.2014.0013

Kalugin O (2008) Bor'ba KGB s emigratsiey, "golosami" i organizatsiya falshivok iz-za rubezha//KGB vchera, segodnia, zavtra. Moskva, 1994, S. 48. In: Shubin AV (ed) Dissidenty, neformaly i svoboda v SSSR. Veche, Moscow

Khlevniuk O (2008) Master of the House: Stalin and His Inner Circle, illustrated edn. (translation Favorov NS). Yale University Press, New Haven, CT

Khrushchev NS (1956) The Secret Speech—On the Cult of Personality. Modern History Sourcebook. https://sourcebooks.fordham.edu/mod/1956khrushchev-secret1.asp. Accessed 23 December 2020

Klajn L (2007) The Past in Present Times: The Yugoslav Saga. University Press of America, Lanham, MD

Koestler A (1994) Darkness at Noon. Rand McNally

Koltai F (1949) Laszlo Rajk and His Accomplices Before the People's Court, 1st edn. Budapest Printing Press

Kopacsi S (1981) Die ungarische Tragödie. Wie der Aufstand von 1956 liquidiert wurde. Frankfurt am Main

Kowalewski D (1980) Human Rights Protest in the USSR: Statistical Trends for 1965-78. Universal Human Rights, 2(1), pp. 5–29. https://doi.org/10.2307/761800

Kuromiya H (2003) Freedom and Terror in the Donbas: A Ukrainian-Russian Borderland, 1870s–1990s. Cambridge University Press, Cambridge, UK

Kuznetsova N, Tiazhkova I (2002) Kurs ugolovnogo prava. Obshaya chast. Tom 1: Uchenie o prestuplenii. Moscow

Levchuk N et al. (2020) Regional 1932–1933 Famine Losses: A Comparative Analysis of Ukraine and Russia, Nationalities Papers, 48(3), pp. 492–512. https://doi.org/10.1017/nps.2019.55

Liszt F, Schmidt E (1932) Franz Liszt: Lehrbuch des deutschen Strafrechts: Einleitung und Allgemeiner Teil. 26. völlig neubearb. Aufl. Reprint 2012. De Gruyter

Lustiger A, Brackman R (2003) Stalin and the Jews: The Red Book; The Tragedy of the Jewish Anti-Fascist Committee and the Soviet Jews. New York

Maksimova O (2014) Revolutionary legal consciousness as source of the soviet law and lawmaking. Associate Professor Moscow University for the Humanities, available in Russian at https://www.gramota.net/materials/3/2014/9-2/21.html. Accessed 16 May 2020

Markovits I (1989) Playing the Opposites Game: On Mirjan Damaška's "The Faces of Justice and State Authority". Stanford Law Review (Damaška MR (ed), 41(5), pp. 1313–1341. https://doi.org/10.2307/1228756

Markovits I (2006) Transitions to Constitutional Democracies: The German Democratic Republic. The ANNALS of the American Academy of Political and Social Science, 603(1), pp. 140–154. https://doi.org/10.1177/0002716205282408

McLoughlin B, McDermott K (eds) (2003) Stalin's Terror: High Politics and Mass Repression in the Soviet Union. 2003 edn. Houndmills, Basingstoke, Hampshire, UK/Palgrave Macmillan, New York

Medushevsky A (2006) Russian Constitutionalism: Historical and Contemporary Development. Routledge, New York

Medushevsky A (2011) Stalinizm kak model. Obozreniye izdatelskogo proekta ROSSPEN. Istoriya stalinizma, *Vestnik Evropy*, no. 30. https://magazines.gorky.media/vestnik/2011/30/stalinizm-kak-model-obozrenie-izdatelskogo-proekta-rosspen-istoriya-stalinizma.html. Accessed 24 December 2020

Millar J (1992) Cracks in the Monolith: Party Power in the Brezhnev Era, 1st edn. Routledge, Armonk, NY

Mishina E (2013) Sacrificial Offering À La Homo Sovieticus. Institute of Modern Russia. https://imrussia.org/en/rule-of-law/378-sacrificial-offering-a-la-homo-sovieticus. Accessed 22 December 2020

Nathans B (2011) Uncertainty and Anxiety: On Khrushchev's Thaw. The Nation. https://www.thenation.com/article/uncertainty-and-anxiety-khrushchevs-thaw/. Accessed 24 December 2020

Orwell G (1961) 1984. Signet Classic, New York, NY

Osakwe C (1979) The Theories and Realities of Modern Soviet Constitutional Law: An Analysis of the 1977 USSR Constitution. University of Pennsylvania Law Review, 127(5), pp. 1350–1437. https://doi.org/10.2307/3311636

Osakwe C (1985) Prerogativism in Modern Soviet Law: Criminal Procedure. Columbia Journal of Transnational Law 23

Osokina E (2002) Economic disobedience under Stalin. In: Viola L (ed) Contending with Stalinism: Soviet Power and Popular Resistance in the 1930s. Cornell University Press, Ithaca

Persak N (2007) Criminalising Harmful Conduct. 2007. Edition. Springer, New York, NY

Přibáň J (2002) Dissidents of Law: On the 1989 Velvet Revolutions, Legitimations, Fictions of Legality and Contemporary Version of the Social Contract, 1st edn. Ashgate Publ Ltd, Aldershot, Hampshire, UK/Burlington, VT

Quigley J (1989) The Soviet Conception of the Presumption of Innocence. Santa Clara Law Review, 29(2), p. 301

Rayfield D (2004) Stalin and His Hangmen: The Tyrant and Those Who Killed for Him, reprint edn. Random House Trade Paperbacks, New York

Raz J (2009) Between Authority and Interpretation: On the Theory of Law and Practical Reason, 1st edn. OUP Oxford

Rebitschek I (2015) Vortrag zum Panel: "Building Socialist Legality: the Judiciary in the Postwar Soviet Union". In: Rahmen des Jahreskongresses der "Association for Slavic, East European, & Eurasian Studies" (ASEEES) in Philadelphia (PA)

Redlich S (1982) Propaganda and Nationalism in Wartime Russia: The Jewish Anti-Fascist Committee in the U.S.S.R. 1941–1948, 1st edn. East European Monographs, Boulder, CO

Rosenbaum K (1962) The German Involvement in the Shakhty Trial. The Russian Review, 21(3), pp. 238–260. https://doi.org/10.2307/126716

Rosenfeldt N (2009) The 'Special' World: Stalin's Power Apparatus and the Soviet System's Secret Structures of Communication. Museum Tusculanum Press, Copenhagen

Rubenstein J (1980) Soviet dissidents: Their struggle for human rights, 1st edn. Beacon Press, Boston, MA

Rubenstein J, Naumov V (eds) (2005) Stalin's Secret Pogrom: The Postwar Inquisition of the Jewish Anti-Fascist Committee, abridged edn. (translation Wolfson LE, Wilson L). Yale University Press, New Haven, CT

Sadurski W (2012) Constitutionalism and the Enlargement of Europe, 1st edn. Oxford University Press, Oxford, UK

Sajó A (2001) Socialist Law. In; Smelser N J, Baltes P B (eds) International Encyclopedia of the Social & Behavioral Sciences. Pergamon, Oxford, pp. 14493–14496. https://doi.org/10.1016/B0-08-043076-7/02776-5

Sakmyster T (2011) Mátyás Rákosi, the Rajk Trial, and the American Communist Party. Hungarian Studies Review; Spring, Vol. 38, Issue 1/2 (Fall): p 45–68, 24p

Sakwa R (2012) Soviet Politics: In Perspective, 2nd edn. Routledge

Sean's Russia Blog (2009) The Kirov Law at 75. https://seansrussiablog.org/2009/12/02/the-kirov-law-at-75/. Accessed 22 December 2020.

Serio J, Razinkin V (1995) Thieves Professing the Code: The Traditional Role of Vory v Zakone in Russia's Criminal World and Adaptions to a New Social Reality. July/August 1995. Vol. 5, Issue. 4. https://archive.is/7IYuP. Accessed 22 December 2020

Service R (2005) Stalin: A Biography. Annotated edition. Harvard University Press, Cambridge, MA

Shizhou W (2010) Rethinking the Purpose of Criminal Punishment. Peking University Journal of Legal Studies 2: 82

Shubin A (2008) Dissidenty, neformaly i svoboda v SSSR. Veche, Moscow

Solomon P (1978) Soviet Criminologists and Criminal Policy: Specialists in Policy-Making. Macmillan, London

Solomon P (1996) Soviet Criminal Justice Under Stalin. Cambridge University Press, Cambridge, UK/New York

Solomon P (2015) Post-Soviet criminal justice: The persistence of distorted neo-inquisitorialism. Theoretical Criminology, 19(2), pp. 159–178. https://doi.org/10.1177/1362480614568746

Spencer I (2000) Lessons from history: the politics of psychiatry in the USSR. Journal of Psychiatric and Mental Health Nursing, 7(4), pp. 355–361. https://doi.org/10.1046/j.1365-2850.2000.00297.x

Szasz B (1971) Volunteers for the Gallows: Anatomy of a Show Trial, 1st edn. Chatto & Windus, London

The Japan Times (2011) The Costly Fallout of Tatemae and Japan's Culture of Deceit. https://www.japantimes.co.jp/community/2011/11/01/issues/the-costly-fallout-of-tatemae-and-japans-culture-of-deceit/. Accessed 24 December 2020

Time Magazine (1978a) Soviet Justice: Still on Trial. When politics enters in, legality goes out the window, 7/31/1978, Vol. 112 Issue 5, p. 46, 1 p. https://content.time.com/time/magazine/0,9263,7601780724,00.html. Accessed 24 December 2020

Time Magazine (1978b) The Shcharansky Trial, July 24, 1978, Vol. 112, No. 4. https://content.time.com/time/magazine/0,9263,7601780724,00.html. Accessed 24 December 2020

Urban G (1982) Stalinism: Impact on Russia and the World, 1st edn. Ashgate Publishing Group, London

Vaksberg A (1990) The prosecutor and the prey: Vyshinsky and the 1930s Moscow show trials, 1st edn. Weidenfeld and Nicolson, London

Viola L (ed) (2002) Contending with Stalinism: Soviet Power and Popular Resistance in the 1930s. Cornell University Press, Ithaca

Viola L (2017) Stalinist Perpetrators on Trial: Scenes from the Great Terror in Soviet Ukraine, illustrated edn. Oxford University Press, New York, NY

Waldron J (2009) Constitutionalism—A Skeptical View. Contemporary Debates in Political Philosophy. John Wiley & Sons, Ltd, pp. 265–282. https://doi.org/10.1002/9781444310399.ch15

Ward C (1993) Stalin's Russia. Edward Arnold

Wood E (2005) Performing Justice: Agitation Trials in Early Soviet Russia, illustrated edn. Cornell University Press, Ithaca, NY

Zachmann UM (2014) Does Europe Include Japan? European Normativity in Japanese Attitudes towards International Law, 1854–1945, Rechtsgeschichte Legal History. Journal of the Max Planck Institute for European Legal History, no. 22: 228–43. https://www.zeitschrift-rechtsgeschichte.de/en/article_id/940. Accessed 24 December 2020

Zviagintsev A, Orlov I (1994) Oko gosudarevo: Rossiiskie prokurory XVIII vek. ROSSPEN, Moscow

Zviagintsev A, Orlov I (1996) Pod seniu russkogo orla: rossiiskie prokurory: vtoraia polovina XIX-nachalo XX v. ROSSPEN, Moscow

Zviagintsev A, Orlov I (1997) Prizvannye otechestvom: rossiiskie prokurory: 1722–1917. ROSSPEN, Moscow

Zviagintsev A, Orlov I (2001) Prigovorennye vremenem: rossiiskie i sovetskie prokurory: XX vek, 1937-1953. ROSSPEN, Moscow

Zweigert K, Kotz H, Weir T (1987) An Introduction to Comparative Law: Volume I: The Framework, 2nd edn. Oxford University Press, Oxford

Chapter 3
Authoritarian Legacy of Twofold Constitutionalism and Its Informal Practices of Politicized Justice in the Former Soviet Republics

Contents

Abstract This chapter seeks to determine what roles totalitarian legacies and their informal practices of politicized justice played in shaping post-communist constitutional developments in the former Soviet republics. In order to illustrate the impact and functions of the communist authoritarian practices in the former Soviet Union, the chapter proceeds with an analysis of the main differences between trials related to politics (political trials) in Western democracies and in transitional former Soviet republics. I provide a concise overview of each trial by conducting a comparative legal analysis of cases selected from Ukraine, Belarus, Germany and Austria. The concluding section compares roles traditionally played by political trials in established democracies with the roles played by such trials in post-Soviet societies that inherited practices of politicized justice from their communist past. Finally, it offers a list of legal criteria to evaluate future allegations about politically motivated justice.

Keywords Post-Soviet constitutionalism · Former Soviet Republics · Established democracies · Totalitarian legacies · Authoritarian practice · Criteria to assess politicized justice · European Court of Human Rights · United Nations Human Rights Council

© T.M.C. ASSER PRESS and the author 2021
A. Galushko, *Politically Motivated Justice*,
https://doi.org/10.1007/978-94-6265-459-4_3

3.1 Introduction

The goal of this chapter is to develop prima facie legal criteria that can be used to assess future allegations about politically motivated justice in transitional former Soviet republics. In order to achieve this goal, the chapter includes the following two categories of legal analysis. *First*, it provides description of facts, procedural history and reasoning behind judgments in selected cases as well as their legal analysis in the framework of the relevant case law by the European Court of Human Rights. The case study includes analysis of cases from the two Western European countries (*Germany* and *Austria*) and the two former Soviet Republics (*Ukraine* and *Belarus*). I analyze cases from Belarus using the legal approach of the European Court of Human Rights as if the country joined the European Convention on Human Rights to find out whether the Council of Europe and the Court could play a significant role in preventing a relapse into politically motivated justice in transitional post-Soviet states. *Second*, the chapter compares the situation with the Rule of Law, fundamental rights and democratic institutions in the selected countries as well as discusses the importance of these institutions for assessing the phenomenon of politicized justice. This analysis tests my hypothesis that, as opposed to Western European democracies, trials against politicians in transitional former Soviet republics often reveal an unwritten Constitution of Soviet extra-judicial conventionalities, judicial and prosecutorial practices that hinder the successful post-communist transition.

The chapter proceeds by describing material facts and legal proceedings in cases chosen in the two Western democracies and the two former Soviet republics. In particular, the cases of *Susanne Winter*, a far-right member of the Parliament for the Freedom Party of Austria (FPÖ), and *Ernst Strasser* of the People's Party (ÖVP), the former Interior Minister of Austria, were chosen to analyze criminal proceedings against politicians in Austria. The cases of *Christian Wulff*, a member of the ruling Christian Democratic Union (CDU), and the latest case of the National Democratic Party (NPD) prohibition under *Article 21(2)* of the German Constitution are examined to illustrate the enforcement of the due process guarantees in political cases in Germany. The landmark decisions by the European Court of Human Rights (ECtHR) in the cases of the former Ukrainian Prime Minister *Yulia Tymoshenko* and the former Interior Minister *Yuriy Lutsenko* are used to show a politically motivated character of criminal proceedings against former opposition politicians in Ukraine. The cases of *Mikalai Statkevitch*, the Belarus opposition leader and the former presidential candidate, as well as the case of the former presidential candidate *Andrei Sannikov* further demonstrate the continuity of Soviet unwritten practices of politicized show trials even after the collapse of the Soviet Union. The comparison of these political cases eventually reveals the communist legacy of an unwritten constitution in the former Soviet republics as opposed to a constitutional dialogue and reconciliation in political cases in Western democracies.

3.2 Germany

3.2.1 The Trial of the Former German President Christian Wulff

The trial of Christian Wulff was an extraordinary event in the modern history of Germany. Never before in the history of post-war Germany such a high-ranking public official as a head of state faced criminal charges and stood before a trial. In the past, only Admiral Karl Doenitz was charged and sentenced as Hitler's successor and the head of state by the Nuremburg tribunal in 1946. Wulff's trial was remarkable due to several reasons. First, the ex-president was suspected of corruption in a politicized case, whose "trifling charges had been trumped up in a conspiracy to tarnish his name".[1] The former president was charged with corruption because he accepted around 700 euros from his friend and film producer David Groenwold, who covered Wulff's family hotel and accommodation expenses during the Oktoberfest in Munich in 2008. In return, Wulff, who was then the regional governor in Lower Saxony, allegedly lobbied for Groenwold's film project by writing a personal letter to the head of 'Siemens' requesting financial support for the project.[2] Shortly after Christian Wulff was elected into the office of the President of Germany in 2010, Wulff and Groenwold faced corruption charges. In particular, the ex-president was charged by the prosecutors of Lower Saxony of "accepting favours while in office[,] which carries a maximum penalty of three years' jail and a fine under German law."[3] Although later prosecutors lowered the charges against Wulff and Groenwold, both of them refused to settle down with the prosecution and pay a fine of 27,000 euros.[4] The ex-president and the film producer wanted to clear their names that, in their opinion, were damaged by media reports.

The second reason why Christian Wulff's trial stood among other similar trials in Germany was that the trial caused a powerful media campaign and public debate that led to Wulff's ultimate resignation. When the prosecutor's office decided to open a criminal case against Mr. Wulff, the media discovered that the former president took a low-interest private loan of 500,000 euros "from the wife of businessman Egon Gerkeens in 2008."[5] Christian Wulff learned that the popular German newspaper Bild was going to publish this story when he was on a foreign trip as the President of Germany. During the trip, the former president has allegedly threatened the management of the Bild when he "left multiple voice-mails for Bild editor Kai Diekmann, saying he would start a "war" if the loan article ran, according to the Süddeutsche Zeitung newspaper."[6] Furthermore, although Christian Wulff later

[1] Deutsche Welle 2014a.

[2] The Irish Times 2013.

[3] Ibid.

[4] Smale 2013.

[5] Tovrov 2012.

[6] Ibid.

apologized to the Bild, die Welt am Sonntag newspaper agued in 2012 that Wulff also "threatened…[this] newspaper with 'unpleasant and public consequences' if an article on Wulff's family and childhood were printed in a June edition."[7] The public criticism caused by these media reports as well as the prosecutor's request to the German parliament to lift Christian Wulff's immunity led to Wulff eventual resignation on 17 February 2012, which had a significant impact on the political life of Germany.

The third and ultimate reason for the outstanding character of Wulff's trial was the political dimension of this trial. At the time when Christian Wulff was nominated to the post of the president, he was a member of the governing Christian Democratic Union (CDU), "a rising star in the CDU and a popular regional leader who was even tipped to succeed Mrs. [Angela] Merkel."[8] The political significance of the case was so large that even Chancellor Merkel had to react to the prosecutor's investigation against Wulff in 2011 by "saying at a press conference in December that 'the president is doing a great job. He has my full support.'"[9] This public support by the Chancellor did not prevent negative political consequences for her party as "[t]he scandal damaged Merkel's Christian Democrats (CDU) and contributed to her party's defeat in the Lower Saxony regional election in January."[10] Besides its impact on national politics, the scandal could have damaged Merkel's international reputation. According to Frank Überall, political analyst from Cologne's University of Applied Sciences HMKW, "[w]hile Germany is lecturing other Europeans on how to run an effective and trustworthy administration, the president she basically chose falls over corruption allegations."[11] After Wulff's resignation, his trial was closely followed by the media and generated useful public debate about corruption in Germany. The political and public controversies around Wulff's trial were reinforced by his resolution to prove his innocence in court, where he "delivered a 50-min statement in which he criticized state prosecutors for a case he called a farce."[12] Two years of legal proceedings in the case and Wulff's subsequent acquittal became an example of a 'political case' resolved through judicial means in Germany.

After a trial, which lasted one year, the state court in Hannover acquitted the former president Wulff of all charges. The presiding judge Frank Rosenow has not found enough evidence, which could prove corruption charges against Christian Wulff and his friend David Groenwold. Instead, the court in Hannover "viewed the relationship between the former president and the film producer as a friendship that included picking up the tabs for each other at different times, and not as a case of official corruption."[13] Furthermore, the court also awarded Wulff "damages

[7] Tovrov 2012.

[8] The Irish Times 2013.

[9] Tovrov 2012.

[10] The Irish Times 2013.

[11] Steininger 2012.

[12] The Irish Times 2013.

[13] Eddy 2014.

for 'losses suffered' during police raid on his home."[14] As the former president of Germany Wulff, therefore, will be entitled to use a government office and receive an annual pension. While the ex-president was satisfied with the ruling, "Wulff's critics claim the trial was necessary to take him to court to prove that no German public official stands above the law."[15] Despite Wulff's acquittal, his resignation and trial show the level of scrutiny accorded to political cases in Germany.

3.2.2 Latest Proceedings to Ban the National Democratic Party (NPD) in 2017

There were two attempts before the German Constitutional Court to ban the ultra-right National Democratic Party (NPD). The first one failed on procedural grounds at the stage of preliminary examination of the case in 2003 when the Federal Constitutional Court "discovered that several of NPD leaders were in fact undercover agents or informers of the German Secret Service."[16] The first application failed on procedural grounds, because "[o]nly three of the seven judges [of the Constitutional Court] voted to reject the government's case [against the NPD], but the court would have needed a two-thirds majority to have continued."[17] German Bundesrat, the upper chamber of the German Parliament, has made the second attempt to ban the NPD in 2017 by submitting an application to the Constitutional Court under *Article 21, Section 2* of the Basic Law (*Grundgesetz*—GG). According to Section 2 of Article 21, "Parties that, by reason of their aims or the behaviour of their adherents, seek to undermine or abolish the free democratic basic order or to endanger the existence of the Federal Republic of Germany shall be unconstitutional."[18] The same provision gives the Federal Constitutional Court the power to ban a political party by declaring it unconstitutional. The second time, as opposed to the previous attempt, the Constitutional Court has found the Bundesrat's application against the NPD admissible on procedural grounds.

The Constitutional Court reasoned that the application was admissible this time, because the German Government and the upper chamber of the Parliament "convincingly demonstrated to the Court that all police informants at the executive levels of the NPD had been already deactivated [Staatsfreiheit], at the latest, at the point in time at which the intention to file an application to prohibit the NPD had to be announced, and that there had been no follow-up aimed at obtaining information."[19]

---

[14] Deutsche Welle 2014b.

[15] Ibid.

[16] Bligh 2014.

[17] CNN 2003.

[18] See the Constitution of Germany, das Grundgesetz, available at https://www.gesetze-im-internet.de/englisch_gg/englisch_gg.html#p0120. Accessed 26 December 2020.

[19] German Constitutional Court, application to establish the unconstitutionality of the National Democratic Party of Germany (NPD) and to dissolve it, Judgement pursuant to Article 21(2) of the

Furthermore, the court has also found that the application will not infringe the principle of the fair trial given that "there have been sufficient precautions to ensure that information obtained incidentally through the observation of the NPD is not used to the party's detriment."[20] In other words, all the previous reasons that were used by the Court to dismiss the previous application against the NPD were not applicable to the new application. All government informants and agents have been removed in advance from their senior positions in the NPD to make sure that the government itself would not be blamed for influencing decision-making processes in the NPD. Furthermore, the absence of government's informers and agents could guarantee the right to a fair trial for the NDP before the Constitutional Court, as the government would not be able to use the surveillance data to undermine the NPD's position in court.

Although the Federal Constitutional Court confirmed procedural admissibility of the second complaint against the NPD, the Court later dismissed it on substantive grounds. The Court took several steps to reach this decision by elaborating on the requirements set in the Section 2 of Article 21 mentioned above. *First*, judges of the Constitutional Court analyzed political aims of the NPD. The Court elaborated that aims of a political party could be "determined chiefly through party manifestos and speeches, works of its influential authors, as well as party publications (BVerfGE 5, 85 at [259])[21] After analyzing the NPD's manifestos, speeches and publications, the Court has found that the NPD indeed pursued anti-Constitutional aims. In particular, anti-Semitic statements by the NPD's leadership as well as political concepts of ethnically-based Volksgemeinschaft (people's community) outlined in NPD publications contradict basic constitutional principles of human dignity and democracy [(BVerfGE 5, 85 at [634])."[22] Thus, the NPD has satisfied the first criteria of having unconstitutional aims of its activities under the Section 2 of Article 21.

The Court has also scrutinized the second criteria related to the behavior of NPD party adherents, "which encompasses party members, supporters, and adherents (BVerfGE 2, 1 at [55]; BVerfGE 5, 85 at [259])."[23] The Court elaborated in this regard that ""[a]dherents" are all persons who support a party's cause and profess their commitment to the party even if they are not members of the party…With regard to statements and acts of rank and file members or of adherents who do not belong to the party, it is decisive whether their behaviour recognisably expresses the party's political will…[which] is generally the case if the behaviour reflects a fundamental

Basic Law (*Grundgesetz*—GG), Article 93(1) no. 5 GG, § 13 no. 2 and §§ 43 et seq. of the Federal Constitutional Court Act, 17 January 2017, Case No. 2 BvB 1/13 (*NPD 2017*). Press Release No. 4/2017 of 17 January 2017, 2 BvB 1/13. https://www.bundesverfassungsgericht.de/SharedDocs/Pressemitteilungen/EN/2017/bvg17-004.html. Accessed 26 December 2020.

[20]Ibid.

[21]Theil 2017.

[22]Theil 2017.

[23]Ibid.

tendency existing in the party, or if the party has expressly adopted such behaviour."[24] Judges of the Constitutional Court observed, however, that "[t]he fact that the NPD, by intimidating or criminal behaviour of members or adherents is [indeed] able to occasionally raise understandable concerns for the freedom of the political process or even fear of violent attacks is undeniable, but it does not reach the threshold determined by Article 21 Section 2 GG."[25] Thus, the behavior of NPD adherents was not enough for the Court to conclude that the behavior of NPD adherents reached the threshold of undermining the free democratic basic order.

The Court has also scrutinized whether the NPR met the third criteria of seeking to undermine or abolish the free democratic order in Germany. In this regard, the Court elaborated on the concepts of seeking to undermine or abolish the basic order.[26] In particular, on the one hand, the Court noted that the criteria of 'abolishing' (beseitigen) is met when activities of a political party abolish "at least one of the constituent elements of the free democratic basic order or…replace…[s] this order with another constitutional order with another constitutional order or another system of government."[27] On the other hand, "[t]he criterion 'undermining' (beeinträchtigen) can be assumed to be met once a party, according to its political concept, noticeably threatens one of the constituent elements of the free democratic basic order."[28] At the same time, the concept that "the party seeks (darauf ausgehen) to undermine or abolish the free democratic basic order…[means that] the party must go beyond its commitment to its anti-constitutional aims in that it exceeds the threshold of actually combatting the free democratic basic order."[29] Furthermore, "there must be specific and weighty indicators that at least make it appear possible that…[such] party's activities will be successful (potentially)."[30] The Court, however, could not help but conclude that the NPD is not capable of achieving its anti-constitutional aims. To support this conclusion, the Court referred to the NPD's "dwindling membership numbers, precarious financial situation, and the NPD's (lack of) electoral success."[31] Therefore, the Court found that the NPD did not meet the criteria of seeking to undermine or abolish the basic order in the meaning of Section 2, Article 21.

Some observers considered the Court's reasoning mentioned above as a departure from the previous case law. In the past, the Court prohibited only two parties.

[24]*NPD 2017*, above no 19. Press Release No. 4/2017 of 17 January 2017, 2 BvB 1/13. https://www.bundesverfassungsgericht.de/SharedDocs/Pressemitteilungen/EN/2017/bvg17-004.html. Accessed 26 December 2020.

[25]Ibid.

[26]See Article 21 (Political Parties), Basic Law of the Federal Republic of Germany (das Grundgesetz), available in English: https://www.gesetze-im-internet.de/englisch_gg/. Accessed 26 December 2020.

[27]*NPD 2017*, above no 19. Press Release No. 4/2017 of 17 January 2017, 2 BvB 1/13. https://www.bundesverfassungsgericht.de/SharedDocs/Pressemitteilungen/EN/2017/bvg17-004.html. Accessed 26 December 2020.

[28]Ibid.

[29]Ibid.

[30]Ibid.

[31]Theil 2017.

The Court banned in 1951 the Socialist Reich Party of Germany (*Sozialistische Reichspartei Deutschlands, SRD*), which followed the ideology of the National Socialism. Although the Communist party of Germany (*Kommunistische Partei Deutschlands, KPD*) was a victim of the Nazi regime, it was banned by the Court in 1956 due to the communist ideology of the 'dictatorship of the proletariat', which could have endangered the existence of the Federal Republic. In line with its KPD judgment, the Court ruled that the prohibition of a political party under the criterion of seeking to abolish the free democratic basic order "does not require…that the party's acts result in a specific danger to the legal interests protected by Article 21 Section 2 sentence 1 GG."[32] However, it appears that the Court departed from its reasoning in the KPD case, when it ruled in the NPD case that there must be "specific and weighty indications suggesting that the…[party] exceeds the boundaries of admissible political struggle of opinions in a manner that would satisfy the criterion of 'seeking'."[33] For the Federal Constitutional Court (FCC) such specific indications may include "violence or criminal acts, which the FCC held would always suffice to meet the criterion of 'seek to', or if the party actions are capable of undermining free and equal participation in the political process, even if only at a regional level (at [588])."[34] Although the KPD and NPD cases did not show any specific and weighty indications suggesting that both parties could actually attain their unconstitutional aims in practice, the Court banned only the KPD, while, in the Court's opinion, the NPD's activities did not meet the criterion of 'seeking' to be prohibited under the Article 21, Section 2.

Although the application to ban the NPD failed in the Federal Constitutional Court, it generated a useful constitutional dialogue among representatives of media legal community, parties to this case and the public. For instance, NPD representatives have requested the Constitutional Court to make a declaration that the NPD is not unconstitutional in its application against both chambers of the German Parliament (Bundestag and Bundesrat) and the Federal Government of Germany. To substantiate its request, the NPD argued that "the effect of the current [public] debate [on a ban (*Verbotsdebatte*)] about a prohibition of the party…and other measures directed against it have the same effect as a ban[, because]…it is too much for a party which is branded as unconstitutional to seek legal protection in every individual case."[35] In other words, the NPD argued that the government's continuous constitutional complaints against it and the debate about its possible prohibition have damaged the NPD's reputation and rights as a political party guaranteed under the Basic Law. The Federal Constitutional Court has refused to make a declaration that the NPD is not

---

[32] *NPD 2017*, above no 19. Press Release No. 4/2017 of 17 January 2017, 2 BvB 1/13. https://www.bundesverfassungsgericht.de/SharedDocs/Pressemitteilungen/EN/2017/bvg17-004.html. Accessed 26 December 2020.

[33] Ibid.

[34] Theil 2017.

[35] German Constitutional Court, Resolution, Application made by the NPD against Bundestag, Bundesrat and Federal Government Unsuccessful, Press Release No. 15/2013 of 5 March 2013, Order of 20 February 2013, 2 BvE 11/12. https://www.bundesverfassungsgericht.de/SharedDocs/Pressemitteilungen/DE/2013/bvg13-015.html. Accessed 26 December 2020.

unconstitutional. Though the Court admitted that the NPD could bring a complaint against other public bodies, the Court proclaimed the application inadmissible due to the reasoning provided by the NPD.

With regard to the NPD's request to declare that it is not unconstitutional, the Court found that "the Federal Constitutional Court's Act does not provide a party with the option to invoke the Federal Constitutional Court's jurisdiction for a declaration of its constitutionality."[36] In other words, political parties can operate as long as they are not declared unconstitutional by the Court and, thus, they do not require a separate 'declaration' of their constitutionality to exercise their rights guaranteed in the Basic Law. In relation to the NPD's claim that the attempts to prohibit it had the same effect as a ban, the Court emphasized the importance of the public debate on such constitutional matters. In particular, the Court reasoned that political parties are expected to participate in the public debate and "[s]tatements on the assessment of a political party as unconstitutional are part of the public dispute…and the party affected can, and must, counter such statements with the means available to it in the struggle of opinions."[37] At the same time the Court acknowledged that such a constitutional dialogue or public debate should be kept within the limits set in the Constitution in the sense that rights of a political party "under Article 21 Section 1 of the Basic Law (Grundgesetz—GG)…[can be] violated if the objective of such a debate [about the party ban] is not to decide this question but to discriminate against the party affected."[38] Therefore, in its decision to dismiss the NPD's complaint the Court emphasized that the NPD had an opportunity to protect its constitutional rights as a political party by presenting its legal defense before the Court, which generated useful constitutional dialogue and public debate related to the NPD's unconstitutionality.

3.3 Austria

3.3.1 The Case of Susanne Winter

Susanne Winter is a member of the Austrian Parliament for the Austrian Freedom Party (FPÖ). In January 2008, Susanne Winter made anti-Islamic comments, as a result of which the prosecutor's office charged her with inciting hate speech, humiliating a religion. In particular, Winter claimed that "In today's [legal] system" the [Islamic] Prophet Muhammad would be considered a 'child molester,' apparently referring to his marriage to a six-year-old child…[and] that it is time for Islam to be

[36]Ibid.

[37]German Constitutional Court, Resolution, Application made by the NPD against Bundestag, Bundesrat and Federal Government Unsuccessful, Press Release No. 15/2013 of 5 March 2013, Order of 20 February 2013, 2 BvE 11/12. https://www.bundesverfassungsgericht.de/SharedDocs/Pressemitteilungen/DE/2013/bvg13-015.html. Accessed 26 December 2020.

[38]Ibid.

'thrown back where it came from, behind the Mediterranean.'"[39] During a discussion with students Winter suggested "that Muslim men should commit bestiality rather than make 'indecent advances' on girls."[40] Furthermore, she speculated that "Austria faces an 'Islamic immigration tsunami'."[41] During the trial, Susanne Winter denied all the charges and pleaded not guilty, "claiming that she 'did not want to insult anyone, but only to point out problems.'"[42] Winter's trial attracted significant media attention and generated a lot of public discussion about standards of political discourse and individual responsibility of politicians for their statements. Arguments used by the parties demonstrated what acceptable standards of political debate must be used by politicians not to infringe rights and freedoms guaranteed by law.

Bernhard Lehofer, Susanne Winter's lawyer, argued in her defense that "[s]he had no intention of preaching hatred…[and] that [her] statements had been taken out of context."[43] Winter further defended herself by arguing that "the simplification of the political message is just good advertising sense…[and] Islam in small doses would be good for Austria, but the size, the excess, that's what she meant by [immigration] tsunami."[44] While Susanne Winter's defense claimed that her statements were entirely permissible under the freedom of speech,[45] the prosecution argued that Winter's case deserves rigorous judicial scrutiny, as it could potentially set a precedent for similar cases in the future. In particular, the state prosecutor Wolfgang Redtenbacher called on the court's responsibility "…to set limits, [because] the background to this case extends far beyond…Vienna."[46] In response to Winter's argument that her behavior is protected by freedom of speech, the prosecution stated "that right is limited by other right".[47] Furthermore, the prosecution insisted that Susanne Winter's public statements went beyond the limits acceptable under the freedom of political speech due to the improper purpose and methods of such statements.[48] In particular, the prosecutor's office concluded that Winter's statements "had only one aim: to get votes, a quite low and nasty method used by Winter and her party to appeal to xenophobic sentiments".[49] Both Susanne Winter's defense and the prosecution had equal opportunity to present evidence and arguments before the court. At the same time, Winter retained her MP status and could continue her work as a politician during the entire trial.

---

[39] The Local 2015.

[40] American Renaissance 2009.

[41] Kern 2011.

[42] American Renaissance 2009.

[43] Gates of Vienna 2009.

[44] Ibid.

[45] Article 13 of the Basic State Law on the General Rights of Citizens. https://ecommons.cornell.edu/bitstream/handle/1813/1443/Austr_Const_1867.pdf?sequence=1&isAllowed=y. Accessed 26 December 2020.

[46] Gates of Vienna 2009.

[47] Gates of Vienna 2009.

[48] The Local 2015.

[49] Gates of Vienna 2009.

The trial court found Susanne Winter guilty of inciting hate speech and insulting religion, as a result of which she was sentenced to a suspended three-month imprisonment and to pay a fine in the amount of 24,000 Euros. Although Susanne Winter has not lost her position in the Parliament over a suspended prison sentence in 2009, "[n]umerous other politicians have called for her resignation."[50] The Austrian Freedom Party (FPÖ) has finally expelled Winter from the party in 2015 when she made anti-Semitic statements in response to a blog post "in reference to an article in which Hungary's Prime Minister Viktor Orban had criticized Jewish financier George Soros for meddling in the politics of the central European country."[51] Therefore, Susanne Winter's trial and the subsequent public debate delineated acceptable limits of political discourse in the Austrian society by demonstrating political as well as legal liability of politicians' for inciting hate speech. Although the court and the public condemned Winter's xenophobic statements, she retained her position in the parliament and was not entirely removed from politics due to her statements.

3.3.2 The Case of Ernst Strasser

Ernst Strasser is the former Minister of Interior (2000–2004) and the former member of the European Parliament from the conservative Austrian People's Party (ÖVP). In March 2011, two British reporters of the Sunday Times newspaper, who pretended to be lobbyists, revealed that Strasser and other MPs[52] were ready to take a bribe in exchange for changing EU legislation. In particular, journalists asked Strasser to amend the EU legislation "on handling electronic scrap and on regulating investments."[53] According to the journalists, Strasser initiated requested from him legislative changes regarding the latter area of legislation and speculated in the video publicized by media that "most MEPs are as lazy as I am and boasted of having five other such customers who pay him on the side."[54] Furthermore, Ernst Strasser justified his work in a video secretly made by journalists by saying "[o]f course I am a lobbyist…This is a wonderful opportunity to learn all the people, to have my own network, and to use this network for my, for my companies. It is a very good combination."[55] The Prosecutor's Office of Vienna has initiated against Strasser a criminal case on charges of corruption. Alexandra Maruna, who represented the Prosecutor's Office, argued that, although he did not actually receive the money from the fake lobbyists, "Strasser claimed € 100,000 a year for …[his] services…[and] offered his vote for money."[56] Arguments presented by the trial parties and the ensuing public debate

---

[50] The Local 2015.

[51] Ibid.

[52] Adrian Severin from Romania, Zoran Thaler from Slovenia and Pablo Zalba from Spain.

[53] Shields 2013.

[54] Pop 2012.

[55] Shields 2013.

[56] Pop 2012.

revealed what conduct of politicians is deemed as unacceptable both in terms of ethics and law in the Austrian society.

Ernst Strasser's lawyer tried to argue during the trial proceedings that it is usual for politicians to be engaged in "what 'thousands of people do daily in Austria, Brussels and worldwide: making contacts and offering to use them'."[57] Austrian Prosecutor Maruna, in her turn, began Strasser's trial by arguing that Ernst Strasser "massively harmed European politics."[58] In response to Strasser's attempts to defend himself by saying that he was just a lobbyist, the Prosecutor opined, "No, you were not. You were a member of Parliament."[59] Trial judge George Olschak agreed with the prosecution when he observed that "[t]here were few people in the...republic who have damaged Austria's image as much as...[Strasser has]."[60] When judge asked the defendant "why he did not tell police about his suspicions, Strasser replied that his experience as interior minister taught him not to trust them."[61] Strasser further defended himself by saying that "he went to expensive dinners and played along in order to expose them as spies from a foreign country, presumably the US."[62] In response to this line of Strasser's defense, trial Judge Olschak said, "[t]hat is probably one of the most outlandish things I have heard in my 20-year career."[63] The trial court in Vienna found Strasser guilty on charges of bribery and sentenced him to four years of imprisonment in January 2013. Though Strasser lost the final appeal against his sentence, in October 2014 the Supreme Court of Austria (*Oberster Gerichtshof*) reduced on appeal his sentence to three years in jail.[64] The sentence had both legal and political consequences for Strasser.

The trial of Ernst Strasser set a precedent and became a warning for other Austrian politicians who may engage in similar corruption activities. In particular, trial judge Olschak argued that Strasser's sentence "would have a deterrent impact on possible copycats, and there are likely a few of those."[65] Under the public pressure Ernst Strasser had to resign from his political positions "while denying wrongdoing...[and] said he wanted to protect the Austrian conservative People's Party, of which he was a senior member."[66] Therefore, Strasser's sentence and his eventual resignation from politics demonstrated both legal and political resolution of this 'politically sensitive' case in Austria. The legal proceedings in the case were accompanied by the public and

---

[57] Pop 2012.

[58] Ibid.

[59] Ibid.

[60] Shields 2013.

[61] Pop 2012.

[62] Ibid.

[63] Shields 2013.

[64] See the reasoning of the Supreme Court of Austria in Ernst Strasser's case available in German. The Austrian Supreme Court, the case of Ernst Strasser, Judgement pursuant to § 266 Abs 1 Strafprozeßordnung 1975 (StPO), 13 October 2014, Case No. 17Os30/14m (*Strasser 2014*). https://www.ris.bka.gv.at/Dokument.wxe?Abfrage=Justiz&Dokumentnummer=JJT_20141013_OGH0002_0170OS00030_14M0000_000. Accessed 27 December 2020.

[65] Shields 2013.

[66] Ibid.

media scrutiny that did not only cover legal aspects related to Strasser's corruption, but also set the red lines for unethical behavior of politicians that engage themselves in dubious lobbying activities in the pursuit of personal material gain.

Both Susanne Winter and Ernst Strasser's case revealed the mechanism of adjudicating 'political cases' in Austria. Winter and Strasser's high political status did not provide them with immunity against political prosecution. On the contrary, it caused an intensive public and media debate among supporters and opponents of both politicians. At the same time, criminal proceedings did not become a tool in the political struggle to 'destroy' completely the personal life and careers of both politicians. Susanne Winter retained her seat in the Austrian Parliament despite the fine and her suspended sentence, while Strasser managed to reduce his imprisonment sentence in the Supreme Court of Austria.[67] Most importantly, the trials, the media and public discourse went along the lines of the Austrian Constitution in the sense that they have not infringed on such fundamental rights (*Grundrechte*) as the equality clause stipulated by *Article 7* of the Austrian Constitution, the freedom of speech and opinion stipulated by *Article 13* of the Basic State Law on the General Rights of Citizens. The constitutional dialogue both inside and outside the courtroom protected Strasser and Winter from arbitrary persecution common in similar cases in the former Soviet Union. This commitment to values and principles of the written constitution became the guarantee that both politicians did not become victims of politicized justice.

3.4 Ukraine

3.4.1 The Trial of the Former Ukrainian Prime-Minister Yulia Tymoshenko

The case of Yulia Tymoshenko could be called a 'political case' due to several considerations. The Prosecutor's Office initiated numerous criminal cases against the former Prime Minister when Tymoshenko lost by a small margin[68] 2010 presidential elections to Viktor Yanukovytch, her main political rival, who became the President of Ukraine. Despite her defeat in the elections, Tymoshenko remained the most popular

---

[67] The Austrian Supreme Court, the case of Ernst Strasser, Judgement pursuant to § 266 Abs 1 Strafprozeßordnung 1975 (StPO), 13 October 2014, Case No. 17Os30/14m (Strasser 2014). https://www.ris.bka.gv.at/Dokument.wxe?Abfrage=Justiz&Dokumentnummer=JJT_20141013_OGH0002_0170OS00030_14M0000_000. Accessed 27 December 2020.

[68] Ms. Tymoshenko received support of 45.47% of voters (11,593,357 votes), while Viktor Yanukovytch received 48.95% (12,480,335 votes), the OSCE/ODIHR Election Observation Mission Final Report, available at www.osce.org/odihr/elections/ukraine/67844. Accessed 27 December 2020.

opposition politician[69] at that time and the main rival of President Yanukovytch at the presidential elections scheduled for 2015.[70] Finally, main criminal charges brought against Yulia Tymoshenko were related to her political activities as the Prime Minister of Ukraine. In particular, in 2011 the General Prosecutor's Office of Ukraine argued that Tymoshenko exceeded her powers of the Prime Minister when she signed a gas contract with the state Russian oil-and-gas company 'Gazprom' on conditions that could have been unfavorable for Ukraine. The 'political nature' of these charges was reinforced with other criminal cases initiated by prosecutors against Tymoshenko's family and members of her political party 'Batkivschyna'.

Other criminal charges against Tymoshenko included accusations of misusing funds received by Ukraine from selling its 'greenhouse emissions quota' to Japan under the Kyoto Protocol. Tymoshenko's governments allegedly used the Kyoto Protocol funds to replenish the state pension fund instead of supporting environmental protection projects as it was agreed with the government of Japan.[71] Prosecutors also accused Tymoshenko of misappropriating state funds by purchasing ambulances for rural areas of Ukraine. [72] In all above-mentioned criminal cases, however, prosecution has never accused Tymoshenko of personally benefitting from her alleged abuse of power. Furthermore, Tymoshenko argued that her family members and supporters also became victims of political persecution. Simultaneously with the criminal investigation initiated against Tymoshenko, the Prosecutor's Office reopened in 2011 an old case against her father-in-law in relation to his work in Tymoshenko's company "United Energy Systems of Ukraine" (UESU). Tymoshenko's husband was granted political asylum in the Czech Republic due to his alleged persecution by the state authorities that allegedly wanted to put Yulia Tymoshenko under psychological pressure.[73] Tymoshenko's lawyer Serhiy Vlasenko has also faced criminal charges related to his divorce, which took place several years before.[74] The Prosecutor's Office initiated similar criminal cases against colleagues and members of Tymoshenko's political party.

Besides Tymoshenko, the following senior members of her party and government have also been prosecuted on various charges ranging from corruption to the abuse of their office: Mr. Filipchuk, the former Environment Minister, Ms. Gritsoun, the

---

[69] A national survey conducted by the Razumkov Center in 2013. https://www.kyivpost.com/content/politics/poll-one-in-three-ukrainians-thinks-tymoshenko-is-opposition-leader-323938.html. Accessed 27 December 2020.

[70] A statement from 31 January 2013 by Mr. Andrij Bychenko, the Director of Sociological Service of the Razumkov Centre, available at https://www.razumkov.org.ua/eng/expert.php?news_id=3867. (link no longer active).

[71] BBC News Europe 2010.

[72] Jurist 2011.

[73] Telegraph 2012.

[74] "Lawyer of former Ukraine PM Yulia Tymoshenko 'faces criminal charges'" from 21 January 2013, available at https://www.theguardian.com/world/2013/jan/21/ukraine-tymoshenko-lawyer-criminal-charges. Accessed 27 December 2020.

state Treasury official, Mr. Ivashchenko, the Minister of Defence,[75] Mr. Lutsenko, the Interior Minister,[76] Mr. Makarenko, the former Head of the State Customs Service of Ukraine,[77] Mr. Korniychuk, First Deputy Minister of Justice,[78] Mr. Didenko, a senior official of the state oil and gas company "Naftogaz", Ms. Kushnir, deputy chief accountant 'Naftogaz'. Prosecution of these senior officials from Tymoshenko's government was also accompanied by the general crackdown on the civil society and opposition media in Ukraine.[79] In 2011 the European Parliament passed a resolution on the prosecution of opposition politicians in Ukraine.[80] According to various international reports "only a few.... low-level, career officials [of then ruling Party of Regions stood before trial for their crimes]."[81] At the same time, criminal cases were initiated "mainly [against] politicians belonging to potential powerful political opposition groups."[82] Manny of these attacks against Ukrainian opposition along with Yulia Tymoshenko's complaint became the subject of judicial review at the European Court of Human Rights.

In 2011, Yulia Tymoshenko was found guilty as charged in the 'gas case' and sentenced to a three-year ban on holding public office and seven years in prison. Furthermore, the Ukrainian court imposed on Tymoshenko the payment of damages in the amount of approximately 140 million EUR. Immediately after the sentence was confirmed on appeal by higher court in Ukraine, the former Prime Minister applied to the European Court of Human Rights (ECtHR). Taking into account seriousness of Yulia Tymoshenko's allegations that her detention was politically motivated, the Strasbourg Court gave priority to her first application, in accordance with the *Rule 41* of the Court Rules.[83] When the applicant submitted the second application related to the criminal trial against her in Ukraine, the ECtHR separated it into a separate case.[84] When reviewing the first application, the Court found that some of the complaints

---

[75] The European Court of Human Rights (ECtHR), Ivashchenko v. Ukraine, 26 October 2012, Case No. 41303/11 (*Ivashchenko* 2012).

[76] ECtHR, *Lutsenko v Ukraine* 2012, 3 July 2012, Case No. 6492/11 (Lutsenko 2012).

[77] ECtHR, '*Makarenko v. Ukraine*', Application No. 622/11.

[78] ECtHR, '*Korniychuk v. Ukraine*', 30 April 2018, Case No. 10042/11 (*Korniychuk* 2018).

[79] Herszenhorn 2013.

[80] See the European Parliament resolution of 9 June 2011 on Ukraine. https://www.europarl.europa.eu/document/activities/cont/201106/20110620ATT21953/20110620ATT21953EN.pdf. Accessed 27 December 2020.

[81] See the *2012 Country Report* on Human Rights and Practices of the US Department of State released by the Bureau of Democracy, Human Rights and Labor. https://www.state.gov/j/drl/rls/hrrpt/humanrightsreport/#wrapper. Accessed 27 December 2020.

[82] Danish Helsinki Committee for Human Rights 2011.

[83] *Tymoshenko* 2013, 30 April 2013, Case No. 49872/11. https://hudoc.echr.coe.int/sites/eng/pages/search.aspx?i=001-119382#{%22itemid%22:[%22001-119382%22]}. Accessed 27 December 2020.

[84] ECtHR, *Tymoshenko v. Ukraine no. 2*, Application no. 65656/12. The ECtHR's decided to strike the application out of its list of cases, 16 December 2014, Decision pursuant to Article 39 (friendly

related to the applicant's detention were inadmissible. In particular, the Court found inadmissible Tymoshenko's complaint about the constant video surveillance (alleged violation of Article 8 ECHR), the lack of medical care in the pre-trial detention center (alleged violation of Article 3 ECHR), where she stayed as well as inadequate conditions of her pre-trial detention (alleged violation of Article 3 ECHR).

The Court used the following reasoning to dismiss inadmissible complaints. Yulia Tymoshenko argued that she did not receive necessary medical care during her stay in the pre-trial detention center, although she had numerous health problems. Tymoshenko alleged that the Government of Ukraine violated Article 3 ECHR (Prohibition of Torture or Degrading Treatment or Punishment) when it used her poor health condition and offered painkillers in exchange for her cooperation with the investigation initiated against her.[85] The Court reasoned that the delay with the medical assistance was Tymoshenko's own fault, because she "was extremely cautious and refused, on a regular basis, to allow most of the medical procedures that were suggested to her."[86] The Court also relied on the external assessment of the European Committee for the Prevention of Torture and Inhuman or Degrading Treatment or Punishment (CPT),[87] whose experts visited Tymoshenko and "had not raised any particular concern with regard to the appropriateness of the medical care provided to [her]."[88] The Court concluded that "Ms. Tymoshenko's health had received considerable attention from the Ukrainian authorities, which had invested efforts far beyond the normal health-care arrangements available for ordinary detainees in Ukraine."[89] The Court, thus, rejected Tymoshenko's complaint about the lack of medical care during her detention on the basis of Article 35 § 3(a) and 4 ECHR.

Yulia Tymoshenko also complained about continuous video surveillance in the state hospital where she stayed and disclosure of private information about her health to the public, which was an alleged violation of Article 8 ECHR (Right to Private Life). The Court dismissed this complain as inadmissible, because the applicant did not exhaust all national remedies available to her in Ukraine. In particular, Tymoshenko could have appealed the decision of the first instance court, which dismissed her complaint about violation of her privacy, in the higher court in Ukraine in line with Article 17 of the Administrative Code of Ukraine. Due to this reasons, the Court dismissed the complaint about the video surveillance on the basis of Article 35 § 3(a) and 4 ECHR. The Court also dismissed Yulia Tymoshenko's complaint

settlements). https://hudoc.echr.coe.int/eng#{%22itemid%22:[%22001-150832%22]}. Accessed 27 December 2020.

[85] *Tymoshenko* 2013, above n 83, p. 46, para 209.

[86] *Tymoshenko* 2013, above n 83, p. 48, para 217.

[87] The Report to the Ukrainian Government on the visit to Ukraine carried out by the European Committee for the Prevention of Torture and Inhuman or Degrading Treatment or Punishment (CPT) from 29 November to 6 December 2011 [CPT/Inf (2012) 30], paras 48–49. https://www.cpt.coe.int/documents/ukr/2012-30-inf-eng.htm. Accessed 27 December 2020.

[88] *Tymoshenko* 2013, above n 83, p. 48, para 215.

[89] *Tymoshenko* 2013, above n 83, p. 48, para 215.

about poor conditions in the detention center where she stayed during the trial. In particular, the applicant complained about lack of light, ventilation, hot and cold water, absence of heating and inadequate quality of food in the detention center. Taking into account that Tymoshenko was unable to walk due to her illness, she also complained that the administration of the detention center did not provide her with opportunities to spend some time outdoors, which she needed to recover from illness.[90] Similar to the dismissal of the complaint about medical treatment, the Court found that, although Tymoshenko experienced some problems related to conditions of her detention, these problems were not serious enough[91] to amount to torture, degrading treatment or punishment in the meaning of Article 3 ECHR.

The Court recognized as admissible the rest of Tymoshenko's complaints related to her forced transfer to the hospital and her pre-trial detention. In particular, Tymoshenko complained that when on 15 March 2012 the Court issued an interim measure under Rule 39 to provide her with necessary treatment in a medical institution in Ukraine, the Government of Ukraine forcefully transferred her from the penal colony to a hospital, which allegedly constituted a violation of her rights under Article 3 ECHR. Tymoshenko further complained that, due to the forceful transfer to a hospital, she sustained injuries and Ukrainian authorities did not conduct proper investigation of this accident. The Court noted that Article 1 ECHR requires national authorities to conduct effective investigations of complaints about possible ill-treatment. However, the Court also observed that the Government of Ukraine could not investigate the matter due to "the applicant's failure to cooperate with the authorities through her persistent refusals to undergo a forensic medical examination, which could have confirmed or rebutted the findings as to the date and cause of the bruising sustained by her."[92] Therefore, the Court concluded that the investigation conducted by the government was effective in the meaning of Article 3 and dismissed Tymoshenko's complaints[93] about her alleged ill-treatment during the transfer to the hospital.

The final complaint made by Yulia Tymoshenko under the first application was related to her detention ordered for an indefinite period of time by the trial court in Ukraine. The trial court in Ukraine ordered Tymoshenko's detention, because she allegedly refused to provide her home address, showed 'disrespect towards the court' by not following trial judge's instructions and interrupting questioning of witnesses, refused to sign a notification about the timing of the next court hearings and came

[90] *Tymoshenko* 2013, above n 83, p. 48, para 215.

[91] *Tymoshenko* 2013, above n 83. See a press-release on the judgment in the Case '*Tymoshenko v. Ukraine*' from 30.04.2013, available at https://hudoc.echr.coe.int/sites/eng-press/pages/search.aspx?i=003-4343134-5208270. Accessed 27 December 2020.

[92] *Tymoshenko* 2013, above n 83, pp. 53–54, para 241.

[93] *Tymoshenko* 2013, above n 83. Judges Spielmann, Villiger and Nussberger wrote a joint dissenting opinion, in which they argued that Tymoshenko's ill-treatment constituted a violation of Article 3 ECHR. The joint dissenting opinion in the case '*Tymoshenko v. Ukraine*', p 72. https://hudoc.echr.coe.int/sites/eng/pages/search.aspx?i=001-119382#{%22itemid%22:[%22001-119382%22]}. Accessed 27 December 2020.

late for seven minutes to one of the hearings in her case.[94] The trial court used the same reasons to extend her detention for an indefinite period of time. Tymoshenko complained before the ECtHR that her detention was arbitrary and unlawful under Article 5 § 1 ECHR. The Court agreed with the applicant that her detention was not justified, because Tymoshenko's alleged contempt towards the trial court is not included into the list of reasons that can be used to justify detention under Article 5. The Court noted that the applicant has also attended all trial hearings in her case and her refusal to sign notifications about next hearings did not obstruct trial proceedings. Moreover, the Court emphasized that it has already found in its previous judgments against Ukraine that a detention for an indefinite period of time contradicts requirements of lawfulness under Article 5 ECHR.[95] Taking into account the above considerations, the Court found that Yulia Tymoshenko's detention ordered by the trial court in Ukraine was unlawful and arbitrary in the meaning of Article 5 § 1 ECHR.

In relation to her detention, Tymoshenko also complained that she did not have an effective remedy to replace her detention with a different preventive measure, which deprived her of the right to judicial review of her detention under Article 5 ECHR. The applicant tried to change her detention to another preventive measure by submitting an appeal both to the trial court and the Appellate City Court of Kyiv. The Court observed that both courts repeated the original grounds for Tymoshenko's detention "being confined in their reasoning to mere statement that no appeal lay against a ruling on change of a preventive measure delivered during the judicial examination of a case".[96] The Court has further noted that it has found in its previous judgments against Ukraine that it is a violation of Article 5 § 4 ECHR not to provide a detained person an opportunity to change a detention order during the examination of a case in court.[97] Therefore, the Court held that the above mentioned deficiency of the Ukrainian judicial review deprived Yulia Tymoshenko of an opportunity to challenge her detention in violation of Article 5 § 4 ECHR.

Yulia Tymoshenko further argued before the Court that, although her liberty was restricted in violation of Article 5 ECHR, she could not exercise her right to compensation guaranteed under Article 5 § 5 ECHR. The procedure for receiving a compensation was not outlined in the State Compensation Act of Ukraine. The Court has already recommended the Government of Ukraine to make the necessary revisions in the Act to make sure it includes a procedure to pay the compensation in case

---

[94] *Tymoshenko* 2013, above n 83, p. 57, para 258.

[95] The European Court of Human Rights (ECtHR), *Yeloyev v. Ukraine*, 6 February 2009, Case No. 17283/02 (*Yeloyev* 2009); ECtHR, *Doronin v. Ukraine*, 19 February 2009, Case No. 16505/02 (*Doronin* 2009); ECtHR, *Solovey and Zozulya v. Ukraine*, 27 November 2008, Case Nos. 40774/02 and 4048/03 (*Solovey and Zozulya* 2008).

[96] *Tymoshenko* 2013, above n 83, p. 60, para 278.

[97] ECtHR, *Molodorych v. Ukraine*, 28 January 2011, Case No. 2161/02 (*Molodorych* 2009). https://hudoc.echr.coe.int/eng#{%22appno%22:[%222161/02%22],%22itemid%22:[%22001-101327%22]}. Accessed 27 December 2020.

Article 5 ECHR was violated. Taking into account that the Government of Ukraine did not fulfill this recommendation, the Court found the violation of Tymoshenko's right to compensation stipulated in Article 5 § 5 ECHR. The applicant also alleged that violation of her rights under Article 5 occurred in conjunction with Article 18 (limitation on use of restrictions on rights). In particular, the applicant claimed that the Government ordered her arrest and detention due to the ulterior political motives. Tymoshenko further argued that the purpose of her arrest and detention was to remove her from political life shortly before the 2012 parliamentary elections campaign and eliminate her as a serious political competitor given that she was "enjoy[ing] widespread support among the population."[98] In other words, Yulia Tymoshenko claimed that she became a victim of politicized justice, whose goal was to eradicate political opposition in Ukraine.

Judges of the European Court of Human Rights carefully considered allegations about politically motivated justice presented by Yulia Tymoshenko's lawyers. The Court reasoned that Article 18 ECHR can be violated only in conjunction with other article of the Convention, which has been already established in the previous case law related to allegations about politically motivated justice.[99] The applicant alleged that her rights were restricted in violation of Article 18 ECHR due to the ulterior motives in conjunction with her complaints about her detention under Article 5 (the first application '*Tymoshenko v. Ukraine*', *no. 49872/11*) and absence of the fair trial in her case (the second application, '*Tymoshenko v. Ukraine no. 2*', *no. 65656/12*). The Court found that Yulia Tymoshenko's alleged contempt towards the trial judge was the only true reason for her detention. This led the majority of judges to conclude that Tymoshenko was detained "not for the purpose of bringing her before a competent legal authority on reasonable suspicion of having committed an offence, but for other reasons".[100] Therefore, the Court found a violation of Article 18 in conjunction with Article 5 ECHR.

While three judges of the Court (Jungwiert, Nussberger and Potocki) agreed that in Yulia Tymoshenko's case Article 18 was violated in conjunction with Article 5 ECHR, the judges argued in a joint concurring opinion[101] that the majority opinion did not sufficiently address Tymoshenko's allegations about politically motivated justice against her. In particular, in the joint concurring opinion the three judges pointed to the 'expedited criminal proceedings' against the applicant that were conducted within less than six weeks, while the applicant had to read more than 4000 pages of case materials as well as attend numerous investigative events and courts hearings. This essentially removed Yulia Tymoshenko from political life shortly before the 2012 parliamentary elections campaign, in the course of which she was supposed to lead the united opposition parties. The three judges argued that the reasons to remove Tymoshenko from political life could be found in her popular support in the

[98] *Tymoshenko* 2013, above n 83, p. 63, para 292.
[99] *Gusinskiy v. Russia*, no. 70276/01, § 75, 19 May 2004.
[100] *Tymoshenko* 2013, above n 83, p. 67, para 300.
[101] *Tymoshenko* 2013, above n 83, the Joint Concurring Opinion, p. 69.

Ukrainian society as one year prior to her arrest and detention she received "45.47% of the popular vote"[102] in the 2010 presidential elections.

It is also mentioned in the concurring opinion that Tymoshenko's party 'Fatherland' (Ukrainian: 'Batkivschyna') was then the strongest opposition force in the country.[103] At the same time, the judges referred to the selective character of criminal prosecution in Ukraine at that time, which targeted many government officials of Ms. Tymoshenko's cabinet and very few low-level official from the ruling 'Party of Regions.'[104] Given the above mentioned considerations, the judges concluded that grounds for Tymoshenko's detention were not only deficient under Article 5 § 1, but have been a result of "other ulterior motives…which were not related to the proper conduct of the criminal proceedings per se, but rather to the applicant's identity and influence as a leading opposition politician in Ukraine."[105] The politically motivated character[106] of the criminal case against Yulia Tymoshenko was also recognized in the friendly settlement on Tymoshenko's second application related to the fairness of her trial shortly after the victory of the 'Euromaidan' revolution, as a result of which Yulia Tymoshenko was released from prison and the former President Yanukovytch fled to Russia in 2014.[107] It is mentioned in the press-release that the Court struck Yulia Tymoshenko's second application out of its list of cases in line with Article 39 ECHR (friendly settlements) referring to "Ukrainian Government's declaration in which they admitted that the criminal prosecution of Ms Tymoshenko had been politically motivated and in which they acknowledged a violation of her Convention rights."[108] The 'political case' of Yulia Tymoshenko has, thus, been resolved through political reconciliation with the new Government of Ukraine.

---

[102] *Tymoshenko* 2013, above n 83, the Joint Concurring Opinion, p. 69.

[103] *Tymoshenko* 2013, above n 83, the Joint Concurring Opinion, p. 69.

[104] See the Ukraine Country Report on Human Rights and Practices of the US Department of State released by the Bureau of Democracy, Human Rights and Labor on 8 April 2011. https://www.state.gov/j/drl/rls/hrrpt/2010/eur/154456.htm. Accessed 27 December 2020.

[105] The Joint Concurring Opinion in *Tymoshenko v. Ukraine*, p. 70. https://hudoc.echr.coe.int/sites/eng/pages/search.aspx?i=001-119382#{%22itemid%22:[%22001-119382%22]}. Accessed 27 December 2020.

[106] The Press Release from 22 January 2015, ECHR 023 (2015). https://hudoc.echr.coe.int/sites/eng-press/pages/search.aspx?i=003-4988882-6120225. Accessed 27 December 2020.

[107] Malkin and Raziye 2015.

[108] ECtHR, *Tymoshenko v. Ukraine no. 2*, Application no. 65656/12. The ECtHR's decided to strike the application out of its list of cases, 16 December 2014, Decision pursuant to Article 39 (friendly settlements). https://hudoc.echr.coe.int/eng#{%22itemid%22:[%22001-150832%22]}. Accessed 27 December 2020.

3.4.2 *The Trial of the Former Ukrainian Minister of Interior Yuri Lutsenko*

Yuri Lutsenko was a prominent opposition leader during the presidency of Viktor Yanukovytch in 2010–2014 and a leader of the political party 'People's Self-Defense' (Ukrainian: *Narodna Samooborona*). He also served as a Minister of Interior in Yulia Tymoshenko's government from 2005 to 2006 and from 2007 to 2010. Along with other opposition leaders, Lutsenko claimed that he became a victim of politically motivated persecution initiated by the former President Yanukovytch and his government. In particular, shortly after Yanukovytch became the President of Ukraine in 2010 the Office of the Prosecutor General charged Lutsenko with abusing his position of the Minister by providing various benefits to his driver. Prosecutors initiated two criminal cases against Lutsenko claiming that he allegedly allocated a state one-room apartment and better police service record for his driver. Shortly afterwards another criminal case was initiated by the General Prosecutor of Ukraine in relation to unlawful search and seizure order allegedly given by Lutsenko when he was a Minister of Interior. The same year police special task force arrested Yuri Lutsenko, who was walking with his dog near his home, in connection to one of the criminal cases initiated against him. The former Minister argued that police neither informed him about reasons for his arrest nor gave him a copy of criminal charges against him.[109] The Ukrainian trial court supported the prosecutor's order for Yuri Lutsenko's detention on the grounds that Lutsenko and his lawyer took a lot of time to study the case and disclosed the information about it to the media, Lutsenko allegedly intervened in the ongoing investigation against him and refused to admit his guilt in the criminal cases brought against him.[110] Ukrainian courts dismissed Yuri Lutsenko's appeals against his detention order. The trial court convicted the former Minister of Interior to four years in prison and confiscation of his property.

Shortly after his arrest and detention, Yuri Lutsenko complained to the European Court of Human Rights arguing that his rights under Article 5 § 1(b), (c), 2 and 3 (Right to Liberty and Security) were violated by the Government of Ukraine. The former Minister of Interior also complained that his right to a fair trial (Article 6 § 1, 2 and 3(a), (b) ECHR) was violated when he was not informed about the subject of criminal proceedings against him prior to one of the court hearings on 27 December 2010. Similar to Yulia Tymoshenko's case, the European Court of Human Rights divided the complaint into two applications related to Lutsenko's detention and his subsequent trial. Furthermore, without specifying any particular Article of the Convention, Lutsenko complained that the Government of Ukraine organized his arrest and detention to remove him from political life prior to the parliamentary elections in 2012.

---

[109] *Lutsenko* 2012, above n 76. https://hudoc.echr.coe.int/sites/eng/pages/search.aspx#%7B%22appno%22:[%226492/11%22]%7D. Accessed 27 December 2020.

[110] *Lutsenko* 2012, above n 76.

In relation to his arrest in the second criminal case initiated against him, Yuri Lutsenko argued that his rights under Article 5 § 1 (arrest) were violated when the court in Ukraine did not examine the lawfulness of the arrest, because the prosecution protested against examination of the arrest in court. The court reasoned that this alone suggested that the purpose of Yuri Lutsenko's arrest was not to bring him before a competent legal authority.[111] Moreover, Lutsenko's arrest was not "necessary to prevent him from committing an offence or fleeing after having done so" in line with Article 5 ECHR.[112] The Court did not receive any evidence from the Government of Ukraine that Lutsenko could influence the process of investigation one year after he left his post of the Minister of the Interior, which would, otherwise, justify his arrest. Furthermore, there was no real danger of Lutsenko's fleeing. He was under the obligation not to abscond and "[d]uring the pre-trial investigation, the applicant appeared for all investigating activities and the investigator had no complaints about his cooperation."[113] This was enough for the Court to conclude that Lutsenko's arrest was arbitrarily arrested in violation of Article 5 § 1 ECHR.

The Court also carefully reviewed grounds for Yuri Lutsenko's detention and found them deficient. One of the reasons of Lutsenko's detention was that he allegedly read his case materials slowly and the Ukrainian trials court had to impose sanctions on him in order not to disadvantage interests of other trial parties. The Court found that by detaining Lutsenko the Ukrainian trial court chose disproportionate response to the allegedly slow examination of the case by him, because under the Ukrainian law "study of a case file is a right and not an obligation of an accused and that the time available to an accused for study of the case file should not be limited (Articles 142 and 218... of the Code of Criminal Procedure...[of Ukraine].)"[114] Another reason for the detention of the former Minister of Interior was that he as a prominent political figure could allegedly influence the process of investigation in his case by making statement in the media. Although this appeared to be one of the most important reasons for Yuri Lutsenko's detention, the Court found that Lutsenko's detention was not necessary to address concerns of the Government about his alleged pressure on trial witnesses. The Court noted that the Government of Ukraine did not explain "in what way the witnesses had been actually threatened by...[Lutsenko's] public statements and why the detention could be considered an adequate response to such statements."[115] In Court's view, it is only expected that a prominent political figure like Yuri Lutsenko should make public statement about his case to explain his position both to his political supporters and opponents.

Another reason for detaining Yuri Lutsenko was his refusal to acknowledge his guilt in the criminal cases initiated by him. The Court noted that it was rather disturbing that the Ukrainian trial court used such a ground for detention. Judges of the Strasbourg Court found that such an approach of the Ukrainian system of criminal

[111] *Lutsenko* 2012, above n 76, p. 27, para 65.

[112] *Lutsenko* 2012, above n 76.

[113] *Lutsenko* 2012, above n 76.

[114] *Lutsenko* 2012, above n 76, pp. 26–27, para 69.

[115] *Lutsenko* 2012, above n 76.

justice "run[s] contrary to such important elements of the fair trial concept as freedom from self-incrimination and the presumption of innocence."[116] This approach of the Ukrainian courts denied Lutsenko an opportunity to rely on the basic principles of the fair trial. By ordering Yuri Lutsenko's detention, the Ukrainian trial court essentially punished him for insisting on his innocence, which is an absolute right of any defendant in a criminal trial. Furthermore, Lutsenko's detention ordered for an indefinite period of time ran contrary to the well-established case law of the Court in the previous cases brought against Ukraine in the context of Article 5 § 1(c).[117] Due to the above-mentioned considerations, the Court could not help but conclude that the grounds for Lutsenko's pre-trial detention were deficient and violated requirements of proportionality and necessity under Article 5 § 1 of the Convention.

The Court noted that despite Yuri Lutsenko's complaints about the unlawfulness of his arrest, the Ukrainian courts did not provide Lutsenko with the judicial control of his detention, which is guaranteed under Article 5 § 3. The Court reiterated that Article 5 § 3 provides for an automatic judicial control of detention and, thus, rejected Ukrainian "Government's objection based on the argument that it was for the applicant to seek the review of the lawfulness of his arrest."[118] Besides the fact that Lutsenko's detention was not examined by a proper judicial authority in Ukraine, "the Court has already established that the applicant and his lawyer were not informed in advance about the subject of the hearing (…para 77…)."[119] Furthermore, Yuri Lutsenko's request to be granted enough time to study documents "brought forward by the prosecution and to prepare his defence was refused without any justification."[120] The Court reasoned that these procedural deficiencies in Yuri Lutsenko's case constituted a violation of Article 5 § 3 ECHR.

Yuriy Lutsenko made an additional complaint that the Government of Ukraine denied him an effective procedure to appeal against his detention order, which is guaranteed under Article 5 § 4 ECHR. The Court noted that, although Yuri Lutsenko made a number of complaints to appeal against his detention order and to challenge grounds for his arrest in Ukraine, "the Kyiv Court of Appeal rejected the applicant's appeal without giving a proper reply to his arguments…[n]either did it give an adequate response to the request signed by the Members of Parliament and supported by the Ombudsman for the applicant's release on bail."[121] The Ukrainian court of appeals simply dismissed Yuri Lutsenko's appeal against his detention order as unsubstantiated and referred to the prolonged examination of the case file by Lutsenko and his lawyer, which was the main reason used by the trial court to order his detention. At the same time, the court of appeals prolonged Lutsenko's detention, "even though the applicant had completed his study of the case-file materials, which had

---

[116] *Lutsenko* 2012, above n 76.

[117] ECtHR, *Kharchenko v. Ukraine*, 10 February 2011, Case No. 40107/02 (*Kharchenko* 2011), para 98.

[118] *Lutsenko* 2012, above n 76, p. 87, para 31.

[119] *Lutsenko* 2012, above n 76.

[120] *Lutsenko* 2012, above n 76.

[121] *Lutsenko* 2012, above n 76, p. 33, para 97.

been the principal reason advanced by the investigating authorities for deprivation of the applicant's liberty."[122] This was enough for the Court to conclude that Yuri Lutsenko was deprived by the Government of Ukraine of an opportunity to receive proper judicial review of his detention in violation of Article 5 § 4 of the Convention.

The final complaint brought by Lutsenko before the European Court of Human Rights was that he became a victim of politically motivated justice, taking into account that the actual goal of his arrest and detention was to remove him from political life shortly before the parliamentary elections of 2012. Although Lutsenko did not refer to any particular provision of the Convention, the Court decided to review this complaint in the context of Article 18 (limitation on use of restrictions on rights). Being a prominent leader of political opposition in Ukraine, Yuri Lutsenko made for the media public statements on criminal cases initiated against him, which was the principle reason why the Ukrainian authorities ordered his arrest and detention. In particular, "[t]he [Ukrainian] prosecuting authorities seeking the applicant's arrest explicitly indicated the applicant's communication with the media as one of the grounds for his arrest and accused him of distorting public opinion about crimes committed by him, discrediting the prosecuting authorities and influencing the upcoming trial in order to avoid criminal liability (... para 26...)."[123] The Court reasoned that such a position of the Ukrainian authorities towards Lutsenko shows "their attempt to punish the applicant for publicly disagreeing with accusations against him and for asserting his innocence, which he had the right to do."[124] This led the Court to conclude that the Ukrainian Government violated Article 18 of the Convention in conjunction with Article 5, when they ordered Yuri Lutsenko's arrest and detention not only to bring him before the competent legal authority in Ukraine "on reasonable suspicion of having committed an offence, but also for other reasons."[125] The 'political nature' of Yuri Lutsenko's case was confirmed shortly after the European Court of Human Rights delivered its judgment on his arbitrary arrest and detention when former President Yanukovych amnestied[126] Lutsenko and Ukrainian courts completely rehabilitated the former Minister after the victory of the "Euro-Maidan revolution' in 2014.

[122] *Lutsenko* 2012, above n 76.

[123] *Lutsenko* 2012, above n 76.

[124] *Lutsenko* 2012, above n 76.

[125] *Lutsenko* 2012, above n 76.

[126] RadioFreeEurope/RadioLiberty 2013.

3.5 Belarus

3.5.1 The Trial of Mikalai Statkevich

Mikalai Statkevich was a presidential candidate in 2010, an opposition activist and the leader of the Social Democratic Party of Belarus (Narodnaya Hramada). On 12 August 1956, the day of the 2010 presidential election in Belarus, Statkevich along with other opposition leaders of Belarus participated in a mass rally against the electoral fraud reported by international observers.[127] The special riot police unit detained Statkevich, other opposition leaders and hundreds of protestors when a group of provocateurs started breaking windows of a government building. In particular, the police detained him "outside of the main post building by dragging him out of a taxi, beating him, and ushering him to a then-unknown location."[128] Mikalai Statkevich was charged with organization and participation in mass riots (Article 293 of the Criminal Code of Belarus), hooliganism (Article 339) and organization and active participation in activities that violate public order (Article 342). The trial court found him guilty as charged and sentenced him to six years' imprisonment in a medium-security prison. The City Court of Cassation in Minsk upheld Statkevich's sentence. The Supreme Court of Belarus and the city Prosecutor dismissed Mikalai Statkevich's appeal against his sentence. Statkevich argued that while he was in prison, "he has been denied medical treatment, beaten pressured to admit his guilt, and forced to engage in hard labor."[129] This book analyzes complaints made by Mikalai Statkevich through rights guaranteed under the European Convention of Human Rights as if Belarus joined the Council of Europe.

If the European Court of Human Rights had an opportunity to review Mikalai Statkevich's complaint, it is very likely that it would declare it admissible if Statkevich did not file his application with the United Nations Human Rights Committee, which is "another procedure of international investigation or settlement."[130] At the same time, in line with the Convention requirements,[131] Statkevich has exhausted all available domestic remedies in Belarus. For instance, after the trial court sentenced him to six years in prison, he unsuccessfully filed an appeal on his sentence to the

[127] Office for Democratic Inst. and Human Rights, Org. for Security and Cooperation in Europe, Republic of Belarus Presidential Election, 19 December 2010, *OSCE/ODHIR Election Observation Mission Final Report*, 4 (22 February, 2011). https://www.osce.org/odihr/elections/75713. Accessed 27 December 2020.

[128] Parfitt 2010.

[129] Individual communication to the United Nations Human Rights Committee in the Case of Mikalai Statkevich against the Republic of Belarus. https://www.freedom-now.org/wp-content/uploads/2013/11/Statkevich-UNHRC-Petition-FINAL-15-Nov-2013.pdf. (link no longer active).

[130] Article 35(2) (b) (Admissibility) of the European Convention on Human Rights (ECHR), opened for signature 4 November 1950 (entered into force 3 September 1953). https://www.hri.org/docs/ECHR50.html. Accessed 22 August 2020.

[131] Article 35(1) (Admissibility) of the European Convention on Human Rights (ECHR), opened for signature 4 November 1950 (entered into force 3 September 1953). https://www.hri.org/docs/ECHR50.html. Accessed 22 August 2020.

court of cassation as well as brought a supervisory appeal to the Head of the Minsk City Court, the Head of the Supreme Court of Belarus, the Deputy Head of the Supreme Court and the Prosecutor's Office of the City of Minsk. Therefore, "under Belarussian law, Mr. Statkevitch has exhausted the domestic legal remedies available to him to vindicate his rights."[132] Accordingly, it is very likely that a Court would not only admit Statkevitch's case as admissible, but also, given the significance of the complaint, would give it a priority under Rule 41 of the Rules of Court.

With regard to his arrest and pre-trial detention, Mikalai Statkevich complained that he "was not informed of the charges against him at the time of his arrest and not promptly brought before a judge for review of whether he should remain detained prior to trial…The decision that he would remain detained was made by the prosecuting attorney."[133] These actions by the authorities of Belarus could potentially constitute a violation of Article 5 ECHR (Right to Liberty and Security). In particular, it could be a violation of Article 5(2) related to the right of an arrested person to be informed promptly about the reasons of arrest or any criminal charge and violation of Article 5 related to the right of the arrested or detained person to be brought promptly before a judge or another competent authority authorized by law to exercise judicial review of such an arrest or detention. In relation to the latter, the first step to analyze Mikalai Statkevich's case would be to see whether he was arrested for the purpose indicated in Article 5 § 1 of the European Convention of Human Rights, which stipulates that a person can be lawfully arrested or detained to bring this person before a competent legal authority "on reasonable suspicion of having committed an offence or when it is reasonably considered necessary to prevent his committing an offence or fleeing after having done so."[134] The Court has also established in its previous case law that the deprivation of liberty under Article 5 § 1(c) must meet the proportionality requirement,[135] according to which the deprivation of liberty must be strictly necessary to ensure the presence of an arrested or detained person in court, while other less strict measures to achieve this goal were not available.

I believe, if the European Court of Human Rights reviewed Statkevich's case under the Convention, it would find a violation of Article 5 § 1. The Court would reason that Statkevich's arrest was contrary to the purpose of the article, because he was not promptly brought before a judge to review his arrest and further pre-trial detention. Instead, only the prosecution authorized his deprivation of liberty for an

---

[132]Individual communication to the United Nations Human Rights Committee in the Case of Mikalai Statkevich against the Republic of Belarus. https://www.freedom-now.org/wp-content/uploads/2013/11/Statkevich-UNHRC-Petition-FINAL-15-Nov-2013.pdf. (link no longer active).

[133]OSCE Trial Monitoring Report, 66-68. In: Individual communication to the United Nations Human Rights Committee in the Case of Mikalai Statkevich against the Republic of Belarus. https://www.freedom-now.org/wp-content/uploads/2013/11/Statkevich-UNHRC-Petition-FINAL-15-Nov-2013.pdf. (link no longer active).

[134]The European Convention on Human Rights (ECHR), opened for signature 4 November 1950 (entered into force 3 September 1953). https://www.hri.org/docs/ECHR50.html. Accessed 27 December 2020.

[135]ECtHR, *Ladent v. Poland*, 18 March 2008, Case No. 11036/03 (*Ladent* 2008); ECtHR, *Ambruszkiewicz v. Poland*, 4 May 2006, Case No. 38797/03 (*Ambruszkiewicz* 2006).

unlimited period of time. Statkevich's arrest and detention were not strictly necessary to ensure his appearance in court. The authorities of Belarus did not even consider measures alternative to detention, while the prosecution did not present any evidence to show the risk of Statkevich's fleeing if he was released from custody. Furthermore, the Government of Belarus has not "provided…any grounds to justify the detention of Mr. Statkevich."[136] Given the above-mentioned facts of the case, it is very likely that the European Court of Human Rights would find that Mr. Statkevich's arrest was arbitrary, because it was made for purposes other than those outlined under Article 5 § 1 of the Convention. Taking into account that Statkevich's detention was ordered for an unlimited period of time in contradiction of the previous case law of the Court,[137] his detention was not reviewed by a proper judicial authority and the Government has not provided proper grounds for his detention, the Court would most probably also find that the entire period of his pre-trial detention was in violation of Article 5 § 1 of the Convention.

I would also argue that Statkevich's trial was in violation of Article 6 (Right to Fair Trial) of the Convention. For instance, in violation of *Article 6 § 2* (Presumption of Innocence), the Government of Belarus made secret recordings of "Mr. Statkevich's statements and made them available to the public before trial, which OSCE concluded "served to provoke negative public reaction and will have undermined [Statkevich's] right to a presumption of innocence."[138] Furthermore, a number of state officials made public statements that presumed Statkevich's guilt long before the trial. For instance, the President of Belarus said before Statkevich's trial that the prosecution of Statkevich and other protestors "was a response to a coup d'état."[139] The state media produced a number of documentaries that portrayed Statkevich and other protestors as criminals that wanted to overthrow the legitimate government.[140] While "[t]he president's office even disseminated the article 'A conspiracy: Behind the Scenes,' which was published in *Sovetskaya Belarus* (Soviet Balrus)…, [o]ther statements [against Statkevich and other protestors] were made by Mr. Lukashenko, officials

---

[136] *Mikalai Statkevich v. Belarus*, Working Group on Arbitrary Detention, Opinion No. 13/2011, U.N. Doc. A/HRC/WGAD/2011/13 (2011). https://hrlibrary.umn.edu/wgad/13-2011.html. Accessed 27 December 2020.

[137] *Kharchenko* 2011, above n 117.

[138] OSCE Trial Monitoring Report, 148–154. In: Individual communication to the United Nations Human Rights Committee in the Case of Mikalai Statkevich against the Republic of Belarus. https://www.freedom-now.org/wp-content/uploads/2013/11/Statkevich-UNHRC-Petition-FINAL-15-Nov-2013.pdf. (link no longer active).

[139] Individual communication to the United Nations Human Rights Committee in the Case of Mikalai Statkevich against the Republic of Belarus, p. 30. https://www.freedom-now.org/wp-content/uploads/2013/11/Statkevich-UNHRC-Petition-FINAL-15-Nov-2013.pdf. (link no longer active).

[140] Amnesty International Report, Security, Peace and Order?, p. 11. In: Individual communication in the Case of Mikalai Statkevich against the Republic of Belarus, p. 30. https://www.freedom-now.org/wp-content/uploads/2013/11/Statkevich-UNHRC-Petition-FINAL-15-Nov-2013.pdf. (link no longer active).

in the ministry of justice, and even a judge of the Supreme Court."[141] Therefore, the authorities of Belarus effectively denied Statkevich's right to the presumption of innocence in violation of Article 6 § 2 of the Convention.

The Court would also find a violation of other elements of Article 6 of the Convention. For instance, Statkevich's right to legal counsel under Article 6 § 4 (c) of the Convention was violated when before his trial "he was not allowed to contact his lawyer for several weeks after his arrest."[142] Moreover, during the pre-trial detention, "[t]he government held him incommunicado for months and denied access to counsel."[143] Therefore, Statkevitch was effectively denied an opportunity to receive legal assistance of his lawyer guaranteed under the Convention. Also, in violation of Article 6 § 4(d), Statkevitch "was denied an opportunity to cross-examine the government's witnesses."[144] Furthermore, Mikalai Statkevich's "attorneys were not permitted to confront the prosecution's key witnesses…, [while t]he prosecution [simply] read the testimony given during the investigation by a number of other witnesses that did not appear court."[145] At the same time, the trial court simply disregarded witnesses on Statkevich's behalf, when "the court did not consider the testimony of witnesses S. N. Kien, A. V. Lebedko, and A. V. Makaev about Mr. Statkevich's electoral campaign and the demonstration on 19 December 2010, including its duration and that protesters were not carrying any dangerous items."[146] The trial court simply followed the Soviet tradition of prosecutorial bias when it "overruled defense motions but granted or sustained every single motion by the prosecution (more than 20)."[147] This, in fact, deprived Statkevich of the basic due process guarantees that are essential for a concept of the fair trial.

In additional to violations of his rights mentioned above, during his detention and subsequent imprisonment Mikalai Statkevich was subjected to ill-treatment, inhumane and degrading treatment that can be characterized as torture under Article 3

[141] Individual communication in the Case of Mikalai Statkevich against the Republic of Belarus, p. 30. https://www.freedom-now.org/wp-content/uploads/2013/11/Statkevich-UNHRC-Petition-FINAL-15-Nov-2013.pdf. (link no longer active).

[142] OSCE Trial Monitoring Report, 159–160. In Individual communication in the Case of Mikalai Statkevich against the Republic of Belarus. https://www.freedom-now.org/wp-content/uploads/2013/11/Statkevich-UNHRC-Petition-FINAL-15-Nov-2013.pdf. (link no longer active).

[143] Individual communication in the Case of Mikalai Statkevich against the Republic of Belarus, p. 26. https://www.freedom-now.org/wp-content/uploads/2013/11/Statkevich-UNHRC-Petition-FINAL-15-Nov-2013.pdf. (link no longer active).

[144] Ibid.

[145] Ibid.

[146] Ibid.

[147] Individual communication in the Case of Mikalai Statkevich against the Republic of Belarus. https://www.freedom-now.org/wp-content/uploads/2013/11/Statkevich-UNHRC-Petition-FINAL-15-Nov-2013.pdf. (link no longer active).

(Prohibition of Torture) of the European Convention of Human Rights.[148] Statkevich's ill-treatment by government agents included both psychological and physical suffering inflicted upon him. In terms of the psychological suffering, police "officers harassed Statkevich and threatened to arrest his wife unless he confessed his guilt."[149] Other forms of psychological pressure the authorities of Belarus "forced him to sleep on the floor with the lights on,...refused him access to a toilet,...kept him in crowded cells with prisoners infected with deadly, communicable diseases,...[or] in isolation for month-long period...[,] transported him to an unknown location, where the officers threatened to render him unconscious."[150] The psychological suffering was complemented with physical mistreatment. For instance, when riot police detained Mikalai Statkevich during the demonstration, he was "physically beaten."[151] Moreover, during the pre-trial investigation "[p]rison officers would march him around in handcuffs or shackles, including with his wrists behind his back so that the officers could lift him from behind in what they called the swallow torture."[152] During his stay in prison, Statkevich "has been denied medical treatment, beaten, pressured to admit his guilt, and forced to engage in hard labor."[153] In order to fall within the scope of Article 3 of the Convention, ill-treatment of a person must reach the minimum level of severity, which, according to the previous case law,[154] depends on "the duration of the treatment, its physical and mental effects and, in some cases, the sex, age and state of health of the victim."[155] I believe the ill-treatment described above reached the level of severity to be classified as torture under Article 3 ECHR.

Furthermore, when a person complains about alleged torture, Article 3 the European Convention of Human Rights requires that national authorities conduct effective investigations into the allegations about such ill-treatment. According to the well-established case law of the Court,[156] "the authorities must always make a serious

---

[148] The European Convention on Human Rights (ECHR), opened for signature 4 November 1950 (entered into force 3 September 1953). https://www.hri.org/docs/ECHR50.html. Accessed 22 August 2020.

[149] Individual communication in the Case of Mikalai Statkevich against the Republic of Belarus, p. 17, available at https://www.freedom-now.org/wp-content/uploads/2013/11/Statkevich-UNHRC-Petition-FINAL-15-Nov-2013.pdf. (link no longer active).

[150] Ibid.

[151] Ibid.

[152] OSCE Trial Monitoring Report, 148–154. In Individual communication to the United Nations Human Rights Committee in the Case of Mikalai Statkevich against the Republic of Belarus. https://www.freedom-now.org/wp-content/uploads/2013/11/Statkevich-UNHRC-Petition-FINAL-15-Nov-2013.pdf. (link no longer active).

[153] Individual communication to the United Nations Human Rights Committee in the Case of Mikalai Statkevich against the Republic of Belarus, p. 27, available at https://www.freedom-now.org/wp-content/uploads/2013/11/Statkevich-UNHRC-Petition-FINAL-15-Nov-2013.pdf. (link no longer active).

[154] ECtHR, *Ireland v. The United Kingdom*, 13 December 1977, Case No. 5310/71 (*Ireland v. The United Kingdom 1977*), para 162.

[155] *Tymoshenko* 2013, above n 83, p. 45, para 197.

[156] ECtHR, *Assenov and Others v. Bulgaria*, 28 October 1998, Case No. 24760/94 (*Assenov and Others* 1998), para 102.

attempt to find out what happened and should not rely on hasty or ill-founded conclusions in order to close their investigation or as the basis of their decisions."[157] The Government of Belarus has not conducted any investigation into Statkevich's complaints about his torture, which could potentially identify and punish persons responsible for it. In particular, the authorities of Belarus have not taken reasonable steps to collect statements from eyewitnesses or relevant forensic evidence, as the Court recommended in its previous case law.[158] Moreover, as a result of such non-investigation of Statkevich's complaints about his alleged ill-treatment, "Mr. Statkevich's health condition deteriorated dramatically…[as] he developed an atrial fibrillation and his eyesight deteriorated significantly."[159] All of the circumstances of the case described above would lead the Court to conclude that Mikalai Statkevich became a victim of ill-treatment that can be classified as torture under Article 3 ECHR.

Finally, Mikalai Statkevich complained that he became a victim of politically motivated justice aimed at him and other critics of President Lukashenka's regime. Thus, the established violation of Statkevich's rights under Articles 5 and 6 of the Convention can be reviewed in conjunction with Article 18 ECHR (Limitation on use of restrictions on rights). Article 18 stipulates that rights guaranteed under the Convention can be restricted only for those purposes that are mentioned in the Convention. Furthermore, in line with the previous case law of the Court,[160] Article 18 can be invoked only in conjunction with other articles of the Convention. The Court also found in the previous cases related to the allegations about politically motivated justice that the Convention is based on the assumption that national governments in members states act in good faith when they enforce rights guaranteed by the Convention.[161] The person who alleges restriction of rights for improper purposes has the burden to produce evidence, which demonstrates "that the whole legal machinery of the respondent State…was ab initio misused, that from the beginning to the end

[157] *Tymoshenko* 2013, above n 83, p. 54, para 234.

[158] ECtHR, *Tanrıkulu v. Turkey*, 8 July 1999, Case no. 23763/94 (*Tanrıkulu* 1999), para 104.

[159] "Even though other suspects testified about the detention conditions and torture by KGB officers, authorities refused to review testimonies and to open an investigation. Article 12 of the Convention Against Torture and Other Cruel, Inhuman or Degrading Treatment or Punishment, 10 December 1984, 1465 U.N.T.S. 85, says the state "shall ensure that its competent authorities proceed to a prompt and impartial investigation, where there is reasonable ground to believe that an act of torture has been committed…The State did not comply with this obligation in Mr. Statkevich's case." In: Individual communication to the United Nations Human Rights Committee in the Case of Mikalai Statkevich against the Republic of Belarus, p. 27, available at https://www.freedom-now.org/wp-content/uploads/2013/11/Statkevich-UNHRC-Petition-FINAL-15-Nov-2013.pdf. (link no longer active).

[160] ECtHR, *Gusinskiy v Russia*, 19 May 2004, Case No. 70276/01 (*Gusinsky* 2004) para 75.

[161] ECtHR, *Khodorkovskiy v Russia*, 31 May 2011, Case No. 5829/04 (*Khodorkovskiy* 2011), para 142. https://hudoc.echr.coe.int/eng?i=001-104983#{%22itemid%22:[%22001-104983%22]}. Accessed 27 December 2020.

the authorities were acting with bad faith and in blatant disregard of the Convention."[162] In other words, the mere suspicion that the applicant became a victim of arbitrary political prosecution would not be enough to find the violation of Article 18. I believe that, similar to Yuri Lutsenko's case discussed above, in violation of Article 18, Mikalai Statkevich's rights have been restricted for political reasons that are not permissible under the European Convention of Human Rights.

The above-mentioned circumstances of Statkevich's case, in my opinion, show that he was punished for his opposition to the Government of Belarus, which has not acted in good faith. Moreover, the national authorities of Belarus were driven by improper political reasons that are contrary to the Convention requirements. In particular, police arrested Statkevich during a peaceful demonstration against alleged electoral fraud, when he was exercising the freedom of assembly and association guaranteed under Article 11 ECHR as well as the freedom of expression under Article 10 ECHR. Therefore, the Government restricted Statkevich liberty not only for the purpose of bringing him before the legal authority on reasonable suspicion of having committed an offence, but also for other improper political purposes in blatant disregard of the Convention. Moreover, statements about Statkevich's guilt made by the President of Belarus and other senior officials prior to the trial demonstrate that the actual purpose of criminal proceedings against Statkevich was to prosecute him for his political activities and attempts to disseminate information about the electoral fraud that the Government tried to conceal from the public. The political nature of Statkevich's case is corroborated by the fact that the President of Belarus amnestied Statkevich along with other prisoners of conscience one day after the deadline[163] set for candidates to submit their applications for the presidential elections in 2015.

3.5.2 The Trial of Andrei Sannikov

Similar to Mikalai Statkevich, Andrei Sannikov was one of the leaders of opposition in Belarus and a candidate in the presidential elections of 2010. Sannikov used to be a career diplomat in the Ministry of Foreign Affairs of Belarus, but resigned from him post in protest to the constitutional amendments that extended powers of President Lukashenka. After his resignation Sannikov established a civic organization 'Charter 97', which protected human rights and criticized the authoritarian regime in Belarus. He has also founded the Coordination Council of Democratic Forces of Belarus, which supported political prisoners and represented various opposition groups. In the 2010 presidential elections, Sannikov received the biggest number of votes among other presidential candidates from the opposition and came second

[162] *Khodorkovskiy* 2011, above n 161, p. 65, para 260.

[163] See the Media Release: Belarusian Politician Mikalai Statkevich Released From Prison, 22 August 2015. https://www.freedom-now.org/news/media-release-belarusian-politician-mikalai-statkevich-released-from-prison/. Accessed 27 December 2020.

after the incumbent president Lukashenko. Like other opposition presidential candidates, Andrei Sannikov was arrested by riot police on 19 December 2010 during a peaceful demonstration, which was interrupted by a group of provocateurs who started breaking windows of the government building. According to witness statements, "the police forces assaulted Mr. Sannikov by pinning him down with a riot shield and jumping on it repeatedly, thereby severely injuring his legs."[164] When Andrei Sannikov and his wife Iryna Khalip tried to leave the place of the demonstration, both of them were arrested and Sannikov was brought to the KGB detention center known as 'Amerikanka'.

Although the majority of arrested protestors were released after several days of detention, Sannikov and other leaders of opposition remained in custody and faced criminal charges. In particular, Sannikov was charged with "organization of mass disorder accompanied by violence against persons, pogroms, arson, destruction of property, or armed resistance of the authority' under Article 293(1) of the Belarus Criminal Code and with 'involvement in riots, as expressed in the immediate fulfillment of actions specified in the first part of this article' under Article 293(2) of the Belarus Criminal Code."[165] Andrei Sannikov other protestors, whom he did not know, faced a trial, which lasted ten days. During the trial Sannikov and other co-defendants were "forced to sit in the courtroom during the proceedings on a hard bench in a barred cage."[166] Similar to Statkevich's case, the court found Sannikov guilty as charged and sentenced him to five years in prison. Andrei Sannikov's appeal on his sentence was dismissed by the Minsk City Court, which did not permit Sannikov to attend the hearing of his case on cassation. Sannikov was subsequently transferred to Novapolotsk penal colony No. 10 to serve his sentence.

Similar to Mikalai Statkevich's case, in my opinion, Sannikov's arrest and detention violated a number of rights guaranteed under Article 5 (Right to Liberty and Security) of the Convention. For instance, at the moment of Sannikov's arrest police did not show him a warrant or any other decision of judicial authority authorizing his arrest. This is not in compliance with Article 5 § 2, according to which "[e]veryone who is arrested shall be informed promptly, in a language which he understands, of

[164]Communication addressed to the Government on 9 February 2012 Concerning Andrei Sannikov, Opinions adopted by the Working Group on Arbitrary Detention at its sixty-third session, 30 April–4 May 2012, No. 14/2012 (Belarus), para 5, p. 2. https://www.freedom-now.org/wp-content/uploads/2012/07/Sannikov-UNWGAD-Opinion-5.4.12.pdf. (link no longer active).

[165]Communication addressed to the Government on 9 February 2012 Concerning Andrei Sannikov, Opinions adopted by the Working Group on Arbitrary Detention at its sixty-third session, 30 April–4 May 2012, No. 14/2012 (Belarus), para 8, pp. 2–3. https://www.freedom-now.org/wp-content/uploads/2012/07/Sannikov-UNWGAD-Opinion-5.4.12.pdf. (link no longer active).

[166]Communication addressed to the Government on 9 February 2012 Concerning Andrei Sannikov, Opinions adopted by the Working Group on Arbitrary Detention at its sixty-third session, 30 April–4 May 2012, No. 14/2012 (Belarus), para 8, pp. 2–3. https://www.freedom-now.org/wp-content/uploads/2012/07/Sannikov-UNWGAD-Opinion-5.4.12.pdf. (link no longer active).

the reasons for his arrest and of any charge against him."[167] Furthermore, Andrei Sannikov's arrest did not meet necessity and proportionality requirements used by the Court to review potential violations of Article 5. Despite Article 5 § 1 requirements, Sannikov was not arrested for the purpose of bringing him before a legal authority on a reasonable suspicion that he committed an offence, or that he could commit such an offence in the future and try to escape prosecution. The Government of Belarus did not manage to demonstrate the necessity of Sannikov's arrest, because it did not produce any evidence that "Sannikov had engaged in or incited any disorder or violence at the demonstration, caused or incited harm to people, or destroyed or incited destruction of property…[while] none of the witnesses identified Mr. Sannikov as a person who committed violence or disobeyed police orders."[168] Given the above-mentioned considerations, the Court would most probably conclude that Sannikov's arrest was arbitrary and in violation of the requirements stipulated under Article 5 § 1 of the Convention.

Andrei Sannikov's subsequent pre-trial detention also appears to be arbitrary, because the prosecution has not provided proper reasons for depriving Sannikov of his liberty. I believe that the Court would conclude that, besides Sannikov's arbitrary arrest, his pre-trial detention was not a proportionate measure, taking into account that the national authorities of Belarus simply disregarded other less strict measures that could have been applied to him. For instance, "[a]ttempts by Mr. Sannikov's attorney to have him released on bail in advance of trial were unsuccessful."[169] Furthermore, similar to Statkevich's case, Sannikov's requests to replace his detention with a different measure were rejected by the trial court without proper justification. According to Andrei Sannikov's complaint, "[d]uring his pretrial detention, Mr. Sannikov sought an order from a Belarusian court for his release, but the court rejected the request."[170] It also appears from Sannikov's complaint[171] that the trial court ordered Sannikov's detention for an unlimited period of time, which contradicts the previous case law, in which the Court found that such a practice is incompatible with the Convention.[172] Due to these reasons, Court would most probably conclude that the entire period of Sannikov's pre-trial detention constituted an arbitrary deprivation of liberty in violation of Article 5 § 1 ECHR.

---

[167]The European Convention on Human Rights (ECHR), opened for signature 4 November 1950 (entered into force 3 September 1953). https://www.hri.org/docs/ECHR50.html. Accessed 27 December 2020.

[168]Petition To: United Nations Working Group on Arbitrary Detention, Human Rights Council United Nations General Assembly, In the Matter of Andrei Sannikov, Citizen of Belarus v. Government of Belarus. https://www.freedom-now.org/wp-content/uploads/2011/11/Petition-re-Andrei-Sannikov-15.09.11.pdf. (link no longer active).

[169]Charter '97 2011a.

[170]Petition To: United Nations Working Group on Arbitrary Detention, Human Rights Council United Nations General Assembly, In the Matter of Andrei Sannikov, Citizen of Belarus v. Government of Belarus. https://www.freedom-now.org/wp-content/uploads/2011/11/Petition-re-Andrei-Sannikov-15.09.11.pdf. (link no longer active).

[171]Ibid.

[172]*Kharchenko* 2011, above n 117, para 98.

The criminal trial in Andrei Sannikov's case has also violated basic principles of the fair trial stipulated under Article 6 of the Convention. Similar to Mikalai Statkevich, the national authorities of Belarus deprived Sannikov of the right to presumption of innocence stipulated under Article 6 § 2 of the Convention when senior government officials made statements that alleged Sannikov's guilt prior to his trial. Besides president Lukashenko, who publicly accused Sannikov and other protestors of organizing coup d'état,[173] "when announcing the charges against Sannikov…, the prosecutors declared this 'guilt was proved in full'."[174] Furthermore, similar to Mikalai Statkevich, Sannikov became a victim of state media propaganda, which portrayed him and other protestors as violent criminals that wanted to overthrow the legitimate government. For instance, "Belarusian state media aired a television special entitled "The Square: Metal Against Glass," which depicted the demonstration as an attempted coup and showed staged photographs of shovels, ice axes, and explosive material allegedly left in the square by the demonstrators."[175] Thus, Sannikov and other arrested opposition leaders became victims of prosecutorial bias, which led the trial court to presume their guilt before it delivered its judgment.

Andrei Sannikov was also denied access to legal counsel in violation of Article 6 § 4(c) of the Convention. During his stay in the KGB pre-trial detention center, "Sannikov was not permitted to see a lawyer in private until he had been in detention for nearly three months."[176] When Pavel Sapelko, who was Andrei Sannikov's lawyer, gave a press-conference "about Mr. Sannikov's "horrendous" condition and the mistreatment done to him during his pretrial detention…[, he] was subsequently disbarred by the Minsk City Bar Association."[177] The national authorities of Belarus have also violated other minimum rights outlined for a fair trial under Article 6 of the Convention in Sannikov's case. For instance, the trial court violated Sannikov's right to have adequate time and facilities necessary for the preparation of his defense outlined in Article 6 § 4(b) of the European Convention on Human Rights.

According to Sannikov's complaint his "lawyers were not provided with any evidence, nor with the Government's official statement of the charges until three weeks before the trial commenced…[which] did not leave…[them] sufficient time

---

[173] Petition To: United Nations Working Group on Arbitrary Detention, Human Rights Council United Nations General Assembly, In the Matter of Andrei Sannikov, Citizen of Belarus v. Government of Belarus. https://www.freedom-now.org/wp-content/uploads/2011/11/Petition-re-Andrei-Sannikov-15.09.11.pdf. (link no longer active).

[174] Communication addressed to the Government on 9 February 2012 Concerning Andrei Sannikov, Opinions adopted by the Working Group on Arbitrary Detention at its sixty-third session, 30 April–4 May 2012, No. 14/2012 (Belarus), para 12, p. 30. https://www.freedom-now.org/wp-content/uploads/2012/07/Sannikov-UNWGAD-Opinion-5.4.12.pdf. (link no longer active).

[175] Petition To: United Nations Working Group on Arbitrary Detention, Human Rights Council United Nations General Assembly, In the Matter of Andrei Sannikov, Citizen of Belarus v. Government of Belarus. https://www.freedom-now.org/wp-content/uploads/2011/11/Petition-re-Andrei-Sannikov-15.09.11.pdf. (link no longer active).

[176] Ibid.

[177] Ibid.

to prepare a proper defence."[178] Furthermore, the trial court displayed prosecutorial bias by providing the prosecution with more favorable treatment than defense, which undermined the equality of arms guaranteed under Article 6 § 1. In particular, "[a]t trial…Mr. Sannikov provided statements that impeached the prosecution's witnesses, but the court ignored the evidence presented by Mr. Sannikov and credited only the government's evidence."[179] Moreover, in relation to witness statements in violation of Article 6 § 3(d) Sannikov could not examine witnesses against him and ensure attendance of witnesses on his behalf. According to experts who observed Sannikov's trial "twenty-nine prosecution witnesses were announced, only eight showed up to testify, with the rest allegedly on 'holiday.'"[180] The trial court simply ignored evidence presented by defense witnesses, "all of whom testified that the demonstration was peaceful and that Mr. Sannikov did not encourage any rioting or violent acts…[and] adopted the prosecution's indictment and statement of evidence verbatim, without referencing the defense evidence."[181] Given the above mentioned procedural irregularities of Andrei Sannikov's trial, it is very likely that the European Court of Human Rights would find that Sannikov's was denied a fair trial in violation of Article 6 ECHR.

Similar to Mikalai Statkevich, Andrei Sannikov suffered from ill-treatment during his arrest and subsequent pre-trial detention. In particular, Sannikov became a victim of police brutality when shortly before his arrest "[p]olice assaulted Mr. Sannikov by pinning him down with a riot shield and repeatedly jumping on it, severely injuring his legs."[182] In detention Sannikov was subjected to both moral and physical ill-treatment. Sannikov experienced physical suffering when "[h]e was beaten up on multiple occasions…[,] was denied access to the toilet…[,] was detained in a freezing cellar…[and] was forced to carry all his personal belongings to…[the] cold cellar where he was made to stand naked by the wall with arms and legs outstretched for long periods and to squat…[,] [d]espite pain in his injured legs, he was not allowed to change position."[183] Sannikov also experienced moral suffering when "Vadim

[178]Communication addressed to the Government on 9 February 2012 Concerning Andrei Sannikov, Opinions adopted by the Working Group on Arbitrary Detention at its sixty-third session, 30 April–4 May 2012, No. 14/2012 (Belarus), para 12, p. 3. https://www.freedom-now.org/wp-content/uploads/2012/07/Sannikov-UNWGAD-Opinion-5.4.12.pdf. (link no longer active).

[179]Petition To: United Nations Working Group on Arbitrary Detention, Human Rights Council United Nations General Assembly, In the Matter of Andrei Sannikov, Citizen of Belarus v. Government of Belarus. https://www.freedom-now.org/wp-content/uploads/2011/11/Petition-re-Andrei-Sannikov-15.09.11.pdf. (link no longer active).

[180]Charter'97 2011b.

[181]Petition To: United Nations Working Group on Arbitrary Detention, Human Rights Council United Nations General Assembly, In the Matter of Andrei Sannikov, Citizen of Belarus v. Government of Belarus. https://www.freedom-now.org/wp-content/uploads/2011/11/Petition-re-Andrei-Sannikov-15.09.11.pdf. (link no longer active).

[182]Petition To: United Nations Working Group on Arbitrary Detention, Human Rights Council United Nations General Assembly, In the Matter of Andrei Sannikov, Citizen of Belarus v. Government of Belarus. https://www.freedom-now.org/wp-content/uploads/2011/11/Petition-re-Andrei-Sannikov-15.09.11.pdf. (link no longer active).

[183]Ibid.

Zaitsev, the head of the KGB, threatened more brutal measures against his wife and child if he did not give incriminatory testimony."[184] As a result of this inhuman and degrading treatment Sannikov's health significantly deteriorated. In particular, "Sannikov sustained on December 19, 2010 and in prison, he has long suffered from a variety of other ailments, such as gout and otitis, which have been exacerbated by his continued abuse."[185] The trial court ignored Sannikov's poor health condition and rejected his multiple requests "to pause the trial so that he could receive medical assistance."[186] The national authorities of Belarus have not conducted effective investigation required under Article 3 ECHR into Sannikov's complaints about his alleged torture and "[t]he [trial] court did not order an investigation of this torture and mistreatment."[187] Given the serious injuries sustained by Andrei Sannikov during his arrest, the deterioration of his health due to the inhuman conditions of his detention, as well as Sannikov's physical and mental suffering, the European Court of Human rights would most probably conclude that Sannikov's ill-treatment reached the minimum level of severity to be classified as torture within the meaning of Article 3 of the Convention.

Similar to other opposition leaders arrested by the riot police on 19 December 2010, Andrei Sannikov claimed that his arrest, subsequent detention and imprisonment were politically motivated. If the European Court of Human Rights had a chance to review Sannikov's case, it would probably address the issue of politicized justice in the framework of Article 18 in conjunction with other articles of the Convention. Similar to Mikalai Statkevich's case, Andrei Sannikov claimed that he was a victim of political, persecution, because he exercised such rights as freedom of expression, freedom of assembly and association that are guaranteed under Articles 11 and 10 ECHR. Although national authorities of Belarus argued that Sannikov and other protestors were detained on December 19th due to national security reasons, "a number of international observers have recognized—and the evidence available

[184] Amnesty International: Four Convicted. Petition To: United Nations Working Group on Arbitrary Detention, Human Rights Council United Nations General Assembly, In the Matter of Andrei Sannikov, Citizen of Belarus v. Government of Belarus. https://www.freedom-now.org/wp-content/uploads/2011/11/Petition-re-Andrei-Sannikov-15.09.11.pdf. (link no longer active).

[185] Petition To: United Nations Working Group on Arbitrary Detention, Human Rights Council United Nations General Assembly, In the Matter of Andrei Sannikov, Citizen of Belarus v. Government of Belarus. https://www.freedom-now.org/wp-content/uploads/2011/11/Petition-re-Andrei-Sannikov-15.09.11.pdf. (link no longer active).

[186] Communication addressed to the Government on 9 February 2012 Concerning Andrei Sannikov, Opinions adopted by the Working Group on Arbitrary Detention at its sixty-third session, 30 April–4 May 2012, No. 14/2012 (Belarus), para 12, p. 3. https://www.freedom-now.org/wp-content/uploads/2012/07/Sannikov-UNWGAD-Opinion-5.4.12.pdf. (link no longer active).

[187] Petition To: United Nations Working Group on Arbitrary Detention, Human Rights Council United Nations General Assembly, In the Matter of Andrei Sannikov, Citizen of Belarus v. Government of Belarus. https://www.freedom-now.org/wp-content/uploads/2011/11/Petition-re-Andrei-Sannikov-15.09.11.pdf. (link no longer active).

has shown—that the protests, in general, and Mr. Sannikov's speech, in particular, did not constitute a threat to the national security of Belarus."[188] Furthermore, statements made by senior state officials of Belarus[189] who blamed Sannikov and other protestors for exercising their freedom of expression prior to the trial demonstrated that Sannikov's arrest, detention and imprisonment were a results of improper political reasons that are not covered by the Convention requirements.

Political motives behind Sannikov's arrest became clear after his release from prison, when "[d]uring a press conference on 21 April 2012, President Lukashenko is quoted as saying in reference to Messrs. Sannikov and Bandarenka, '[o]ne more [act of] pressure and those blabbermouths, who have been set free and should say thanks for that, may return to prison. If they blabber, they will go back there.'"[190] The open threat of the re-arrest, thus, showed that the national authorities of Belarus did not act in good faith when they arrested and prosecuted Andrei Sannikov and other participants of the peaceful demonstration against the electoral fraud. Such statements made by the head of state also convincingly show that from the beginning to the end of Andrei Sannikov's trial the whole legal machinery was misused to punish Sannikov for his criticism of the Government of Belarus in blatant disregard of the European Convention of Human Rights as well as Belarus' own Constitution, the International Covenant on Civil and Political Rights and the Universal Declaration of Human Rights.[191] I believe that Andrei Sannikov produced evidence that goes beyond a mere suspicion and would be sufficient to convince the European Court of Human that his rights were restricted for improper political reasons. Therefore, it is very likely that, similar to Mikalai Statkevich's case, the Court could find that Andrei

---

[188]Communication addressed to the Government on 9 February 2012 Concerning Andrei Sannikov, Opinions adopted by the Working Group on Arbitrary Detention at its sixty-third session, 30 April–4 May 2012, No. 14/2012 (Belarus), para 5, p. 2. https://www.freedom-now.org/wp-content/uploads/2012/07/Sannikov-UNWGAD-Opinion-5.4.12.pdf. (link no longer active).

[189]For instance, when Sannikov and other protestors were arrested, President Lukashenko made a public statement, "That's enough of that. There won't be any more silly democracy, muddle-headed democracy in the country." In Amnesty International Report, Petition To: United Nations Working Group on Arbitrary Detention, Human Rights Council United Nations General Assembly, In the Matter of Andrei Sannikov, Citizen of Belarus v. Government of Belarus. https://www.freedom-now.org/wp-content/uploads/2011/11/Petition-re-Andrei-Sannikov-15.09.11.pdf. (link no longer active).

[190]Communication addressed to the Government on 9 February 2012 Concerning Andrei Sannikov, Opinions adopted by the Working Group on Arbitrary Detention at its sixty-third session, 30 April–4 May 2012, No. 14/2012 (Belarus), para 35, p. 6, available at https://www.freedom-now.org/wp-content/uploads/2012/07/Sannikov-UNWGAD-Opinion-5.4.12.pdf. (link no longer active).

[191]In particular, fundamental freedoms of peaceful assembly and association stipulated under *Articles 21* and *22* of the *International Covenant on Civil and Political Rights* (ICCPR), adopted and opened for signature 16 December 1966 (entered into force 23 March 1976); *Article 20* of the *Universal Declaration of Human Rights* (UDHR), adopted and proclaimed by UN General Assembly Resolution 217 A (III) of 10 December 1948 during the 183rd plenary meeting, and *Article 35* and *36* of the Constitution of Belarus, the right to a fair trial under *Article 14* of the ICCPR, *Articles 10* and *11* of the UDHR and *Article 26* of the Constitution of Belarus as well as the freedom of thought and expression under *Articles 18* and *19* of the ICCPR and UDHR and *Article 33* of the Constitution.

Sannikov's rights were restricted for other reasons than those permissible under the European Convention of Human Rights.

3.6 Prima-Facie Criteria to Assess Politically Motivated Justice

Based on the case study of political trials analyzed in the previous sections, the goal of this section is to outline prima-facie criteria that can be used in the future to evaluate allegations about politically motivated justice. Taking into account that the European Court of Human Rights (ECtHR) has already reviewed a substantial number of cases related to politically motivated justice in the former Soviet Union,[192] it would make sense to develop a list of potential prima-facie criteria using the language from the case law of the Court. These criteria are, in turn, closely connected with the major components of criminal proceedings. Overall, the book discerns five essential components of such proceedings: (1) Pretrial Investigation; (2) Goal of a Trial; (3) Procedural Safeguards; (4) Outcome of the Trial; (5) Enforcement of the Sentence Delivered by Court. Assessment of these components gives an opportunity to develop the list of criteria to evaluate 'political trials' in transitional post-Soviet republics and developed Western democracies from a comparative perspective. The first stage of the pre-trial investigation sheds light on important differences that exist among trials related to politics in the former USSR and in Western Europe.

The *first criterion* of the pre-trial stage is connected with the question whether a suspect in a 'political case' has been detained or arrested and whether a political party has to stop its activities during proceedings aimed at banning the party. If the suspect has been deprived of his or her liberty, it is essential to clarify in this regard whether the measures alternative to detention such as release on bail or house arrest have been effectively available at the pre-trial stage. In transitional post-Soviet states, the overwhelming majority of politicized trials involve the detention of a suspect before and during a trial.[193] In established Western democracies, on the contrary, a suspect in a 'political case' is not necessarily kept in detention. For instance, the Austrian representative in the European Parliament Ernst Strasser, the Austrian far-right MP Susanne Winter and the Former German President Christian Wulff were not deprived of their liberty during the trial proceedings. Furthermore, the National Democratic

---

[192] In particular, ECtHR Ilgar Mammadov v Azerbaijan, 22 May 2014, Case No. 15172/13; ECtHR, Tymoshenko v Ukraine, 30 April 2013, Case No. 49872/11; ECtHR, Lutsenko v Ukraine, 3 July 2012, Case No. 6492/11; ECtHR, *Khodorkovskiy v Russia,* 31 May 2011, Case No. 5829/04 and ECtHR, *Gusinskiy v Russia,* 19 May 2004, Case No. 70276/01.

[193] In all cases selected for this book from Belarus and Ukraine ('Tymoshenko v Ukraine' App no 49872/1 and 'Lutsenko v Ukraine' App no 6492/11 from Ukraine, Mikalai Statkevich and Andrei Sannikov from Belarus), the detained opposition leaders have been detained before or shortly after the beginning of their politicized show trials. Ukrainian and Belarus courts routinely rejected, without giving any specific reasons, the defendants' applications for measures alternative to detention.

Party of Germany (NPD) could continue its political activities, while the German Constitutional Court was deciding whether to ban the NPD due to the party's far-right activities in Germany.[194] It appears that post-Soviet ruling elites often use the prolonged deprivation of liberty to put pressure on political opponents, who are then at 'full disposal' of detention authorities, label detained opposition representatives as 'dangerous criminals' in the public discourse as well collect self-incriminatory evidence and confessions from suspects to justify their arrest and detention post-factum. Thus, the unavailability of the measures alternative to detention can render proceedings in such political cases arbitrary.

Moreover, the deprivation of liberty as such can also be called politically motivated if charges against a detained opposition politician do not amount to a 'reasonable suspicion' within the meaning of *Article 5 § 1(c)* of the European Convention on Human Rights. Although, according to the case law of the Court, "high political status does not grant immunity",[195] the Convention requirement that the deprivation of liberty must be based on a 'reasonable suspicion' can protect a suspect from arbitrary persecution. In this context, the 'reasonable suspicion' "mean[s] the existence of facts or information which would satisfy an objective observer that the person concerned may have committed the offence".[196] Therefore, if the suspect's pre-trial detention in a 'political case' is not based on a reasonable suspicion and he or she cannot effectively apply for measures alternative to detention, the deprivation of liberty can point to the politicized nature of the pre-trial component of criminal proceedings in a given case.

The *second criterion* to evaluate politically motivated justice would be the overall goal of criminal proceedings. In other words, why is a trial organized in the first place and what do trial parties attempt to achieve? It appears that in developed Western democracies the goal of a 'political trial' (i.e. a trial related to politics) is more or less similar to that of a non-political trial. In general, in democratic countries the goal of an independent system of judiciary in political as well as in non-political cases is to give both prosecution and a defendant an opportunity to present their arguments and evidence in order to determine guilt or innocence of the defendant. In pluralistic democratic societies, a political trial can often attract significant public attention and provoke an open debate in the media. This, in turn, may motivate a judge in such a trial to consider how to ensure access of media and the public to trial hearings without disadvantaging one of the trial parties and compromising confidentiality of trial records prior to the court verdict. The theatricalization of politicized trials in transitional former Soviet republics reveals a different goal of criminal proceedings in such cases. One goal of politicized trials in such countries is to send a 'warning message' to a larger group of political opposition (anti-corruption campaigners, protest artists,

---

[194] Bligh 2014.

[195] *Khodorkovskiy* 2011, above n 161, p. 62, para 251.

[196] *Khodorkovskiy* 2011, above n 161, p. 62, para 251. https://hudoc.echr.coe.int/sites/eng/pages/search.aspx#{%22appno%22:[%225829/04%22],%22itemid%22:[%22001104983%22]}. Accessed 27 December 2020.

'foreign agents' etc.), which is affiliated with a defendant. Another goal of politicized proceedings is to remove the defendant from politics as well as destroy him or her through physical and psychological pressure, public humiliation, torture[197] and denial of medical treatment.[198] The language used by the European Court of Human Rights provides useful guidance in this regard.

The Court talks, in particular, about "a 'hidden [political] agenda', [which can rebut]…the presumption…[that member states act in] good faith."[199] According to the case law of the Court, the burden of proof lies on an applicant, who alleges that criminal charges against him or her were politically motivated (i.e. pursued a hidden political agenda). In order to prove the presence of such a hidden political agenda and rebut the presumption of good faith, the applicant must present to the Court direct and incontrovertible proof "that the whole legal machinery of the respondent State in the present case was ab initio misused, that from the beginning to the end the authorities were acting with bad faith and in blatant disregard of the Convention."[200] Although the standard of proof required by the Court is quite high, the criterion of the goal of criminal proceedings could reveal essential characteristics of politicized justice. *First*, this criterion can help generally assess whether authorities organize a trial against a politician to intimidate a broader group of political opposition. *Second*, by examining the goal of criminal proceedings in a politicized criminal case, it is possible to find a hidden political agenda, which may uncover the abuse of the entire legal machinery in a given country by national authorities that blatantly violated the Convention.

The *third criterion* would be a flow of proceedings in a political case. Similar to other criteria, in democratic states criminal proceedings do not substantially differ from each other in political and non-political cases. Whether a trial is held against a politician or not, judges in such states follow usual procedures prescribed by law. It also means that defendants are neither put in a disadvantageous position nor enjoy any special status due to their involvement in politics. For instance, similar to suspects in non-political cases, politicians who face criminal charges in Western democracies and their legal counsels have sufficient time to study the case file and prepare for the defense. In transitional post-Soviet states, on the contrary, political cases stood out, as they involve a range of irregularities and expedited extra-judicial procedures

---

[197]See, for example, the report prepared by the European Committee for the Prevention of Torture and Inhuman or Degrading Treatment or Punishment (CPT) on the visit to Ukraine from *29 November to 6 December 2011*, which addressed issues of alleged torture and outlined problems related to the provision of medical treatment to then imprisoned leaders of the Ukrainian opposition Ms. Tymoshenko and Mr. Lutsenko. https://rm.coe.int/1680698448. Accessed 27 December 2020.

[198]See also the request made by the European Court of Human Rights under Rule 39 of its Rules of Court on 15 March 2012, "indicating to the Ukrainian Government that her medical treatment in an appropriate institutionalised setting should be ensured." A press-release on the judgment in the Case '*Tymoshenko v. Ukraine*' d.d. 30 April 2013. https://hudoc.echr.coe.int/sites/eng-press/pages/search.aspx?i=003-4343134-5208270. Accessed 27 December 2020.

[199]See the final judgment in the case "Khodorkovskiy v. Russia", p. 65, para 260, available at https://hudoc.echr.coe.int/eng#{%22tabview%22:[%22document%22],%22itemid%22:[%22001-104983%22]}. Accessed 27 December 2020.

[200]Ibid.

that are aimed at disadvantaging the defense and undermining the equality of arms principle.

In a typical politicized trial and accused person has a very short time to familiarize himself or herself with the case file, as all proceedings are accelerated in contrast with non-political cases, where the same proceedings are usually prolonged and repeatedly delayed due to the case overload in courts and ineffectiveness of investigative authorities. For instance, in their joint concurring opinion Jungwiert, Nussberger and Potocki noted that then the leader of the united opposition forces in Ukraine Yulia Tymoshenko faced 'accelerated pre-trial investigation' that was conducted within less than six weeks, while Ms. Tymoshenko had to read more than 4000 pages of case materials as well as attend numerous investigative events and courts hearings.[201] Similar to Ms. Tymoshenko, at the same time another leader of the Ukrainian opposition Yuri Lutsenko faced akin procedural irregularities. In particular, a Ukrainian court ordered Mr. Lutsenko's detention, because he allegedly tried to disadvantage other trial parties by reading 'too slowly' *forty-seven volumes* of his case-file. The European Court of human rights reasoned that this decision of the Ukrainian court was disproportionate, taking into account that under the Ukrainian law "study of a case file is a right and not an obligation of an accused and that the time available to an accused for study of the case file should not be limited (Articles 142 and 218… of the Code of Criminal Procedure…[of Ukraine].)"[202] Therefore, such arbitrarily applied procedural irregularities and accelerated proceedings could point to the presence of politicized justice in a given case.

The *fourth criterion* to assess a political case is an outcome of a trial. In developed Western democracies even in cases of politicians, who lost public support and faced substantial criticism in the media, there is still a fair chance that the defendant could be exonerated as a result of the trial,[203] or that defendant's sentence could be reversed, suspended or reduced by the higher court.[204] Ruling elites of transitional post-Soviet states, on the contrary, use dependent judiciary to arrange a verdict against representatives of political opposition well before a trial. Representatives of the political opposition, who face a politicized show trial in such countries, are usually 'doomed'

---

[201] *Tymoshenko* 2013, above n 83, the Joint Concurring Opinion.

[202] *Lutsenko* 2012, above n 76, pp. 26–27, para 69. https://hudoc.echr.coe.int/sites/eng/pages/search.aspx#%7B%22appno%22:[%226492/11%22]%7D. Accessed 27 December 2020.

[203] For instance, although the former German President Christian Wulff had to resign from his position as a result of media criticism, which questioned his work ethics, the German court acquitted him of all charges after a long trial. In Tovrov 2014. See also "the Former German President Wulff acquitted on corruption charges," 27 February 2014, https://www.dw.com/en/former-german-president-wulff-acquitted-on-corruption-charges/a-17460629. Accessed 27 December 2020.

[204] For example, the senior Austrian politician Ernst Strasser, whose case was reviewed in this book, was found guilty on charges of bribery and corruption and sentenced to four years in jail, lost the final appeal against his sentence. Nevertheless, the Supreme Court of Austria still reduced Strasser's sentence to three years. See the reasoning of the Supreme Court of Austria in Ernst Strasser's case available in German: https://www.ris.bka.gv.at/Dokument.wxe?Abfrage=Justiz&Dokumentnummer=JJT_20141013_OGH0002_0170OS00030_14M0000_000. Accessed 27 December 2020.

to receive a guilty verdict.[205] Taking into account that the outcome of politicized show trials is pre-determined in transitional post-Soviet countries regardless of the actual guilt or innocence of an accused opposition politician, this is a blatant violation of *Article 6* (the Right to a Fair Trial) of the European Convention of Human Rights (ECHR) and the principle *Nullum Crimen, Nulla Poena Sine Lege* (no punishment without law).

The proposed criteria of the trial outcome can reveal politicized justice depending on very particular circumstances of each case. Various factors such as other show trials interconnected with each other, the intensity of a smear campaign against a defendant and criminalization of 'socially dangerous actions' not penalized under law should be reviewed in their totality in each particular case. For instance, Yulia Tymoshenko, whose case was reviewed in this text, faced criminal charges in Ukraine for signing a contract on import of Russian gas on allegedly unfavorable for the state conditions, which has never been criminally prosecuted in similar cases in the history of independent Ukraine. Although Tymoshenko was not charged with committing corruption, fraud or other crimes penalized under the Ukrainian law, as prosecutors did not charge her with obtaining a personal profit from the gas deal, the Ukrainian court violated her Convention rights by arbitrarily recharacterizing Tymoshenko's actions as the abuse of official powers and sentencing her to seven years in prison.[206] The 'outcomes' of the criminal proceedings against Tymoshenko, such as her removal from politics shortly before the parliamentary elections of 2012, her arbitrary detention,[207] simultaneous prosecution of more than eight senior members of her Cabinet and a state sponsored smear campaign against her, could altogether demonstrate that "there were other ulterior [political] motives...of the relevant authorities which were not related to the proper conduct of the criminal proceedings per se."[208] Therefore, the outcome of a trial can shed light on potential ulterior motives of authorities that brought charges in a given political case.

The *fifth criterion* to assess politically motivated justice would be the enforcement of a sentence delivered in a political case. In particular, I argue that it is important to know whether the court sentence has been actually enforced and, if yes, how. In

---

[205]The best example would be the case of Ilgar Mammadov, whose right to the presumption of innocence guaranteed under Article 6 § 2 of the European Convention on Human Rights (ECtHR) was violated when the Prosecutor General and the Ministry of Internal Affairs of Azerbaijan issued a press statement, which alleged Mammadov's guilt before his trial was conducted. See the final judgment '*Ilgar Mammadov v. Azerbaijan*' para 143. https://hudoc.echr.coe.int/eng#{"appno":["15172/13"],"itemid":["001-144124"]}. Accessed 27 December 2020.

[206]See the Statement from 22 January 2015 by the ECtHR on the friendly settlement and the Ukrainian Government's declaration in which they admitted that the criminal prosecution of Ms Tymoshenko had been politically motivated and in which they acknowledged a violation of her Convention rights, available at https://hudoc.echr.coe.int/eng#{%22itemid%22:[%22001-150832%22]}. Accessed 27 December 2020. See also Tymoshenko 2013, above n 83.

[207]See the Press Release of the European Court of Human Rights from 30.04.2013. Former Prime Minister of Ukraine was arbitrarily detained. http://hudoc.echr.coe.int/webservices/content/pdf/003-4343134-5208270. Accessed 27 December 2020.

[208]See *Tymoshenko* 2013, above n 83, the Joint Concurring Opinion by *Judges Jungwiert, Nussberger and Potocki.*

democratic countries, defendants that are found guilty and sentenced by courts in both political and non-political cases usually observe their verdicts without any privileges or exemptions. Furthermore, powerful politicians and common criminals do their time in prison under the same conditions. For instance, Ernst Strasser, who used to be the Minister of Interior of Austria, became a simple librarian in a prison library after the Austrian court sentenced him to imprisonment on corruption charges.[209] In transitional post-Soviet states even sentenced opposition politicians still keep their 'elite status' and sometimes receive a privileged treatment even in prisons. For instance, Ms. Tymoshenko, whose case has been analyzed in this book, argued in her application to ECtHR that she suffered torture due to the lack of medical care provided to her in prison in violation of Article 3 ECHR.

The Court, however, rejected her complaint on the grounds that "Ms. Tymoshenko's health had received considerable attention from the Ukrainian authorities, which had invested efforts far beyond the normal health-care arrangements available for ordinary detainees in Ukraine."[210] Very often in post-Soviet republics the political nature of criminal proceedings against opposition politicians is also finally confirmed when the government arbitrarily amnesties or pardons only some prisoners in violation of previous practice and procedure. Such quasi-legal amnesties are supposed to show the 'leniency' of the ruling elites and their readiness to cooperate with the international community. For instance, although the President of Azerbaijan has released few political prisoners in order to receive an invitation to attend the Nuclear Security Summit in Washington in the US, in 2016,[211] according to the estimates of human rights observers, *one hundred forty-two* political prisoners are still deprived of their liberty in prisons of Azerbaijan.[212] Similar quasi-legal amnesties occurred in Belarus. In 2015, President of Belarus Alexander Lukashenka also pardoned six political prisoners to receive foreign financial aid and international recognition of his fifth term in office.[213] The former presidential candidate Mikalai Statkevich, whose case has been reviewed in this text, was also pardoned by Lukashenka just one day after the deadline for submitting applications for the

---

[209] See "Former Minister Now a Prison Librarian", 18 November 2014. https://www.thelocal.at/20141118/former-minister-now-a-prison-librarian. Accessed 27 December 2020.

[210] See *Tymoshenko* 2013, above n 83, para 214. https://hudoc.echr.coe.int/sites/eng/pages/search.aspx?i=001-119382#{%22itemid%22:[%22001-119382%22]}. Accessed 27 December 2020.

"Government representatives also argued in Tymoshenko's case that her "cell had been equipped with a supply of hot and cold water, a separate toilet and a washing stand with a tap and had been equipped with central heating…The Government observed that while, according to the general rule, each detainee was provided with access to bathing facilities for thirty minutes once every seven days, the applicant had been permitted to have a shower several times a week." See Tymoshenko 2013, above n 83, paras 42–44. https://hudoc.echr.coe.int/sites/eng/pages/search.aspx?i=001-119382#{%22itemid%22:[%22001-119382%22]}. Accessed 27 December 2020.

[211] Ismayilova 2016.

[212] See the Press-Release "Working Group presents update list of political prisoners in Azerbaijan", 22 March 2018. https://www.humanrightsclub.net/en/prisoners/2018/707/. Accessed 27 December 2020.

[213] See Deutsche Welle 2015.

presidential elections in 2015.[214] Therefore, if applied, amnesties, pardons and other arbitrary quasi-legal decisions, aimed at relieving a person from a sentence delivered by court in a political case, would strongly indicate the presence of politicized justice.

Given the above-mentioned considerations, it is, thus, possible to argue that five criteria could be used to make a prima-facie assessment of allegations about politically motivated justice against a politician or a political party at various stages of criminal proceedings. *First*, during the pre-trial stage, it is essential to determine whether a person suspected of committing an offence was deprived of liberty and then could effectively apply for measures alternative to detention. In transitional post-Soviet states, arrest and detention of opposition politicians usually signal that ruling elites use politicized justice in order to remove their competitors from politics prior to elections, 'label' the opposition as criminal as well as put additional psychological and physical pressure on government critics during their prolonged detention before and during a trial. *Second*, in order to reveal the politicized nature of criminal proceedings against a politician, it is necessary to identify the true goal of such proceedings. If a state uses an entire legal machinery against a defendant by arbitrarily rejecting all defense motions, tacitly supporting or openly ignoring a smear campaign against the defendant in the media, interrupting defendant's political activities during criminal proceedings as well as using such proceedings to intimidate other opposition representatives, all of this could constitute direct and incontrovertible proof that the state was not acting in good faith and there was a 'hidden political agenda' behind the criminal proceedings.

Third, the flow of criminal proceedings could include various politically motivated procedural irregularities such as a very short time allocated to a defendant and his or her counsel to study a case file, accelerated proceedings in political cases in contrast with prolonged proceedings in non-political cases. *Fourth*, the eventual outcome of a trial against a politician could demonstrate whether allegations about politicized justice were true in the first place. While in established democracies a trial against a politician often leads to his or her acquittal, reduction or reversal of sentence on appeal, in transitional states 'show trials' against opposition usually end with a well-anticipated politicized guilty verdict, which removes an opposition politician from politics shortly before elections and establishes a 'precedent' to criminalize 'socially dangerous' political activities, to justify the continuous persecution of opposition. *Fifth*, a subsequent enforcement of a verdict in a 'political case' could finally confirm or reject allegations about politicized justice. In post-Soviet states, politicians sentenced to prison by court often enjoy certain privileges that are not available to other common inmates. Besides better conditions of their incarceration, some political prisoners are arbitrarily 'pardoned' by ruling elites that seek closer cooperation with the international community despite other political prisoners remaining in jail.

---

[214] See the Media Release: Belarusian Politician Mikalai Statkevich Released from Prison, 22 August 2015. https://www.freedom-now.org/news/media-release-belarusian-politician-mikalai-statkevich-released-from-prison/. Accessed 27 December 2020.

3.7 The Role of the Council of Europe in Preventing a Relapse into Politicized Justice

Based on the case study of trials from Western Europe and the former Soviet Union analyzed in this book, it is possible to argue that the membership in the Council of Europe and the ratification of the European Convention on Human Rights (ECHR) could play an important role in preventing a relapse into politically motivated justice in post-Soviet states. In particular, the European Court of Human Rights (ECtHR) provides a forum for strategic litigation as a means of political pressure[215] on those post-Soviet member states of the Council of Europe, where rights of political opposition are violated. The case law of the European Court of Human Rights identifies issues related to politically motivated justice common for many post-Soviet states. By condemning politically motivated prosecution of political opposition in the former Soviet republics, the ECtHR could act as the 'court of last instance' for opposition leaders, whose complaints have been routinely disregarded by national authorities.[216] As a sign of this positive influence, courts of many post-Soviet states that joined the Council of Europe learned how to apply and follow the case law[217] of the European Court of Human Rights in relation to the freedom of speech and complaints submitted by representatives of political opposition. Furthermore, the supervision of the Council of Europe over ECtHR's judgments execution and the possibility of infringement proceedings against non-implementing member states often appear to be the only help that persecuted opposition politicians and human rights activists[218] could receive after submitting a complaint about their politicized justice to the court in Strasburg. The membership in the Council of Europe appears to be beneficial for democratic transformations in the former Soviet republics.

In particular, the membership in the Council of Europe gives an opportunity to ratify its other basic agreements and conventions[219] that could promote the Rule of Law and post-Soviet democratic transformations. In addition to the European Court of Human Rights, member states can benefit from other institutions of the Council of Europe that could help them dismantle old authoritarian practices. In particular, member states could receive advice and support from the European Commission

---

[215]See an example, how the Council of Europe put political pressure on Azerbaijan in the strategic litigation case of 'Ilgar Mammadov v. Azerbaijan'. In Andreas Zimmermann and Julie-Enni Zastrow. "EJIL: Talk!—Council of Europe's Committee of Ministers Starts Infringement Proceedings in Mammadov v. Azerbaijan: A Victory for the International Rule of Law?" Accessed 19 February 2018. https://www.ejiltalk.org/council-of-europes-committee-of-ministers-starts-infringement-proceedings-in-mammadov-v-azerbaijan-a-victory-for-the-international-rule-of-law/#more-15857. Accessed 27 December 2020.

[216]For example, national courts simply rejected complaints made by *Tymoshenko, Lutsenko* and *Khodorkovskiy.*

[217]Neshataeva 2013.

[218]Remezaite 2017.

[219]For example, since the time of its accession to the Council of Europe in 1995, Ukraine has joined the European Social Charter, the Framework Convention for the Protection of National Minorities and European Charter for Regional or Minority Languages.

for Democracy through Law (the Venice Commission), the Congress of Local and Regional Authorities and other organizations of the Council of Europe. The Council of Europe institutions do not only deal with the issues of criminal justice, but could also advise on decommunization legislation, the decentralization of government, election observation and other issues essential for successful post-communist democratic transformations. These activities are important, because by joining the Council of Europe, former Soviet republics undertook certain obligations such as the protection of "a common [European] heritage of the Rule of Law",[220] which is essential for the removal of the Soviet practices of arbitrary political persecution. The obligations do not remain just empty statements, given that the Council of Europe takes all necessary steps to monitor their practical implementation.

The monitoring mechanism of the Parliamentary Assembly of the Council of Europe and, in particular, the Special Committee on the Honoring Obligations and Commitments, prepare once in two years monitoring reports about the progress achieved by the member states in honoring the above-mentioned obligations.[221] Moreover, the Parliamentary Assembly continues a political 'post-monitoring dialogue' with non-compliant countries.[222] It helps address pending issues related to ongoing political persecutions in many former Soviet republics not only at the level of ECtHR case law, but also at the informal political level of the parliamentary 'peer-review' conducted by the Assembly. Although monitoring reports of the Assembly can lead to sanctions[223] against a non-compliant state, the monitoring procedure is in general a softer mechanism, which allows addressing sensitive political issues of the member states such as politicized trials against opposition. It is also important that former Soviet republics that joined the Council of Europe aspire to reach the human rights standard common for all member states. In particular, the Council of Europe has rejected the idea to create a two-tier system of human rights protection to accommodate a lower human rights standard in transitional post-Soviet countries like Russia, because "it would give the governments of the existing member states more latitude in weakening their own commitment to the Strasbourg system."[224] Therefore, the European Convention on Human Rights does not differentiate between initial members of the Council of Europe and new member states that recognized the jurisdiction of the European Court of Human Rights shortly after the collapse of the Soviet Union.

It is also true that the Council of Europe is not so powerful in terms of its political and financial capacities, which has recently led to an open confrontation with

---

[220]See the European Convention on Human Rights (ECHR), opened for signature 4 November 1950 (entered into force 3 September 1953). https://www.hri.org/docs/ECHR50.html. Accessed 22 August 2020.

[221]Malfliet and Parmentier 2010, p. 44.

[222]Ibid., p. 45.

[223]For example, such sanctions may include suspension of the voting rights of the non-compliant state and even its ultimate expulsion from the Council of Europe.

[224]Malfliet and Parmentier 2010, p. 192.

Russia over its financial contributions.[225] However, one cannot underestimate the symbolic importance of the Council of Europe as a regional organization, which sets the common human rights standard for the majority of European countries, except the 'pariah state' like Belarus or the semi-recognized state of Kosovo. Even the Government of Russia,[226] which makes continuous threats to leave the Council of Europe, still attempts to regain its voting rights in the Parliamentary Assembly and preserve its influence within the organization. None of this would take place, if the membership does not bring international recognition and ability to engage effectively with other states on the international plane.[227] Therefore, it is possible to conclude that the membership in the Council of Europe could provide useful mechanisms to reveal, prevent and fight against old communist practices of politically motivated justice in transitional former Soviet republics. Furthermore, republics like Belarus that have not yet joined the Council of Europe are more likely to retain strong repressive practices of politicized justice inherited from the Soviet Union.

3.8 Conclusion

Based on the above analysis of 'political cases' from Austria, Belarus, Germany and Ukraine, this research used the language of the European Court of Human Rights to formulate five prima-facie legal criteria that can be applied to evaluate future allegations about politically motivated justice at various stages of criminal proceedings in the former Soviet Union. The *first criterion* of detention can help assess during the pre-trial stage whether the deprivation of liberty is arbitrarily used by national authorities to put prolonged physical and psychological pressure on a suspect in order to remove him or her from politics as well as obtain 'self-incriminatory evidence', while no measures alternative to detention are effectively available. The *second criterion* of the goal of criminal proceedings can be used to reveal a hidden political agenda of a politicized trial. This hidden agenda usually manifests itself through a government-sponsored smear campaign against an accused person in the media, violation of the equality of parties' principle by a trial court and other government institutions that belong to the state legal machinery misused by ruling elites for the sake of political expediency.

The *third criterion* of the flow of criminal proceedings could point to such politically motivated procedural irregularities as accelerated proceedings in 'political cases' as opposed to prolonged proceedings in similar 'non-political cases', very short time allocated to the defense to study a case file and other quasi-legal techniques aimed at disadvantaging a defendant. The *fourth criterion* of the eventual outcome of proceedings may demonstrate a pre-determined verdict in a 'political case' when political activities are arbitrarily recharacterized/criminalized as 'socially dangerous

225 Deutsche Welle 2018.

226 Mälksoo and Benedek 2017.

227 Buckley 2017.

actions' and guilty verdicts against opposition politicians are well expected before major election campaigns. Finally, the *fifth criterion* of the enforcement of a verdict in a 'political case' could be the ultimate proof of politically motivated charges in a given case when only some representatives of opposition are arbitrarily pardoned or amnestied, while others sentenced in similar 'political cases' remain in prison. Although the application of the above-mentioned criteria does not guarantee that a given trial can be then categorically classified as 'politicized' or 'fair', the offered criteria rather provide a guidance what elements of criminal proceedings one should focus on to reveal the phenomenon of politicized justice.

The comparative analysis of cases from the two Western democracies and the two transitional former Soviet republics has also demonstrated the positive role played by the Council of Europe (CoE) and the European Court of Human Rights (ECtHR) in preventing and confronting cases of politically motivated justice. In particular, political opposition from the countries that joined the Council of Europe could use the ECtHR as a forum for strategic litigation and the 'court of last instance' to support arbitrarily detained and imprisoned opposition representatives. The Court in Strasbourg has already identified common issues with politicized justice in its case law, which has been already applied and followed by many national courts. Besides interim measures and recommendations given by the ECtHR to the member states, the Council of Europe (CoE) offers a monitoring mechanism to oversee the actual implementation of court's judgments by national authorities. The infringement proceedings against non-compliant states as well as the political 'post-monitoring dialogue' conducted by the Parliamentary Assembly with such countries gives an opportunity to address sensitive issues of 'political trials' that could not be otherwise resolved through the legal means. It appears, thus, that the Council of Europe plays an important role as an 'umbrella organization' for many democratic initiatives in transitional post-Soviet states.

Apart from the ECtHR's case law on 'political trials', the Council of Europe institutions can advise transitional post-Soviet republics on various legal initiatives related to the decommunization, the decentralization of government, election observation and other issues of democratic transition, which is essential for the prevention of politically motivated justice. The European Commission for Democracy through Law (the Venice Commission), the Congress of Local and Regional Authorities and other organizations of the Council of Europe played an important role of international arbiters and experts that scrutinized national legislative initiatives and developments. Most importantly, the former Soviet republics that joined the Council of Europe made serious international commitments such as the protection of "a common [European] heritage of the Rule of Law",[228] which is indispensable for the elimination of old communist practices of arbitrary persecution against political opponents. Being effectively excluded from these cooperation and monitoring mechanisms, post-Soviet states like Belarus are more likely to retain old communist practices

[228]The European Convention on Human Rights (ECHR), opened for signature 4 November 1950 (entered into force 3 September 1953). https://www.hri.org/docs/ECHR50.html. Accessed 22 August 2020.

of politicized justice inherited from the Soviet Union. Therefore, the key conclusion of this chapter is that politically motivated justice is a complex phenomenon, which requires a comparative analysis of qualitative and quantitate data in the context of dynamic social, political and legal developments in those countries where opposition faces persecution.

References

American Renaissance (2009) Austrian Far-Right Legislator Convicted of Anti-Muslim Incitement—American Renaissance. https://www.amren.com/news/2009/01/austrian_far-ri/. Accessed 26 December 2020

BBC News Europe (2010) Ukraine ex-PM Yulia Tymoshenko faces investigation, 15 December, available at https://www.bbc.co.uk/news/world-europe-12001004. Accessed 27 December 2020

Bligh G (2014) Defending Democracy: A New Understanding of the Party-Banning Phenomenon. Journal of Transnational Law, Vanderbilt University. https://www.semanticscholar.org/paper/Defending-Democracy%3A-A-New-Understanding-of-the-Bligh/9366fae2cc78500c6c1a505cec6e352a201ef779

Buckley N (2017) Russia Tests Council of Europe in Push to Regain Vote. Financial Times, 26 November. https://www.ft.com/content/3cccaf92-d12c-11e7-b781-794ce08b24dc. Accessed 27 December 2020

Charter '97 (2011a) Andrei Sannikov remains in KGB jail till trial (18 April). https://charter97.org/en/news/2011/4/18/37816/. Accessed 27 December 2020

Charter '97 (2011b) Five-Year Trial against Sannikov: Evidence for defence not attached to case (29 April 2011). https://charter97.org/en/news/2011/4/29/38164/. Accessed 27 December 2020

CNN (2003) Bid to Ban German Far Right Fails. https://edition.cnn.com/2003/WORLD/europe/03/18/germany.far.right.reut/. Accessed 26 December 2020

Danish Helsinki Committee for Human Rights (2011) Legal Monitoring in Ukraine II, available at https://khpg.org/en/index.php?id=1313446474. Accessed 27 December 2020

Deutsche Welle (2014a) Former German President Wulff acquitted on corruption charges. https://p.dw.com/p/1BGJ3. Accessed 26 December 2020

Deutsche Welle (2014b) Former German President Wulff acquitted on corruption charges. https://www.dw.com/en/former-german-president-wulff-acquitted-on-corruption-charges/a-17460629. Accessed 26 December 2020

Deutsche Welle (2015) Freed Belarus Opposition Figure Delivers Warning about Lukashenko, 24 August. www.dw.com/en/freed-belarus-opposition-figure-delivers-warning-about-lukashenko/a-18669993. Accessed 27 December 2020

Deutsche Welle (2018) Russia Withholds Payments to the Council of Europe. https://www.dw.com/en/russia-withholds-payments-to-the-council-of-europe/a-42792673. Accessed 22 August 2020

Eddy M (2014) German Ex-Leader Acquitted of Graft Charges from His Time as Governor. https://www.nytimes.com/2014/02/28/world/europe/christian-wulff.html. Accessed 26 December 2020

Gates of Vienna (2009) Susanne Winter Found Guilty. https://gatesofvienna.blogspot.com/2009/01/susanne-winter-found-guilty.html. Accessed 26 December 2020

Herszenhorn DM (2013) Journalist Is Beaten in Latest Attack on Ukrainian Opposition, the New York Times. https://mobile.nytimes.com/2013/12/26/world/europe/ukraine.html?emc=edit_tnt_20131225&tntemail0=y. Accessed 27 December 2020

Ismayilova K (2016) Don't Let Azerbaijan Use Political Prisoners as Props. *Washington Post*, 31 March, sec. Opinions. https://www.washingtonpost.com/opinions/president-obama-hold-the-azeri-president-accountable-for-political-prisoners/2016/03/31/91720c50-f68f-11e5-9804-537defcc3cf6_story.html. Accessed 27 December 2020

Jurist (2011) Ukraine prosecutors launch new investigation of ex-PM Tymoshenko, 28 January. https://jurist.org/paperchase/2011/01/ukraine-prosecutors-launch-new-investigation-of-ex-pm-tymoshenko.php. Accessed 27 December 2020

Kern S (2011) A Black Day for Austria. Gatestone Institute. https://www.gatestoneinstitute.org/2702/sabaditsch-wolff-appeal. Accessed 26 December 2020

Malfliet K, Parmentier S (eds) (2010) Russia and the Council of Europe: 10 Years After. Palgrave Macmillan UK

Malkin B, Raziye A (2015) Vladimir Putin Saved My Life, Says Ousted Ukrainian President Viktor Yanukovych—Telegraph. https://www.telegraph.co.uk/news/worldnews/europe/russia/11692593/Vladimir-Putin-saved-my-life-says-ousted-Ukrainian-president-Viktor-Yanukovych.html. Accessed 27 December 2020

Mälksoo L, Benedek W (eds) (2017) Russia and the European Court of Human Rights: The Strasbourg Effect. Cambridge University Press (European Inter-University Centre for Human Rights and Democratisation), Cambridge, UK. https://doi.org/10.1017/9781108235075

Neshataeva T (2013) Decisions of the European Court of Human Rights: novelties and influence on legislation and legal practice [Resheniya Evropeyskogo Suda po pravam cheloveka: novelly i vliyanie na zakonodatel'stvo i parvopriminitel'nuyu praktiku]. Norma, Moscow

Parfitt T (2010) Belarus cracks down on 600 opposition protesters, The Guardian (London), 22 December

Pop V (2012) Former MEP on Trial in Cash-for-Amendments Scandal. Accessed 3 October 2017, available at https://euobserver.com/justice/118325. Accessed 26 December 2020

RadioFreeEurope/RadioLiberty (2013) Ukraine: Yanukovych Pardons Lutsenko. https://www.rferl.org/a/ukraine-yanukovych-lutsenko-pardon/24950001.html. Accessed 27 December 2020

Remezaite R (2017) EJIL: Talk—Azerbaijan: Is It Time to Invoke Infringement Proceedings for Failing to Implement Judgments of the Strasbourg Court? https://www.ejiltalk.org/azerbaijan-is-it-time-to-invoke-infringement-proceedings-for-failing-to-implement-judgments-of-the-strasbourg-court/. Accessed 27 December 2020.

Shields M (2013) Strasser jailed for bribery in European parliament sting. https://www.reuters.com/article/us-europe-corruption-strasser/strasser-jailed-for-bribery-in-european-parliament-sting-idUSBRE90D0QT20130114. Accessed 26 December 2020

Smale A (2013) Former German President Goes on Trial. https://www.nytimes.com/2013/11/15/world/europe/christian-wulff-trial-in-germany.html. Accessed 26 December 2020

Steininger M (2012) German President Wulff resigns amid scandal, diverting Merkel's attention. https://m.csmonitor.com/World/Europe/2012/0217/German-President-Wulff-resigns-amid-scandal-diverting-Merkel-s-attention-video. Accessed 26 December 2020

Telegraph (2012) Tymoshenko's husband wins asylum in the Czech Republic, 6 January. https://www.telegraph.co.uk/news/worldnews/europe/ukraine/8997723/Yulia-Tymoshenko-husband-wins-asylum-in-Czech-Republic.html. Accessed 27 December 2020

The Irish Times (2013) Ex-German president Christian Wulff on trial for corruption. Former Merkel ally charged with accepting €700 for hotel and meals during beer festival. https://www.irishtimes.com/news/world/europe/ex-german-president-christian-wulff-on-trial-for-corruption-1.1595252. Accessed 26 December 2020

The Local (2015) FPÖ MP Expelled for Anti-Semitic Remarks. https://www.thelocal.at/20151102/winter-retreats-from-her-anti-semitic-remarks. Accessed 26 December 2020

Theil S (2017) A Vote of Confidence for the German Democratic Order: The German Federal Constitutional Court Ruling on the Application to Ban the National Democratic Party, UK Constitutional Law Association. https://ukconstitutionallaw.org/2017/01/31/stefan-theil-a-vote-of-confidence-for-the-german-democratic-order/. Accessed 26 December 2020

Tovrov D (2012) German President Christian Wulff's 'War' with the Media. 01.03.2012. https://www.ibtimes.com/german-president-christian-wulffs-war-media-390126. Accessed 26 December 2020

Tovrov D (2014) German President Christian Wulff's 'War' with the Media, 1 March 2012, available at https://www.ibtimes.com/german-president-christian-wulffs-war-media-390126. Accessed 27 December 2020

Conclusions

The research for this book has been motivated by recent trials against prominent representatives[1] of political opposition in transitional former Soviet republics. Although these countries have adopted democratic constitutions and established constitutional courts shortly after the fall of Communism, opposition often accuse governments there of staging arbitrary criminal proceedings that brought a feeling of *déjà vu* of politically motivated Soviet show trials against the so-called 'people's enemies'. The puzzle to address in this regard is the absence of similar practices of politically motivated justice in established Western democracies that have also experienced a communist or another totalitarian regime in the past. In this book, I analyze the Soviet legacy of politically motivated justice, whose goal is 'not only legal but also political in a direct sense…[, because] the law was being used merely as an alibi.'[2] In particular, this text focuses on the 'legal history' and 'traditions' of communist politically motivated justice from early Soviet 'agitation trials' in 1919–1933 to show trials against dissidents in the late Soviet Union in 1960–1982 (see Table 1).

As a result of this research, I identified various ***types of Soviet politically motivated trials*** (see Table 2) such as *trials against class enemies* (trials against representatives of the bourgeoisie, independent farmers etc.), the Communist Party Purge against political competitors (*Moscow show trials*), *rural* (*raion*) *trials*, *anti-Semitic trials* (the so-called 'Doctors' Plot' and the 'Jewish Antifascist Committee'), *military trials* and criminal *prosecution of dissidents* in the late Soviet period. Taking into account that these politically motivated trials pursued different political goals and agendas, I argue that trials against class enemies, rural (raion) trials, anti-Semitic trials, military trials and trials against Soviet dissidents had indirect political goals, because these

[1] In particular, ECtHR (the European Court of Human Rights), *Ilgar Mammadov v Azerbaijan,* 22 May 2014, Case No. 15172/13; ECtHR, *Tymoshenko v Ukraine*, 30 April 2013, Case No. 49872/11; ECtHR, *Lutsenko v Ukraine*, 3 July 2012, Case No. 6492/11; ECtHR, *Khodorkovskiy v Russia,* 31 May 2011, Case No. 5829/04 and ECtHR, *Gusinskiy v Russia,* 19 May 2004, Case No. 70276/01.

[2] See Christenson R (1999) Political Trials: Gordian Knots in the Law, revised, expanded, subsequent edn. Routledge, New Brunswick, NJ, p. xiii.

© T.M.C. ASSER PRESS and the author 2021
A. Galushko, *Politically Motivated Justice*,
https://doi.org/10.1007/978-94-6265-459-4

Table 1 Milestones of politically motivated justice under communism

Show trials, relevant legislation	Year
Code of Criminal Procedure of RSFSR	1923
Fundamental Principles of Criminal Legislation of the USSR and the Union Republics[a]	1924
Fundamental Principles of Criminal Procedure of the USSR and the Union Republics	1924
Criminal Code of the RSFSR	1926
Shakhty Affair	1928
Industrial Party Case	1930
Mensheviks' Trial	1931
Metropolitan-Vickers Case	1932
The FirstMoscow Show Trial	19–24 August 1936
Adoption of ***Stalin's Constitution***	6 December 1936
The second Moscow Trial	25–30 January 1937
The third Moscow Trial	2–13 March 1938
László Rajk's Show Trial	September 16–24, 1949
Fundamental Principles of Criminal Legislation of the USSR and the Union Republics[b]	1958
Fundamental Principles of Criminal Procedure of the USSR and the Union Republics	1958
Criminal Code of the RSFSR	1960
Code of Criminal Procedure of the RSFSR	1960
Brezhnev's Constitution of 'Developed Socialism'	7 October 1977
Anatoliy Shcharansky's Trial	1977
Zviad Gamsakhurdia's Trial	1977
Andrei Sakharov's Case	1978
The Affair of 'Young Specialists'	1982

Source The author
[a]Berman (1966)
[b]Ibid

trials pursued a broader political and social mission of reorganizing the structure of Soviet society by eliminating or excluding from politics entire social classes and groups. The book focuses rather on the second narrow category of show trials against political rivals, whose goal was directly political, namely to 'weaponize' criminal justice against actual or potential political opposition.

In this regard, my research has identified ***seven core practices*** (see Table 3) of Soviet politically motivated show trials.

(1) *Ex Parte Communication* between prosecutors, judges and organizers of show trials; (2) '*Judicial Prerogativism*', which disfavored actual and potential opponents of the ruling elites at all stages of criminal proceedings; (3) '*Prosecutorial or*

Table 2 Categorization of 'Political Trials' during the communist regime

Types of political trials	Goals of politically motivated justice	
	Scapegoating[a]	Removing actual or potential threats
1. The Moscow trials	V	V
2. The Communist Party Purge	V	V
3. Rural (raion) trials	V	V
4. Military trials		V
5. Anti-semitic trials	V	V
6. Dekulakization (liquidation of middle-income peasantry). *NKVD order # 00447* of July 30, 1937, 'About repressions against former kulaks, criminals, and other anti-Soviet elements'	V	V
7. Trials against dissidents in the late Soviet period		V

Source The author
[a]For instance, "Stalin played very skillfully on the peasants' need to find scapegoats…for everything that had gone wrong during or after the collectivization campaign." In: Urban (1982)

Accusatorial bias', according to which a defendant was presumed guilty; (4) '*Confessions and Self-indictment*' that replaced any objective evidence of defendant's guilt or innocence; (5) *Accelerated and simplified* '*summary*' *criminal proceedings* conducted by extra-legal bodies; (6) A doctrine of '*Crime by Analogy*', which later transformed into arbitrary recharacterization of criminal offences in violation of the principle *Nullum Crimen* (no punishment without law); (7) A '*political amnesty*' or a 'pardon' granted in some political cases. Furthermore, taking into account that the Soviet practices had a supreme legal standing and could trump any written law including constitutional provisions, I conclude that these informal and mostly unwritten practices of politically motivated criminal justice created a parallel legal order within the Soviet legal system.

Other countries of the communist bloc replicated politicized practices "superimposed on the rules of written law"[3] to consolidate the power of the communist regime. László Rajk's trial in communist Hungary became a 'blueprint' for similar Soviet-like show trials in Bulgaria, Poland, Czechoslovakia and East Germany. These and other trials demonstrated that the Soviet model of politicized justice was not a unique 'phenomenon' inherent only to the Soviet Union under Stalin, but rather a 'toolkit' of practices that could be shared between similar non-democratic regimes. The show trials exposed the split into two parallel legal orders: an official decorative order used by the Communist Party to maintain the appearance of legality and an

[3]ECtHR, *Streletz, Kessler and Krenz v. Germany*, 22 March 2001, Case Nos. 34044/96, 35532/97 and 44801/98 (*Streletz, Kessler and Krenz* 2001). http://hudoc.echr.coe.int/app/conversion/pdf/?library=ECHR&id=001-59353&filename=001-59353.pdf. Accessed 27 December 2020.

Table 3 Legal features of Soviet Political Trials

Legal features	Stages of criminal proceedings				
	Preliminary investigation	Indictment	Trial	Judgment	Appeal
1. ***Ex parte communication*** (telephone law, clandestine connections between the judiciary and members of Politburo and other government agencies)	X	X	X	X	X
2. Judicial '***Prerogativism***', which "operate[s] either in favor of the litigant, if he happens to be privileged, or to his detriment, if he is a member of a disfavored class."[a]	X	X	X	X	X
3. ***Confessionsandself-indictment*** to prevent "an ideologically sophisticated defendant with fire in his belly…[from] turn[ing] his trial into a trial of the regime trying him."[b]	X	X	X		
4. ***Accelerated and simplified criminal proceedings***[c]	X	X	X	X	X
5. Applying the principle of '***crime by analogy***' and '***arbitrary recharacterization***'	X	X	X	X	X
6. ***Prosecutorialor accusatorial bias*** of Soviet judges and prosecutors who often presumed that "defendants are usually guilty."[d] A judge could not acquit the defendant in order not to 'spoil' legal proceedings	X	X	X	X	X
7. Political leadership granted '***politicalamnesty***' or 'pardoned' some defendants					X

Source The author
[a]Osakwe (1985)
[b]See n 5, p. 120.
[c]"As the historian Anton Antonov-Ovseenko has described it: a case was dealt in a few minutes, the members of the [Supreme Court] Collegium would then withdraw to "deliberate", a process that merely consisted in their signing the already determined sentence". In: Rosenfeldt (2009)
[d]Kovalev (2010)

informal order of mostly unwritten practices of political persecution and domination unconstrained by written formal law.

Previous researchers have already described the phenomenon of duality. For instance, *Ernst Fraenkel* found the dual state (German: *der Doppelstaat*) in Hitler's Germany, which was split into normative and prerogative states.[4] While in the normative state, economic relations strictly followed law, in the prerogative state politicized quasi-judicial practices like "healthy folk sentiment"[5] or '*gesundes Volksempfinden*' always prevailed over law to prosecute 'enemies of the state' and to promote the ideology of National Socialism. *Robert Sharlet* has also offered his concept of the dual state in the Soviet Union.[6] Sharlet saw the duality in the Soviet system of justice, which was split into the 'Communist Party law' applied only to resolve cases of senior party members out of ordinary courts and the socialist legality (Russian: *sotcialistichеskaya zakonnost*) applicable to the rest of the Soviet society. *Richard Sakwa* detected a dual state in modern Russia after the fall of Communism.[7] Sakwa's model described an administrative state, which overrides the written law and coexists with the constitutional state, where the public is supposed to follow the formal written constitution. Most recently, in her study of everyday law *Kathryn Hendley* also reported on the traditional for Russia phenomenon of legal dualism when she mentioned that "this dualism has rarely been acknowledged.…A look back at Russian law in the tsarist and Communist periods reveals the long standing role of dualism, a syndrome that undergirds present-day attitudes."[8] *Alexei Trochev* agrees with Hendley when he observes that constitutional dynamics in the country "have one feature in common: the duality of the Russian state and its legal system."[9] I concur with these authors and use their concepts to develop my own theoretical framework for analyzing the Soviet legacy of politically motivated justice.

The split of the legal system in the Russian Empire and the Soviet Union could also be explained by conventional for Russia "'split consciousness' or a 'dual soul' (*dvoedushie*)…[when i]ndividuals possessed multiple identities."[10] The Soviet Union magnified this split consciousness through its multiple social realities of the black

[4] Fraenkel E (2010) The Dual State: A Contribution to the Theory of Dictatorship. Lawbook Exchange edn.(translation Shils EA, Lowenstein E). The Lawbook Exchange, Ltd., Clark, NJ.

[5] See "Law and Justice in the Third Reich" in the Holocaust Encyclopedia available at http://www.ushmm.org/wlc/en/article.php?ModuleId=10005467. Accessed 27 December 2020.

[6] Sharlet R (1998) Stalinism and Soviet Legal Culture, Stalinism. Routledge. https://doi.org/10.4324/9781315130217-7, pp. 155–179.

[7] Sakwa R (2013) Systemic Stalemate: Reiderstvo and the Dual State. In: Robinson N (ed) The political economy of Russia. Rowman & Littlefield, Lanham, MD, pp. 59–67.

[8] Hendley K (2017) Everyday Law in Russia, illustrated edn. Cornell University Press, Ithaca/London, p. 5.

[9] Trochev A (2017) The Russian Constitutional Court and the Strasbourg Court: judicial pragmatism in a dual state. In: Mälksoo L, Benedek W (eds) Russia and the European Court of Human Rights: The Strasbourg Effect. Cambridge University Press (European Inter-University Centre for Human Rights and Democratisation), Cambridge, pp. 125–149. https://doi.org/10.1017/9781108235075.007.

[10] Hellbeck J (2019) Writing the Self in the Time of Terror: Alexander Afinogenov's Diary of 1937, Self and Story in Russian History. Cornell University Press, pp. 69–93. https://doi.org/10.7591/9781501723933-006.

market with its parallel world of hidden economy,[11] the Thieves' World (Russian: *vorovskoy mir*)[12] with its rules alternative to the official legal system, the communist propaganda machine of the perfect communist society[13] and the 'alternative psychiatry' with its 'punitive medicine'[14] for dissidents. There is no wonder that individuals as well as institutions developed multiple identities in order to be able to navigate in the various social realities. In his novel '1984', George Orwell offered the concept of '*doublethink*',[15] which accurately described the split consciousness in a totalitarian society. The roots of the Soviet and Russian duality could also be traced back to the Asian culture of formal and informal norms of behavior. Japan followed concepts of *Honne* (a person's true intentions) and *Tatemae*[16] (opinions displayed in public), when it combined[17] outward compliance (*Tatemae*) with laws borrowed from Europe and the customary devotion (*Honne*) to godlike Emperors.

My analysis of the above-mentioned Soviet practices of politicized justice led me to the conclusion that the Soviet legal system included ***two coexisting legal orders*** of formal (written) and informal (unwritten) norms. The first 'formal legal order' included written constitutions that remained only on paper and played a ceremonial role necessary for the legitimization of the Soviet ruling elites at home and abroad. The second 'informal legal order' was mostly unwritten and included customary law as well as other conventionalities of political justice, which was justiciable in Soviet courts and superior to written laws. A special role played by the informal practices of politicized justice in the Soviet Union and other communist states has been already recognized in the previous research conducted by Alena Ledeneva,[18]

[11]Osokina E (2002) Economic Disobedience Under Stalin. In: Viola L (ed) Contending With Stalinism: Soviet Power and Popular Resistance in the 1930s. Cornell University Press.

[12]Serio JD, Razinkin VS (1995) Thieves Professing the Code: The Traditional Role of Vory v Zakone in Russia's Criminal World and Adaptions to a New Social Reality. July/August – 1995.Vol# 5 - Issue# 4, available at http://archive.is/7IYuP. Accessed 12 March 2021.

[13]Ebon M (1987) The Soviet Propaganda Machine, 1st edn. McGraw-Hill, New York.

[14]Spencer I (2000) Lessons from history: the politics of psychiatry in the USSR. Journal of Psychiatric and Mental Health Nursing, 7(4), pp. 355–361. doi.org/10.1046/j.1365-2850.2000.00297.x.

[15]"DOUBLETHINK means the power of holding two contradictory beliefs in one's mind simultaneously, and accepting both of them…To tell deliberate lies while genuinely believing in them, to forget any fact that has become inconvenient, and then, when it becomes necessary again, to draw it back from oblivion for just so long as it is needed, to deny the existence of objective reality and all the while to take account of the reality which one denies…Even in using the word DOUBLETHINK it is necessary to exercise DOUBLETHINK. For by using the word one admits that one is tampering with reality; by a fresh act of DOUBLETHINK one erases this knowledge; and so on indefinitely, with the lie always one leap ahead of the truth." In: Orwell G (1961) 1984. Signet Classic, New York, NY.

[16]*Tatemae* literally means *façade* in Japanese.

[17]Zachmann UM (2014) Does Europe Include Japan? European Normativity in Japanese Attitudes towards International Law, 1854–1945", Rechtsgeschichte Legal History - Journal of the Max Planck Institute for European Legal History, no. 22 (2014): 228–43, available at http://www.zeitschrift-rechtsgeschichte.de/en/article_id/940. Accessed 12 March 2021.

[18]Ledeneva A (2001) Unwritten Rules: How Russia Really Works, CER Essays. Centre for European Reform, London, p. 2.

Table 4 Distortion of criminal law principles in the Soviet system of political justice

Essential elements of a fair trial	Inverted principles of the soviet system of justice
1. **Presumption of innocence** *Ei Incumbit Probatio Qui Dicit, Non Qui Negat* (the burden of the proof lies upon him who affirms, not he who denies)	Presumption of guilt
2. **Principe of legality** *Nullum Crimen, Nulla Poena Sine Lege* (no punishment without law)	Doctrine of analogy and arbitrary recharacterization
3. **Judicial duty of care, the right to a fair hearing** *Audi Alteram Partem* (hear the other side)	Judicial prerogativism
4. **Equality of arms** *Libra Justa Justitiam Servat* (a just balance preserves justice)	Prosecutorial or accusatorial bias

Source The author

Immo Rebitschek,[19] Inga Markovits,[20] Peter Solomon[21] and others. In contribution to the previous research, this book offers a *novel concept of **'Twofold Constitutionalism'***, which argues that informal practices attained in the Soviet Union a supra-constitutional rank in the sense that they became an unwritten Soviet constitution capable of overriding formal constitutions and any written law for the sake of political expediency and flexibility of law favored by the Communist Party.

This book asserts that the duality of the Soviet legal system manifested itself through the ***inversion of the fair trial principles*** (see Table 4), ***politicization of the goals of criminal proceedings*** (see Table 5) and the ***duplication of all branches of government*** (see Table 6) in the Soviet Union.

In particular, the two coexisting legal orders of formal and informal norms inverted the maxims of criminal law and procedure into their complete opposites. In the Soviet system of political justice, the presumption of innocence was turned into presumption of guilt, the principle of no punishment without law was replaced with the doctrine of analogy and arbitrary recharacterization, the judicial duty of care transformed into judicial prerogativism and the principle of the equality of arms was substituted with the accusatorial bias. The Soviet dual legal system has also led to politicization of the conventional goals of criminal punishment. Deterrence, restitution, retribution, education and rehabilitation were replaced with directly political

[19]Rebitschek I (2015) Vortrag zum Panel: "Building Socialist Legality: the Judiciary in the Postwar Soviet Union". In: Rahmen des Jahreskongresses der Association for Slavic, East European, & Eurasian Studies (ASEEES), Philadelphia (PA).

[20]Markovits I (2006) Transitions to Constitutional Democracies: The German Democratic Republic. The Annals of the American Academy of Political and Social Science, 603(1), pp. 140–154. https://doi.org/10.1177/0002716205282408.

[21]Solomon P (1992) Soviet Politicians and Criminal Prosecutions. The Logic of Party Intervention. In: Millar J (ed) Cracks in the Monolith: Party Power in the Brezhnev Era, 1st edn. Routledge, Armonk, NY.

Table 5 Goals of politically motivated punishment under communism

Conventional goals of criminal punishment	Inverted goals of criminal punishment under communism	Activities to reach the inverted goals of politically motivated justice
Retribution	• **Political retribution** • **Monopolization of state power**	Eliminating political competitors, actual and potential opponents
		Prosecuting people that represent 'hostile' ideologies or social groups even if these people are publicly condemned and sentenced *in absentia*
		Putting a 'public stigma' of criminality on opponents and rivals
Rehabilitation, restitution	• **Regime's self-rehabilitation** • **Restitution of political status quo** • **Legitimization of existing regime**	Scapegoating and shifting the blame for ineffective policies to imaginary external and internal enemies
		Gaining 'public support' by playing on popular fears, xenophobia and prejudices in trials against marginalized groups and ethnic minorities, manipulating the public opinion
Deterrence, education	• **Deterrence of political disobedience** • **Political education** • **Enforcement of regime's ideology and policies**	Boosting obedience/discipline of the Communist Party top brass (*Nomenclatura*) through purges of its 'deviant members'
		Communicating regime's new social rules and ideology to the general public

Source The author

goals of political retribution, monopolization of power, regime's self-rehabilitation, restitution of status quo, regime's legitimization, deterrence of disobedience, political and ideological education.

Taking into account that the Soviet Union did not have the true separation of powers between different branches of government, but rather a measurable separation of work between various institutions, I argue that the Soviet legal duality also led to the establishment of shadow extra-legal bodies that duplicated all branches of government. For instance, to deal with political cases, the communist leadership set up secret political departments, *troikas* and *dvoikas* in already repressive government

Table 6 'Twofold Constitutionalism' in the USSR[a]

LAYER I (*Official Separation of Powers under the Nominal Written Constitutions of the USSR*)

LEGISLATIVE BRANCH	EXECUTIVE BRANCH	JUDICIAL BRANCH
The Supreme Council of the USSR (Russian: *Verkhovny Sovjet SSSR*) - the supreme legislative body of the Soviet Union. **Republican Councils of Soviet People's Republics**	**The Council of Ministers (1946-1990) or the Government of the USSR** (Russian: *Verkhovny Sovjet SSSR*): - General Procuracy; - OGPU/ NKVD/ Ministry of Internal Affairs. - Republican Procuracies and Criminal Bodies	- **The Supreme Court of the USSR**; **-Republican Supreme Courts;** - **Military Tribunals;** - **District Courts.**

LAYER II (***Unofficial System of Political Criminal Justice under the Unwritten Constitution of the USSR***)

LEGISLATIVE BRANCH	EXECUTIVE BRANCH	JUDICIAL BRANCH
'Politburo' of the Soviet Leadership - A shadow quasi-legislative body; - Issued secret guidelines on political repressions; - Delivered verdicts before a trial.	- **Secret political departments** at various governmental agencies; - ***Troikas* and *dvoikas, and other extrajudicial summary proceedings*** run by OGPU, NKDV and KGB.	- **Special boards** (Russian: *osoboiyesoveshaniya*), **secret tribunals** and **collegiums** within the structure of the Supreme and ordinary republican courts.

Source The author
[a]The chart outlines the separation of powers under the Soviet Constitutions adopted in 1937 and 1977

agencies like OGPU, NKVD and KGB. Special boards and collegiums often adjudicated political trials instead of ordinary courts. The Politburo of the Soviet leadership became a shadow quasi-legislative body, which issued secret guidelines on political repressions and even delivered verdicts before any 'trial'. Classified communication between extra-judicial bodies and their official counterparts was supposed to create an illusion of a pseudo-independent singular system of justice, which was actually divided into two parallel legal orders.

This book looked into the ***interplay between formal and informal norms*** during the Soviet times and found that the informal norms of politically motivated justice usually prevailed over formal written norms depending on the following three factors. **Factor 1**: 'distribution of political forces' that either rejected or supported the use of informal norms (flexibility of law) in a given political situation. **Factor 2**: the interpretation of legality by different state agencies as well as their willingness to enforce written formal norms and limit political interventions through informal practices in the so-called 'Steered Justice System'[22] "by means of [continuous] conflict and negotiations."[23]**Factor 3**: the legal system undergoes radical transformations after revolutionary events or other systemic changes that give an opportunity to adopt a very broad definition of *corpus delicti* in line with considerations of political expediency.

My argument that Soviet informal practices of politicized justice became part of an unwritten constitution is based on *Joseph Raz*' ***characterization of a constitution***, which "in a thick sense of the word is (1) *constitutive of the legal and political structure*, (2) *stable*, (3) *written*, (4) *superior to other law*, (5) *justiciable*, (6) *entrenched*, and (7) *express common ideology*."[24] Practices of politicized justice were indeed constitutive of the Soviet legal and political culture, because the Soviet state came into existence through politically motivated 'class struggle' against class enemies. Politically charged quasi-legal concepts of 'revolutionary vigilance', 'Soviet legal conscience', 'flexibility of law', the swift and severe punishment of 'people's enemies', the doctrine of analogy and arbitrary recharacterization became the building blocks of the Soviet legal structure from its inception. This system of politicized justice was extremely stable given that practices of political persecutions remained in use well beyond Joseph Stalin's death even at times of mild liberalization during the so-called Khrushchev thaw, Brezhnev's stagnation and Gorbachev's perestroika. Though the intensity of these repressions varied over time, they ensured the continuity of the communist regime and its ideology until the very collapse of the Soviet Union.

Although Soviet practices of politicized justice were mostly unwritten, according to Joseph Raz, customary law could still become an unwritten part of the constitution. Raz himself gives an example of the United Kingdom, whose constitution includes both unwritten common law and the written documents such as "the Bill of Rights of 1689, the Act of Union between England and Scotland of 1706...[and] the European Communities Act of 1971."[25] Thus, despite their mostly unwritten form, Soviet practices of politicized justice could still be called a constitution in a thick sense of this word. With their 'supra-constitutional rank' the practices of politicized justice were also superior to other law, taking into account that the Communist Party could disregard all Soviet written laws and written constitutions to persecute 'people's enemies' at any time for the sake of political expediency. In the same vein, the afore-mentioned traditions of politically motivated justice were justiciable in Soviet courts that followed practices of ex-parte communication, judicial prerogativism, accusatorial bias and presumption of guilt rather than written law.

---

[22]See n 26.

[23]Ibid.

[24]Raz J (2009) Between Authority and Interpretation: On the Theory of Law and Practical Reason, 1st edn. OUP Oxford; Sadurski W (2012) Constitutionalism and the Enlargement of Europe, 1st edn. Oxford University Press, Oxford, UK, p. 45.

[25]See n 32, p. 325.

As the analysis of Soviet show trials and recent 'political cases' from former Soviet republics demonstrates, communist practices of politically motivated justice were so entrenched both in terms of their longevity and influence on the Soviet legal culture that they manifested themselves throughout the entire existence of the Soviet Union (1922–1991) and even after its collapse. Such longevity of Soviet politicized justice took place, because it expressed ideology common for all Soviet people or *Homo Sovieticus*, whose mindset and mentality transformed in the course of the communist social engineering experiment. The above-mentioned considerations, thus, show that practices of politicized justice occupied such a special and privileged place in the Soviet legal hierarchy that they could be characterized as an unwritten constitution in a very real sense of the word.

In addition to Joseph Raz' definition of a constitution, my research has also identified several characteristics of communist politically charged practices that demonstrate their constitutional status in transitional post-Soviet states. In particular, the practices of politically motivated justice have a '***Radiating Effect***' in these countries in the sense that at any moment they can prevail over all social norms and rules. As Alena Ledeneva rightly formulated it, "[Soviet] practices that have come to be known as extra-legal or informal ... [influence or radiate over such key areas of life as] elections, ..., the media, ... industry and business, ... legal and security spheres."[26] In other words, given their privileged status in all spheres of life, the informal practices have a profound impact on entire transitional post-Soviet societies and underlie their legal systems. Such a privileged status of informal practices can also be explained by their '***Ubiquitous Nature***'. The informal practices are ubiquitous in transitional post-Soviet societies, because they are routinely applied by virtually everyone including public officials, representatives of judiciary and legal enforcement agencies, while this application is "based on shared expectations about formal rules... and on mutual understanding about informal norms of friendship or other relationship."[27] Given the pervasive nature of unwritten informal practices in the post-Soviet space, one should not underestimate their role in social, political and legal transformations after the fall of Communism.

When after the collapse of the Soviet Union written laws were routinely disregarded by virtually everyone, criminal punishment became suspended but arbitrarily enforceable at any time. As Ledeneva rightly observes, the deficiencies of post-Soviet laws in combination with the traditional disrespect of law have led to the situation when "[i]nformal practices are often justified as a rational response to perceived defects in formal rules and their enforcement... both producing and resulting from patterns of distrust in public institutions and disregard for formal rules."[28] The negative outcome of overriding formal norms by informal ones is that the arbitrary nature of informal norms can subvert democratic principles enshrined in written constitutional provisions. This '***Subversive Character***' of politically charged practices means that they replace democratic values of written constitutions with an opposite

---

[26] See n 25, p. 189.

[27] Ibid., p. 16.

[28] Ledeneva A (2006) How Russia Really Works, 1st edn. Cornell University Press, Ithaca, p. 27.

set of standards that can potentially undermine all post-Soviet reforms. According to Sakwa, such subversion is possible, because the parallel informal legal order "do[es] not repudiate the formal constitutional framework but operate[s] within its institutional constraints while subverting its spirit."[29] Thus, it means that the Soviet political practices compromise the entire process of post-communist democratization.

In order to reveal the communist legacy of politicized practices, my book includes ***qualitative case studies of trials*** against opposition politicians in the two transitional former Soviet republics (Ukraine and Belarus). In this regard, I have analyzed cases from Belarus using the legal approach of the European Court of Human Rights (ECtHR) as if the country joined the European Convention on Human Rights to find out whether the Council of Europe (CoE) and the Court could assist in preventing a return to communist traditions of politicized justice in transitional post-Soviet states. Furthermore, I have selected two 'political cases' from established Western democracies (Germany and Austria) to answer **the main question posed by this book** about roles played by 'political trials' in former Soviet republics and in Western democratic countries.

As a result of these case studies, the book offers ***three findings***. *First*, recent trials against political opposition leaders in the former Soviet Union demonstrate that the communist legacy of '*Twofold Constitutionalism*' has survived the collapse of the Soviet Union in transitional post-Soviet states, whose legal systems are still split into two legal orders of formal and informal norms. *Second*, the case studies confirmed my ***hypothesis*** that trials related to politics play different roles in transitional post-Soviet states and in established Western democracies. As opposed to transitional post-Soviet states, whose informal practices and conventionalities create a parallel system of justice with its 'political trials' that have directly political goals to eliminate political rivals and a potent opposition, in Western democracies trials against politicians and political parties play a non-politicized role within the rule of law in the sense that such trials usually lead to an open public discussion of important legal and political matters, reconciliation and dialogue in line with democratic principles enshrined in written constitutions. *Third*, practices of politicized justice can potentially delay the post-communist transition of former Soviet republics from the totalitarian 'dual state' to the genuine, rather than the declaratory rule of law.

My research complemented the qualitative analysis of the 'case studies' with ***international quantitative ratings*** to compare the overall situation with criminal justice, independence of judiciary, protection of fundamental rights and adherence to the rule of law in transitional post-Soviet states and established democracies. Quantitative rankings by the Freedom House, the World Justice Project (WJP) and the World Economic Forum demonstrate that, as opposed to the developed Western democracies like Germany and Austria that received high scores in 2010–2015, scores of transitional post-Soviet republics like Ukraine and Belarus were deteriorating during the same period when both countries had trials against political opposition. Though it is not sufficient to use quantitative rankings alone to confirm or reject

[29] Sakwa R (2013) Systemic Stalemate: Reiderstvo and the Dual State. In: Robinson N (ed) The political economy of Russia. Rowman & Littlefield, Lanham, MD, pp. 59– 467.

allegations about politicized justice, such rankings reveal a great variety of factors that contribute to persecutions against opposition.

I also determined that despite their nominal and formal character, written constitutions still play important roles in transitional and authoritarian states. Although informal practices of politicized justice often override provisions of written constitutions in non-democratic states, even nominal authoritarian constitutions continue to perform roles of the 'operating guide' to coordinate activities of state agencies, the 'billboard' to present a favorable image of the country at home and abroad as well as became a 'consumption activity' of ruling elites that collect information through constitution writing.[30] All these roles of written yet nominal constitutions are essential for ensuring the legitimization and longevity of non-democratic regimes. Unlike democratic states, where law and practice follow aspirational goals set in constitutions, in authoritarian or transitional states, informal practices turn written constitutions and their 'democratic aspirations' into 'hollow vessels', 'window-dressing' and 'constitutional cheap talk'.

The book concludes that the Soviet legacy of politicized justice (see Table 7) has significant ***repercussions for transitional former Soviet republics***.

If the communist practices of politicized justice have the supreme rank within the legal hierarchies of the transitional post-Soviet states, their written constitutions as the supreme written law can be easily disregarded for the sake of political considerations. The phenomenon of this legal duality, thus, affects not only victims of politically motivated justice, but also ordinary citizens, whose constitutional rights and freedoms can be routinely violated, as they remain only on paper. Although many authoritarian post-Soviet governments were quick to declare that they observed the Rule of Law by adopting new democratic constitutions and establishing constitutional courts shortly after the fall of Communism, '*Twofold Constitutionalism*' exposes the declaratory nature of these 'imitated democracies' and questions the legitimacy of political regimes in these countries. Furthermore, resemblance of these political regimes to the dual state found by Ernst Fraenkel at the time of National Socialism in Germany could potentially have far-reaching consequences for international peace and security in general. In this context, 'political trials' are the ultimate and effective test to check whether a transitional state has attained the genuine rather than the declaratory Rule of Law.

The main outcome of this research is ***a list of seven prima facie criteria*** based on the ECtHR case law that can be used to assess future allegations (see Table 8) about politicized justice at various stages of criminal proceedings in the former USSR.

First, during the pre-trial stage, in politicized criminal proceedings a suspect is usually subjected to a prolonged deprivation of liberty and cannot effectively apply for other measures alternative to detention. Therefore, an arrest and a prolonged deprivation of liberty not based on a 'reasonable suspicion' that the suspect committed an offence could signal that ruling elites use politicized justice in order to remove

[30] Ginsburg T and Simpser A (eds) (2013) Constitutions in Authoritarian Regimes. Cambridge University Press (Comparative Constitutional Law and Policy), Cambridge. https://doi.org/10.1017/cbo9781107252523.

Table 7 Questions to identify the Soviet legacy of 'Twofold Constitutionalism'

#	A checklist of questions to be asked	Similarities with Soviet Political Trials
1.	Do criminal proceedings target only a single person or a large group of individuals that are judicially disadvantaged or even tried *in absentia* by a national system of criminal justice?	In the USSR victims of politically motivated justice belonged to the following broad social categories that were openly disadvantaged through judicial prerogativism: (1) representative of bourgeoisie and capitalists (class enemies); (2) stigmatized ethnic minorities such as the Soviet Jewish community; (3) Defiant social groups like middle income peasants (*kulaks*); (4) Popular military commanders; (5) Political dissidents that openly criticized government policies etc.
2.	Do political decision makers have ex-parte communication with a court?	Politburo meetings went as far as sending 'premade verdicts' in political cases to trial courts
3.	Do essential elements of a fair trial such as presumption of innocence, principle of legality, judicial care and equality of arms become 'inverted'?	Soviet show trials were notorious for their 'inversion' of criminal law maxims into their complete opposites (i.e. presumption of guilt, doctrine of analogy, judicial prerogativismand prosecutorial bias)
4.	Are there accelerated and simplified extra-legal criminal proceedings that violate the national legislation in force?	In the USSR, simplified summary procedures were used against those who were too unimportant or too unpredictable to be brought to a public trial
5.	Are there elements of theatricality such as public confessions, retracted confessions and repentance?	Stalinist show trials were based not on evidence, but on confessions obtained under torture
6.	Was a trial accompanied by a public smear campaign against a defendant?	All Soviet show trials triggered propaganda campaigns against 'internal and external enemies'
7.	Does a criminal punishment pursue retribution, rehabilitation, restitution, deterrence and education or opposite 'political goals'?	Unlike conventional goals of criminal punishment, show trials scapegoated defendants for government failures and removed political opponents
8.	Were political amnesty and pardon arbitrarily granted?	Some victims of Soviet show trials were arbitrarily pardoned or amnestied often post-mortem to demonstrate ostentatious leniency of Soviet justice
9.	Does a national legal system have signs of *'Twofold Constitutionalism'*?	Under the Soviet system of 'Twofold Constitutionalism' the written constitution played only a nominal role, while mostly unwritten norms of political justice were superimposed on all formal laws through clandestine directives that had a supra-constitutional rank

Source The author

Table 8 Possible differences between trials against politicians in established democracies and trials against political opposition in transitional post-Soviet states

Essential components of proceedings	Trial against politicians in established democracies	Trials against political opposition in transitional post-Soviet Republics
1. **Pretrial detention**	A defendant is not necessarily kept in detention before and during the trial. Measures alternative to detention such as release on bail or house arrest can usually be applied	The defendant is usually already kept in detention at the stage of criminal investigation, or is constantly under the threat of detention if he or she does not 'cooperate' with the investigation to 'acknowledge' his/her 'guilt'. Courts reject measures alternative to detention despite the existing case law and defendant's previous record
2. **Goal of the trial**	The goal of the trial is to give both prosecution and the defendant an opportunity to present their arguments and evidence in order to determine guilt/innocence of the defendant. The defendant can often continue his or her political career even after the trial	The goal of the trial is to remove the defendant from politics, to destroy the defendant as a person and a politician through public humiliation, denial of medical treatment, torture, physical and psychological pressure. The trial usually targets a larger group of political opposition (anti-corruption campaigners, protest artists, 'foreign agents' etc.), which is affiliated with the defendant
3. **Proceedings**	Trials usually follow criminal procedures prescribed by law. Defendants and their legal counsels are given enough time to study the case file and prepare for the defense. Representatives of media are allowed to cover essential stages of criminal proceedings	The defendant is given very little time to study the case file due to accelerated procedures. Trials are turned into shows that are characterized by public confessions, repentance, invented facts and fiction as well theatricality displayed by both the prosecution and the defense
4. **Outcome of the trial**	There is a fair chance that the defendant could be exonerated as a result of the trial, or that defendant's sentence could be reversed, suspended or reduced by the higher court	The outcome of the trial is certain in advance, as the ruling elites have communicated the 'guilty verdict' and even defendant's sentence to the court prior to the trial. The trial is usually accompanied by a smear campaign against the defendant

(continued)

Table 8 (continued)

Essential components of proceedings	Trial against politicians in established democracies	Trials against political opposition in transitional post-Soviet Republics
5. **Sentence**	If sentenced, the defendant observes the court's judgment without any privileges or exemptions	Political prisoners can often be pardoned or amnestied in total disregard of the existing law and practice in order to demonstrate leniency of the ruling elites and their readiness to cooperate with international partners

Source The author

their rivals from politics shortly before elections, stigmatize opposition leaders as common criminals and put them under psychological and physical pressure in the course of their detention before and during a trial.

Second, a goal of criminal proceedings could also reveal the politicized nature of a trial against a politician or a political party. If one alleges that national authorities pursue political goals when they initiate criminal proceedings against opposition, he or she should present direct and incontrovertible proof that the given state was not acting in good faith, because there was a 'hidden political agenda' behind the criminal proceedings. Such a political agenda or goals manifest themselves when the state *ab initio* misuses its entire legal machinery against a defendant by arbitrarily rejecting all defense motions, tacitly supporting or openly ignoring a smear campaign against the defendant in the media, interrupting defendant's political activities during criminal proceedings as well as using such proceedings to intimidate other opposition representatives. If the state, accused of pursuing a political agenda against opposition, commits the afore-mentioned blatant violations of the due process standards, victims of the persecution have every right to raise the red flag and inform the public about such instances of politically motivated justice.

Third, various procedural irregularities, aimed at disadvantaging a defendant and undermining the equality of arms principle, could be yet another indicator of politically motivated justice in cases related to politics. In particular, in transitional post-Soviet states opposition politicians that face numerous criminal charges usually have very little time to study their case files and go through accelerated proceedings in contrast with conventionally prolonged proceedings in non-political cases. ***Fourth***, outcomes of a trial related to politics could be analyzed in their entirety to see the 'bigger picture' of social and political factors that led to politicized justice in a given case. For instance, in Western democracies 'political trials' often lead to a defendant's acquittal, reduction or reversal of sentence on appeal, while a politician or a political party still have an opportunity to continue their professional activities throughout a trial. In transitional post-Soviet states, on the contrary, the outcome of a 'political trial' is predetermined with an expected 'guilty verdict', which establishes a 'precedent' for prosecuting other members of opposition. The situation, when in transitional post-Soviet states opposition politicians are usually 'doomed' to be found guilty regardless of their actual guilt or innocence, is, of course, a violation of the right to a fair trial (*Article 6 ECHR*) and the principle of legality *Nullum Crimen* (no punishment without law).

Fifth, whether and how a verdict is actually enforced could eventually confirm or remove allegations about politicized justice. While in established Western democracies politicians sentenced in political cases usually abide by sanctions imposed by their verdicts without any exceptions or privileges, in transitional post-Soviet states politicians sentenced by court often retain their 'special status' even in prison. It means that representatives of political opposition may have either better or worse conditions of their incarceration in comparison with other inmates sentenced in non-political cases. Furthermore, some of the imprisoned representatives of political opposition may be arbitrarily amnestied or pardoned in violation of formal norms and usual practice applied in non-political cases. An amnesty of a political prisoner may be a positive development, which shows the readiness of national political elites to soften repressions in response to international criticism. However, the arbitrary nature of such occasional amnesties only emphasizes that 'politicized cases' are resolved not by means of law but rather by means of opaque decisions and 'back-room deals' that cannot prevent politicized justice in the future.

To provide an explanation of the ***differences between politics and administration of justice*** in transitional post-Soviet states and in established democracies, this research drew upon Macnaughton-Smith's concept of the 'Second Code',[31] which is an informal set of unwritten rules routinely used by any complex society to label a person as a perpetrator of the first code of official written norms. Though the content of the 'Second Code' is usually uncertain, it can be determined by studying practices, conventionalities and customs of a given society. Politicized trials against opposition from Ukraine and Belarus demonstrate that in transitional post-Soviet states the division between the administration of justice and politics is blurred or absent in 'political cases', because the 'Second Code' of national legal traditions was replaced in these countries with Soviet politically charged practices. 'Political trials' from Germany and Austria show, on the contrary, that in established democracies both the first and the second 'codes' proscribe a clear line between politics and administration of justice. Taking into account that the administration of justice performs political functions in transitional former Soviet republics, in these countries the system of justice becomes a mere surrogate and an extension of politics.

This book offers ***three ways to overcome the Soviet legacy*** of '*Twofold Constitutionalism*' and its arbitrary politically motivated trials. ***First***, the duality of politicized criminal justice can be removed by implementing democratic values and principles enshrined in written constitutions that are systematically disregarded during arbitrary trials against political opposition. However, this 'national legal avenue' does not seem very promising now, given the high level of corruption, the lack of independent judiciary as well as deficient or absent reforms in many transitional post-Soviet

[31] Macnaughton-Smith P (1968) The Second Code: Toward (or Away from) an Empiric Theory of Crime and Delinquency. Journal of Research in Crime and Delinquency, 5(2), pp. 189–197. https://doi.org/10.1177/002242786800500208.

states. ***Second***, if a former Soviet republic joined the Council of Europe, strategic litigation in the European Court of Human Rights in combination with the international pressure can facilitate the removal of communist practices of politicalized justice. ***Third***, in the long run, a true decommunization campaign combined with restorative and reparatory justice measures could rehabilitate political prisoners as well as prevent politically motivated trials in the future.

The communist legacy of show trials has become useful for many post-Soviet ruling elites. In line with Garfinkel's theory of a degradation ceremony,[32] similar to Soviet politicized justice modern show trials are supposed to cause the moral indignation against political rivals for their violation of informal norms, demonstrate to the public that 'self-proclaimed' political opponents are in fact deviants and become a place of the 'ritual destruction' of a denounced opposition. The goal of these degradation ceremonies is to belittle government critics by reconstituting their identity as 'foreign agents' and 'common criminals' as well as showing how helpless and vulnerable they are in their confrontation with the state apparatus. Instead of using 'non-legal means' by simply eliminating political opponents and turning them into martyrs, repressive post-Soviet regimes often use the old Soviet practices of show trials to convert any political opposition into easily intelligible crimes and, thus, undermine the ability of opposition to lead the popular dissent.

The book concludes that transitional former Soviet republics have not yet learned their lessons from the history of the communist totalitarian regime. The presence of the Soviet practices of politicized justice in spite of democratic constitutions demonstrates that the legacy of '*Twofold Constitutionalism*' lives on nowadays. The Rule of Law or the equality of all before law is most apparent when the national system of justice does its best to ensure that the most powerful and the most vulnerable members of society are equally subject to the laws in place. Post-communist ruling elites that persecute their opponents should go no further than the history of the Soviet dissident movement, which was prosecuted, partly because it identified causes of the Soviet Union collapse long before it actually happened. By discarding dissenting opinions of political opposition, all non-democratic states eventually lose an opportunity to improve overtime and learn from those who challenge them.

---

[32]Garfinkel H (1956) Conditions of Successful Degradation Ceremonies. American Journal of Sociology, 61(5), pp. 420–424. https://doi.org/10.1086/221800.

Index

© T.M.C. ASSER PRESS and the author 2021
A. Galushko, *Politically Motivated Justice*,
https://doi.org/10.1007/978-94-6265-459-4

CPSIA information can be obtained
at www.ICGtesting.com
Printed in the USA
LVHW051832120421
684238LV00002B/225

9 789462 654587